Jews in the South

Jews *in the* South

Edited by *Leonard Dinnerstein* and *Mary Dale Palsson*

Louisiana State University Press
Baton Rouge

*To Rose and Abe Dinnerstein
and Gerald Palsson*

ISBN 0–8071–0226–1
Library of Congress Catalog Card Number 72–89114
Copyright © 1973 by Louisiana State University Press
All rights reserved
Manufactured in the United States of America
Printed by The TJM Corporation, Baton Rouge, Louisiana
Designed by Dwight Agner

Contents

Acknowledgments

"South Carolina from Shaftesbury to Salvador," from Abram Vossen Goodman, *American Overture*, copyright, 1947, by The Jewish Publication Society of America. Reprinted by permission. "Further Light on Jacob Henry," by Ira Rosenwaike, reprinted from *American Jewish Archives* (November, 1970), by permission. "David L. Yulee, Florida's First Senator," by Leon Hühner, reprinted from *Publications of the American Jewish Historical Society*, XXV (1917), by permission of Minna Hühner Schulz and the American Jewish Historical Society. "Jews and Negro Slavery in the Old South, 1789–1865," by Bertram Wallace Korn, reprinted from *Publications of the American Jewish Historical Society*, L (March, 1961), by permission of the author and the American Jewish Historical Society. "American Judaeophobia: Confederate Version," reprinted from Bertram Wallace Korn, *American Jewry and the Civil War*, pages 176–88, copyright, 1951, with the permission of The Jewish Publication Society of America. "The Post-Civil War Economy in the South," by Thomas D. Clark, reprinted from *American Jewish Historical Quarterly*, LV (1966), by permission of the author and the American Jewish Historical Society. "Atlanta in the Progressive Era: A Dreyfus Affair in Georgia," reprinted with permission of The Macmillan Company from *The Age of Industrialism in America*, by Frederic C. Jaber (ed.). Copyright © 1968 by The Free Press, a Division of The Macmillan Company.

"'The Jew's Daughter': An Example of Ballad Variation," by Foster B. Gresham, reprinted by permission from *Journal of Ameri-*

can Folklore, XLIV (1934). "Slow Revolution in Richmond, Va.: A New Pattern in the Making," by David and Adele Bernstein, reprinted from *Commentary*, by permission; copyright, 1949, by the American Jewish Committee. "Southern Jews: The Two Communities," by Theodore Lowi. This paper was first published in the *Jewish Journal of Sociology*, VI (July, 1964), and is reprinted by permission of the editor of the *Jewish Journal of Sociology*. "Mixed Marriages in the Deep South," by Sidney I. Goldstein, reprinted by permission of *Reconstructionist*, XXX (March 6, 1964), 15 West 86 Street, New York, N.Y. 10024. "The New Orleans Jewish Community," by Leonard Reissman. This paper is reprinted from the *Jewish Journal of Sociology*, IV (No. 1, 1962), and is reprinted by permission of the author and of the editor of the *Jewish Journal of Sociology*. "Southern City," by Joshua A. Fishman, from *Midstream*, VII (Summer, 1961), reprinted by permission of the author and of the editor. "The Dilemma of the Southern Jew," from the *Reconstructionist*, XXIV (January 9, 1959), reprinted by permission. "Virginia Jewry in the School Crisis," by Murray Friedman, reprinted from *Commentary*, by permission; copyright © 1959 by the American Jewish Committee. "Mississippi Marranos," by Marvin Braiterman, from *Midstream*, X (September 1964), reprinted by permission of the author and of the editor. "Rabbis and Negro Rights in the South, 1954–1967," by Allen Krause, from *American Jewish Archives*, XXI (April, 1969), copyright © by permission.

Jews in the South

Introduction

THE FIRST Jewish community in the South developed during the settlement of Georgia in 1733. Even before that, individual Jews had lived in the region. Yet, despite their residence of at least two and a half centuries, southern Jews and their historic development have received scant attention from historians. In fact they have usually drawn thoughtful analysis only during times of crisis when they became objects of prejudice and scorn. Except for different religious practices, Jews made every effort to become absorbed into the activities of their adopted home. Their life-style closely resembled that of their gentile neighbors, and this is one reason they have failed to attract the attention of historians interested in the uniqueness of minority groups.

One other important factor explains their unsung existence in the South. From colonial times to the present, Jews have comprised less than 1 percent of the whole southern population. By the time of the Revolution, they probably totaled fewer than five hundred people.[1] Many of them resided in Charleston, South Carolina, which contained one of the largest Jewish communities in the United States.[2] During the next several decades, however, increasing numbers of Jewish immigrants chose to live in the North. In spite of the influx of German

1. Ira Rosenwaike, "An Estimate and Analysis of the Jewish Population of the United States in 1790," *Publications of the American Jewish Historical Society*, L (1960), 34.
2. Ira Rosenwaike, "The Jewish Population of the United States as Estimated from the Census of 1820," *American Jewish Historical Quarterly*, LIII (1963), 138–52 *passim*.

Jews into the South after 1836, fewer than fifteen thousand Jews lived there by 1860.[3] The total increased moderately as the region began to industrialize after the Civil War, and at the present time the Jewish population in the South is less than four hundred thousand.[4]

Regardless of their numerical limitation, Jews contributed substantially to the expansion of the South. Even though they did not always gain full social acceptance, their prosperity and enterprise supported growing communities. They deserve study on this basis alone. Moreover no understanding of the Jewish experience in America would be complete without an appreciation of their history in the South. The unevenness and dispersion of research to date make an attempted overview difficult. Nevertheless the articles in this collection were gathered for the purpose of illuminating the major facets of this long-neglected subject.

In several respects the experiences of Jews in the South paralleled those of their coreligionists elsewhere in the United States. As Morris Schappes has so aptly noted: "Jewish life here has developed distinctively as a part of the economic, political, social and cultural life of a nation developing under capitalist relations—with slavery and its aftermath of anti-Negro restrictions as the only pre-capitalist institution to play a major role in that development."[5] Although settlers retained their Old World prejudices, most of them realized the need for a diversified economy, and they welcomed the special talents and skills attributed to the Jews. In the North as well as in the South, many Jews prospered, especially as artisans, financiers, and merchants. The ghetto, a product of European feudalism, existed nowhere in this country.

As their economic position became increasingly secure, Jews sought to expand their civil and political privileges, but they met resistance in every region that they inhabited. In 1740 the British Parliament greatly advanced their cause by permitting the naturalization of Jews in all British colonies.[6] Nonetheless equal rights were slow in coming.

3. Uriah Zevi Engelman, "Jewish Statistics in the U.S. Census of Religious Bodies (1850–1936)," *Jewish Social Studies*, IX (1947), 131.

4. *American Jewish Yearbook*, XXXII (1930–31), 220; XLII (1940–41), 227–28; LXIX (1968), 282–83.

5. Morris U. Schappes, *A Documentary History of the Jews in the United States, 1654–1875* (New York: Citadel Press, 1950), xi.

6. Nathan Glazer, *American Judaism* (Chicago: University of Chicago Press, 1957), 17.

Despite the small number of Jews, all of the colonial legislatures—
North and South—circumscribed their liberties to some extent. Denial
of the Trinity subjected Jews to imprisonment in Virginia and to
death in Maryland. A Virginia statute of 1705 prohibited them from
obtaining full citizenship and barred their appearance as court witnesses.[7] In 1723 the Maryland law code read: "If any person shall
hereafter within this province deny our Savior, Jesus Christ, to be the
true Son of God, or shall deny the Holy Trinity, he should for the
first offense be fined and have his tongue bored, and . . . for the third
offense be put to death." [8] In 1703 one hundred and fifty inhabitants
of Colleton County, South Carolina, protested an election in which
"Jews, Strangers, Sailors, Servants, Negroes, and almost every French
Man in Craven and Berkley County" participated in the voting.[9] The
ruling powers subsequently curtailed the franchise: after 1716 only
Christians could vote in South Carolina.[10] Maryland and North Carolina barred Jews from the legal profession and that disability continued
into the nineteenth century.[11] These examples seem to prove what
other scholars have already stated with certainty, that at no time in
the colonial period did Jews enjoy equal status with gentiles.[12]

The humane and rational aspects of the American Revolution
represented a great stride toward human rights for the Jew. Inspired
by the rhetoric of democracy, such states as Virginia in 1787, South
Carolina in 1790, and Georgia in 1798 granted them voting rights.[13]

7. Jacob Rader Marcus, *Early American Jewry: The Jews of Pennsylvania and
the South* (Philadelphia: Jewish Publication Society of America, 1953), 160.
8. Paul Masserman and Max Baker, *The Jews Come to America* (New York:
Bloch Publishing Co., 1932), 88.
9. William Rivers, *A Sketch of the History of South Carolina to the Close of the
Proprietary Government by the Revolution of 1719* (Charleston, S.C.: McCarter Co.,
1856), 459.
10. Marcus, *Early American Jewry*, 522; Charles Reznikoff and Uriah Z. Engelman,
The Jews of Charleston (Philadelphia: Jewish Publication Society of America, 1950),
7–8.
11. Leon Hühner, "Jews in the Legal and Medical Professions in America Prior to
1800," *Publications of the American Jewish Historical Society*, XXII (1914), 149. And
see Anita Libman Lebeson, *Jewish Pioneers in America, 1492–1848* (New York: Bren-
tano's, 1931), 187.
12. Marcus, *Early American Jewry*, 554; Anson Phelps Stokes, *Church and State in
the United States* (3 vols.; New York: Harper & Row, Publishers, 1950), I, 857.
13. Marcus, *Early American Jewry*, 525.

Yet, the constitutions of North Carolina in 1776, Maryland in 1776, and Massachusetts in 1780 denied Jews the right to hold office.[14]

By the time of the Civil War, overt civil and political barriers had disappeared both in the North and the South, with the exceptions of North Carolina and New Hampshire, which did not grant full political rights to Jews until 1868 and 1877, respectively. Complete social integration, however, proved elusive. This problem received national attention in 1877, when Joseph Seligman protested being denied a hotel room in Saratoga, New York, because of his faith.[15] By the 1890s numerous clubs began to exclude Jews from membership. "Social mobility was always an important characteristic of the American scheme for living," Oscar Handlin states. He further explains that "his exceptional mobility and the fear of his strangeness made the Jew the most prominent and the most vulnerable target of all the minorities discriminated against." [16]

The problem of social acceptance is one facet of a greater difficulty Jews throughout the United States have encountered from time to time—that of antisemitism. Since antisemitism in this country has never reached the virulent level encountered in Europe, most American historians have neglected the subject completely. When they have investigated it, they have usually expressed a conclusion similar to John Higham's statement that such active bigotry "happened only in moments of crisis, when war or depression sharpened resentment at the trader and profiteer." [17] Outbreaks were therefore most violent during the Civil War, the depression of the 1890s, World War I and its aftermath, and the Great Depression of the 1930s. Ideological antisemitism, Higham maintains, should be distinguished from the traditional American xenophobia. Americans have always displayed an antagonism toward the arrival of masses of immigrants. Thus the large influx of Jews in the 1840s, and again between the 1870s and the 1920s, resulted in

14. Joseph L. Blau and Salo W. Baron (eds.), *The Jews of the United States, 1790–1840: A Documentary History* (New York: Columbia University Press, 1963), I, 15–20.

15. Stephen Birmingham, *Our Crowd* (New York: Harper & Row, Publishers, 1967), 143ff.

16. Oscar Handlin, *Adventure in Freedom: Three Hundred Years of Jewish Life in America* (New York: McGraw-Hill Book Company, 1954), 197–98.

17. John Higham, "American Anti-Semitism Historically Reconsidered," in Charles Herbert Stember (ed.), *Jews in the Mind of America* (New York: Basic Books, Inc., 1966), 248.

occasional vehement outbursts stemming from a native fear of foreign influence.[18]

Considering the occurrence of discrimination within the broad categories of economic, political, and social activities, the Jewish experience in both the North and South was similar, at least up to the present century. In both regions they encountered obstacles that they have either overcome or have learned to accept.

One other important similarity merits attention. During the nineteenth century, Jews throughout the United States considered complete assimilation into the American way of life their most important goal. They discovered opportunities for advancement that had not been offered to them in any other country of the world. Being a good American meant erasing cultural distinctions that had previously set them apart. Increasingly they conformed to the middle-class standards of their adopted home.

The formation of the short-lived Reformed Society of Israelites in South Carolina in 1824 illustrates the extent to which Judaism was becoming Americanized. Influenced by the religious liberalism of Charleston, forty-seven members of the Beth Elohim congregation petitioned the elders for the use of instrumental music, English prayers, and English sermons in their services. Their request was denied and they set about establishing their own congregation.[19]

Later in the century, the German Jews of New York had become so assimilated that they regarded the mass migration of their East European coreligionists as a threat to their status in society. As Moses Rischin explains: "In the years of the great Jewish migration, to be identified as a Jew became more and more irksome. The hosts of uncouth strangers, shunned by respectable New Yorkers, seemed to cast a pall upon all Jews." [20]

As the twentieth century progressed, however, Jews in America began to be concerned with the problem of maintaining their own

18. *Ibid.*, 248–50. See also Leonard Dinnerstein (ed.), *Antisemitism In The United States* (New York: Holt, Rinehart & Winston, 1971).

19. Allan Tarshish, "The Charleston Organ Case," in Abraham J. Karp (ed.), *The Jewish Experience in America*, II, 285–00.

20. Moses Rischin, *The Promised City: New York's Jews, 1870–1914* (New York: Harper & Row, Publishers, 1970), 95. And see Ande Manners, *Poor Cousins* (New York: Coward McCann and Geoghegan, Inc., 1972)

identity. During the last few decades the ideal of assimilation has become suspect, especially in the North. Awareness of their own minority status has also caused increased solicitude among some Jews for the welfare of other minorities. As a growing number of Jews in the North have become associated with liberal causes, their experience has diverged from that of Jews in the South. Of course the numerical superiority of northern Jews accounts for much of this activity, but these people have hardly been touched by three potentially powerful forces that have always affected the lives of southern Jews.

Agrarianism is the first major factor. Even though Carl Bridenbaugh demonstrates that there was no South prior to 1776, he admits that the rural nature of the region constituted one of the two conditions foreshadowing the South that was to be. By the time of the Revolution, Charleston's population had grown to twelve thousand, but it was the single large community south of Philadelphia.[21] The lack of urban centers deterred Jewish settlement in the southern states. Since most Jews preferred to be merchants rather than farmers, they generally elected to live in the port cities. Thus, by the end of the colonial period, the only substantial Jewish communities existed in New York, Philadelphia, Savannah, Charleston, and Newport, Rhode Island.[22] As the North became industrialized, the number of jobs for unskilled workers multiplied, and Jews found the opportunities for economic advancement in this region much more numerous than in the South. Furthermore, most of the ships from Europe docked in the harbors of Boston, New York, and Philadelphia, thereby facilitating northern settlement.

The predominantly agrarian society in the South helped conserve a typically American bias that favored the producers rather than the financiers.[23] Such an attitude occasionally militated against the Jews during the early days of the Republic and in the Populist movement of the 1890s. Thus in the 1820s, when the Jews were still fighting to eliminate political restrictions in the Maryland Constitution, *Niles'*

21. Carl Bridenbaugh, *Myths and Realities: Societies of the Colonial South* (Baton Rouge: Louisiana State University Press, 1952), 59.
22. Nathan Glazer *et al.*, "Social Characteristics of American Jews," in *The Characteristics of American Jews* (New York: Jewish Education Committee Press, 1965), 12.
23. Higham, "American Anti-Semitism," 248.

Weekly Register commented on why gentiles often restricted Jewish activities: "They will not sit down and labor like other people—they create nothing and are mere consumers. They will not cultivate the earth, nor work at mechanical trades, preferring to live by their wit in dealing, and acting as if they had a home no where." [24] A mistrust of all those engaged in finance and a desire to restrict the power of urban voters caused the farmers to protest the right of Jews to hold state office.[25]

During the 1890s, when the Populist Party achieved great strength in the Midwest and South, agrarian members sometimes voiced a similar prejudice. Some of them became convinced of an international Jewish financial conspiracy. As Higham concludes: "The few Populists who gave vent to anti-Semitic diatribes were extravagantly susceptible to fears of anarchy, of a breakdown of the whole civilized order." [26]

Fortunately these prejudices did not prevent the Jews from attaining a high standing in southern communities. The rural nature of the South did indeed discourage a large number of Jews from settling there, but the second major force—slavery—was an equally important factor. It also affected the Jewish experience in other ways.

By the time of the Revolution, slavery had become a potent element in southern society. After the war the rapid growth of the slavery-based plantation system meant that new immigrants, who usually had very little capital, were more attracted to northern areas where free labor prevailed. Jews who did migrate to the South customarily settled in the urban areas or traveled the countryside peddling their wares. Almost none of them became plantation owners. After the invention of the cotton gin, slavery became entrenched in the South and many residents declared their devotion to the principle.

The northern attack on slavery further stimulated a "rigid conformity of thought." [27] Increasing sectional antagonism reinforced support for this institution and engendered intolerance toward any

24. Quoted in *ibid.*
25. Edward Eitches, "Maryland's 'Jew Bill,'" *American Jewish Historical Quarterly*, LX (March, 1971), 258, 278.
26. Higham, "American Anti-Semitism," 248.
27. Clement Eaton, *The Mind of the Old South* (Baton Rouge: Louisiana State University Press, 1964), 82.

questioning of existing mores.[28] The test of the true southerner became his acceptance of Negro bondage. Southern Jews had no ambivalence on this score. Most either kept silent or gave wholehearted support to the southern ideology. In contrast northern Jews could be found on both sides of the issue.[29]

In spite of the fact that the southern economy became increasingly diversified after the Civil War, southerners maintained a closed mind on the subject of race. In the present century, most of them are still concerned with keeping the Negroes in a subordinate position. Consequently, white minorities in the South have found the greatest acceptance when they have assumed the dominant values of the society. Even white Christian liberals were often reluctant to speak out on race relations.

Southern Jews who have taken positions that differ from the majority have often been censured by others of their faith who feel that criticism of established mores jeopardizes the entire Jewish community. A case in point is that of Rabbi Benjamin Goldstein, formerly of Montgomery, Alabama's Temple Beth Or, who in the 1930s protested against the injustices heaped upon the Scottsboro boys (nine Negro youths accused of raping two white women). The boys had been found guilty despite medical evidence that made the charge of rape absurd. The members of Goldstein's congregation demanded that he cease his public protestations of the court verdict or resign from his position. He resigned. Subsequently members of the Temple admitted to newspaper reporters that they agreed with Rabbi Goldstein's remarks, but they viewed their airing as an "open threat to the welfare of the congregation." [30]

In city after city, Jews have refused to endorse publicly the 1954 Supreme Court ruling calling for school integration. As one Mississippian put it:

We have to work quietly, secretly. We have to play ball. Anti-Semitism is always right around the corner. . . . We don't want to have our Temple

---

28. *Ibid.*, 241.

29. Bertram Wallace Korn, *American Jewry and the Civil War* (Philadelphia: Jewish Publication Society of America, 1951), chap. 2.

30. Dan T. Carter, *Scottsboro: A Tragedy of the American South* (Baton Rouge: Louisiana State University Press, 1969), 258–59.

bombed. If we said out loud in Temple what most of us really think and believe, there just wouldn't be a Temple here anymore. They [the gentile neighbors] let it alone because it seems to them like just another Mississippi church. And if it ever stops seeming like that, we won't have a Temple. We have to at least pretend to go along with things as they are.[31]

Members of the local B'nai B'rith lodge in Waycross, Georgia, withdrew from the national organization, largely because of its liberal position toward civil rights. They believed that such a commitment jeopardized their position in society.[32]

Nevertheless, several southern Jews have spoken out on integration and other liberal causes, some even risking economic security to do so. Unfortunately their numbers are few. Among the more vigorous supporters of integration have been Rabbis Jacob Rothschild of Atlanta and Charles Mantinband, who has ministered to Jews in Alabama, Mississippi, and Texas. But most southern Jews prefer to remain inconspicuous.[33]

Joining agrarianism and racism as major determinants in the course of southern Jewish history is the dominant religious element, Fundamentalist Protestantism. Carried to the southern interior by rugged frontiersmen, it posed a major threat to all other faiths. In Bridenbaugh's opinion, "the compelling religious feature of the entire interior was the existence in its most virulent form of a fierce sectarianism." [34] Fundamentalist Protestantism had little effect on life in the coastal towns, and the Jews of Charleston lived in an atmosphere of religious tolerance. But during the nineteenth century, the South's two major sects, the Methodists and Baptists, became strongholds of conservatism. Most southern churches began to resist, strongly and eloquently, the intrusion of alien peoples, ideas, and institutions.[35]

Religious intolerance often centered on the Jews. Many Baptist

---

31. Marvin Braiterman, "Mississippi Marranos," see below, pp. 355–56.
32. James Lebeau, "Profile of a Southern Jewish Community: Waycross, Georgia," *American Jewish Historical Quarterly*, LVIII (June, 1969), 234–35.
33. Leonard Dinnerstein, "Jews and the Desegregation Crisis in the South," *American Jewish Historical Quarterly*, LXI (March, 1973).
34. Bridenbaugh, *Myths and Realities*, 181.
35. Joseph H. Fichter and George L. Maddox, "Religion in the South, Old and New," in John C. McKinney and Edgar T. Thompson (eds.), *The South in Continuity and Change* (Durham: Duke University Press, 1965), 360–64.

and Methodist ministers accused Jews of killing the Savior.[36] Two southerners, describing their boyhood religious experiences, recalled that "the veriest infant was made acquainted with the lapses of the ancient Jews, and all God's wrath at their behavior was thundered in his ears." [37] Wilbur J. Cash, a perceptive commentator on regional characteristics, added in 1941, "All the protests of scholars have been quite unavailing to erase from the popular mind, in the South as elsewhere, the notion that it was the Jew who crucified Jesus." [38] Such attitudes are still fervently held by Southern Baptists today, as a 1965 survey conducted by Charles Y. Glock and Rodney Stark reveals. Only 8 percent of those questioned were found free of antisemitic traits, while an overwhelming 80 percent sincerely believed that "the Jews can never be forgiven for what they did to Jesus until they accept Him as the True Savior." For this last belief, affirmative Protestant and Catholic responses nationwide averaged only 33 percent and 14 percent respectively.[39] At the Jewish-Baptist Scholars Conference held in Louisville, Kentucky, in August, 1969, Baptist minister Bob Adams acknowledged: "It is probably and tragically only too true that many Southern Baptists are as Anti-Semitic as their portrayal in the Glock and Stark report." [40]

Regardless of this hostile attitude toward their beliefs, many Jews received a warm welcome in southern communities. One peddler recalled that many Christians held him in special regard. Frequently asked about the Bible, he was often required to settle religious disputes because, in his words, "I was a Jew and they all looked upon me as an authority." He also noted that some rural southerners were so backward that they considered him as some sort of Christian. "I remember well," he reminisced, "being asked time and again 'Are you a Baptist

36. William J. Robertson, *The Changing South* (New York: Boni and Liveright, 1927), 98–99.

37. Broadus Mitchell and George Sinclair Mitchell, *The Industrial Revolution in the South* (Baltimore, 1930), 273.

38. Wilbur J. Cash, *The Mind of the South* (New York: Alfred A. Knopf, Inc., 1941), 342.

39. Charles Y. Glock and Rodney Stark, *Christian Beliefs and Anti-Semitism* (New York: Harper & Row, Publishers, 1966), 63, 202; Rabbi Arthur Gilbert, "Prejudice and Social Justice" (Paper delivered at Southern Baptist-Jewish Scholars Conference, held in Louisville, Ky., August 20, 1969), 3.

40. Bob Adams, "Christians, Racism and Anti-Semitism" (Paper delivered at Southern Baptist-Jewish Scholars Conference), 5.

Jew or a Methodist Jew?'" Harry Golden, insisting that the South has had a tradition of philosemitism, wrote that in the rural South, people held the Jewish citizenry almost as private possessions: "He is 'our Jew' to small-town southerners, and they often take care of him with a zeal and devotion otherwise bestowed only on the Confederate monument in the square." [41]

Such factors as ruralism, Fundamentalist Protestantism, and slavery, with its aftermath of racism, have certainly affected the Jewish experience in the South; but their effect has not been totally adverse. Even though religious prejudice existed, countervailing American ideals stressed the essential equality of all white men and the abundance of opportunities for those who worked hard. Thus most Jews found that life in the South afforded many pleasures and economic advantages.

Many of the Jewish immigrants began as peddlers and then purchased small shops; a few eventually acquired large emporiums. Morris Rich, who had performed numerous odd jobs before embarking upon a career as traveling salesman, opened a small retail dry goods business in Atlanta in 1867. This store, still owned by Rich's descendants, is today one of the largest merchandising establishments in the South.[42] Jews also successfully participated in other economic endeavors. They owned quarries in Virginia, functioned as cotton brokers in Alabama, and pioneered in the production of men's ready-made clothing. The Lehman family amassed a comfortable sum from investments in Alabama banks, railroads, and cotton mills; a Texas Jew prospered as a coffee importer; and a number of Jews owned slaves. There were also Jewish auctioneers, slave-traders, doctors, lawyers, and craftsmen.[43]

During the nineteenth century, three southern Jews, David Yulee of Florida, Franklin Moses of South Carolina, and Judah P. Benjamin of Louisiana, reached high public office. Yulee's wife, the former

41. Harry Golden, *Forgotten Pioneer* (Cleveland: World Book Publishing Co., 1963), 66–67; Golden, *A Little Girl Is Dead* (Cleveland: World Book Publishing Co., 1965), 226; Golden, "Jew and Gentile in the New South: Segregation at Sundown," *Commentary*, XX (November, 1955), 403–404.

42. Henry Givens Baker, *Rich's of Atlanta* (Atlanta: University of Georgia Press, 1953), 9, 11, 12, 15, 270, 274.

43. Allan Tarshish, "The Economic Life of the American Jew in the Middle Nineteenth Century," in *Essays in American Jewish History* (Cincinnati: American Jewish Archives, 1958), 278–79, 282, 283; Rosenwaike, "The Jewish Population of the United States," 149.

Nancy Wickliffe, daughter of a Kentucky governor, allegedly demanded, as part of the conditions of marriage, that he change his surname to Yulee, presumably because she objected to the Jewish nature of his original name, Levy. Despite antisemitic attacks, Yulee won election to Congress as territorial delegate from Florida in 1841, and United States Senator in 1845.[44] Little is known about Franklin Moses except that he served as chief justice in antebellum South Carolina.[45] Senator Judah P. Benjamin of Louisiana, the most prominent southern politician of Jewish birth before the Civil War, refused an appointment to the United States Supreme Court that President Franklin Pierce offered, and eventually became secretary of state in the Confederacy.[46]

As their record indicates, the Jews adapted readily to the southern environment. Wherever they settled they contributed to the development of the community. Most of the literature demonstrates that they considered assimilation of great importance, and consequently intermarriages between Jews and Gentiles were frequent. Jewish politicians served as southerners first, and as American citizens second.

A study of their history reveals that while the experiences of Jews in the South roughly parallel those of Jews in the North in general instances, they are not identical. Moreover, a closer examination of the Jewish story in the South brings into focus the vicissitudes of a minority group seeking a place within the rigid structure of a closed society.

When the Jews first arrived in Georgia in 1733, they came without the approval of the trustees of the colony who resided in London. Fearing that the Jews would damage the colony's reputation, these

44. Leon Hühner, "David L. Yulee, Florida's First Senator," *Publications of the American Jewish Historical Society*, XXV (1917), 18–19; New York *Tribune*, October 11, 1886, p. 5; James Leon Alderman, "David Levy Yulee: Ante-Bellum Florida Leader (1810–1886)" (M.A. thesis, University of North Carolina, 1946), 9; Moses Elias Levy, Yulee's father, attempted to explain his son's change of name in a letter to a correspondent: "Some of my people find the name [Levy] an inconvenient traveling one, even in the most tolerant countries in the world." Moses Elias Levy to James M. Gould, February 19, 1846, quoted in Arthur W. Thompson, "David Yulee: A Study of Nineteenth Century American Thought and Enterprise" (Ph.D. dissertation, Columbia University, 1954), 9.

45. Harry Simonhoff, "1868: Franklin J. Moses: Chief Justice of South Carolina," *Journal of the Southern Jewish Historical Society*, I (November, 1958), 23; Cincinnati *American Israelite*, April 18, 1873.

46. *Jewish Encyclopedia* (12 vols.; New York: Funk and Wagnalls Co., 1912), III, 28–30.

trustees sent word to the proprietor, Governor James Edward Oglethorpe, to get rid of them as soon as possible.[47] After consulting lawyers in Charleston, Oglethorpe concluded that the Jews had a legal right to stay in his colony. He then proceeded to assign parcels of land to them.[48]

Apparently they adapted more readily to their surroundings than they did to each other. Although Jews may have numbered at least eighty-three, an enormous rift developed between the two segments of their population, those of German ancestry and those of Spanish-Portuguese descent. The Ashkenazic Germans not only spoke a different language, but they also differed from the Sephardic Iberians in their religious observances. While it was not uncommon for both groups to worship together in other colonies, these particular families in Georgia became so hostile toward each other that one resident complained: "The Spanish and Portuguese Jews persecuted the German Jews [there] so much that no Christian could persecute another like that." [49] By the 1740s many Jews and gentiles became disillusioned with the severe restrictions placed upon them by the trustees—prohibition of slavery being the most important—and they sought greater freedom in South Carolina.

Most of the disgruntled Savannah Jews settled in Charleston, where at least a handful of Jews had resided since 1695. Finding themselves numerous enough to form an organized congregation, they established a place of worship, *Beth Elohim Unveh Shallom*, in the fall of 1749. It had the distinction of being the second synagogue in North America, the first having been erected in New York.[50] By 1800 Beth Elohim had the largest membership in the United States, totaling 107.[51]

Notwithstanding the political obstacles in Maryland and North Carolina, Jews led active lives in most regions of the South during the early years of the Republic. Moreover, although antisemitic remarks

47. Leon Hühner, "The Jews of Georgia in Colonial Times," *Publications of the American Jewish Historical Society*, X (1902), 71.
48. Abram Vossen Goodman, *American Overture: Jewish Rights in Colonial Times* (Philadelphia: Jewish Publication Society of America, 1947), 176.
49. *Ibid.*, 184, 189, 191.
50. Rufus Learsi, *The Jews in America: A History* (Cleveland: World Publishing Co., 1954), 33; Thomas J. Tobias, "Joseph Tobias of Charles Town: 'Linguister,'" in Karp (ed.), *The Jewish Experience in America*, I, 118.
51. Rosenwaike, "An Estimate and Analysis of the Jewish Population," 32.

occasionally crept into the literature of the period, most gentiles seem to have accepted Jews into their communities.

The Civil War aggravated tensions between Christians and Jews. The conflagration aroused strong feelings of in-group solidarity, exacerbating demands for unity and producing a heightened sense of nationalism both in the North and the South. Bertram Korn believes that "anti-Jewish prejudice was a characteristic expression of the age, part and parcel of the economic and social upheaval effectuated by the war." [52] Northern Judaeophobes, e.g., a writer in *Harper's Weekly*, denounced all Jews as "secessionists, copperheads, and rebels," [53] while southerners accused them of being "merciless speculators, army slackers, and blockade-runners across the land frontiers to the North." [54] South Carolina's Governor James Orr believed that the Jews in the Confederacy were loyal to the Union and "generally averse to rendering military service . . . or upholding the rebel cause." [55] Judah P. Benjamin, the secretary of state, aroused the ire of numerous southerners. One observer believed it "blasphemous" for a Jew to hold such an important position, while another was certain that the "prayers of the Confederacy would have more effect if Benjamin were dismissed." [56] Denunciation of Jewish merchants was a common practice in many towns in Georgia, and the *Southern Illustrated News* observed, "all that the Jew possesses is a plentiful lot of money, together with the scorn of the world." [57]

Active antagonism toward the Jews subsided after the war. In fact gentiles who wished for commercial growth in the hope of emulating northern industrial accomplishments welcomed Jews into their community. The Sandersonville *Central Georgian* hailed their presence "as an auspicious sign." The newspaper observed, "Where there are no Jews, there is no money to be made." Virginia's Richmond *Whig* noted that "a sober, steadier, and more industrious and law abiding

52. Korn, *American Jewry*, 156.   53. *Ibid.*, 157.

54. E. Merton Coulter, *The Confederate States of America, 1861–1865* (Baton Rouge: Louisiana State University Press, 1950), 233.

55. New York *Times*, June 7, 1871, p. 1.

56. Korn, *American Jewry*, 177; Hudson Strode, *Jefferson Davis: Confederate President* (New York: Harcourt, Brace & Co., 1959), 150.

57. Quoted in Rudolph Glanz, *The Jew in the Old American Folklore* (New York: privately published, 1961), 54.

class of population . . . [does] not exist." [58] In 1900 a leading Atlanta merchant was upheld as "a typical exponent of the characteristics of his race [who] has happily exemplified that spirit and progressive enterprise for which his people are noted all over the world." [59]

In rural areas the peddler with his canvas bag of goods became a familiar sight during the latter part of the nineteenth century. Thomas D. Clark claims that "the Alsatian Jew was a hero and he has remained largely unnoted and unsung by the historians," since "many a Southern store had its beginning in a humble peddler's pack." [60] Although southerners actively endeavored to attract immigrants to their region, their attempts remained largely unsuccessful. Perhaps newcomers to the United States dreaded competition with the Negro, or feared that they could not grow the staple crops of cotton and tobacco.[61] Yet the Jews who ventured into the area often achieved great success as merchants and as leaders in the town. As Clark boasts: "They were members of the lodges, served on all sorts of boards and committees, were sources of advice, and oftentimes gave a sound leadership in the organization of banks." [62]

Regardless of such evident goodwill, hostile attitudes also emerged. Despite its economic growth, the South continued to be plagued by low incomes and crop failures, and to be subservient to northern bankers and manufacturers. Southerners sometimes gave vent to their frustrations by blaming the Jews for economic reverses. Moreover, the greatest amount of criticism seemed to center on religious differences.

These problems intensified during the 1890s, a period of great social turbulence throughout the country, and persisted in the South through the early decades of the 1900s. Two leading southerners, W. W. Thornton, president of the University of Virginia, and Zebulon Vance, United States Senator from North Carolina, discussed possible reasons for the hostility toward Jews in the South.

In an 1890 interview, Thornton attributed anti-Jewish feeling to racial and religious differences. "The mere fact of difference," he em-

58. E. Merton Coulter, *The South During Reconstruction* (Baton Rouge: Louisiana State University Press, 1947), 203.

59. Baker, *Rich's of Atlanta*, 225.

60. Thomas D. Clark, "The Post-Civil War Economy in the South," *American Jewish Historical Quarterly*, LV (1966), 427.

61. *Ibid.*, 429.   62. *Ibid.*, 428–29.

phasized, "is a persistent cause." Elaborating, the university president noted that "Jews certainly care less for what is embraced in the term culture than Christians who are equally well off." He had never seen "a really scholarly" Jewish student. Thornton thought that the prejudices might subside if Jews married Christians and accepted the true faith. "All intelligent Christians," he replied to the editors of the *American Hebrew*, "deplore the fact that the historical evidences for Christianity have so little weight with your people." [63]

Senator Vance, an outspoken critic of antisemitism, attested to its significance by pleading for tolerance of Jews in a speech, "The Scattered Nation," delivered in more than fifty towns and cities of the country between 1874 and 1890. Responding to the queries put to him by the *American Hebrew*, Vance wrote that although the various southern churches may not have preached antisemitism,

Sufficient care is not taken to point out with reference to the crucifixion, the injustice of holding responsible a whole people, generation after generation, for the acts of a few. No doubt this unconsciously lays a foundation of prejudice, which is largely added to by the jealousy of Gentile rivals in business. Nothing is so satisfactory to a man as to be able to excuse an unworthy motive by referring it to a love of God and his religion. This prejudice is also increased by the unreasonable propensity to consider the Jew under all circumstances as a foreigner, in which case we veneer our motive with a love of country.[64]

Naturally antisemitism was not limited to one particular region, but Jews reacted to these outbursts more vociferously in the North than in the South. At the beginning of the twentieth century, two incidents occurred which reveal these regional differences. In 1902, at a funeral for a Jewish rabbi in New York City, Irish workmen began throwing bricks and other objects at the passing cortege. Police called to the scene also pummeled the mourners for "inciting a riot." The Jewish community protested the action of both the brick throwers and the police. Mayor Seth Low immediately responded by appointing five prominent citizens, including two Jews, to an investigating committee; and within six weeks they published their report, accusing both the workmen and the police of antisemitism. Northern Jews, even

63. Thornton, *American Hebrew*, XLII (April 4, 1890), 191.   64. *Ibid.*, 196–97.

though subject to discrimination, felt sufficiently secure to denounce the bigots and demand public retribution.[65]

The Leo Frank case, which dominated the news in Atlanta between 1913 and 1915, presents a marked contrast. Shunning publicity, Jews confined to themselves their feelings about the rabid antisemitism that existed in the city. Only through gentile spokesmen did they voice their concerns. Frank had been convicted of murder in a sensational trial, highlighted by the state's use of a Negro as its main witness. Subsequent judicial appeals to alter the verdict failed, but John Slaton, governor of Georgia from 1913 to 1915, commuted the death penalty to life imprisonment. This action led to the most vitriolic outbursts of antisemitism ever witnessed in the South. The Georgia Jews, instead of protesting or demanding government intervention, sent their wives and children to relatives in other states until quiet was restored.[66]

In the twentieth century, many Jews, well organized in trade unions and other institutions, led by articulate, forceful men, and commanding resources of status, education, and money, have become politically powerful in cities like New York, Chicago, Boston, Philadelphia, and Detroit. The countervailing strength of ethnic groups in the North has fostered the development of a public rhetoric committed to an acceptance of cultural pluralism. In some areas this rhetoric has even produced nondiscrimination laws.

In the South open hostility toward Jews is still acceptable. Sam Massell, a Jew who was elected mayor of Atlanta (the first Jew to ever hold this position) in 1969, charged some of his opponents with antisemitism. He felt that reporters and newscasters were less than friendly when they referred to him as "the Jewish liberal" from the "synagogue district" of the city.[67] In some sections of the South, antisemitic candidates still run for major office without hiding their prejudices. In 1970 one such gubernatorial entrant finished fourth in a nine-man Democratic primary in Georgia; an unsuccessful candidate for Congress in Alabama campaigned against American support for Israel (an

65. New York *Times*, July 31, 1902, p. 1; August 1, 1902, p. 14; *American Hebrew* (September 19, 1902), 497–99.

66. Leonard Dinnerstein, *The Leo Frank Case* (New York: Columbia University Press, 1968).

67. New York *Times*, October 22, 1969, pp. 1, 6; October 23, 1969, p. 61.

unthinkable position for any statewide aspirant in the northern industrial regions); and in Louisiana Democrat John R. Rarick, an archsegregationist who had the support of known antisemites, won a seat in the United States House of Representatives without even having to face an opponent.[68]

Several studies reflect a feeling of insecurity among southern Jews. These reports often disguise both the names of Jews and their places of residence to avoid embarrassment or harassment.[69] Reminders that they are "being merely tolerated," [70] make Jews cautious in their public activities. They are continually apprehensive that some Jew might offend members of the dominant group. As Harry Golden notes: "The mildest New Deal expression in a 'letter to the editor' signed with a Jewish name sends a shiver through the entire Jewish community—('now we've got someone else to worry about'). But the greatest fear of all is that the next Jewish newcomer to town may be an 'agitator,' a 'pink,' an organizer for the CIO, or even a worker for some Negro cause." [71]

Jews who live in rural areas face a life of religious isolation. Liberal observers fear that such a situation hastens homogenization and brings a loss of Jewish identity. Yet many of these people are descendants of families who have lived in the area for a hundred years or more. The fact that they have kept the faith for generations is no indication that they will continue to do so, but it is a cause for hope.

The essays in this volume are intended to help the reader understand the experiences of Jews in the South, although their 250-year presence in this region defies a single exhaustive analysis. Regardless of the generalizations in this introduction, the southern Jews cannot be neatly discussed and dismissed in a few short essays.

A great obstacle in understanding southern Jews is the uneven nature of the research pertaining to them. Sources for the colonial and antebellum South give only a partial glimpse of their experiences

68. *American Jewish Yearbook*, LXXII (1971), 133–34.
69. Benjamin Kaplan, *The Eternal Stranger* (New York: Bookman Associates, 1957), 104, 156; "U.S. Journal: New Orleans," *New Yorker*, March 9, 1968, pp. 138–43.
70. Kaplan, *The Eternal Stranger*, 127.
71. Harry L. Golden, "The Jews of the South," *Congress Weekly*, XVIII (December 31, 1951), 10.

during that period. Therefore comprehensive conclusions cannot be drawn. Furthermore most of the available analyses have been prepared by Jews who often reflect a bias that has changed with the times. Liberal Jews, writing today, sadly note the lack of liberalism among their fellows in the South, and they seem shocked that these people have often appeared more southern than Jewish. Scholars and observers who wrote during the first few decades of the century, however, seemed pleased at the phenomenal success of their people in this region and applauded their efforts to become assimilated. Those who have looked for antisemitism found it in abundance; while those who believe these outbreaks to be only a small portion of the total history have often stated that blatant antisemitism has been far less prevalent in the South than in the North.

Moreover stereotyped images of southerners, which include their agrarian attitudes, their racial bigotry, and their fundamentalist beliefs, often do a great disservice. Not all Protestants hate Jews, and Jews have frequently received greater acceptance in rural communities than in the industrial cities. Sadly, racism is not confined to the South. Perhaps liberals feel more reluctant to speak out on this issue in the South than elsewhere, but this reluctance is common to both Jew and Gentile.

The South is now changing. The abolition of legal segregation may finally break the shackles that a caste society imposed on both whites and blacks. Many northern industries have moved south and large numbers of northerners have followed them. The growth of research and educational centers in the South, like the Raleigh-Durham-Chapel Hill (North Carolina) triangle, has brought in scientists and scholars. Southern universities in Virginia, Tennessee, Florida, Louisiana, and Texas are able to compete favorably for outstanding scholars with almost any university in the nation. The growth of the federal government's programs has also increased the size of its bureaucracy, especially around Washington, D.C., and the space centers in Florida and Texas.

This large population movement is also reflected in the centers of Jewish population in the South. Jews have been leaving the rural communities and the more politically conservative areas and have flocked to the growing cities and thriving regional areas. At present there are approximately 378,000 Jews in the South. Of this number slightly more than 300,000 of them are concentrated in Florida, Georgia, Texas, and Virginia. Many of these people—precise figures are unavailable—are migrants from the North attracted to sunny Florida; the regional centers like Dallas, Houston, and Atlanta; and in the case of federal government employees, the suburbs of Washington, D.C., in northern Virginia.

As the following charts show, the Jewish population has been declining in some southern states and also in its ratio to the rest of the population.

Jewish Population in the South[72]

State	1927	1937	1967
Alabama	12,891	12,148	9,465
Arkansas	8,850	6,510	3,065
Florida	13,402	21,276	175,620
Georgia	23,179	23,781	25,760
Kentucky	19,533	17,894	11,200
Louisiana	16,432	14,942	15,630
Mississippi	6,420	4,603	4,015
North Carolina	8,252	7,333	9,200
South Carolina	6,851	5,905	7,155
Tennessee	22,532	25,811	16,716
Texas	46,648	49,196	63,680
Virginia	25,656	25,066	37,300

Percent of Jews in the State Population

Alabama	0.5	0.42	0.27
Arkansas	0.46	0.32	0.16
Florida	0.98	1.27	2.93
Georgia	0.73	0.77	0.57
Kentucky	0.77	0.61	0.35
Louisiana	0.85	0.70	0.43
Mississippi	0.36	0.23	0.17
North Carolina	0.28	0.21	0.18
South Carolina	0.37	0.31	0.28
Tennessee	0.91	0.89	0.43
Texas	0.86	0.80	0.59
Virginia	1.01	0.92	0.82

72. *American Jewish Yearbook*, XXXII (1930), 220; XLII (1940–41), 227–28; LXIX (1968), 282–83.

Whether the above figures indicate an especially low birthrate, a relatively high number of intermarriages, or simply a concentration of the southern Jewish population is impossible to pinpoint. We do know that Rabbi Louis Bernstein, president of the Rabbinical Council of America, the largest of the nation's Orthodox rabbinic groups, is alarmed by the "frightening increase in intermarriage." In June, 1972, he warned that "assimilation and intermarriage constitute grave perils to the survival of American Jewry. . . . Statistics indicate that a substantial proportion of American Jews will be lost to us during this generation unless drastic measures are adopted." [73] A few days after Rabbi Bernstein's dire prediction, David M. Blumberg of Knoxville, Tennessee, the international president of B'nai B'rith, a Jewish fraternal order, acknowledged that "intermarriage is a very serious problem for us." [74]

Jewish organizations do not like to reveal certain types of statistics, making it very difficult to get accurate, up-to-date figures on intermarriage or on how long a Jewish family has lived in a particular community. What percentage of southern Jews is third or fourth generation, and what percentage constitutes immigrants from the North and Europe have not been ascertained. Certainly in-depth demographic studies would help us understand who the southern Jews are and where they came from. They might suggest as well whether southern Jewry is a vital or withering group.

Readers of these essays should keep the aforementioned limitations in mind. Disregarding such restrictions, however, the articles in this collection do provide a picture of the chief aspects of Jewish life in the South. They were selected to show the problems encountered by the Jews, their successes, what they thought about their life in this region, and what other southerners thought about them. Of course, they cannot cover every facet of southern Jewish development, nor are they intended to. They do reflect, to a considerable extent, what it has meant to be a southern Jew.

---

73. New York *Times*, June 25, 1972, I, 25.   74. New York *Post*, June 27, 1972, p. 16.

Section 1 Jewish Life in the Antebellum and Confederate South

Jews in the colonial South lived, for the most part, like others in the community save for their religious practices and the political restrictions placed upon them. They earned their living as merchants, traders, storekeepers, artisans, sawmill operators, butchers, and even plantation owners. They exhibited, in the words of Jacob Marcus, the dean of American Jewish historians, "a readiness, if not an eagerness, to adapt themselves to the life and culture about them" and hence modified a number of Old World religious practices. For example, although orthodox Judaism decrees a day of rest on the seventh day, a number of Jews conducted business on Saturdays.

Records of Jewish experiences in the colonial South are scanty, and many assumptions have been made on the basis of guesswork. People have been identified as Jewish if they had Jewish-sounding names, but no one knows how many Jews lived in the southern colonies. Five hundred is a maximum guess, although there may not have been even three hundred at the time of the American Revolution. Intermarriage with Christians occurred; there is, however, no record of its frequency. Bertram Korn, noted rabbi and scholar, indicated in his book *American Jewry and the Civil War* that "the majority of the descendants of colonial Jews disappeared into the non-Jewish environment."

Three Jewish communities thrived in the colonial South. The first dates from 1733, when forty Jews landed in Savannah, Georgia, but seven years later most of the Jews in the Savannah settlement moved on to Charleston, South Carolina. During the 1780s a third Jewish community developed in Richmond, Virginia. The Jews of Charleston quickly achieved prominence in that city, and some of their activities are described by historian Abram Vossen Goodman in this section. Of all these early communities, the one in Charleston deserves the most attention. Not only did it contain the largest number of Jews, about two hundred by the time of the Revolution, but also its history received the greatest documentation.

Jews did not have equal political rights in any of the thirteen colonies. After the American Revolution, New York became the first state to eliminate religious tests for voting and officeholding. In the South, Virginia, in 1785, and South Carolina and Georgia, before the end of the eighteenth century, followed suit. It is noteworthy, however, that the two southern colonies with the fewest Jews in the eighteenth century, Maryland and North Carolina, were the last to allow them full participation in government.

In North Carolina a Jew, Jacob Henry, served one term in the House of Commons, but after his reelection in 1808, his right to retain his seat was challenged. Opposition united behind the state constitutional provision that state officials must accept the divinity of the New Testament, which of course no professing Jew could do. Henry defended himself so eloquently that the legislature allowed him to remain.

The Maryland Constitution of 1776 prohibited Jews from voting, officeholding, and even from serving as jurors and witnesses in court. Beginning in 1797 Jews repeatedly, but unsuccessfully, petitioned the General Assembly for equal rights. Until its passage in 1826, the "Jew bill" remained an issue of serious political concern in the state. Baltimore representatives consistently favored granting equal suffrage; rural districts staunchly opposed the idea. Interestingly most of the Jews in Maryland resided in Baltimore at this time.

Jewish life in the South between the end of the American Revolution and the end of the Civil War did not differ significantly from that of other urban whites of similar economic background. By 1820 the five hundred Jews in Charleston, constituting 5 percent of the city's white population, participated fully in the social and economic life of the city. At one time two of Charleston's four newspapers were edited by Jews. Other Charleston Jews founded a steamship line between that city and Havana, reestablished the Chamber of Commerce, introduced illuminating gas to the city, and pioneered in other industrial enterprises.

During the 1850s the Jewish population grew rapidly; according to census figures, Jewish synagogues in the South increased from six to seventeen. Upon the advent of war, there were thriving Jewish communities in Louisville and Wilmington, North Carolina; Augusta, Columbus and Macon, Georgia; Mobile and Montgomery, Alabama; and New Orleans.

Jews, for the most part, occupied a secure place in pre–Civil War society. The success of David Yulee, the first Jew ever elected to the United States Senate, illustrates this point. His entrance into Florida politics is described by Leon Hühner, a pioneer in the writing of American Jewish history. Judah P. Benjamin, another Jewish politician, rose to great prominence in Louisiana and eventually occupied several high positions during the life of the Confederacy. Unfortunately for Benjamin, however, the Civil War produced widespread Judaeophobia, and he experienced bitter criticism. As sociologist Benjamin Kaplan asserts: "He did his utmost to absorb himself into the structure of the South . . . yet managing to maintain a 'free space' around himself that somewhat protected him from the intolerance, jealousy, and hate he felt from all directions."

The activities of both Yulee and Benjamin prove a point that Bertram Korn makes: "No Jewish political figure of the Old South ever expressed reservations about the justice of slavery or the rightness of the Southern position." This distinguished scholar advances this damning notion about all southern Jews: "There is no iota of evidence, no line in a letter, no stray remark, which would lead us to believe that these Jews gave conspicuous support to the slave system out of fear of arousing anti-Jewish prejudice." Acceptance of slavery was an aspect of southern life common to nearly all of its white inhabitants.

The Civil War brought immeasurable suffering to participants on both sides, but it was notably hard on the Jews. Just prior to the conflict, an enormous wave of immigrants flooded the country. The total Jewish population in the nation swelled conspicuously to about 150,000, providing a greater target for the xenophobic American society. Traditional fears of the Jews intensified during the 1860s, as evidenced by numerous vitriolic attacks. The 15,000 Jews of the South suffered no less than their coreligionists in the North, as Korn demonstrates in the concluding essay of this section.

The following articles highlight the key aspects of southern Jewish experiences in the antebellum and Confederate periods.

Abram Vossen Goodman

South Carolina from
Shaftesbury to Salvador

CAROLINA owes its origin to the time in 1663 when eight English noblemen, on profit bent, secured a grant of land between Virginia and Spanish Florida. This great tract they proposed to colonize. How else could they make money?

It was not as easy to secure settlers for the southern wilderness as for the more inviting stretches of New England and the Middle Colonies. The proprietors must have recognized that their best prospects were among the dissenters, for their first charter proclaimed that, along with public worship according to the forms of the Anglican Church, the proprietors were ready to make such concessions as they saw fit to nonconformists of good behavior.[1]

A second charter, dating from 1665, went a step farther. It guaranteed that no person should be molested or punished for differences in belief or practice if given indulgence by the proprietors.[2] Neither document required settlers to be Christians or Protestants, but decisions in matters of religion were left completely in the hands of Carolina's owners.

The first faltering policies were terminated in 1669, when Lord Ashley assumed leadership and began to steer a more determined course. Ashley, later to become the Earl of Shaftesbury, was an inscrutable politician who belonged to a different school from the typical courtier of the Restoration age. He was endowed with a keen mind

---

1. *Colonial Records of North Carolina*, I, 32 f.   2. *Ibid.*, I, 113 f.

and independent judgment, and had a broad sympathy for religious toleration.

One of the most productive friendships in the history of English thought developed between him and the philosopher John Locke. Out of a fortuitous meeting in Oxford in 1666 the two men were drawn together, and Locke became the statesman's confidant and physician. One may see Ashley's influence at work in Locke's writings.[3] This is particularly true of his *Epistola de Tolerantia*, which someone has called the most original of Locke's works,[4] with its plea for the recognition of absolute liberty.[5]

When Ashley became the head of the enterprise, it was only natural for him to make his close friend, John Locke, chief secretary of the company of the lords proprietors.[6] Accordingly, Locke put on paper "my lord's" ideas and his own, and the net result was *The Fundamental Constitutions for the Government of Carolina* which Locke wrote in his own hand.[7]

The *Constitutions* which were prepared in 1669, with their seignories and baronies, their landgraves and caciques, seem to the uninitiated a melange of archaic concepts. Sixteen of the articles concern matters of religion, and they make rewarding reading.

The *Constitutions* set up the Church of England as the established faith, the only one to be supported by taxes.[8] In the very next article they provided that "seven persons agreeing in any religion shall constitute a church." There are extensive reasons given why this form of liberalism should prevail:

1. The natives were heathens whose lack of Christianity gave the newcomers "no right to expel them or use them ill."
2. It would be unreasonable to keep out any of the prospective settlers who would be of different religious opinions.
3. There should be civil peace and a compact with all men whatever

---

3. H. R. Fox Bourne, *The Life of John Locke* (London, 1876)), I, 238 f.; Louise Fargo Brown, *The First Earl of Shaftesbury* (New York, 1933), 156. There seems to be some doubt concerning the authorship of *The Fundamental Constitutions*. See Charles McLean Andrews, *The Colonial Period of American History* (4 vols.; New Haven: 1934-38), III, 212.

4. Alexander Campbell Fraser, *Locke* (Edinburgh, 1890), 90.

5. J. H. Locke, *Four Letters on Toleration* (London, n.d.), 1.   6. Bourne, I, 236.

7. *Ibid.*, I, 239.   8. Article 96, *Colonial Records of North Carolina*, I, 202.

their backgrounds, to avoid offense to God and scandal to the true religion.

4. "Jews, Heathens and other dissenters from the purity of the Christian religion" should obtain a chance to acquaint themselves with its doctrines and "by good usage and persuasion . . . be won over to embrace . . . the truth." [9]

This article offered as cordial a welcome to Jews as Roger Williams himself might have extended, even if the object was to win them over to Christianity.

The *Constitutions* did not obligate a man to embrace a particular denomination, but they required him to have some religion. Each person above the age of seventeen had to identify himself with a religious group or else forfeit the protection of the law.[10] Atheism as such was under a ban, but all religions were to be respected. "Abusive language against any religion" was forbidden, "that being the certain way of disturbing the peace, and of hindering the conversion of any to the truth." [11]

So much for the religious philosophy of Locke's *Constitutions*. The truth is that this fabric of government was never accepted by the settlers of Carolina. Five times the proprietors sought the adherence of the Assembly, but their efforts proved futile on each occasion.[12] A final version of the *Fundamental Constitutions* was proffered as late as 1698 in somewhat abridged form. The same religious conditions as before were in evidence, but the Jews as such were not mentioned.[13]

Shortly afterwards the division of the province into North and South Carolina was achieved. For some time the settlements to the north had suffered because of remoteness from the government at Charleston. In fact, it was easier for them to ship their tobacco by way of Virginia. Isolation bred separatism, until finally the official break was completed in 1712 when Edward Hyde became first governor of North Carolina.[14]

9. *Ibid.*, I, 202 f.   10. Article 101, *ibid.*, I, 203.   11. Article 106, *ibid.*, I, 204.
12. Andrews, *Colonial Period of American History*, 220 f.
13. *Colonial Records of North Carolina*, II, 856 f.
14. R. D. W. Conner *et al.*, *History of North Carolina* (6 vols.; Chicago, 1919), I, 97.

There were practically no Jews in North Carolina during the colonial period.[15] Such as came there lived under a regime with a hateful established church whose treatment of dissenters was harsh. Of more interest to Jews was their struggle for complete emancipation after freedom and statehood had been achieved.[16] This was not entirely realized until 1868 when Jews were permitted to hold office under the state constitution, a product of Reconstruction days.[17]

South Carolina's record, on the other hand, has been outstanding, with its treatment of the Jews more uniformly favorable than that of any other colony where they settled in numbers. Few indeed were the rebuffs faced, while the story of the rights enjoyed by the Jews establishes South Carolina as the first community in the modern world where Jews might vote. It was also the first government where a Jew was elected to office by his Christian neighbors.

The first Jew mentioned was living in South Carolina in 1695, fifteen years after the founding of Charleston. In that year the Yamassee tribe, which was friendly to the English, took four Indians from Spanish Florida their prisoners and brought them to Charleston, where Governor John Archdale had them questioned. The governor wrote: "They could speak *Spanish*, and I had a *Jew* for an Interpreter, so upon examination I found they profess'd the Christian Religion as the Papists do." They were accordingly rescued from the prospect of slavery and sent to St. Augustine.[18] As for the unnamed Jew, he was assumedly Sephardic, and therefore well qualified to translate such Spanish as was spoken by the Indians.

The early Jewish arrivals were a tiny segment of the heterogeneous population of South Carolina, which showed a marked diversity

15. Leon Hühner's article, "The Jews of North Carolina prior to 1800," mentions but one indisputable Jew in pre-Revolutionary North Carolina, although he lists a number of Jewish-sounding names, signifying nothing. *Publications of the American Jewish Historical Society*, hereinafter cited as *P.A.J.H.S.*, XXIX, passim.

16. Stephen Beauregard Weeks, *Church and State in North Carolina* (*Johns Hopkins University Studies*, 11th series), passim.

17. Hühner, "The Struggle for Religious Liberty in North Carolina," *P.A.J.H.S.*, XVI, 68.

18. John Archdale, "A New Description of that Fertile and Pleasant Province of Carolina," in B. R. Carroll, *Historical Collections of South Carolina* (New York, 1836), II, 106.

from the beginning. Most conspicuous among the dissenters were the Huguenots who entered the province in large numbers following the revocation of the Edict of Nantes in 1685.[19] By 1700 they numbered one-twelfth of the population.[20] For our study the place of the Huguenots in South Carolina life is important. In their political struggles, they served as shock troops in the battle for the rights of aliens. If we search for a clue to explain the enjoyment of civil rights by the Jews of South Carolina on a large scale, it is found in the part played by these French-speaking foreigners.

Unfortunately for the peace of mind of the Huguenots themselves, they plunged into partisan politics. In France these Protestants had fought for the cause of Calvinism; under English rule they associated themselves with the political fortunes of the Anglican Church.[21] It so happened that in South Carolina the dissenters and the Church of England party were pretty evenly matched, so that the Huguenots occupied a key place in the party strife.[22]

Quite understandably the Huguenots as foreigners were in an exposed position and became the butt of agitation by the dissenters. The latter went so far as to question the validity of French marriages and the legitimacy of the offspring of Huguenots. What is more, their opponents insisted that since the French settlers were aliens, their estates would revert to the proprietors upon death.[23]

Of course the Huguenots appealed to the proprietors in England for support and received a reply that stiffened their resistance. The French settlers, said the authorities overseas, "have Equall Justice wth English men and Injoy the Same Privilidges."[24]

The Huguenots must have listened with satisfaction when Governor Joseph Blake, a Puritan, addressed the Assembly on February 23, 1697, and urged that the lawmakers unify the population by passing various measures that would improve the standing of aliens by securing their estates.[25] A joint committee of both chambers set to work

---

19. Arthur Henry Hirsch, *Huguenots of Colonial South Carolina* (Durham: 1928), 10 ff.

20. *Ibid.*, 113 f. 21. *Ibid.*, 90 ff., 105. 22. *Ibid.*, 113.

23. *South Carolina Commons Assembly Journals*, 1693, p. 36. 24. *Ibid.*

25. *Commons Assembly Journals*, 1697, p. 5 f.

immediately[26] and, by the time the Assembly adjourned on March 10, the act they proposed had become law.[27]

The statute declared that religious persecution had forced some aliens to settle in South Carolina and these people had proved themselves law-abiding and industrious. "All Aliens, male and female, of what nation soever, which now are inhabitants of South Carolina," it declared, should have all the rights of anyone born of English parents.[28]

It is asserted that since certain settlers had come in the hope of securing freedom of conscience, all Christians (Papists excepted) should enjoy full freedom of worship. They were not, however, to disturb the public peace or interfere with the religious services of others.[29]

It should be noted that freedom of conscience was granted only to Protestants, but the full rights of British subjects in all other respects were extended to every alien who applied by petition to the governor within the next three months. Those who became naturalized in this way were required to swear allegiance to the king.[30]

Included with the text of the law were the names of sixty-four men who had already petitioned the General Assembly for the benefits now accorded. The list has a distinct Huguenot flavor except for the four names at the end. The conclusion is as follows: "Simon Vallentine merchant, ——— [undecipherable] merchant, Jacob Mendis merchant, and Avila merchant." [31]

There is every reason to believe that these were four Jewish merchants, some of whom—probably all—were of Spanish and Portuguese descent. The first of them, Simon Valentine, may be positively identified. Under the name of Simon Valentyn Vander Wilde, a Jew, he was recorded in New York as receiving his burgher right in 1682.[32] His South Carolina naturalization papers too have been preserved. They read in part as follows:

GREETEING

KNOW Yee that Simon Valentine Mercht: an alien of ye Jewish Nation borne out of the Crown of England hath Taken his oath of allegiance to our Sovereign Lord William ye Third . . . And is fully . . . Qualified and

---

26. *Ibid.*, 6.   27. *Ibid.*, 18.   28. *Statutes of South Carolina*, II, 131.
29. *Ibid.*, II, 133.   30. *Ibid.*, II, 132.   31. *Ibid.*
32. Hühner, "Asser Levy," *P.A.J.H.S.*, VIII, 22 n.

Capacitated to have use and Enjoy all the rights Priviledges Powers and Immunityes Given . . . any Alien then Inhabitant of South Carolina . . .

The document is dated May 26, 1697—two and a half months after the law was enacted—and is signed by the governor, John Blake.[33]

We have a shred of information about Abraham Avilah, one of the other three merchants whose names accompanied Valentine's on the petition. In 1698 Avilah empowered Valentine to serve as his attorney.[34] This lends further probability to the hypothesis that Avilah was Jewish.

The act of naturalization was truly a historic event. Many years were to elapse before 1740 when Parliament would pass its law to naturalize foreign Protestants and Jews in the colonies. We recall that when a similar attempt to naturalize Jewish aliens in England was made in 1753, the act was revoked following furious demonstrations of popular resentment. Note 1697, the year of Jewish naturalization in South Carolina, as a milestone in Jewish history.

A second important right secured by the Jews of South Carolina was the franchise, which was also highlighted by the political battles of the Huguenots. For the mass naturalizations did not end the party struggles, which continued as bitterly as ever.

From the very earliest times, the qualifications of voters had been defined in exceptionally broad terms. The *Fundamental Constitutions* had declared merely that no one owning less than fifty acres of freehold[35] should be able to participate in the election of a member of Parliament, as the General Assembly is there called. In 1692 the Assembly extended the franchise to anyone who would swear that he was worth ten pounds. Although the text has been lost,[36] we know what became of the measure. The proprietors vetoed it, claiming the bill was so loosely worded that even the pirates of the Red Sea would have been qualified to vote in Carolina.[37] If the pirates of the Red Sea might vote, why not the Jews in the province?

The voting situation became a crucial issue as the outgrowth of one

---

33. Barnett A. Elzas, *The Jews of South Carolina* (Philadelphia, 1905), 20 f.
34. *Ibid.,* 21 f.   35. *Colonial Records of North Carolina,* I, 199.
36. *Statutes of South Carolina,* II, 73.
37. William James Rivers, *A Sketch of the History of South Carolina* (Charleston, 1856), 437.

of the fights which flourished between the dissenters and the Church of England party. In 1702 there was quite a commotion in the Assembly when the dissenters claimed that Governor James Moore had organized a military expedition against St. Augustine in order to enslave Indians for private gain.[38] At the time, half the members walked out, so that a quorum was lacking to approve the debts incurred during the campaign.[39] Later there was a riot, or rather a brawl, which resulted in one casualty, a woman's miscarriage.[40]

This was all very trivial. But in the tense atmosphere of South Carolina it was deemed sufficiently serious to demand redress from the proprietors in England. Accordingly one hundred and fifty inhabitants of Colleton County, including Assembly members, gathered together on June 26, 1703, and signed a long address of grievances which they sent to London by John Ash, one of the dissenter leaders. They hoped thus to gain the support of the lords proprietors in the battle against the Anglican party.[41] After describing the course of Governor Moore's troubles and the abortive riot in Charleston, they went on to tell of the election procedures in the province.

They felt that foreigners had infringed on the "fundamental rights & unquestionable Privileges belonging to *English-men*," for no alien, unless properly qualified, should have the right to vote. Yet in the Berkeley County election of November, 1701, aliens, free Negroes, and servants had participated.[42]

But things were even worse in the election of 1703.

For at this last Election, Jews, Strangers, Sailors, Servants, Negroes, & almost every *French* Man in Craven & Berkly County came down to elect, & their Votes were taken; & the Persons by them voted for were returned by the Sheriff, to the manifest wrong & prejudice of other Candidates.[43]

The protest concluded with a passionate appeal for that relief which could not be found in Carolina. "When Foreigners & Strangers shall make our laws," it declared, ". . . when, in a word, Force is made the Arbiter of all differences . . . it is surely a time, if ever there be one, for a people to complain." [44]

It goes without saying that the Jewish issue was dragged into the

38. *Ibid.*, 456.   39. *Ibid.*, 457 f.   40. *Ibid.*, 458 f.
41. *Ibid.*, 453 ff.   42. *Ibid.*, 455.   43. *Ibid.*, 459.
44. *Ibid.*, 459 f.

controversy because the Jews were not lined up with the dissenters. Had they voted on the other side, the ballots to which they were entitled by law would have been respected and not denounced. Because they were anxious to confound the governor's followers, the dissenters had to impeach the character of all associated with him.

This same procedure was pursued in a rabid pamphlet, entitled *Affairs in Carolina*, which was begun by John Ash, the representative of the dissenters in London. Death intervened before the work was finished, but Ash got far enough to accuse Simon Valentine, the Jew naturalized in 1697, of serving as go-between for Governor Moore in a shady deal. It concerned the collection of money from John Martin to foster illegal trade with the French at a time when a state of war existed between the two nations.

Ash admitted that he could not prove his charges in a court of law.[45] Mr. Alexander Salley, who edited his pamphlet, stated that the abuse and bias of the brochure rendered it unreliable as a historical source.[46] Ash makes clear, however, which side Valentine (and other Jews) espoused in the great provincial struggle.

After Ash's death Joseph Boone continued agitation in England on behalf of the dissenters, first before the proprietors and then before the House of Lords.[47] He presented a memorial to that body which described the role of the Jews in the election in almost the same language as Ash had employed.[48] At this time he engaged England's outstanding public relations counsel of the day, Daniel Defoe. The author of *Robinson Crusoe* turned out a pamphlet called *Party-Tyranny* for the benefit of the two houses of Parliament.[49] There, too, appears the account of the Jewish voters.[50]

While the dissenters were carrying their futile protests to England, the Anglican group at home made reprisals in their own way. In 1704, they passed an act to exclude dissenters from the Assembly by requiring all nonconformist members to receive the sacrament of the Lord's Supper according to the usage of the Church of England. At

45. Alexander S. Salley, *Narratives of Early Carolina*, (New York, 1911), 275.
46. *Ibid.*, 268.   47. Rivers, 222 f.
48. Frederick Dalcho, *An Historical Account of the Protestant Episcopal Church in South Carolina* (Charleston, 1820), 64 f.
49. Salley, 223 f.   50. *Ibid.*, 245.

the same time, Anglican assemblymen were excused from the sacrament altogether.[51]

On November 4, 1704—six months later—the Anglicans had their revenge. They set up a church establishment (quite in harmony with the provisions of the *Fundamental Constitutions*),[52] they passed a new naturalization law, and they authorized new standards for suffrage. The new naturalization regulations added two restrictions not found in the act of 1697. First, a candidate for naturalization must take the oath of allegiance to Queen Anne and that of abjuration to the house of Stuart "on the Holy Evangelists or otherwise according to the form of his profession." The "otherwise" was the loophole which provided for such exceptions as Jews. The second provision was more significant in that it would not permit naturalized subjects to serve in the Assembly.[53]

The new suffrage requirements demanded that voters be twenty-one years of age, own fifty acres of land or be worth ten pounds, and reside in their precincts for three months.[54] This law allowed aliens to vote as before.

The act to keep dissenters out of the Assembly did not have a long life, for it was based on party vengeance. Repeal was brought about on November 30, 1706.[55]

The election law, however, was not replaced until September 19, 1721. The new statute declared that "every free white man . . . professing the Christian religion" who was at least twenty-one years of age, able to meet the property requirements, might vote after a year's residence in the province.[56]

The same act did not include Christianity among the qualifications for membership in the Assembly, nor was there any Christological phrase in the oaths taken by those elected. But each successful candidate had to be sworn "on the holy evangelists." [57] In addition each member was expected to take "the usual oaths" and conform to other regulations which were beyond fulfillment by any believing Jew.

There is no evidence to indicate that the Jews were under con-

51. *Statutes of South Carolina*, II, 232 f.   52. *Ibid.*, II, 252 f.
53. *Ibid.*, II, 252 f.   54. *Ibid.*, II, 249.   55. *Ibid.*, III, 140.
56. *Ibid.*, III, 136.   57. *Ibid.*, III, 137.

sideration when this new legislation became effective. There were so few of them in the colony at the time that, in 1723, a full account of the state of religion in South Carolina did not see fit so much as to mention the Jews.[58]

The fact was that a long period elapsed before Charleston might be described as having a Jewish community. We know already of the four Jews who were naturalized in 1697. Barnett Elzas, who wrote on the Jews of South Carolina, found only two additional Jewish names in Charleston during the next thirty-five years.[59] During the thirties of the eighteenth century a thin trickle of Jewish immigrants flowed in and, beginning with 1750, Jewish names occur more frequently in Elzas' catalogue.[60] Many of the newcomers came from England, some of them belonged to the malcontents who abandoned Savannah, and a few, no doubt, sailed to Charleston from the West Indies.

In 1750, the community was large enough to establish a congregation, known as Beth Elohim,[61] which acquired a synagogue during its first decade of existence.[62] Probably this house of prayer was a converted dwelling. At any rate, it was the second synagogue on the North American continent, the first being in New York. In South Carolina there never seems to have been an attempt to bar Jews or any other sect, save Catholics, from worshiping as they pleased.

Isaac Da Costa, who came over from London in 1750, was representative of the community in two important fields of activity: religion and trade. He was *hazzan* of the congregation, while serving as shipping agent and merchant, dealing in European and Indian goods.[63]

Moses Lindo, probably the most unusual of the Jewish merchants, laid claim to an education at the Merchant Taylor's School in London.[64] He became an expert in indigo and asserted that he had been summoned before Parliament to testify on the qualities of the Carolina product.[65]

In 1756, he removed to Charleston[66] where he exercised his talents as sorter of the indigo which was now being grown in ever-increasing quantities, since the British government offered a bounty for the colo-

58. Hirsch, 315 ff.   59. Elzas, 277.   60. *Ibid.*
61. Nathaniel Levin, "Beth Elohim," *Charleston Year Book, 1883*, 301.
62. *Ibid.*, 302.   63. Elzas, 35 f.   64. *Supra*, 62 f.
65. Elzas, 48.   66. *Ibid.*, 49.

nial crop.[67] Seventy-four prominent men of South Carolina signed a testimonial which declared Lindo to be the only man qualified to grade the indigo properly, and Governor Thomas Boone (at Lindo's own request) made him "Surveyor and Inspector-General of the Indico" of South Carolina.[68]

There are other examples of Lindo's flair for histrionics. One was his correspondence with the authorities of the College of Rhode Island, to which he promised a munificent endowment if Jewish students were made welcome.[69] Another was the dispatch of a large water sapphire or topaz, purchased for a trifle, to the queen of England, since he deemed one of lesser rank unworthy of so precious a stone.[70] Lindo died in 1774.[71]

Turning from business to the social life of Charleston, we find little if any discrimination against Jews. Moses Solomon became one of the members of St. Andrew's Society, a Scottish social and philanthropic organization to which men of other stocks gained admission.[72] And Isaac Da Costa, the *hazzan*, in 1759, was made treasurer of King Solomon's Lodge, No. 1, the oldest regularly constituted lodge in the Masonry of South Carolina.[73]

There was even a Jewish officer, named Joseph Levy, commissioned lieutenant in the South Carolina Regiment of Foot in 1757. During the Cherokee War of 1760 and 1761, we find Lieutenant Levy enrolled in Colonel Middleton's South Carolina Regiment.[74] This conflict was a training school for some of the state's heroes of the Revolution. Henry Laurens, William Moultrie, Francis Marion, Isaac Huger, and Andrew Pickens were officers who served as comrades in arms with Levy.[75]

During these years the political pattern of South Carolina had been changing. The election law of 1721, which required voters to be Christian, came to be replaced by one in 1745 which raised the property

67. *Charleston Year Book, 1883*, 403.   68. Elzas, 53 ff.
69. *Supra*, 61 ff.   70. Elzas, 64.   71. *Ibid.*, 66.
72. Mrs. St. Julien Ravenel, *Charleston* (New York, 1906), 119 f.; Elzas, 28.
73. Elzas, 36.   74. *Ibid.*, 42.
75. Edward McCrady, *The History of South Carolina under the Royal Government, 1719–1776* (New York, 1899), 350.

qualifications,[76] and by one in 1759 which made Protestantism a requirement.[77] Maybe the arrival of a contingent of Acadian exiles was responsible for this.[78] Were Jews being deprived of the vote during this period? There is no evidence that they were prevented from casting their ballots, and when we note that one Jew, Francis Salvador, was actually elected to office, we may be sure that any restriction on voting had become a dead letter.

Salvador, who was born in England, belonged to one of the most prominent Jewish families in the country.[79] His grandfather, Francis Salvador, Jr., had been associated with the effort to send Jews to Georgia at the outset of Oglethorpe's undertaking.[80] Young Salvador—he was probably only twenty-six at the time[81]—landed in Charleston, 1773,[82] and set himself up as a planter on some of his family-in-law's land in the Ninety-Six district.[83]

The neighborhood was seething with agitation against Parliament and King George, and Salvador, newcomer though he was, played an active part in the patriot cause. Perhaps he recognized that out on the Carolina frontier a man was rated at his own worth, while across the sea in England all his family's prestige and influence could not wipe away the stigma of being a Jew. At any rate, his district made him their representative to the First and Second Provincial Congress in 1774. There he was named to various committees concerned with the conduct of the war.[84] He was the first Jew in American history, and probably the first Jew in the modern world, to serve in an elective office.

Early in the Revolution, Salvador was slain in a border clash with Indians who had taken the warpath under British instigation.[85] His career was not so much a tribute to the man himself as it was a symbol of the atmosphere of good will which prevailed in South Carolina.

76. Albert Edward McKinley, *The Suffrage Franchise in the Thirteen English Colonies in America, Publications of the University of Pennsylvania, Series in History* (Philadelphia, 1905), II, 155.

77. *Ibid.,* 157. 78. McCrady, 326 ff. 79. Elzas, 68 ff.
80. *Infra,* 172 ff. 81. Elzas, 76 n. 21. 82. Elzas, 68.
83. *Ibid.,* 70.
84. *Journal of Provincial Congress, 1775,* p. 29.
85. John Drayton, *Memoirs of the American Revolution . . .* (2 vols.; Charleston, 1821), II, 338 ff.

The state of religion that existed there on the eve of the Revolution was almost idyllic, if we may judge by the picture which William Gerard de Brahm painted. De Brahm established a German community at Bethany, Georgia, and built the fortifications of Charleston. His service as surveyor for South Carolina, Georgia, and East Florida gave him the background for a descriptive work with the bizarre title of *Philosophico-Historico-Hydrogeography of South Carolina, Georgia, and East Florida*.[86]

Said de Brahm of Charleston:

The city is divided in two parishes, has two churches, S^t. Michal's and S^t. Philip's, and six meeting houses, vid^t an Independent, a Presbyterian, a French, a German, and two Baptist; there is also an assembly for Quakers, and an other for Jews; all which are composed of several nations, altho' differing in religious principels, and in the knowledge of salvation, yet are far from being incouraged, or even inclining to that disorder which is so comon among men of contrary religious sentiments in many other parts of the world, where that pernicious spirit of controversy has laid foundation to hatred, persecution, and cruel inquisition, in lieu of ascertaining thereby how to live a godly life. A society of men (which in religion, government, and negotiation avoids whatever can disturbe peace and quietness) will always grow and prosper: so will this City and Province, whoose inhabitants was from its beginning renound for concord, compleasance, courteousness, and tenderness towards each other, and more so towards foreigners, with out regard or respect of nation or religion.[87]

This tradition is more glorious than anything in South Carolina's annals about the craft of a Marion or the brilliance of a Calhoun, or all the heroism of her sons during the dark days of the War Between the States.

---

86. *Philosophico-Historico-Hydrogeography*, Plowden Weston, ed. (*Documents Connected with History of South Carolina*), 161 f.
87. *Ibid.*, 195 f.

Jacob Henry's Speech, 1809

PETITION TO VACATE THE SEAT OF JACOB HENRY*
NORTH CAROLINA

In House of Commons 5th December, 1809

Whereas it is contrary to the freedom and independence of our happy and beloved Government, that any person should be allowed to have a seat in this Assembly or to watch over the rights of a free *People*, who is not constitutionally qualified for that purpose. It is therefore made known that a certain JACOB HENRY, a Member of this House, denies the divine authority of the New Testament, and refused to take the Oath prescribed by Law, for his qualification, in violation of the Constitution of the State—

Resolved, that the said JACOB HENRY is not entitled to a seat in this Assembly, and that the same be vacated.

Jacob Henry's Speech, 1809

I certainly, Mr. Speaker, know not the design of the Declaration of Rights made by the people of this State in the year 1776, if it was not to consecrate certain great and fundamental rights and principles which even the Constitution cannot impair; for the 44th section of the latter instrument declares that the Declaration of Rights ought never to be violated, on any pretence whatever; if there is any apparent difference between the two instruments, they ought, if possible,

---

* From minutes of North Carolina House of Commons.

to be reconciled; but if there is a final repugnance between them, the Declaration of Rights must be considered paramount; for I believe it is to the Constitution, as the Constitution is to law; it controls and directs it absolutely and conclusively. If, then, a belief in the Protestant religion is required by the Constitution, to qualify a man for a seat in this house, and such qualification is dispensed with by the Declaration of Rights, the provision of the Constitution must be altogether inoperative; as the language of the Bill of Rights is, "that all men have a natural and inalienable right to worship ALMIGHTY GOD according to the dictates of their own consciences." It is undoubtedly a natural right, and when it is declared to be an inalienable one by the people in their sovereign and original capacity, any attempt to alienate either by the Constitution or by law, must be vain and fruitless.

It is difficult to conceive how such a provision crept into the Constitution, unless it is from the difficulty the human mind feels in suddenly emancipating itself from fetters by which it has long been enchained: and how adverse it is to the feelings and manners of the people of the present day every gentleman may satisfy himself by glancing at the religious belief of the persons who fill the various offices in this State: there are Presbyterians, Lutherans, Calvinists, Mennonists, Baptists, Trinitarians, and Unitarians. But, as far as my observation extends, there are fewer Protestants, in the strict sense of the word, used by the Constitution, than of any other persuasion; for I suppose that they meant by it, the Protestant religion as established by the law in England. For other persuasions we see houses of worship in almost every part of the State, but very few of the Protestant; so few, that indeed I fear that the people of this State would for some time remain unrepresented in this House, if that clause of the Constitution is supposed to be in force. So far from believing in the Thirty-nine Articles, I will venture to assert that a majority of the people never have read them.

If a man should hold religious principles incompatible with the freedom and safety of the State, I do not hesitate to pronounce that he should be excluded from the public councils of the same; and I trust if I know myself, no one would be more ready to aid and assist than myself. But I should really be at a loss to specify any known religious principles which are thus dangerous. It is surely a question between a man and his Maker, and requires more than human attributes to pronounce which of the numerous sects prevailing in the world is most acceptable to the Deity. If a man fulfills the duties of that religion, which his education or his conscience has pointed to him as the true one, no person, I hold, in this our land of liberty, has a right to arraign him at the bar of any inquisition: and the day, I trust, has long passed, when principles merely speculative were propagated by force; when the sincere and pious were made victims, and the light-minded bribed into hypocrites.

The purest homage man could render to the Almighty was the sacrifice of his passions and the performance of his duties. That the ruler of the universe would receive with equal benignity the various offerings of man's adoration, if they proceeded from the heart. Governments only concern the actions and conduct of man, and not his speculative notions. Who among us feels himself so exalted above his fellows as to have a right to dictate to them any mode of belief? Will you bind the conscience in chains, and fasten conviction upon the mind in spite of the conclusions of reason and of those ties and habitudes which are blended with every pulsation of the heart? Are you prepared to plunge at once from the sublime heights of moral legislation into the dark and gloomy caverns of superstitious ignorance? Will you drive from your shores and from the shelter of your constitution, all who do not lay their oblations on the same altar, observe the same ritual, and subscribe to the same dogmas? If so, which, among the various sects into which we are divided, shall be the favored one?

I should insult the understanding of this House to suppose it possible that they could ever assent to such absurdities; for all know that persecution in all its shapes and modifications, is contrary to the genius of our government and the spirit of our laws, and that it can never produce any other effect than to render men hypocrites or martyrs.

When Charles V, Emperor of Germany, tired of the cares of government, resigned his crown to his son, he retired to a monastery, where he amused the evening of his life in regulating the movements of watches, endeavoring to make a number keep the same time; but, not being able to make any two go exactly alike, it led him to reflect upon the folly and crimes he had committed, in attempting the impossibility of making men think alike!

Nothing is more easily demonstrated than that the conduct alone is the subject of human laws, and that man ought to suffer civil disqualification for what he does, and not for what he thinks. The mind can receive laws only from Him, of whose Divine essence it is a portion; He alone can punish disobedience; for who else can know its movements, or estimate their merits? The religion I profess, inculcates every duty which man owes to his fellow man; it enjoins upon its votaries the practice of every virtue, and the detestation of every vice; it teaches them to hope for the favor of heaven exactly in proportion as their lives have been directed by just, honorable, and beneficent maxims. This, then, gentlemen, is my creed, it was impressed upon my infant mind; it has been the director of my youth, the monitor of my manhood, and will, I trust, be the consolation of my old age. At any rate, Mr. Speaker, I am sure that you cannot see anything in this Religion, to deprive me of my seat in this house. So far as relates to my life and conduct, the examination of these I submit with cheerfulness to your candid and liberal construction. What may be the religion of him who made this objection against me, or whether he has any religion or not I am unable to say. I have never considered it my duty to pry into the belief of other members of this house. If their actions are upright and conduct just, the rest is for their own consideration, not for mine. I do not seek to make converts to my faith, whatever it may be esteemed in the eyes of my officious friend, nor do I exclude any one from my esteem or friendship, because he and I differ in that respect. The same charity, therefore, it is not unreasonable to expect, will be extended to myself, because in all things that relate to the State and to the duties of civil life, I am bound by the same obligations with my fellow-citizens, nor does any man subscribe more sincerely than myself to the maxim, "whatever ye would that men should do unto you do ye so even unto them, for such is the law and the prophets."

Ira Rosenwaike
Further Light
on Jacob Henry

NORTH CAROLINA'S Constitution of 1776 denied public office to individuals unable to affirm the "truth of the Protestant religion" or the "divine authority" of the New Testament. In 1809, however, Jacob Henry was able to prevent his seat in the House of Commons, the lower chamber of the state legislature, from being declared vacant because, as a Jew, he could not make such affirmations. Henry's successful effort has long been celebrated as a victory of the principle that the right to public office is not dependent on religious belief. The impressive speech Henry delivered when the House debated the issue is credited with persuading the legislators to reject the resolution that would have deprived him of his seat. The speech has been reprinted continually, since at least 1814,[1] in collections of addresses and documents and in histories. So limited, however, has our knowledge of Henry himself been that modern-day historians are still unable to assess the validity of the statement by a mid-nineteenth-century North Carolina chronicler that Henry's speech was reportedly "the production of [the state's] Chief Justice Taylor."[2] John

1. In a note accompanying the most recent reprint as of this writing, Joseph L. Blau indicates that the first reprinting probably appeared in a collection of addresses, *The American Speaker*, published at Philadelphia in 1814. See also Daniel J. Boorstin (ed.), *An American Primer* (2 vols.; Chicago, 1966), I, 220. On the North Carolina state Constitution of 1776, see *American Jewish Archives*, X (1958), 30–31.

2. John H. Wheeler, *Historical Sketches of North Carolina from 1584 to 1851* (2 vols.; Philadelphia, 1851), II, 74.

Louis Taylor, a native of Ireland and a Roman Catholic, may conceivably have feared that, if a Jew could lose his position, so might a Catholic, for failure to subscribe to "the truth of the Protestant religion" as specified in Article 32 of the state constitution.[3]

In general all historical accounts note that Jacob Henry, first elected a member of the House of Commons from Carteret County in 1808, was reelected in 1809 and that during his second term an attempt was made to vacate his seat. Then biographical data very nearly cease, without so much as the mention of a date or place of birth or of death. It is my intention now to sketch in chronological sequence some events in Henry's life as revealed through census material, vital records, obituaries, and wills. Through such means, at least a skeletal outline may be rendered, one which must suffice until a much-needed, full-blown portrait can be supplied.

That Jacob Henry was the son of Joel and Amelia Henry has been documented on the basis of Joel Henry's will.[4] Joel Henry is listed in the first Federal census, that of 1790, as head of a household of three in Carteret County.[5] It may be assumed that the younger male in the household, a lad under sixteen years of age (the only age classifications were over or under sixteen), was Jacob Henry. At the 1800 census, Joel Henry was again listed as head of a household, in Beaufort town, Carteret County.[6] Since the Henry family then consisted of only one white male and one white female (plus ten slaves), it may be surmised that at the time their son Jacob was not living at home. Jacob was clearly in Carteret County in 1801, however, for county marriage bond records show his application to marry Esther Whitehurst that year. The records are dated February 9, 1801.[7]

At the 1810 census, for the first time Jacob Henry headed a household in Beaufort town.[8] The household consisted of five white males,

---

3. *Ibid.*, p. 129; Boorstin, pp. 219–20.

4. See Morris U. Schappes (ed.), *A Documentary History of the Jews in the United States, 1654–1875* (New York, 1950), 597.

5. United States Bureau of the Census, *Heads of Families at the First Census of the United States taken in the year 1790. North Carolina* (Washington, D.C., 1908), 129.

6. "Population Schedules of the Second Census of the United States: 1800. North Carolina" (Ms., National Archives, Washington, D.C.).

7. Schappes, 597.

8. "Population Schedules of the Third Census of the United States: 1810. North Carolina" (Ms., National Archives, Washington, D.C.).

five white females, and twelve slaves. The household's oldest white male, apparently, Jacob Henry, was in the twenty-six to forty-five age category; the oldest white female, apparently Esther Henry, was in the sixteen to twenty-five age group. By 1820 the Jacob Henrys have disappeared from the census rolls of North Carolina, but other sources indicate the family's migration to Charleston, South Carolina, where one household in 1820 was indeed headed by a Jacob Henry. This household contained four white males, seven white females, and fifteen slaves. The white adults included one male in the forty-five and over age category, one female in this age group, and one female between twenty-six and forty-five years of age.[9]

The *City Gazette* of Charleston for July 31, 1823, reported the following obituary:

On the 16th inst. departed this transitory life, in the 37th year of her age, after an illness of 16 days, Mrs. Esther Henry, the wife of Mr. Jacob Henry of this city. Mrs. Henry was a native of Beaufort, in North Carolina, but has resided in this city for several years.[10]

Two years later almost to the day, the *City Gazette* for July 28, 1825, lamented

the loss of Mrs. Amelia Henry, a native of the Island of Bermuda, but for many years a truly respectable resident in this city to which she was brought in early life, with exception of a few years' residence in Newburn and Beaufort, N. C. She pursued practice of midwifery in this city. She departed on the morning of June 25th.[11]

Amelia, Jacob Henry's mother, was seventy years old at the time of her death, according to the Charleston death records. Both she and her daughter-in-law Esther—who was called "Hester" in the official city records and listed as thirty-eight years of age—were interred in the "Hebrew" cemetery.[12] Amelia's will, dated April 19, 1824, indicates the composition of the Henry family a year before her death. Mentioned are her son Jacob, who is named coexecutor, and seven grand-

9. "Population Schedules of the Fourth Census of the United States: 1820. South Carolina" (Ms., National Archives, Washington, D.C.).
10. Cited in *South Carolina Historical Magazine*, LIII (1952), 172.
11. *Ibid.*, 174.
12. "Return of Deaths within the City of Charleston 20 July 1823 to 27 February 1825, 27 February 1825 to 9 July 1826" (Ms., County Department of Health, Charleston, S.C.).

children: Denah, named coexecutrix, Joel, Philip Jacob, Samuel, Judah (Judith), Cordelia, and Sarah Henry.[13]

Two of Henry's children were next to appear in the obituary columns. The *Charleston Courier* of November 11, 1835, reported the death, at the residence of her brother in Orangeburg District, of "Miss Judith J. Henry, second daughter of J. Henry, Esq. of this city, aged 26 years." Judith's will, dated October 1, 1835, named her brother Philip J. Henry as executor.[14] In a lengthy eulogy, the *Charleston Courier* of May 26, 1842, recorded the death of Philip J. Henry in his thirty-fifth year; he had been "a native of Beaufort, North-Carolina, but for many years a resident of this city."

Perhaps historians have failed to note the date of Jacob Henry's death because the Charleston press published no obituary to mark the passing of this long-term Charleston resident. Nor, strangely, has any record of the probating of a will appeared, but a funeral notice in the *Charleston Courier* of October 14, 1847, is of moment in this connection:

The relatives, friends and acquaintances of Jacob Henry and of his son S. W. Henry, and the Masonic Fraternity, are particularly requested to attend the funeral of the former, from the residence of his son, Meeting-st., opposite Circular Church, this afternoon at 4 o'clock, without further invitation.

It seems clear that this announcement refers to Jacob Henry, the former North Carolina legislator. S. W. Henry, his son, would have been Samuel [Whitehurst?] Henry. Furthermore, Henry's Masonic associations as early as his North Carolina years are known; one study has pointed out his membership in a lodge in Beaufort County in 1807 and in New Bern in 1812.[15]

Jacob Henry's age at the time of his death in 1847 can be calculated from census sources as about seventy-two or seventy-three. In 1790, as a child in his father's household, he was under sixteen, indicating a birth year not earlier than 1774. In 1820 he was enumerated

13. "Charleston County Will Book" (Ms., Charleston, S.C.).
14. *Ibid.*
15. Samuel Oppenheim, "The Jews and Masonry in the United States before 1810," *Publications of the American Jewish Historical Society*, XIX (1910), 75.

in the age classification "forty-five and upward," which would mean a birth year not later than 1775 (assuming the accuracy of the tally). Why should Jacob Henry have fallen into such obscurity during his lifetime that his death—unlike that of his wife, or of his mother—produced no obituary? That is not clear. What can be stated is that his contemporaries were unaware of the lasting place Jacob Henry was to achieve in the annals of American history.

Leon Hühner

David L. Yulee,
Florida's First Senator

Ιτ IS A curious fact that so little has been written concerning the career of several Southern statesmen who were potent figures in our national history during the period immediately preceding the Civil War. Men whose names in their day were familiar throughout the land are to-day well nigh forgotten, and even so brilliant a personality as that of Judah P. Benjamin had no fitting biography until Prof. Pierce Butler's comparatively recent work appeared.

Though by no means so prominent as Benjamin, David L. Yulee was nevertheless a noteworthy figure in his day. It is, therefore, remarkable that, beyond a dozen lines or so, nothing has ever been written concerning his career with the exception of an article by his son, C. Wickliffe Yulee, which, however, is mainly of a reminiscent and personal character.[1] In preparing this paper, therefore, it was necessary to go through original documents on file in various government departments, the public reports of Senate and House Committees, and the writings of distinguished contemporaries.

Not only had Senator Yulee the distinction of having been a prominent factor in national affairs for over twenty years, but to him belonged in large measure the honor of having obtained the admission of Florida into the Union, and of being her first Senator. Besides this, he is of additional interest because he was the first Jew ever elected to the United States Senate.

---

1. C. Wickliffe Yulee, "Senator Yulee," *Publications of the Florida Historical Society*, Jacksonville, 1909, vol. ii, nos. 1 and 2.

The father of the subject of our sketch never bore the name of Yulee. The family name was Levy, and as David Levy the future Senator first distinguished himself in the affairs of Florida.[2] His father, Moses Elias Levy, was a native of Morocco, born at Mogador about 1782.[3] He emigrated to the Island of St. Thomas about 1800, at the age of eighteen, and there engaged in the lumber business, accumulating a considerable fortune. In 1816 he removed to Havana, Cuba, where he was a government contractor in supplying troops.[4] Two years later he paid his first visit to the United States.[5]

C. Wickliffe Yulee, in the sketch above referred to, claims a rather fanciful ancestry for his family. To quote from his article—the Senator's grandfather was a Portuguese, who "became a high official in the Emperor of Morocco's court, and as such had been given the rank of prince. Upon the death of the Emperor, whose side he had espoused against the intriguing heir, he was obliged to fly at a moment's notice to England, taking with him his wife, an English Jewess, and their infant son." This child was Moses Levy. He was educated in an English university, but became a tradesman; and his mother "who had exaggerated ideas as to the importance of the princely title, insisted upon his dropping the name of Yulee temporarily, and adopting that of Levy," her own maiden name. This name he retained to the day of his death—although he approved of the resumption of the family name by the Senator.[6]

In connection with the above statement it must be borne in mind that Senator Yulee married out of his faith and that his children were brought up as Christians. In fact the article referred to shows a desire to

2. George B. Utley, "Origin of the County Names of Florida," *Magazine of History*, vol. viii, 79.

3. See *House Document*, no. 10, 27th Congress, 1st Session, p. 17, and Report by Mr. Halsted; House Document, no. 510, 56th Congress, 2d Session; Chester H. Rowell, *A Historical and Legal Digest of All Contested Election Cases in the House of Representatives of the United States* (Washington, 1901); *Barton Report*, 27th Congress, 114.

4. "Contested Election Case of David Levy," *House Report*, no. 450, 27th Congress, 2d Session, vol. ii.

5. *Ibid., Barton Report.* At the date of the birth of his son, Moses Levy was a subject of the King of Denmark. Nathan Levy, who was United States Consul at St. Thomas in 1832, may have been a relative. See *Committee Report*, no. 705, 24th Congress, 1st Session, vol. iii; *Committee Report*, no. 87, 25th Congress, 2d Session, vol. i; *Report*, no. 238, 25th Congress, 3d Session, vol. i; *House Report*, no. 72, 26th Congress, 1st Session, vol. iv.

6. Yulee, *supra*, no. 1, pp. 26, 28.

escape the recognition of a Jewish ancestry as much as possible, and, aside from the fanciful statement as to how the name Levy came into the family, it even claims that the princely grandfather was not a Jew at all, but a Mohammedan by the name of Yulee.[7]

The fact remains, however, that the Senator's father was never known by any other name than Moses E. Levy, and was always devoted to the ancient faith.[8] When he visited the United States about 1818, he became enthusiastic over our free institutions, and contemplated settling here, but his affairs at the time did not permit him to remove. Even before Spain had ceded Florida to the United States, he had decided to settle in the Eastern portion of that Territory, and in August, 1820, through his agents Hernandez and Cheavitean purchased about 45,000 acres of land for which it appears he paid about $40,000.[9] His plan was to bring families from Europe to settle on his plantation, "and in 1820 he instructed his agent in London that the colonists designed for his settlement might be sent on." [10]

On June 8, 1821, he appeared in Philadelphia before the United States Circuit Court, and there declared his intention of becoming a citizen of the United States.[11] About this time he also visited New York, and became acquainted with prominent Jews there; among others, Daniel L. M. Peixotto.[12]

Leaving Philadelphia he went to St. Augustine by way of Charles-

7. *Ibid.*, 28.
8. The *Occident* for Sept., 1856, speaks of the senator from Florida as "the son of a professing Jew, the late Moses Elias Levy."
9. See "Contested Election case of David Levy," *House Report*, no. 450, 27th Congress, 2d Session, vol. ii, pp. 5, 56. Part of the purchase price was only payable after the cession of Florida to the United States. See *House Document*, no. 10, 27th Congress, 1st Session, Exhibit 12; *Levy v. Aredondo*, in Transcript of Records of Supreme Court of United States, Jan. Term, 1838, Part 2, pp. 912, 933, 936 and *ibid.*, Jan. Term, 1839, Part 2, p. 614; 56th Congress, *House Document*, no. 510; Rowell, *supra: Barton Report*; *Executive Documents*, vol. xi, 18th Congress, 1st Session, 74; *Levy v. United States*, in which the report recommends the confirmation of his claim to 36,000 acres in Alachua County; also, *ibid.*, 84, confirming 14,500 acres.
10. "Contested Election Case of David Levy," *supra*, 5, *Barton Report*; *House Document*, no. 10, *supra*, Exhibit 17; Rowell, *supra*, *Barton Report*. Several of the settlers thus obtained came from France, as was the case with the Chateauneuf family, and some of his colonists came directly from New York and New Jersey. See *Executive Documents*, vol. xi, *supra*, 70, 343–44. A road was built and other improvements were made. *Ibid.*, 323, 325, 333–37, 343–44, 349, 350, 355. And see *infra*, 132 *et seq.*
11. See authorities given in note 9.
12. *House Report*, no. 450, *supra*, 59. He was the son of the minister of the Spanish and Portuguese synagogue at New York.

ton and arrived there about the time of the change of sovereignty.[13] He purchased Negroes and commenced sugar planting at a place called Volutia about eight miles above Lake George on the St. John's River, and also at a place opposite this, which he named Hope Hill.[14] As early as 1822, he figured extensively in large land transactions in that portion of the Territory.[15]

Andrew Jackson became Governor of the Territory, and in March, 1823, issued an ordinance which enabled those persons who were inhabitants of Florida at the time of the change of flags to become American citizens at once by complying with certain formalities. Under this ordinance Levy renounced his allegiance to the King of Denmark, to whom St. Thomas belonged, and took the oath of allegiance to the United States, receiving a certificate of citizenship at St. Augustine.[16] It was this method of obtaining his citizenship which subsequently proved to be a source of infinite trouble both to himself and his son.

When Moses Levy visited the United States, he brought with him his son David.[17] Like Alexander Hamilton, therefore, the future Senator was born in the West Indies, the date of his birth being June 2, 1810.[18] As the father desired to give his children the best possible education, he did not take them with him to Florida, but took the boy to Norfolk, Virginia, where he placed him with his intimate friend Moses Myers,[19] then a leading citizen of Norfolk, who had held distinguished office, and who at one time had represented the French Republic in the United States.[20] David Levy attended school and continued to reside at

13. "Contested Election Case of David Levy," *supra; House Document*, no. 510, *supra*; Rowell, *supra*.

14. *Ibid.; House Report*, no. 450, *supra*, Exhibit 26, p. 74.

15. *Ibid.; House Report*, no. 450, *supra*, Exhibit 12, p. 49; *Executive Documents*, vol. xi, *supra*, 130, 223, 256, 258, 311–16. It is interesting to note that among those figuring in his real estate transactions were Abraham M. Cohen and Antonio Mier, probably Meyer. The former was a resident of Philadelphia.

16. *Ibid.; House Report*, no. 450, *supra;* House of Representatives, 38th Congress, 2d Session, *Miscellaneous Document*, no. 57; Bartlett, *Cases of Contested Elections in Congress*, 1834–65 (Washington, 1865).

17. *Ibid.; House Report*, no. 450, *supra*, 56.

18. *Ibid.; House Document*, no. 510, *supra*; Rowell, *supra*. The place of his birth was St. Thomas.

19. See *House Report*, no. 450, *supra*; 133, Affidavit of Dr. Francis Mallory; *House Document*, no. 510, *supra*; Rowell, *supra; House Document*, no. 10, *supra*; Exhibit 11.

20. See "The Jews of Virginia," by the present writer, in *Publications of the American Jewish Historical Society*, no. 20.

Norfolk from 1819 to 1827, with the exception of occasional trips to the West Indies.[21]

In the meantime his father had become one of the foremost citizens of St. Augustine. He had purchased extensive lands in the interior and was considered one of the most influential men in the Territory. From the affidavit of Judge Elias B. Gould,[22] printed in one of the Government publications, it appears that as early as 1822 Moses E. Levy took an active part in the politics of Florida, particularly on the subject of education, and from time to time contributed to the daily press on various subjects using as a pen name, the words "Youlee," "Eubates" and similar forms.[23] He even succeeded in 1824 in bringing about certain reforms in the administration of the law.[24]

When, in 1825, Letamendi, the Spanish consul in Florida, celebrated the adoption of the Spanish Constitution by a great function, we learn that the street decorations and other portions of the arrangements were gotten up under Levy's direction, and that the account of the event in *The Florida Herald* was, in part, written by him.[25] We have Isaac Leeser's statement for the fact that he was a professing Jew,[26] and it further appears that he was repeatedly engaged in religious controversial literature, which called forth a book by Captain Thrush, published in England, entitled "Letters to the Jews, particularly addressed to Mr. Levy of Florida." [27] In 1827 and 1828 he appears to have been in England, and to have engaged in a similar controversy with one Forster. This correspondence, which was subsequently published, indicates that Moses Levy had made quite a reputation both as a speaker and a writer. But even aside from these religious controversies, he seems to have created a stir by a plan he devised for the abolition of Negro slavery.[28]

21. See *Miscellaneous Document*, no. 57, *supra*, 41 *et seq.*; *House Document*, no. 510, *supra*; Rowell, *supra*; *House Report*, no. 450, *supra*; *House Document*, no. 10, Exhibit C.

22. Gould's father was the founder of the *East Florida Herald*. See *ibid.*

23. *Ibid.*; *House Report*, no. 450, *supra*, vol. ii, 66; Bartlett, "Contested Election Cases," *supra*; Rowell, *supra*.

24. *Ibid.*   25. *House Report*, no. 450, *supra*, 67.   26. See *Occident*, 1856.

27. See Th. Thrush, late Captain R. N., *Letters to the Jews with a copy of a Speech said to have been delivered by Mr. Levy of Florida* (New York, 1829). This book is mentioned in Jacobs and Wolf's *Bibliotheca Anglo-Judaica*, no. 431, p. 74. I am indebted to Albert M. Friedenberg for calling my attention to it.

28. See "Letters concerning the Present Condition of the Jews. Being a Correspondence between Mr. Forster and Mr. Levy," 1829. In the preface appears the following

About 1822, the family of Moses E. Levy consisted of four children, all of whom resided in London,[29] with the exception of David who was being educated at Norfolk, Virginia, as already stated. Later on, however, the other children were brought to America, and the eldest son, Elias, placed at Harvard College.[30] For some unknown reason, however, Moses Levy cut short the education of both his sons in 1827. The reasons given by his grandson is that his action was prompted by "a condition of religious socialism." [31] Young David, instead of going to St. Augustine, went to a plantation of his father's in the interior of Florida, which he and his brother managed for some years, so that, even as late as 1831, we find him residing in Alachua County, in the interior of East Florida.[32] He frequently visited St. Augustine, however, and made friends with many of the old Spanish families, though by this time he seems to have become quite estranged from his father.[33] He finally removed to St. Augustine, studied law with Judge Robert R. Reid, and was admitted to the bar in 1832.[34] Entering the political arena, he soon became an important factor and obtained the position of Clerk to the Territorial Legislature.[35] In 1834, he attracted attention by a public Fourth of July oration.[36] During the Seminole troubles he was active in protecting the interests of the white settlers, and was present at important negotiations with the Indians. To him we are indebted for the report of the conference of 1834 between General W. Thompson, the United States Agent, and the Seminole chiefs, among whom was the

---

statement: "Mr. Levy has by his conduct and discourses at meetings of Jews and Christians over which he presided and by his writings of the subjects of discussion at these meetings as also by his plan for the abolition of negro slavery, made his name so well known as to render any further introduction of him to public notice unnecessary." In this work Levy's letters are signed M. E. Levy and, in the last of them, he mentions that he is on the eve of his departure for America. I am indebted to Mr. Friedenberg for calling my attention to this book.

29. See *House Report*, no. 450, *supra*, 56, 58; Bartlett, *supra*; Rowell, *supra*.

30. *Ibid.*; *House Report*, no. 450, *supra*, 67; Yulee, *supra*, no. 1, p. 28. Elias is probably identical with Elias Yulee who subsequently became Receiver of Olympia, Washington Territory. See *Senate Report*, no. 381, 35th Congress, 2d Session, vol. i, Feb. 18, 1859; *ibid.*, no. 123, 36th Congress, 1st Session, vol. i.

31. Yulee, *supra*, no. 1, p. 28.

32. *House Report*, no. 450, *supra*; *Miscellaneous Document*, no. 57, *supra*, 41.

33. Yulee, *supra*, no. 1, p. 28.

34. See *House Report*, no. 450, *supra*; Bartlett, *supra*; Rowell, *supra*.

35. *Ibid.*

36. See affidavit of Elias B. Gould in *House Report*, no. 450, *supra*.

famous Osceola, together with the addresses delivered on that occasion.[37] A contemporary work by an army officer, describes Levy at this time as "not only one of the most enlightened, but also one of the most patriotic inhabitants of Florida." [38]

Thenceforth his political advancement was rapid. In 1836 he was elected to the Legislative Council from St. John's County, and served during the session of 1837; in the latter year he was elected to the Legislature, continuing during the session of 1838.[39] In that year he was elected one of the delegates of St. John's County to the Convention which framed the Constitution of Florida, his name being appended to the first Constitution adopted.[40] He was chosen Delegate in Congress for Florida for the next two years, and from the start appears to have been the soul of the movement to obtain the admission of Florida into the Union.

Like all public men, however, he had many enemies, and it was while a member of the Constitutional Convention in 1838 that one of the defeated candidates raised the question that neither he nor his father was legally a citizen of the United States.[41] The question was decided in his favor, but in 1841, an order to show cause why his name should not be stricken from the roll of attorneys for the same reason was obtained by some of his opponents. The Court of Appeals sustained Levy's citizenship.[42] As the question was still unsettled, however, when he was about to take a trip to Cuba in 1840, he applied for a passport, stating all the facts to the Department of State. The passport was granted; [43] but the question of the regularity of his father's naturalization, through

37. M. M. Cohen [an Officer of the Left Wing], *Notices of Florida and the Campaigns* (Charleston, 1836), 57, 62.

38. *Ibid.*, 62.

39. See *House Document*, no. 10, *supra*, Exhibit C; *House Report*, no. 450, *supra*.

40. See *The Acts and Resolves of the First General Assembly of the State of Florida. Published under the Direction of the Attorney General of the State* (Tallahassee, 1845). The Constitution was adopted Dec. 3, 1838, and signed Jan. 11, 1839. See *House Document*, no. 10, *supra*.

41. *Miscellaneous Document*, no. 57, *supra*, 41 *et seq.*; *House Report*, no. 450, *supra*; *House Document*, no. 10, *supra*; *House Document*, no. 510, *supra*; Rowell, *supra*.

42. *Ibid., Barton Report.*

43. *Ibid.* "The letter of the Delegate to the Secretary of State dated July 25, 1840, will show that in making application for a passport, he referred the attention of the Department distinctly to the proceedings on file there."

which he claimed citizenship, continued to harass him for many years to come.

In 1840, one David R. Dunham brought the question before the Grand Jury on the ground that his vote should not have been received by the Inspectors of Election. Here, too, Levy was successful,[44] but in 1841, while sitting in the 27th Congress as Delegate from the Territory of Florida, the question again came up in its most serious form. Mr. Dunham on that occasion presented a remonstrance to the House of Representatives against Levy's right to a seat. A committee was appointed, and this body decided against him, declaring his seat vacant.[45] The young Delegate, however, obtained permission to present further testimony, with the result that the committee, by Mr. Barton, of Virginia, presented a majority report in his favor, while Mr. Halsted, of New Jersey, submitted a minority report against him. The House took no action on this report, and so Levy retained his seat.[46]

The question involved in this contest may here be mentioned. It seems that the ordinance issued by General Jackson, under which Levy's father had been naturalized, had been declared void; and a subsequent law had been passed which granted citizenship to all who had been *inhabitants* of Florida at the time of the change of sovereignty, on complying with certain formalities. It was contended, however, that Levy's father was not an inhabitant on July 17, 1821, when American sovereignty commenced, but that he had come to Florida a few days later and could not, therefore, claim the benefit of this legislation.[47] The evidence as to this point was hopelessly conflicting. The only theory, on which the majority report proceeds, was that the Delegate was a child at the time, that his father had purchased land before the formal

44. *Ibid.* The question was also tested and decided in his favor by the unanimous decision of the Territorial Court of Florida, Feb. 13, 1841.

45. *Ibid., Halsted Report.*

46. *Ibid.* Barton's Report is dated March 15, 1842. See Rowell, *supra*, 41–47, 114; also *House Document*, no. 10, *supra*; the entire contest and testimony are given in full in the authorities mentioned, particularly in *House Report*, no. 450, *supra*.

47. *Ibid.* It is interesting to note that the evidence in this election contest also disclosed the names of several Florida settlers, naturalized there in 1821 and who were probably Jews. They were George Levy, aged 26, a planter from London, Lewis Solomon, aged 30, a watchmaker from London, Levy M. Rodenburg, aged 29, a grocer from Amsterdam, and Isaac Hendricks, a planter from South Carolina. See *Report*, no. 450, *supra*, 123.

transfer, and declared his intention at Philadelphia of becoming a citizen, coupled with the fact that there was doubt as to whether or not the father was in Florida at the date mentioned, whereas there was no doubt that he had continually resided there for many years. It was only fair, therefore, that the leaning of the committee should be in favor of his citizenship, on the ground that the spirit of the naturalization policy of this country had been fully satisfied.[48]

It is interesting to note that in this contest David Levy enlisted every possible influence. He procured affidavits from Daniel Levi Maduro Peixotto of New York and several from his father.[49] From the language of the latter's affidavit however, as well as from some of his father's letters about this time, it appears that Moses Levy had become completely estranged from his son. Even after the contest had been decided in Levy's favor, General P. S. Smith endeavored to reopen the matter for the purpose of presenting further evidence against Levy.[50] On this point Smith wrote to Levy's father, and the latter's reply shows that the relations between father and son were far from cordial. Moses Levy wrote: "The irritating subject of David Levy is become troublesome to me beyond measure. . . . The subject begins to make me unhappy indeed." [51] He concluded by saying that the whole thing was of no interest to him, and later in a deposition which he gave to General Smith, he spoke of his early purchase of land "in this, to me, unhappy country." [52]

In the House of Representatives David Levy attracted attention almost from the start, and, owing to the fact that his views on many subjects were exactly opposed to those of John Quincy Adams, he seems at once to have incurred the dislike of this distinguished statesman. The

48. See authorities cited in note 41. Judge James M. Gould, one of the oldest inhabitants of St. Augustine, testified: "I have always been on intimate terms with the old inhabitants of St. Augustine, especially the Spanish portion and the most prominent, and among them have never heard the citizenship of David Levy doubted. They are truly American people who adopted the American laws and have watched with a jealous eye any infringement of them, and who do more towards sustaining them than many native-born Americans. They have generally supported David Levy at the elections and considered him as much a citizen as themselves." Joseph Manucy and other old inhabitants gave similar testimony.

49. *Ibid.; House Report*, no. 450, *supra*, 24, 59.

50. *Ibid.;* 27th Congress, 3d Session, *House Document*, no. 15, Dec. 14, 1842.

51. *Ibid*. The letter is dated St. Augustine, Nov. 13, 1842.

52. *Ibid*. Moses E. Levy's deposition is verified Oct. 31, 1842, and in both letter and deposition he never speaks of the Delegate as his son but always alludes to him as David Levy.

earliest mention of the new Delegate appears in Adams' *Diary* under date of June 21, 1841, in the following words:

Pickens introduced David Levy as Delegate from the Territory of Florida. Morgan objected to his being sworn and presented papers contesting his election, and denying that he is a citizen of the United States. The Speaker called for credential and upon inspection of it swore him in. The papers presented by Morgan were referred to the Committee of Election. Levy is said to be a Jew, and what will be, if true, a far more formidable disqualification, that he has a dash of African blood in him, which, *sub rosa*, is the case with more than one member of the house.[53]

This last remark was probably due to the fact that Levy may then already have made the claim that his grandfather was a prince and a Mohammedan. In September, 1841, Levy tried to enlist Adams' favor in his contested election case, but Adams seems to have considered the matter desperate.[54]

For some years prior, the Seminole Indians had been harassing settlers in Florida, and the government had made war upon them. Just at this time, however, there were bills in the House for the withdrawal of troops from Florida, on the ground that security had been restored. Levy foresaw that this would leave settlers at the mercy of the Indians and vehemently opposed the bills mentioned. He made several speeches in the House and called for official documents in the War Department relating to the situation. The earliest of these speeches was made during his election contest and within a month after being sworn in. John Quincy Adams mentions them repeatedly in his *Diary* thus: August 3, 1841, "I found Levy, the Delegate from Florida attempting to get up for consideration his resolution of inquiry upon the Secretary of War";[55] May 16, 1842, "I found Levy, the Jew Delegate from Florida, making a red hot speech against the President's message declaring his intention to put an end to the Florida war";[56] May 25, "In the House David Levy, the alien Jew Delegate from Florida, moved a call for correspondence of the commanding officer of the Army in Florida . . .

53. Charles Francis Adams (ed.), *Memoirs of John Quincy Adams comprising his Diary from 1795 to 1848* (Philadelphia, 1877), vol. x, 483.

54. *Ibid.*, vol. xi, 6, 7.   55. *Ibid.*, vol. x, 520.

56. *Ibid.*, vol. xi, 155. Even before this Levy had presented a resolution calling on the Secretary of War for information concerning Indian troubles in Florida. See *H. R.* 1, 27th Congress, 1st Session, July 29, 1841.

and a resolution that there should be no cessation of hostilities till the Seminoles should have been effectively subdued. He told of a whole family butchered since the 1st of this month";[57] on June 4, 1842, "Long speech of Pope for a reduction of the army. David Levy, delegate from Florida loquacious against it." [58] As time went on Adams' dislike became more and more pronounced, until in February, 1843, we find him writing: "Weller moved a reconsideration to let Levy make another hour speech, which he did. I was provoked to the boiling point, but made no reply." [59]

In February, 1844, Levy distinguished himself in a very able speech concerning the termination of the tenth article of the Ashburton Treaty, which involved the subject of slavery and the extradition of slaves. Adams in his *Diary* stated: "David Levy, the Jew Delegate from Florida with much apparent agitation and awful length of face, moved a suspension of the rules to enable him to offer a resolution requiring the President to give notice to the British Government that the United States wish to terminate the tenth article of the Ashburton Treaty." Adams expressed his fear that this would bring up the subject of slavery and added that he was full of anxiety on that account.[60] Despite these sneering references, we have Edward Everett's tribute to Levy's address when writing in January, 1845: "Levy's argument is so clear and satisfactory that I have not attempted to improve upon it." [61] Shortly afterward, Everett, writing on the Ashburton Treaty to the Earl of Aberdeen, said: "The undersigned instead of any argument of his own to that effect, invites Lord Aberdeen's attention to the extract herewith

57. *Ibid.*, vol. xi, 162. It was quite natural that Levy should feel very strongly on this subject, for in 1835 his father's sugar houses and one of his plantations had been destroyed by hostile Indians. Some property which had been saved and removed to Micanopy was ordered burnt by the commanding officer of the United States troops when he abandoned the place, so as to prevent it from falling into the hands of the enemy. Moses E. Levy had presented a claim to Congress for property thus destroyed but his claim had been disallowed on the ground that the property had been lost by the fortunes of war. See *Committee Report*, no. 236, 25th Congress 3d Session, vol. i, Jan. 26, 1839.

58. *Memoirs of John Quincy Adams, supra*, vol. xi, 168, 170.

59. *Ibid.*, 316.

60. *Ibid.*, 500. Adams frequently referred to Levy simply as "the Jew Delegate from Florida." See *ibid.*, vol. xii, 164.

61. Edward Everett to Secretary of State, Jan. 31, 1845, quoted in letter from Levy to Westcott, Mar. 21, 1845, original in writer's possession.

transmitted from a speech of Mr. Levy, Delegate from Florida to the Congress of the United States in which the sufficiency of an indictment is very ably maintained." [62]

His most important work, however, on which his whole heart and soul centered, was that of obtaining the admission of Florida into the Union. In this cause he worked incessantly for several years until his efforts were finally crowned with success. He aroused public sentiment in the Territory in order to get the necessary support, arranged meetings, and sent circulars even to the most distant parts. [63]

Some years ago the present writer purchased a collection of autograph letters written by Yulee about this period and subsequently. Some of these relate to his criticism of the administration, some to the admission of Florida, and others to general political affairs. One of the earliest, written in 1842, resented the appointments made by President Tyler without consulting the representatives of the section affected. He wrote:

The fact is that Mr. Tyler is a weak man, with good impulses but no clearness of principle and no enlargement of purpose. I have become satisfied that as a Democrat I cannot confess any political sympathy with him. If I could, I could do something in the way of office, but it is a game I cannot play. . . . The design is, I suppost, to make a Tyler and Webster presidential party, but it is a small beer concern that will become flat by exposure. Sometimes he consults me, but I wash myself of responsibility for his appointments, and shall shortly come out with a letter upon the subject.

He also spoke of Polk as a presidential candidate. [64]

This letter, though written three years before Florida was actually admitted into the Union, shows his activity in that regard. He wrote: "As it will be next to impossible to bring Florida in alone, it has been thought best to get our matter under way in this session, and not risk a defeat, but to be in train for immediate action in the next session." The letters in my possession were addressed to various public men, most of them to James D. Westcott, subsequently his colleague in the Senate.

62. Jan. 30, 1845, quoted in *ibid.*
63. See *Circular Letter of D. Levy to the People of Florida relative to the admission of Florida into the Union* (Washington, 1844), 24 pp.; *Executive Document*, no. 71, 25th Congress, 3d Session, vol. iv., Jan. 11, 1839; original letters in writer's possession.
64. Original in writer's possession.

His correspondence included the foremost men of his day, George Bancroft, Polk, Pierce, Benjamin, Buchanan and the rest.[65] One of the most important of these letters, dated February 22, 1845, only a few days before the actual admission of Florida, was addressed to Westcott, and in part reads as follows:

I took up this measure at the only time when there was a hope of uniting the people—came out wholly in the fact of unanimous opposition in my own district, on the favor of which I was so dependent for my prospects in life—took the stump upon the subject—wrote my friends in its support—got the measure reported in the only shape it could have passed—have now got it through the House with a triumphant vote—have been laboring like a slave to overcome the party policy by which we were to be buried in the Senate, and am now satisfied it has been successfuly overcome and that we will be admitted—and with all this evidence of my sincerity I am to be blamed if by unavoidable circumstances it should fail. . . . This disposition to blame me may be owing to my not continuing to make incessant noise about it. It is not according to my way to do so. I have my own manner of accomplishing things. I came out upon the subject and kept it going, until public sentiment at home was ripe for the movement. That was one step, and I stopped when that was sufficiently done. I then turned to the accomplishment of the measure here and worked in quiet until it was time to make a noise and demonstration here, and then did it, and succeeded. Never judge me to be inactive because I am silent.[66]

As already stated Florida was admitted a few days after this letter was written and Levy at once began a very vigorous campaign, which resulted in his election as the first Senator from the State. One of the letters in my possession mentions the numerous attacks upon him, and he advised his manager to assure the people that he "has procured positive assurances from Mr. Polk that only Florida men will be appointed in Florida as soon as the State is organized." This campaign was one of the most bitter ever fought. All sorts of charges were made against Levy and continued even after his election. In one of the letters addressed to Westcott in July, 1845, he said: "They write me from St. Augustine that our Democratic friends are all well satisfied with your selection. They write me also that General Hernandez and General Worth in the

65. See Polk Papers, Bancroft Collection, New York Public Library, no. 332; Polk Papers, Library of Congress; *Calendar of Papers of Martin Van Buren* (Washington, 1910), 385; see *Publications, supra*, no. 22, p. 100.
66. Original in writer's possession.

same room where I happened to be, said that the party had elected two blackguards—so you see we both have to mend our morals in the Senate. I was in hopes my labors would be confined to improving my mind but it seems I shall have to look to my morals also." All the letters thus far referred to are signed *David Levy*, or simply *Levy*.[67]

On March 10, 1845, the new State named one of her counties in his honor, so that, though he subsequently changed his name, his memory is perpetuated in the old name only, for Levy County and the town of Levyville in Florida have continued without change to the present time.[68]

The year 1845 was a landmark in Yulee's career. He had been for several years a familiar figure in Washington and had access to good society there, becoming acquainted among others with the family of ex-Governor Wickliffe of Kentucky, formerly a member of Tyler's Cabinet. He married Miss Wickliffe. Up to the time of his election as Senator, he had been known by no other name than that of David Levy. Shortly after being elected to the Senate, however, and just prior to his marriage, it was stated that Miss Wickliffe made it a condition that he change his name.[69] In compliance with her request he assumed the name of Yulee, so that while he served in the House of Representatives as Levy, in his subsequent career he was known as Yulee. The act of the legislature by which his name was changed may be found in volume 1 of the Laws of Florida. It reads: "Whereas, David Levy memorialized this General Assembly stating that his proper patronymic is *Eulee*, and that his father prior to his birth, dropped the same, and assumed that of Levy, and that he is desirous of resuming the said name of *Eulee*. Be it therefore enacted by the Senate and House of Representatives of the State of Florida in General Assembly convened, that the name of David

67. *Ibid.*

68. See Leslie A. Thompson, *A Manual or Digest of the Statute Laws of the State of Florida* (Boston, 1847), 18. It seems that this county had been originally established and organized by the Acts of the Governor and Legislative Council of the Territory of Florida, and simply was confirmed when the state government was established. See George B. Utley, "Origin of the County Names of Florida," *supra*; J. M. Hawk, M.D., *The Florida Gazetteer, 1871*, p. 56; Charles Ledyard Norton, *A Handbook of Florida* (New York, 1892), 54. Norton, however, is mistaken as to the date of naming Levy County. See *The Acts and Resolves of the First General Assembly of the State of Florida* (Tallahassee, 1845), 37, 38.

69. See obituary notice in *New York Tribune*, Oct. 11, 1886.

Levy be altered and changed to David Levy Eulee." He seems, however, to have altered the spelling at once, substituting the letter *Y* for *E*.
This law became effective December 29, 1845,[70] and immediately afterward he married Miss Wickliffe.[71]

This change of name appears also from the letters in my possession.
The earliest, as already stated, are signed *David Levy* or simply *Levy*,
but the signature became *David Levy Yulee*, in 1846, as appears from
one written to George Bancroft a few days after the enactment of the
law above referred to. Later on the letters are signed simply *D. L. Yulee*.
From this period on, the senator seemed to have no longer associated
with the Jewish members of his family. Thereafter no mention was ever
made of his father, and though he never formally joined any other
church, it is doubtful whether he ever took any interest in Jewish affairs. His children were brought up in the Christian faith.[72]

The lady whom Yulee married belonged to one of the distinguished
families of the day. We have the authority of Mrs. Clay that she was
called the "Wickliffe Madonna." [73] Shortly after their marriage they
made a tour through some of the Northern states, being entertained
among others by Governor Winthrop at his home near Boston.[74]

Yulee took his seat in the Senate December 1, 1845, almost a month
before his change of name became effective. He became chairman of
the Naval Committee in 1846, and was one of the earliest champions of
iron vessels.[75] It is interesting, too, to find that he was also one of the
strongest opponents of the movement for abolishing flogging in the
Navy.[76] Among the bills he introduced and succeeded in passing was

70. Acts and Resolves, *supra*. It has also been stated that the name Yulee was obtained by transposing the letters of the name Levy. As, however, the name Yulee is a
well-known Jewish name among Portuguese Jews, the chances are that it may have
been the ancestral name.

71. Yulee, *supra*, no. 1, p. 34.   72. *Ibid.*

73. She was so called because she was so devoutly religious. See Mrs. Virginia Clay,
A Belle of the Fifties (New York, 1904), 54.

74. Yulee, *supra*, no. 1, p. 34.

75. *Ibid.*, 35. It is interesting to note that he reported adversely on the claim of
Captain John Ericsson for superintending the construction of the steamer *Princeton*.
See Poore's *Index*, 576.

76. Yulee, *supra*, no. 1, p. 35. It is a curious fact that the brutal system of flogging
in the navy was finally abolished through the efforts of another Jew, Commodore
Uriah P. Levy.

the one authorizing the Grinnell Expedition in search of Sir John Franklin.[77]

Later he became chairman of the Committee on Post Offices and Post Roads, and was one of the earliest champions of cheap ocean postage.[78] Of his ability we have the estimate of Floyd, Buchanan's Secretary of War, that he possessed "an energy and zeal which commanded unusual success." [79]

Though Yulee's father had been an advocate of the abolition of slavery, the Senator, like most Southern statesmen, became affiliated with the pro-slavery element. During a trip on the Ohio he became acquainted with Edwin M. Stanton, whom he tried to convert to his views on that subject, and there is extant a letter written to Stanton in 1848 along the same lines.[80]

His term expired in 1851. At the following election, however, he was defeated by Stephen R. Mallory in one of the closest contests ever witnessed in this country. There were 59 members of the legislature and a resolution had been adopted requiring a majority vote for choice. On the first ballot Yulee received 29 votes, and there were 29 blanks. The second and third ballots had the same result. Yulee claimed that he was the only qualified person voted for and should have been declared elected. Finally Mallory received 31 as against Yulee's 27. The contest was bitterly fought in the Senate by Yulee's counsel, Reverdy Johnson and Edwin M. Stanton, but the Senate's decision was adverse, though the question was considered so close that in 1853 the Senate voted that Yulee receive from the contingent fund a sum equal to his *per diem* as Senator from the commencement of the session to August, 1852, when the case was finally decided.[81]

77. *Ibid.*, 35. The writer has been unable to verify this statement. Yulee, however, was interested in the Wilkes Exploring Expedition. See "Report on the Wilkes Exploring Expedition," *Senate Report*, no. 29, 30th Congress, 1st Session.

78. Yulee, *supra*, 36.

79. *Ibid.* Additional particulars of his career in the Senate are given in Milo Milton Quaife (ed.), *The Diary of James K. Polk, 1845–49* (Chicago, 1910), vol. i, 28, 30–32, 149, 184, 211, 262–63; vol. iii, 194; *The Works of James Buchanan* (Philadelphia, 1911), vol. vii, 130; vol. viii, 368; vol. xi, 124, 126–32.

80. See George C. Gorham, *Life and Public Services of Edwin M. Stanton* (New York, 1899), vol. i, 73, where the letter is given in full.

81. *Ibid.* The report is an elaborate document of about 300 pages. See 49th Congress, 1st Session, *Senate Miscellaneous Document*, no. 47: "Compilation of Senate

He now devoted his entire energy to the development of his State; he drew up the "Internal Improvement Act" and planned an extensive system of railroads. The Florida Railroad, incorporated in 1853, was his special favorite. It crossed the State from the Gulf to the Atlantic and, as he figured, would be utilized in connection with the commerce of New York and the Mississippi Valley. A system of fast steamers would carry products from Florida and Georgia to the North and at the same time attract immigrants.[82]

He was re-elected to the Senate in 1855 and served continuously till 1861, when he resigned to join the Confederate cause.[83]

It may fairly be said that among the statesmen of the South, none saw more clearly the inevitable conflict between the North and South on the question of slavery than did Yulee. Shortly after the adoption of the Wilmot Proviso, in February, 1848, he offered a resolution in reference to New Mexico and Southern California, protesting against the abolition of slavery in that section on the ground that these territories belonged to *all* the citizens of all the states and that slave property could therefore rightfully be brought into them.[84] Writing to Calhoun in 1849, he suggested that if an amendment to the Constitution protecting the South against aggression were not adopted, he thought it "the best policy to take steps at once for a separation." [85] These radical views earned for him the title of the "Florida Fire Eater." [86] Among his closest friends was Stephen A. Douglas whom he supported in the leadership

---

Election Cases, 1789–1885," by George S. Taft, 143–47; 38th Congress, 2d Session, *House Miscellaneous Document*, no. 57: "Cases of Contested Election," by D. W. Bartlett, 32d Congress, 1st Session, 608. The debate may be found in the "Appendix" to the *Congressional Globe*, 32d Congress, 1st Session, 1170–76; E. M. Stanton, "Argument before the Select Committee of the United States Senate," Washington, 1852; *Senate Miscellaneous Document*, no. 2, 32d Congress, Special Session, I; *Senate Report*, no. 349, 32d Congress, 1st Session, vol. ii, and *Senate Miscellaneous Document*, no. 109, 32d Congress, 1st Session, vol. i.

82. Obituary notice in *New York Herald*, Oct. 11, 1886; Yulee in *supra*, no. 1, p. 37.

83. Nicolay and Hay's *Life of Lincoln*, vol. iii, 181; *New York Herald*, Oct. 11, 1886.

84. Yulee, *supra*, no. 1, p. 34.

85. *Ibid.* See *Senate Miscellaneous Document*, no. 6, Part 2, 30th Congress, 1st Session, vol. i.

86. See *New York Herald*, *supra*.

until the latter repudiated secession.[87] Yulee was one of the ten Southern statesmen, including Jefferson Davis, who in 1850 signed an agreement to oppose by any and all means the admission of California unless upon certain conditions agreeable to the South.[88]

After Lincoln's election no Southern statesman more fully realized the gravity of the situation than did Yulee. He at once held repeated conferences with Ex-President Tyler and others, and early in January, 1861, while still a United States Senator, joined the foremost senators of the South in a plan to form a confederacy. On January 5, 1861, he wrote a letter which was to be delivered to Joseph Finnigan or Governor Call of Florida,[89] and this has since become an historic document. He therein advised the taking of all United States strongholds before the Federal Government was able to strengthen its position. The letter reads as follows:

Washington, January 5, 1861.

My dear Sir:

The immediately important thing to be done is the occupation of the forts and arsenals in Florida. The Naval Station and forts at Pensacola are first in consequence. For this a force is necessary. I have conversed with Mr. Toombs on the subject. He will start this work for Georgia and says if the Convention or Governor will ask Governor Brown of Georgia for a force, he will immediately send a sufficient force and take the Navy Yard and forts.

The occupation of the Navy Yard will give us a good supply of ordnance and make the capture of the forts easier. Major Chase built the forts and will know all about them. Lose no time, for my opinion is, troops will be very soon despatched to reinforce and strengthen the forts in Florida. The arsenal at Chattahoochee should be looked to, and that at once, to prevent the removal of arms deposited there.

87. Yulee, *supra*, 38. He was a jealous defender of all that related to the South. Mrs. Archibald Dixon in *The True History of the Missouri Compromise* (Cincinnati, 1899), 232–34, mentions how in 1850 Yulee bitterly opposed the printing of a resolution of the Legislature of Vermont against slavery on the ground that its language was insulting to the South.

88. This agreement was still extant in 1900 and in possession of John G. Parkhurst. It was originally found by scouts at Winchester, Tenn., in 1863. See *Report of American Historical Asssociation, 1900,* vol. i, p. 603.

89. Colonel George W. Call. The letter is given in full in *New York Herald, supra,* and may also be found in Nicolay and Hay, *supra,* 180.

I think that by the 4th of March all the Southern States will be out, except perhaps Kentucky and Missouri, and they will soon have to follow.

What is advisable is the earliest possible organization of a Southern Confederacy and of a Southern Army. The North is rapidly consolidating against us upon the plan of force. A strong government, as eight States will make, promptly organized, and a strong army with Jeff. Davis for General in Chief, will bring them to a reasonable sense of the gravity of the crisis.

Have a Southern government as soon as possible, adopting the present Federal Constitution for the time, and a Southern army. I repeat this because it is the important policy.

Virginia and Maryland and Tennessee are rapidly coming up to the work. God speed you.

I shall give the enemy a shot next week before retiring. I say enemy. Yes. I am theirs and they are mine. . . .

Yours in haste,
D. L. Yulee.[90]

On January 7 he wrote another letter to General Finnigan of the Sovereignty Convention, enclosing a copy of resolutions adopted at a conference of the senators from Georgia, Alabama, Louisiana, Arkansas, Texas, Missouri and Florida. In this letter he said:

The idea of the meeting was that the States should go out at once and provide for the early organization of a Confederate Government, not later than the 15th day of February. This time is allowed to enable Louisiana and Texas to participate, and volunteer bills might be passed which would put Mr. Lincoln in immediate position for hostilities, whereas by remaining in our places until the 4th of March, *it is thought we can keep the hands of Mr. Buchanan tied, and disable the Republicans from effecting any legislation which will strengthen the hands of the incoming administration.*

The resolutions which he enclosed read as follows:

Resolved, that in our opinion, each of the Southern States should as soon as may be, secede from the Union.

Resolved, that provision should be made for a Convention to organize a Confederacy of the seceding states, the Convention to meet not later than the 15th day of February, at the City of Montgomery, in the State of Alabama.

Resolved, that in view of the hostile legislation that is theatened against the seceding states, and which may be consummated before the 4th of

90. *Ibid.*

March, we ask instructions whether the delegates are to remain in Congress for the purpose of defeating such legislation.[91]

These letters were found among Yulee's effects when his home in Fernandina was taken by Union troops in 1862.

Florida passed her ordinance of secession on January 10, 1861, and Yulee's was the first speech in the Senate to announce the secession of a Southern state. This was on January 21, 1861. The question before the Senate was the admission of Kansas. Yulee asked permission to address that distinguished body on a personal matter, and when permission was given, he delivered a dignified address announcing his resignation and stating that Florida withdrew because she "was not willing to disturb the peace of her associates by an inflamed and protracted struggle within the Union. The people of Florida will ever preserve a grateful memory of past connection with this Government and just pride in the continued development of American society." [92]

Mrs. Clay, an eyewitness, in her *Memoirs* thus describes the memorable scene: "As one by one, Senators Yulee, Mallory, Clay and Jefferson Davis rose, the emotion of their brother Senators and of us in the galleries increased; as each Senator, speaking for his state, concluded his solemn renunciation of allegiance to the United States, women grew hysterical and waved their handkerchiefs . . . men wept and embraced each other mournfully. . . . Scarcely a member of that Senatorial body but was pale with the terrible significance of the hour." [93]

Yulee's plan seems to have been that the Union be split into three parts, the East, the West and the South, all of which might possibly

91. See obituary notices in *New York Times*, and *New York Tribune*, Oct. 11, 1886, where the letter and resolutions are given in full. The rapid secession of several of the southern states compelled the senators to retire sooner than they had anticipated. See also Nicolay and Hay, *Life of Lincoln*, vol. iii, 180.

92. See *New York Herald*, *supra*; Nicolay and Hay, *supra*, 181; Yulee, *supra*, no. 1, p. 42. On Jan. 22, 1861, a motion was submitted that the *Journal* be so corrected as to record the fact that Messrs. Davis, Mallory, Yulee, Clay and Fitzpatrick had announced that the states from which they were senators respectively had seceded and that they thereupon withdrew from the Senate. An amendment was offered that these names be stricken from the list of senators. Both motions were tabled, and on Mar. 13, 1861, a resolution was adopted that these senators having withdrawn from the Senate, their seats in this body became vacant. This resolution, however, did not include Yulee, whose term of office had expired on Mar. 3, 1861. See Senate, 36th and 37th Congresses, 195.

93. See Clay, *A Belle of the Fifties*, *supra*, 147.

form a defensive and commercial league, each, however, to work out its own salvation.[94]

Months before Lincoln's election, he had resolved to retire from public life and devote himself to the development of his State. The railroad he had established was completed, and the merchant ships in connection with it were ready, but the latter were soon seized by the Federal Government and used for conveying Union troops.[95]

Yulee now joined his family at Fernandina, and took an active part in the organizing of troops.[96] Later he sent his wife and children to his sugar plantation at a place called Homosassa, situated on a small river flowing into the Gulf of Mexico. He joined them there when Fernandina was captured and there he remained in retirement during the early years of the war, Homosassa becoming one of the shelters of refuge for blockade runners, after Cedar Keys had been taken.[97]

Though he was repeatedly consulted by Southern statesmen throughout the struggle, he took no active part in the war. While he and his family were absent on one occasion, Federal troops appeared and his house was destroyed by fire,[98] but the army officers disclaimed all responsibility.

His friendship with Jefferson Davis had been a very close one in the early days, and a letter written by the latter after some misunderstanding during Pierce's administration closed with the words

You are too near to me by many ties, and your kindness has been too often shown, to permit me to leave you for an hour in doubt as to the affectionate regard with which I am as ever,

Your friend,
Jefferson Davis.[99]

During Buchanan's administration, however, their relations became somewhat strained, because Yulee was instrumental in securing Johnston's appointment as Quartermaster-General in preference to Colonel Robert E. Lee, who was Davis' candidate. Later still, after the commencement of the war this estrangement became a permanent breach.[100]

94. Yulee, *supra*, no. 2, p. 3.   95. *Ibid.*, no. 1, p. 38.
96. See *New York Herald, supra.*
97. Norton, *supra*, 233; Yulee, *supra*, no. 2, p. 4; *Proceedings of the Convention of the People of Florida, 1861*, p. 15.
98. This is denied by Norton, *supra*, 233. See, however, Yulee, *supra*, no. 2, p. 7.
99. Yulee, *supra*, no. 2, p. 8.   100. *Ibid.*, 8, 9.

Despite the fact that Yulee took no active part in the war, the Federal Government regarded him from the start as one of the chief offenders, and made repeated efforts for his capture.[101]

After Appomattox, the Governor of Florida appointed him one of a commission to go to Washington and confer with the President as to the reestablishment of Florida in the Union.[102] Before reaching Washington, however, he was arrested at Gainesville, Georgia, and sent a prisoner to Fort Pulaski, near Savannah.[103] The letters above mentioned, found at Fernandina, were the basis of his arrest, and though many prominent men interceded with President Johnson he remained a prisoner. Even his friend Stanton refused at first to stir in his behalf.[104] The State of Georgia in Convention memorialized the President in behalf of Yulee, Davis and the few remaining prisoners of state.[105] A whole year elapsed, yet though most prisoners of war had been set at liberty, the only ones that remained in confinement were Davis, Clay and Yulee.[106] The last-named was finally liberated through the efforts of his old friend General Joseph E. Johnston, who induced General Grant to intercede for him.[107] Thereafter he took no active part in politics though it is stated that he was again offered the United States Senatorship.[108] He joined his family at Fernandina and continued to devote all his time to building up the ruined railroad system of Florida, retiring finally with a comfortable fortune.[109] Removing to Washington in 1880, Yulee was received into the circle of his former friends and associates, Fish, Frelinghuysen, Hamlin and others.[110] His wife died in 1884 and he followed her two years later, on October 10, 1886. Both were interred in

101. *Ibid.*, 9; *New York Herald*, *supra*, states that "he did all in his power to organize troops for the defense of the state and took such an active and prominent part in the rebellion that at its close he was incarcerated." See also *New York World*, Oct. 11, 1886.

102. Yulee, *supra*, no. 2, p. 10.   103. *Ibid.*   104. *Ibid.*, 14.

105. See *Confederate Records of Georgia* (1865), 147: Resolution of Oct. 26, 1865; Report of Committee, *ibid*, 197.

106. Yulee, *supra*, no. 2, p. 14.

107. *Ibid.*, 15. He was pardoned by President Johnson who had been one of his colleagues in the Senate. See *New York Tribune*, *supra*.

108. Yulee, *supra*, 16.

109. *Ibid.*; *New York Herald*, *supra*, states: "After the War, he accepted the situation and did all in his power to restore the prosperity and commerce of the state." See George R. Fairbanks, *Florida, its History and its Romance* (Jacksonville, 1898), 204.

110. Yulee, *supra*, 17.

Georgetown Cemetery, at Washington. He left four children, C. Wickliffe Yulee, Mrs. C. A. Reid, the Misses Florida and Mary Yulee.[111]

Though he can be regarded as a Jew by race only, yet his name deserves to be remembered because he was the first of his race to be a member of the United States Senate and because his career incidentally brings to view the career of his father, Moses Elias Levy, an observant Jew, who was one of the influential pioneers in the early history of the Territory of Florida.

---

111. He died at the Clarendon Hotel, New York, where he was stopping on his way from Bar Harbor, Me., to Washington. See obituary notices in the *Sun*, and the other New York daily newspapers, cited herein, of Oct. 11, 1886.

Benjamin Kaplan
Judah Philip Benjamin

IF THIS ESSAY bore a subtitle it would surely have to be "The Story of a Disillusioned Hero." From his unpretentious birth in a poor Orthodox Jewish home, to his elegant burial in the Catholic cemetery of Pérelachaise in Le Mans, France; from hearing his father read from the Torah (Leviticus, 25:10): "Proclaim liberty throughout all the land unto all the inhabitants thereof," to his vociferous stand in favor of slavery; from being one of the chief architects of the Confederacy, to escaping ignominiously to England after Appomattox, this wandering Jew, an exotic and mysterious personality, is one of contradictions, controversies, and legend. His true character may remain a secret for a long time to come, and Benjamin himself was partly responsible for the mystery. His distrust of biographers was strong enough to cause him to destroy many of his letters and documents, making it difficult to achieve a total picture of Benjamin the man.

Hated by his opponents, adored by his friends, charming, aggressive, egotistical, and brilliant, one of the most powerful and enduring forces of the Confederacy, he was a man acquainted with grief, tortured with doubt about his mission in life. Wherever he went he was applauded, yet he must have felt alien to that social and political atmosphere. He did his utmost to absorb himself into the social, political, economic, and military structure of the South, yet managed to maintain a "free space" around himself that somewhat protected him from the intolerance, jealousy, and hatred he felt from all directions. All the while, he searched painfully for personal identity, recognizing that in reality he was a stranger among those whom he served.

History has a way of reciting the fortunes of a nation in terms of the leaders who seem to have determined the fate of its people. And no history is complete without some understanding of the motives, drives, and inner thoughts of the persons involved. This would be particularly true in a historical sketch of the life and meteoric career of one of the most inscrutable and fascinating leaders of the Confederacy, who after more than a century, is still wrapped in obscurity and myth.

Had the South won the Civil War, the name of Judah P. Benjamin would surely have been one of the great ones of history. As it is, he is mainly remembered today by some lawyers, a few southern historians, and, dimly, by the Jews of the South. In a sense, Benjamin was a product of the South, where passion for oratory, settling one's honor on the dueling field, and an almost universal enjoyment of Sir Walter Scott's novels influenced codes of conduct and colored southern life with a romantic cast.

Judah Philip Benjamin was born August 6, 1811, on the island of St. Thomas, British West Indies. His parents were Orthodox Jews. His mother, Rebecca de Mendes, was of Spanish ancestry, with a Sephardic background; his English father, Philip Benjamin, was a Talmudic scholar, naïve, lackluster, far more concerned with study than with making a living for his impoverished wife and seven children.

Rebecca Benjamin had an uncle, Jacob Levy, who was a merchant living in Wilmington, North Carolina, and the family soon settled in nearby Fayetteville where Philip continued his unsuccessful career as storekeeper. Rebecca, who seemed to be of tougher fiber than her husband, was determined that her son Judah, who even when a child demonstrated an eager and acute mind, would receive the best education possible. He was sent to the Fayetteville Academy, considered to be one of the finest preparatory schools in the South at that time. There young Judah, under the guidance of Colin McIver, a Scottish minister, made outstanding progress; and in 1825, at the age of fourteen, he entered Yale University to complete his studies.

At Yale he quickly made it apparent that he had not only a keen mind but a precise, sagacious, and provocative one. He soon began to

assert some independence of thought and to indulge in some minor re-
bellions. At seventeen he already felt an urgent sense of purpose, which
he maintained throughout his life, an urgency that he found challenging
and thrilling. At the end of his third year, he left Yale without earning
a degree because of "a violation of the laws of the college." Many an
abolitionist newspaper later charged that Benjamin had been forced to
leave college because of dishonesty. Benjamin's explanation was that he
left because his father was financially unable to keep him there and biographers have been inclined to believe his explanation.

At seventeen this colorful, aggressive youth found himself in New
Orleans, which for him must have seemed exotic, spicy, and picturesque, with its French language, Spanish architecture, and Creole
aristocracy.

At this point it would be well to portray briefly the "social climate"
in which the Jews of Louisiana in particular and of the South in general
found themselves at this period of American history. The growth of
Jewish communities, such as existed in New York, Pennsylvania, Virginia, South Carolina, and Georgia, was prohibited in Louisiana by
Bienville's Black Code. The *Code Noir* was issued in March, 1724, and
remained in effect until the United States acquired Louisiana in 1803,
and its first article decreed the expulsion of Jews. After the Louisiana
Purchase, the Black Code continued, although the jurisdiction of the
United States Constitution negated its religious implications. Not until
1868, however, did the Louisiana Constitution proclaim that "every
person has the right to worship God according to his conscience."

Because they were foreign born and were non-Christian, Jews were
regarded as "different," and different they were, which inevitably resulted in a "social distance" between them and their neighbors. The host
culture of the greater community had its own customs, holidays, and
calendar rhythm, but many Jews knew another set of calendar observances. These characteristics plus the rapidity with which Jews rose in
socioeconomic areas tended to intensify the sense of differences between them and the non-Jewish on all levels. These conditions made
them vulnerable targets for discrimination, despite the fact that most
Jews were friendly with their non-Jewish neighbors and were eager to
conform to the American way of living and to be integrated into the
American cultural pattern.

In the meantime the new Republic, with sharp internal quarrels over states' rights and slavery, was tending rapidly toward disintegration, and in 1861 the divergence between the North and the South grew into civil war. There were no specifically Jewish attitudes in regard to this bitter struggle. The Jews who lived in the South usually defended the concept of states' rights and the institution of slavery. On the other hand, those Jews who lived in the North defended Lincoln's policies and vehemently denounced slavery. Bertram Wallace Korn, in his well-documented *American Jewry and the Civil War*, discusses at length the economic tensions, personal fears and frustrations, and mass passions which strengthened and heightened reaction to Jews in the North as well as the South.

Judah Benjamin's first job in New Orleans was in a commercial house and, while he did not particularly care for such work, it gave him valuable experience and enabled him to make many important contacts throughout the city. He was determined, however, to become a lawyer, a profession in which he believed he could find greater possibilities of self-fulfillment, a sense of power, leadership, independence, and opportunities for creative, intellectual enterprise. Indeed it was already being said of him, that he was a "devilish smart young fellow." Judah studied law in his spare time, and in 1832, at twenty-one, he was admitted to the bar.

At this point in his life, he fell in love with Natalie St. Martin, whom he had been teaching English. Miss St. Martin considered herself a Creole, a devout Catholic; she was beautiful, spoiled, and extravagant. They were married on February 12, 1833. If Judah had any interest in his ancestral religion, it was now broken, at least overtly, and he had little or no contact with the Jewish community of New Orleans.

Selfish and shallow, Natalie, at sixteen, was little interested in her husband and his endeavors, except for the money he could earn. She was intellectually much inferior to him and she had only an elementary education. In truth, she had little love for her short, stout husband with his cherubic face and perpetual smile, who was far removed from her social plane and her religious proclivities.

Benjamin carefully concealed from the world his private life with its disappointments, turmoil, misery, and loneliness. In some fashion he had to compensate for his failure in marriage, which all his days he was to consider the one great void in his life. For ten years they lived together miserably; then Natalie moved to Paris where their only child, Ninette, was born, and they met at infrequent intervals until he fled to Europe at the end of the Civil War. There is little doubt that to a large degree his success in law, business, and politics grew out of his need to support his wife and daughter and to compensate for the painful failure of his marriage.

Thus Judah P. Benjamin turned with even greater intensity and aggressiveness to the outside world. He became more than ever involved in the stream of whirling human experiences around him, no matter the costs, the risks, or the sacrifice. From his ancestors he must have learned the age-old lesson of survival: one has no choice—there was nothing to do but to face up to the most harassing discouragements. So he drove himself deeper into law, politics, business, farming, and eventually wartime politics. His most formidable weapons of defense and attack were shrewd wit, stubborn courage, verbal skill, a body of knowledge, a veiled magnetism, a shy manner; he perhaps had a deep-seated dream to return "home," a dream secretly held by most Jews throughout their long and difficult history.

It is interesting to note that this compulsion for self-assertion and mastery, this zealousness that bordered on evangelism, created in him an extreme individualism that inevitably resulted in a sort of alienation from those whom he served and whom he so ardently wanted to impress. Stephen Vincent Benét portrays Judah P. Benjamin skillfully, succinctly in his narrative poem, "John Brown's Body":

> Judah P. Benjamin, the dapper Jew
> Seal-sleek, black-eyed, lawyer and epicure,
> Able, well-hated, face alive with life . . .

But not even Benét, with his keen insight into human nature, could penetrate the secrets of Judah's heart nor fathom the subconscious motives underlying his life.

From the very beginning, Benjamin's law career was an outstanding success, and he seemed to glory in his achievements. His great juristic knowledge, his eloquence and sheer force of personality, his legal skill, and his urgent need to succeed soon made him the leading commercial lawyer in New Orleans. In 1842 he acquired a national reputation when he argued the legal cases that arose out of the mutiny of a group of slaves on the brig *Creole*.

Despite his phenomenal success as a lawyer, Benjamin decided in 1842 to go into politics, and without much difficulty he was elected as a Whig to the lower house of the state legislature. In 1844 he was one of the delegates to the Louisiana constitutional convention, at which time he played an important role in the founding of a state university which subsequently became Tulane University. He was also responsible in large measure for locating this institution in New Orleans.

During these years he achieved a reputation as a public speaker. It was said of him: "As a speaker, he was calm, collected, forcible, though sometimes a little too rapid in his elocution. His voice has a silvery, mellifluous sweetness and seldom jars upon the ear by degenerating into a shrill or harsh tone while his manner and gestures are graceful and finished." [1] However, at best his oratory was never more than subsidiary to Benjamin's legal and political interests, but even these activities did not wholly satisfy his need for action. He became interested in and bought a colorful plantation known as Belle Chasse, situated below New Orleans. He hoped that his wife would be happy living in such luxury, but she found it boring and distasteful, and it was at this time that she moved to Paris, where she remained permanently. This move hurt Benjamin deeply.

It is interesting to note that after Natalie left, Judah tore down the old Belle Chasse house and built a larger one. It was said that he would not be content until he had a great mansion, with many rooms, imposing columns, and accommodations for a great number of guests.

And indeed the structure was grandiose—more like a Greek temple. It was built of Louisiana cypress and had fifteen-foot-wide galleries which surrounded the building and protected it from the sun and rain; huge white columns lent grandeur and dignity to the mansion. It contained twenty rooms, with high ceilings, tall windows, sparkling chandeliers, and strong, massive doors. One hundred slaves maintained the three-hundred-acre plantation.

---

1. Rywell Martin, *Judah Benjamin: Unsung Rebel Prince* (Ashville, N.C.: The Stephens Press, 1948), 16.

Alongside the main buildings were a brick smokehouse, a gas-manufacturing plant to light up the many rooms, and a very special plantation bell containing two hundred silver dollars melted into it to give it a "silvery" tone.

About this time Benjamin received another setback. His sight became seriously impaired. It was a bitter blow to his pride and to his ambitions and, for a time, caused him to be moody and despondent.

The production of cane sugar was in its infancy in Louisiana at that period, and most plantations were mainly concerned with cotton farming. Benjamin early became interested in the possibility of developing better techniques for cane cultivation and sugar manufacturing. His discoveries proved most valuable, and he was able to apply them at his plantation. In 1846 and 1848, he wrote a series of articles for *De Bow's Review*, the important publication of antebellum planters, in which Benjamin set forth his new theories and methods relating to the sugarcane industry. The Louisiana Agriculture Society awarded him its first prize for his contribution.

But success escaped him once more, for the bankruptcy of a friend, whose note for sixty thousand dollars he had endorsed, cost him his plantation and threw him back upon his law practice. Thereafter, until the end of his life, his devotion to law, in which he attained the highest eminence, was tempered only by his interest in politics.

After the loss of Belle Chasse, he was ridiculed, but his courage, vision, sensitivity, and hard work helped restore him. Indeed disappointment seemed to make his mind more precise and more provocative than ever.

In 1852 he entered national politics at which time he was elected to the United States Senate. Before he took office in March, 1853, President Franklin Pierce nominated him as an associate justice of the United States Supreme Court. This must surely have been the highest public honor received by an American Jew up to that time. He declined the offer stating that he preferred a more active political career. But the political career alone did not truly satisfy him, and he began to have great dreams about the development of commerce, not only in Louisiana but in all America. He became involved in the organization of the Jackson Railroad, from New Orleans to Jackson, Mississippi (now known as the Illinois Central), and another railroad to run across the Isthmus of Tehuantepec in Mexico. Benjamin early recognized the need to link New Orleans with areas farther north and the value of a route by which the gap between the Atlantic and Pacific oceans could be bridged. The Panama route was shorter, but the distance across the Isthmus of Tehuantepec was only 125 miles, and it was much closer to the center of trade. However, because of financial complications in New Orleans and unstable political conditions in Mexico, this project failed. Judah Benjamin did play an important role in the development of the Central Pacific Railroad. It was constructed eastward from Sacramento to join the western portion of the Union Pacific.

Benjamin was not the first Jewish senator from the South. David L. Yulee of Florida had been elected some years previously, but it was the consensus among leaders of that day that Benjamin was by far one of the most outstanding men who served in that body. It was not long before he was recognized by his colleagues to be among the ablest members of the United States Senate, and by 1859 he was chairman of the Committee on Private Land Claims and a member of the Judiciary Committee.

Despite the fact that Benjamin had little to do with Judaism, he found that he could not escape from its label. Records of the Jewish congregations in New Orleans indicate that he did not attend services and was not listed among those Jews prominent in social and civic affairs in the Jewish community. Little if any mention is made in his biographies regarding anti-semitic attitudes he may have encountered in his younger days. He himself had little to say about this, and it was not until he became famous that he faced the problem. Korn makes the point that at that time most any Jew who rose above the ordinary level had to pay for his conspicuous position by suffering attacks on his background and the faith of his folk. Judah Benjamin learned this lesson quickly. Often, during his triumphs or his failures, he was reminded of his religious origin—sometimes subtly and sometimes brutally, sometimes in jest and sometimes in sordidness. Usually he ignored these references but there were times when some deep, sensitive nerve was touched, and he could neither smile nor keep his clenched hands in his pockets. Martin Rywell tells a story that graphically illustrates his convictions: "In [Benjamin's] life the tentacles of religious preju-

dice often lashed him. There are several versions of the following anecdote credited to him. General Henry Gray was his opponent for
election to the United States Senate in January, 1859. Toward the
close of the campaign they met at Shreveport. General Gray said of
Benjamin: 'His forefathers have crucified the Savior of the world.' To
which Benjamin replied: 'It is true that I am a Jew, and when my
ancestors were receiving the Ten Commandments from the immediate hand of Deity, midst the thunderings and lightnings of Mount
Sinai, the ancestors of my opponent were herding swine in the forest
of Great Britain.' " [2]

There must have been moments when Judah Philip Benjamin, the
brilliant orator, the competent jurist, the successful politician, the fanatical proponent of the dream of southern grandeur, felt that he was
neither fish nor fowl, that the life of a Jew is a strange paradox. On
the one hand, he has been the eternal wanderer, yet he lives according
to a pattern that seems to be geared to permanence. Judah's conduct
indicates that he must have resolved fervently to bend where other
people break. And bend he did, becoming more urbane, more aggressive—and more lonely.

In 1861 Benjamin's career in the Senate came to an end. With the
election of Abraham Lincoln to the presidency in November, 1860,
the southern states made preparations to secede from the Union. During those stormy days, Benjamin was one of the earliest of the southern senators to advise secession. On December 8, 1860, he particularly
advocated separate secession by Louisiana. On December 14 he signed
the famous address by southern members of Congress, "To Our Constituents." This was followed by an impassioned defense of the rights
of secession and of southern policy that further enhanced his reputation as a defender of states' rights. Shortly after the secession of Louisiana, he made his brilliant and emotional speech to the Senate. It was
not an ordinary political address; it was, in truth, a sincere effort to
hold the Union together. But it failed and seventy-two years after the
adoption of the Constitution to form "a more perfect Union," the
Union dissolved and the Confederacy was formed.

Benjamin's last spirited oration sounded a little like Moses' "Let

2. *Ibid.,* 35.

my people go." There is little doubt that Judah was sincere in his argument, but the question arises: how much of his attitude was influenced by policy and how much by genuine conviction?

As Benjamin entered the ferment surrounding secession and war, his zeal burned with a fire that did not always seem a pure flame. This writer believes that his fervor was made to serve a purpose of which most biographers are as yet unaware. It would be dramatic, at least, to know how his rationalization developed and what patterns it took. The struggle between the South and the North quickly ceased to be a thing of the head and became a thing of the heart, and Judah threw himself with all his might into what the South considered the life's blood of the issue—slavery. It is true that it was a time of confusion and heartache, that men, women, and even children were faced with bewildering choices between alternatives of action and attitudes that seemed mutually incompatible and inconsistent. Yet the irritating question persists: what is the role of the Jew in the matter of slavery? Benjamin's dedication to slavery seems a contradiction in one who came from a home where Judaism and its traditions held freedom as an inherent right of every person. Young Judah must have heard his father expound the Talmud, wherein it is emphasized again and again that although man may be the most miserable of creatures, he is God's creation and therefore possesses rights and dignities of his own. Judah very likely read in a child's history of the Jews that they have always struggled to be free and that they have become the very incarnation of the spirit of liberty. Once when he was involved in a suit relating to slaves, he said: "What is a slave? He is a human being. He has feelings and passions and intellect. His heart, like the white man's swells with love, burns with jealousy, aches with sorrow, pines under restraint and discomfort, toils with revenge and even cherishes the desire of liberty." Judah P. Benjamin must have remembered well the words put into Shylock's mouth by Shakespeare. The mysteries of Benjamin's true feelings about slavery—the conflict in his mind and its effect on his psyche—all make the "Sphinx of the South" a difficult subject for the historian.

As soon as the Confederacy was established, Benjamin was appointed attorney general, a position for which he was not at all suited, for the reason that it was too inconsequential for a man of his ability.

It was the lowest cabinet position and, so far as Benjamin was concerned, a wasteful, futile one.

President Jefferson Davis thought highly of Judah Benjamin, despite the fact that Benjamin had once challenged him to a duel after Davis spoke in a derogatory manner about him. Davis, his anger passed, deeply regretted the wrong he had committed; he declined the duel as not justifiable and made a public apology. Both men behaved so scrupulously, according to their accepted "code," that the incident began a genuine friendship. Years later when Jefferson Davis was writing about his relationship with Benjamin, he said: "Mr. Benjamin, of Louisiana, had a very high reputation as a lawyer, and my acquaintance with him in the Senate had impressed me with the lucidity of his intellect, his systematic habits and capacity for labor." [3]

It is a generally accepted fact that until he became a member of the Confederate cabinet, Judah Benjamin was quite popular. For some time he had been recognized as leader of the entire New Orleans legal community. However, his brief tenure as attorney general offered him no opportunity to utilize his legal ability, and he instead spent a great deal of time advising Davis on matters pertaining to the presidency, a situation that created much jealousy. Davis soon appointed him secretary of war. It was part of Benjamin's strange fate to enter this office under conditions that made it impossible for him to succeed.

The southern generals had no confidence in him, and serious breaks occurred between the general staff and the secretary of war. So sound was Benjamin's judgment and so precise his logic that often he angered the military leaders by making them appear incompetent. It is agreed by most students of history that no other southern leader saw the problems of the desperate Confederate government with the same objectivity and relentless detachment as did Judah Benjamin. Indeed, many of the men around him interpreted his objectivity as too liberal toward states' rights and slavery.

Most of all, Benjamin angered and baffled General Joseph E. Johnston and consequently embarrassed Louisiana's popular hero, General Pierre Gustave Toutant Beauregard. "Old Bory," was believed by many to be no less than the reincarnation of one of Napoleon's grand

3. Jefferson Davis, *The Rise and Fall of the Confederate Government* (New York: D. Appleton and Co., 1881), I, 242.

marshals. Johnston once wrote to the Confederate President: "The course of the Secretary of War has not only impaired discipline, but deprived me of the influence in the army, without which there can be little hope of success." [4]

Benjamin held his office for six stormy months, during which time he reorganized the department, but many of the unrealistic and over-optimistic generals were opposed to his demanding administration. The relationships grew so bitter and the dissension so deep that in March, 1862, President Davis appointed Judah Benjamin secretary of state, a position he held until the dream of a Confederate empire died.

To a sensitive person like Benjamin, the cruelties of the fratricidal struggle must have been painful. As the war progressed, he could not but realize that all his zealousness, diligence, perseverance, and devotion brought few good results. Until the very end of the Confederacy, he remained an enigma to his associates—he was loved, envied, and hated, invariably the center of controversy; he was a man about whom strong, often bitter views were expressed both by friend and foe. Only President Davis never lost faith in him. As a matter of fact, during the war years Benjamin was the President's closest adviser, his cheerfulness and overt optimism helping to strengthen his gloomy and temperamental leader. Davis later said of Benjamin that he was "my chief reliance among men."

As secretary of state, Benjamin did his best to obtain recognition for the Confederacy from Great Britain and France and endeavored to secure foreign aid wherever he thought possible, but European countries were pessimistic about the South's chances for success and remained aloof.

Few peoples in the history of man have fought with more courage and intensity for what they believed than did the people of the South. They poured out their blood and they sacrificed their homes for a cause that was doomed from the beginning. With Appomattox, Judah Benjamin found that there was no place for him to go. He was convinced that he was considered by many Yankees as the leader of the southern rebellion and that if he were captured he would be treated cruelly. In a letter to his sister, he stated that he preferred to die trying

4. *The War of the Rebellion: A Compilation of the Official Records of the Union and Confederate Armies* (Washington, D.C., 1881), Ser. I, Vol. V, 1087.

to escape rather than fall into the hands of the northern army. He claimed that he knew of a proclamation in which a large reward was offered for the capture of President Davis and his cabinet. Davis was accused of having been involved in the plot to assassinate Abraham Lincoln. This must have been a frightful blow to Benjamin.

The man who built Belle Chasse, who stood before the Supreme Court of the land, who was twice elected to the Senate of the United States, who was considered by many to be the heart and brains of the Confederacy no longer had a home. The man who held three different positions in the cabinet of the Confederacy, who had been hailed as a brilliant orator and often called the most outstanding Jew of his time, the man who must have, at his father's Passover service, thanked God for the delivery of his ancestors from Egypt, yet who stood up and fought for a slavocracy, found himself an outcast, running and hiding, once again a stranger in a strange land.

Disguised as a Frenchman, he acquired a horse and wagon, crossed Georgia, and entered Florida whence he planned to escape by sea to the West Indies. He managed to hire a small fishing boat, which was stopped and searched by a northern gunboat. Benjamin escaped capture by posing as a cook, and after a number of narrow escapes, he reached England. He did not settle in France where his wife and daughter lived, for he was convinced that they cared little for him, a tragic fact that tortured him for many years, and one which he never overcame.

By the sheer force of his personality, determination, and knowledge of foreign legal systems, he soon became well known in London, and in 1870 Judah P. Benjamin was made queen's counsel for the county of Palatine of Lancaster. One can only imagine the thrill he must have experienced as he received this rank from the queen herself. Before he left England a few years later, he was honored at a banquet given by the bar of England in the Inner Temple Hall. This was the occasion for the expression of an unprecedented "collective farewell" to a man who was considered by his colleagues to be outstanding in mental endowments and argumentative power.

In the summer of 1883, Judah Benjamin became ill and moved to Le Mans, France to be reunited with his wife and daughter. After a lifetime of wandering, he was with the women whom he dearly loved but who never returned that love. He was, as always, gracious and forgiving, and the smiling mask on his chubby face covered the tragedies of his life.

During the winter he became critically ill and on May 6, 1884, he died. His wife had always regretted that he was not a Catholic, and a few moments before he died, she, believing that he had become one, had the final Roman Catholic rites administered to him. A Catholic service was held for him in the church of St. Pierre De Chaillot, and he was buried in the cemetery of Pérelachaise.

Bertram Wallace Korn

Jews and Negro Slavery in the Old South, 1789–1865

Introduction

As WE INAUGURATE this five-year-long observance of the Civil War*, there is certain to be no diminution of the quantity of historical volumes already flooding forth from the nation's presses. One of the major subjects will undoubtedly continue to be the question of the causes of the Civil War. Some writers will favor political interpretations; others will emphasize economic factors; still others will cite social ingredients. Some will blame the North, and others the South. Some will denounce fool-hardy leadership in the South, or in the North, or both. Others will underline the failure of ordinary citizens in both sections to express their feelings and desires. Many of these writers will be so enamored of their theories that they will overlook the all-pervasive influence of the crucial problem: slavery. Political, economic, social, psychological, and other currents *were* present as contributory factors, but they were *all* related in one way or another to the persistence of the slave system. Had Negro slavery not been an integral aspect of the life of the Old South, there would have been no conflict, no secession, no war. Differences there might have been, but not violence and bloodshed. Slavery was the single indigestible element in the life of the American people which fostered disunion, strife,

* Address delivered at the Fifty-Ninth Annual Meeting of the American Jewish Historical Society at the Jewish Museum of the Jewish Theological Seminary of America, New York City, February 18, 1961.

and carnage, just as the concomitant race problem has continued to an important degree to be a divisive force in American life to this day.[1]

Previous students of the American Jewish scene have appeared to be reluctant to investigate the question of Jewish participation in the slave system. Works on local Jewish history in Southern communities, in particular, have either glossed over or altogether ignored this basic aspect of the life and experiences of the Jews of the Old South. It is my purpose to attempt to survey the following themes: Jews as planters, and as owners of slaves; the treatment of slaves by Jews; the emancipation of slaves by Jews; Jews as harsh taskmasters; business dealings of Jews with slaves and free Negroes; Jews as slave dealers; cases of miscegenation involving Jews and Negroes; and opinions of Jews about the slave system.[2]

1. See Lee Benson and Thomas J. Pressly, *Can Differences in Interpretations of the Cause of the Civil War Be Resolved Objectively?* (mimeographed text of paper presented at the Annual Meeting of the American Historical Association, Dec. 29, 1956), for an extensive presentation of differences in the interpretation of pre-War patterns of thought and action.

2. I begin with 1789 for the following reasons: firstly, before discussing Jewish ownership of slaves in the colonies, it would be necessary to consider the question of Jewish legal status in the colonies in order to investigate the problems of all property ownership by Jews; secondly, the Colonial period was the hey-day of slave importation from Africa, and northern Jews were far more active in this aspect of the slave-trade than southern Jews; and thirdly, Jewish settlers in the West Indian colonies were at least as influential as those on the North American mainland, and a study of slavery during that time would therefore require extensive reference to those non-southern Jewish communities. This study is terminated with the end of the Civil War, because the nature of Jewish life in the Reconstruction period was far different from that of the antebellum period. Only in a few instances has material before or after these dates been utilized, and these data are clearly germane. An additionally complicating factor has been avoided through the elimination of reference to the Jews of the border states, Maryland, Kentucky, and Missouri, which were at least as much a part of the North as they were of the South, as the Confederate leaders eventually discovered.

The following abbreviations will be used for works frequently cited: *AJA* = American Jewish Archives files; *AJAM* = *American Jewish Archives* [journal]; *E* = Barnett A. Elzas, *The Jews of South Carolina* (Philadelphia, 1905); *EL* = Herbert T. Ezekiel and Gaston Lichtenstein, *The History of the Jews of Richmond from 1769 to 1917* (Richmond, 1917); *HTC* = Helen Tunnicliff Catterall, *Judicial Cases Concerning American Slavery and the Negro* (4 vols.; Washington, 1926-36); *JNH* = *Journal of Negro History*; *MC* = Jacob Rader Marcus, *American Jewry. Documents. Eighteenth Century* (Cincinnati, 1959); *ME* = Jacob Rader Marcus, *Early American Jewry: The Jews of Pennsylvania and the South, 1655-1790* (Philadelphia, 1953), *MM* = Jacob Rader Marcus, *Memoirs of American Jews, 1775-1865* (3 vols.; Philadelphia, 1955-56); *OCC* = *The Occident and American Jewish Advocate*; *PAJHS* = *Publications of the American Jewish Historical Society*; *R* = Joseph R. Rosenbloom, *A Biographical Dictionary of Early American Jews* (Lexington, 1960); *RE* = Charles Reznikoff with Uriah Z. Engelman, *The Jews of Charleston* (Philadelphia, 1950).

1   Jews As Planters and As Owners of Slaves

Only a small number of Jews in the Old South were planters. Socio-logical and economic factors explain why so few Jews achieved this characteristic Southern status of ownership and occupation. History had ordained that European Jews could not own land; the selection of occupations in which Jews could train their sons was severely delim-ited. Most Jews, out of natural inclination and the pressure of circum-stances, felt safer in urban areas, where they could share each other's fellowship and find support in each other's presence. If Jews desired to be loyal to their ancestral faith, they could fulfill this need only where other Jews resided, not in the rural areas. An additional pressure was the poverty which accompanied most immigrant Jews when they came to America. The average Southern Jew was, therefore, a peddler or store-keeper, with comparatively slim resources, who tended to live in a town or city, and would not even think of aspiring to the ownership of a plantation.

Some Jews found their way to the highest rung of the economic and social ladder through prosperous careers as merchants or profes-sional men. Among this small number of men, probably the best-known was Judah P. Benjamin, the brilliant New Orleans attorney, who pur-chased an extensive plantation twenty miles below the city in 1844, in partnership with Theodore Packwood, who served as the resident man-ager. Not content with the rather smallish mansion house, Benjamin re-built Belle Chasse into a magnificent house which finally fell victim to a housing development in 1960. Benjamin's home, in which he installed his sisters after his wife and daughter moved to Paris, was an elegant example of ante-bellum grace, with "great, double-leveled porches, al-most fifteen feet across, a parade of massive, rectangular pillars and everything else in proportion; curving stairways of mahogany, massive carved decorations, silver-plated doorknobs, extensive rose gardens be-tween the house and the levee, and an enormous bell into which Ben-jamin was said to have dropped five hundred silver dollars during the melting, to 'sweeten the tone.' " Though Benjamin continued to prac-tice his legal profession, he devoted great interest to his plantation, unlike the typical absentee landlord, and wrote articles and delivered speeches on the problems of sugar-planting. Belle Chasse was staffed with one hundred and forty slaves, of whom about eighty were field-hands. Benjamin sold the plantation after his election to the Senate.[3]

Another well-known Jewish planter was Major Raphael J. Moses who owned land at Esquiline Hill, near Columbus, Georgia. Moses, who became Chief Commissary Officer of Longstreet's Corps during the war, wrote in his memoirs that "when the war broke out, I had forty-seven slaves, and when it ended I had forty-seven freedmen—all left me except one, old London, who staid with me until he died." [4]

Other Jewish planters were: Nathan Nathans, who was a President of Beth Elohim Congregation of Charleston, South Carolina, with a plantation on the Cooper River; Isaiah Moses, who worked thirty-five slaves on his farm at St. James, Goose Creek, South Carolina; Mordecai Cohen, who had twenty-seven slaves on his plantation at St. Andrews, South Carolina, and his two sons Marx and David, both of whom owned nearby farms; Isaac Lyons, of Columbia, South Carolina; Barnet A. Cohen of King's Creek, South Carolina; and Chapman Levy, who turned from the law to planting when he moved to the Mississippi Territory. Various members of the Mordecai family had plantations in North Carolina and Virginia. Among other large plantation holdings, Moses Levy owned a magnificent home, "Parthenope," on a plantation at the juncture of the Matanzas River and Moses Creek, in Florida, which he sold to Achille Murat, the French refugee. One of the few lady planters was Abigail Minis, who had a small plantation near Savannah on which she employed seventeen slaves. The only Louisiana planter other than Benjamin whom we have been able to discover was J. Levy of Ascension Parish, with forty-one slaves working his fields.[5]

3. Robert Douthat Meade, *Judah P. Benjamin, Confederate Statesman* (New York, 1943), 57, 63, 90; J. Carlyle Sitterson, *Sugar Country: The Cane Sugar Industry in the South, 1753–1950* (Lexington, 1953), 131, 154; *The Life of Judah Philip Benjamin, A Publication of the Louisiana State Museum* (New Orleans, 1937); Harnett T. Kane, *Deep Delta Country* (New York, 1944), 68–69; Baton Rouge *Advocate*, March 27, 1960, magazine section, 1.

4. *MM*, I, 184.

5. Addendum on "Absentee Ownership of Slaves in the United States in 1830," in Carter G. Woodson, *Free Negro Owners of Slaves in the United States in 1830* (Washington, D.C., 1924), 61; 1840 Mss. Census Returns for New Orleans and Vicinity, National Archives; *RE*, 92; *E*, 51, 143; *R*, 25, 89; *ME*, 385; A. J. Hanna, *A Prince in Their Midst: The Adventurous Life of Achille Murat on the American Frontier* (Norman, 1946), 86; Leon Hühner, "David L. Yulee: Florida's First Senator," *PAJHS*, no. 25

There were probably a number of other Jewish owners of plantations, but altogether they constituted only a tiny proportion of the Southerners whose habits, opinions, and status were to become decisive for the entire section, and eventually, for the entire country. In contradistinction, it is astonishing to discover even one Jew who tried his hand as a plantation overseer even if only for a brief time. He was the much-traveled, restless and adventurous Solomon Polock, a member of the well-known Philadelphia family, who worked on a plantation near Mobile in the late 1830s.[6]

But the typical Jew had no thought of working on a plantation, much less of owning one. He was likely to be a petty trader, trying to eke out a marginal living in an occupation which ranked quite low on the social scale of the Old South. He considered himself fortunate if he could pay his bills on time; and rated it a high accomplishment to own his shop with a few rooms on the floor above where his family could live. If he were as yet unmarried, he and a brother or uncle or nephew would live in a room behind the store, and the men would try to save up enough money to make their future more secure. Such men as these had no reason to invest their small capital in a slave, nor had they any need for a slave's services. Take, for example, young Samuel Adler and his brother who had a store in Talladega, Alabama. These two men, both unmarried, slept in the room behind their store, while two or three young clerks lived upstairs. They sent their laundry out, and ate their meals at a local hotel, except on Sunday, when their food was sent over to the store. What would the Adlers have done with a slave even if they could have afforded one?[7] Or consider the fourteen Jewish men who lived in a Mobile, Alabama, boarding house. They were all between the ages of nineteen and thirty-nine, and earned their living as shopkeepers or clerks, with one tailor added for good measure. These men might be served at table by a slave, but

---

(1917), 4–7. Hühner, however, reports that Moses Levy favored the abolition of slavery, despite his extensive ownership of slaves.

6. Letter, Barnett Polock to Sarah Polock, Sept. 6, 1836, in collection of Edwin Wolf, II.

7. We know about the Adler brothers' laundry and meals from 26 Ala. 145, quoted in *HTC*, III, 201. On Dec. 2, 1854, a slave, Vincent, broke into their store and stole some goods; the trial revolved around the question of whether the slave had actually rifled a store or a residence. If the latter, the penalty would, of course, be much more severe.

this was the extent of their need. Furthermore, a slave would only be in the way in their little stores.[8]

On the other hand, Jews who were more firmly established in a business or professional career, as well as in their family relationships, had every reason to become slave-owners, although, of course, some socially prominent families took pride in employing white servants in their homes.[9] Precise statistics concerning the ownership of slaves by Jews are hard to locate. Census records must be used with caution, because certain Jews known from other sources to be resident in a specific area at a given time were not listed at all; peddlers and traveling merchants, for example, were apt to be on the road when the census was taken; some of the manuscript census returns are quite illegible; and, in addition to frequent misspelling, the identification of Jewish names will always constitute a problem.

It is possible, nevertheless, to gain some information of value from the census returns. My colleague, Dr. Malcolm Stern, has investigated the 1790 manuscript census returns in his genealogical researches, and has generously provided me with the relevant data. Unfortunately, the returns for Georgia and Virginia were destroyed, but the South Carolina data provide valuable insight. Seventy-three census heads of households have been identified as Jewish; of these, at least thirty-four owned one or more slaves, to a total of 151 slaves. The only large holdings of slaves were possessed by Jacob Jacobs of Charleston (11), and Abraham Cohen (21), Solomon Cohen (9), and Esther Myers (11), all of the Georgetown District.[10]

The returns for other censuses have not yet been subjected to in-

8. 1850 Mss. Census Returns for Mobile County, National Archives.

9. This is an aspect of southern social life about which little has been written. Among the Jews of Mobile, according to the 1850 Mss. Census Returns, some of the most prosperous Jews reported white servants—Solomon I. Jones (the brother of Israel Jones) kept two white servants, and Philip Phillips had "four female Irish" in help—undoubtedly needed to take care of his large brood of children.

10. It is a misfortune that Ira Rosenwaike did not see fit to reproduce the data about slaves in his "An Estimate and Analysis of the Jewish Population of the United States in 1790," *PAJHS*, L, no. 1 (Sept., 1960), 23–67. Dr. Stern's notes have not been published; they do offer, however, an interesting contrast between ownership of slaves in South Carolina and other states. These statistics are as follows: of twenty-three Jewish heads of household in the New England states, five owned a total of 21 slaves; of sixty Jewish heads of household in New York, twenty owned a total of 43 slaves; of thirty-one Jewish heads of household in Pennsylvania, only three owned a total of 6 slaves; and of eight Jewish heads of household in Maryland, three owned a total of 3 slaves.

tensive investigation for Jewish data. But some guidance may be obtained from the results of a cursory sampling of the returns for New Orleans over a period of twenty years. In the 1820 manuscript census records for New Orleans, it has been possible to identify only six Jews. Each of these owned at least one slave, and the six owned twenty-three slaves altogether. By 1830, twenty-two Jews can be identified in the census returns—a very low number, since there were about sixty-six Jews in the area when the newly established congregation published its list of contributors in 1828, although some of the donors were not permanent residents. More than half of these twenty-two did not own slaves, but ten of them owned a total of seventy-five slaves. Obviously some of the newly arrived Jewish settlers could not afford to own slaves. By 1840, when sixty-two Jews can be identified in the census returns—again a very small number, since there must have been at least several hundred Jewish families in the community by that time—the newcomers had prospered to so great a degree that only seven reported that they owned no slaves. The fifty-five identifiable Jewish slaveowners of New Orleans in 1840 held a total of three hundred and forty-eight Negroes in bondage, an index to growing prosperity.[11]

A large proportion of the early Jewish settlers in New Orleans were migrants not from foreign countries, but from well-established communities like Charleston. This was not true of Mobile, where only a small number of Jews were other than German and Polish immigrants, who were likely to be less prosperous and less assimilated than the New Orleans residents. Yet, according to the Mobile 1850 census, which lists seventy-two identifiable Jewish heads of family, thirty-one Jews were owners of slaves, to a total of ninety slaves. The proportion is even higher in view of the fact that we include in the figure for heads of families, nineteen young clerks and peddlers who lived in the homes of relatives, and fourteen Jewish bachelors who lived in a single boarding-house.[12]

11. 1820, 1830, and 1840 Mss. Census Returns for New Orleans and Vicinity, National Archives. The statistics for 1830 are somewhat deceptive: of the ten slaveowners, one, L. Jacoby, owned thirty slaves, and another, Samuel Hermann, owned seventeen. More accurate approximations of the Jewish population of New Orleans are obtainable from city directories, congregational records, and newspaper advertisements, but these, of course, give no data on the ownership of slaves.

12. 1850 Mss. Census Returns for Mobile, National Archives.

Another statistical indication of Jewish ownership of slaves, probably more accurate in terms of proportions than the census returns, are references to slaves in Jewish wills. Over the years, Professor Jacob R. Marcus has assembled at the American Jewish Archives, one hundred and twenty-nine wills of identifiable Southern Jews who died during the period of our interest. Of these, thirty-three refer to the ownership and disposition of slaves. This would mean, if it is a reliable index, that perhaps one-fourth of Southern Jewish adults were slave-owners. It is instructive that this matches the Federal figures for the 1860 census, namely, that three-fourths of the white population of the South were not slave-owners. Equally important, however, is the fact that only one-seventh of Southern Negroes were domiciled in towns or cities. The proportion of Jewish slave-owners, then, was possibly even larger than that of non-Jews, since the overwhelming majority of Southern Jews lived in the towns and cities.[13]

It would seem to be realistic to conclude that any Jew who could afford to own slaves and had need for their services would do so. Jewish owners of slaves were not exceptional figures. Slavery was an axiomatic foundation of the social pattern of the Old South. Jews wanted to acclimate themselves in every way to their environment; in both a social and psychological sense, they needed to be accepted as equals by their fellow-citizens. It was, therefore, only a matter of financial circumstance and familial status whether they were to become slave-owners.

II   The Treatment of Slaves by Jews

How did these Jewish slave-owners treat their Negroes? What did they feel towards them as human beings? Were they inclined to be lenient masters, motivated by tender sympathy, or were they, like other Southerners, sometimes kindly, sometimes harsh—but always masters?

It is obviously hard to secure answers to these questions. But some

13. The thirty-three wills refer specifically to one hundred and thirty-two slaves; in two cases slave children are not enumerated or named; in a number of others, only a few slaves are referred to by name, while unspecified numbers are grouped together in general categories. It is quite likely that some of the ninety-seven remaining decedents owned slaves and lumped them together with all other types of property, but this can neither be proved nor disproved without extensive reference to the estate inventories. The Federal statistics are derived from John Hope Franklin, *From Slavery to Freedom* (2nd ed.; New York, 1956), 185, 189.

indication of the feelings of Jews towards their slaves may be derived from a detailed study of the wills to which we have alluded.

Apologists for the slave system have often contended that the cruel master was an exception, and that most slave-owners were considerate, kindly, and thoughtful. Much depends on the definition of a word like consideration. However kindly a man might be as a master, what of the future of his slaves after his death? In nineteen of these thirty-three wills, more than half, slaves were merely bequeathed to relatives or friends without specific instructions; in five, the executors were instructed to sell them. In the majority of these wills, then, slaves were treated like other property, to be retained if convenient and expedient, to be sold if that seemed the judicious course. The word kindness surely cannot encompass any relationship where a faithful servant could be torn away from familiar moorings and sold to a stranger who might or might not be a "good" master. It was probably typical that the executor of the estate of Emanuel Stern, who died in New Orleans in 1828, sold off his twelve-year-old slave, Mathilda, at auction, for $400. This was a profitable transaction, for in the inventory, Mathilda was valued at $250.[14]

On the other hand, although the kindly feelings of some slave-owners cannot possibly be regarded as justification for the slave system, it is important to realize that some masters went far beyond a commercial attitude in their relationships with slaves. The proof of this is to be found in numerous cases of loyalty even after the emancipation which was produced by the Civil War. One example of this reciprocated regard is to be found in old London's decision to stay with his former master, Major Moses. Another is revealed in a letter which Emma Mordecai received in 1867 from a former slave, Sarah P. Norris. The letter itself, beautifully composed and written, is evidence of Emma's opinion of the law which forbade whites to teach reading and writing to slaves. Sarah sends Emma news of the family and acquaintances in Richmond. But more, she assures her erstwhile mistress that she and her husband are looking after the family graves in the Richmond cemetery, and that all is well. "I never could forget my

---

14. Not in the Marcus collection at *AJA*. Data from Inventory of Estate of Emanuel Stern, Record Room, Civil District Court, New Orleans. Stern did not own Mathilda's parents.

people," she writes, "I loved them then, I love them now." [15] It would be pure prejudice to gainsay the humane motivations of slave-owners like Miss Mordecai.

Nine of the Archives' wills contain specific provisions relating to Negroes which reflect feelings of warm generosity. In his last testament, proved on February 18, 1796, Philip Hart of Charleston bequeathed freedom to his slave Flora. Jacob Cohen of Charleston emancipated his slave Tom, in his will proved on June 6, 1800. Samuel Jones of Charleston, in his will proved on January 20, 1809, instructed his executors to emancipate his slave Jenny and her son Emanuel, if he had not already done so in his lifetime, and bequeathed to Jenny his "Bed, Sheets, Bedstead, Blankets, Tables, Pots, Plates, Chairs, Looking Glass," allowing two other slaves such part of these possessions as they might desire. Jones also bequeathed the income from certain properties to Jenny and her son, and to six slaves who were not to be emancipated. A further provision stipulated that "it is my further desire not to drive Jenny and her children out of my House in King Street, until they have time to Procure a Place for their abode." Jones gave no indication of his reason for failing to emancipate his other slaves.

Col. Chapman Levy's mother, Sarah Levy of Kershaw District, South Carolina, who died in 1839, revealed a special affection for two old slaves in her will. "It is my directions, desire and earnest request," she wrote, "that old Kennedy shall be kept with his wife and each treated with kindness and all reasonable indulgence and if my son Chapman Levy shall desire to purchase him to add to his happiness it is my directions that he shall have him at the price of three hundred dollars." Rachel D'Azevedo of Charleston, whose will was proved on February 23, 1843, did her best to assure the contentment of her slaves, Maria, Rose, Dinah, and Flora, despite the adamant provisions of state law. She bequeathed these slaves and their issue to her daughter, Mrs. Sarah A. Motta, "with the express, and particular Conditions, that immediately after the death of the said Mrs. Sarah A. Motta, the Servants aforesaid with their issue or increase Shall work for their own use and time or services, being the same to all intents and purposes as if they were entirely free." She also asked that her executor, Abraham Moïse,

15. Letter, dated Nov. 23, 1867, Mordecai Collection, Duke University Library.

act as "a kind protector to my Servants Should they require his Valuable Services."

Dr. Jacob De La Motta of Charleston, whose will was proved on February 22, 1845, directed that his sister Rachel treat his slaves, Ann Maria Simmons, and her son Augustus, "with lenity," that she allow them to work at their own option, that they pay her only "moderate" wages, "and on no account to be sold on account of their being family servants born and bred in the same."

Benjamin Levy, the New Orleans printer and publisher, directed in his will, probated just after his death on January 10, 1860, that his slave Richard White, a barber, be given the opportunity to purchase his freedom for $500. If this were not possible during his son, Alexander Levy's lifetime, White was to be set free after the son's death. Levy furthermore stipulated that the slave was "never to be sold, Mortgaged, or hired out for a longer term than one Year at a time, and never to be hired out of the State of Louisiana." Another provision in Levy's will expressed his hope that a token of esteem be given by his family to each of the eight slaves who had been his property, and now belonged to other members of the family, as a "Small Memorial of their old Master."

Two of the wills refer to free Negroes. Benjamin Davis of Charleston, in his last testament which was proved on September 26, 1831, bequeathed one hundred and fifty dollars "for her faithful Services" to "a free colod woman named Elsey." Far more unusual was a provision in the will of David Perayra Brandon of Charleston, proved on April 24, 1838: "I recommend my faithful Servant and friend Juellit or Julien free Negro, to my dear Rachel [his stepdaughter] and W. C. Lambert [her husband] my friend and request them to take him under their protection to treat him as well as they would do me and to give him Such portion of my Cloths as they will think useful to him and never forsake him being the best friend I ever had." How many white men in the Old South would have wanted to describe a Negro as their "best friend" in the most permanent document of their lives, and how many would have dared do so?

These wills are ample evidence that some Jewish Southerners were deeply sensitive to the human character of their Negroes, and thought of them as fellow men rather than as cattle or merchandise.

III Emancipation of Slaves by Jews

No matter what kindnesses were bestowed upon slaves by their masters, only one gift was permanently meaningful, the gift of freedom. Fortunately, Samuel Jones, Jacob Cohen, Philip Hart, and Benjamin Levy were not the only folk who wanted to emancipate their slaves. Isaiah Isaacs of Charlottesville, Virginia, whose firm had once been compelled to take a Negro slave as security for a debt, outlined an elaborate program for the freeing of his slaves in his will which was proved in April, 1806:

Being of opinion that all men are by nature equally free and being possessed of some of those beings who are unfortunate[ly] doomed to slavery, as to them I must enjoin upon my executors a strict observance of the following clause in my will. My slaves hereafter named are to be and they are hereby manumitted and made free so that after the different periods hereafter mentioned they shall enjoy all the privileges and immunities of freed people. My slave Rachel is to go free and quit all manner of claim of servitude from and after the first day of January, which shall be in the year [1816], James from and after the first day of January [1820], Polly on the first day of January [1822], Henry on the first day of January [1830], and William on the first day of January [1834], and should either of my females slaves Rachel or Polly have a child or children before the time they become free such issue is to serve to the age of thirty-one, and then to be discharged from servitude; the said slaves are not to be sold, but to remain the property of my children and to be divided in the same manner as directed as to the division of my real estate; each one of my slaves are to receive the value of twenty dollars in clothing on the day of their manumission.[16]

No comparable Jewish will exists, with so complete a plan of emancipation, but in 1796, Samuel Myers of Petersburg, Virginia, purchased a mulatto woman, Alice, from the trustees of the estate of a neighbor, with the obvious intention of emancipating her, which purpose he fulfilled a little over a year later.[17] A similar case of purchasing a slave

16. *EL*, 15, 327–29.
17. Photostat of deed of emancipation, *AJA*. But Myers did not free all his slaves. Louis Ginsburg, *The Jews of Petersburg* (Petersburg, 1954), 7, offers data on a number of his slaves, and in 1830, Myers' firm in Richmond was listed as owning eighty-two slaves: Woodson, "Absentee Ownership of Slaves in the United States in 1830," p. 73. Professor Jacob R. Marcus suggests to me that Myers may have purchased Alice as a concubine in view of his first wife's death just four months before. The relevant dates are as follows: Sarah Judah Myers died on Oct. 12, 1795; Myers bought Alice on Jan. 4, 1796; Myers married Judith Hays on Sept. 27, 1796; he sold Alice on Oct. 2,

for rapid emancipation was that of Joseph Tobias of Charleston who, on July 23, 1798, bought a slave named Jenny for $500 from Dr. James Cletherall, and promptly freed her "for former services rendered me." Perhaps she had nursed him during an illness while she was still the physician's property.[18] In the same year, Solomon Raphael of Richmond, and his partner, freed their slave Sylvia and her child; and six years later Raphael emancipated another slave, Priscilla.[19] In 1812, Solomon Jacobs, also of Richmond, freed his slave Esther.[20]

A Northern owner of Southern slaves,[21] Jacob I. Cohen, formerly of Richmond, and now of Philadelphia, provided for the emancipation of his slaves in his will which was probated in Philadelphia on October 31, 1823. Cohen directed that his slaves "Dick, Spencer, Meshack, Fanny and Eliza together with their children be manumitted from slavery immediately after my decease; and I do give and bequeathe to the said Dick, Spencer, Meshack, Fanny and Eliza twenty-five dollars each. But if any of my said Negroes will not accept their freedom I do then will and direct that they have the choice of their own master." Cohen also directed that the children of Mary Andrew, a slave who was to be freed at a later time, be regarded as "free from their birth." [22]

It will be noticed, of course, that these examples of emancipation were all quite early. This is no coincidence, since most of the Southern states gradually tightened their restrictions until it was virtually impossible to free a slave except through stratagem or deceit. Those who

---

1797. There is, of course, no documentary evidence of Myers' purpose, nor of the relationship.

18. Deeds from Vol. 3-L, 174, Miscellaneous Records, South Carolina Archives Department, Columbia, in Thomas J. Tobias' collection of photostats of family papers.

19. *EL*, 78, 80. 20. *EL*, 85.

21. Historians have failed to express any interest in northern owners of property in the South, property which frequently included Negro slaves. Michael Hart of New York City, for instance, who died in September, 1861, owned a plantation in Virginia. His son, Henry, went South, and "fearing that Richmond would be taken . . . left the city, and went to North Carolina, taking with him most of the slaves belonging to the estate"; 25 Grattan 795 ff., cited in *HTC*, I, 265. The well-known naval officer, Commodore Uriah P. Levy, who was so proud of his part in the agitation for the abolition of flogging in the American navy, was apparently not an abolitionist when slavery was under discussion. He held title not only to Jefferson's Monticello, a fact which has been well publicized, but also to a Virginia plantation known as Washington Farm, on which Negro slaves were worked; 3 A.K. Marsh 480, cited in *HTC*, I, 296.

22. *EL*, 330-32.

believe that the Civil War could have been avoided through a general realization of the coming collapse of the slave economy ought to be compelled to read the enactments of the various states which were contrived to make the slave system a one-way street with no escape. It is quite possibly true that the expansion of slavery was economically unfeasible, but there is no indication that Southern leaders and framers of law were prepared to make emancipation easy. To the contrary, they bent every effort to keep the slaves in chains, and gradually encroached on the lives and activities of free Negroes, as well.

IV   Jews as Harsh Taskmasters

Acts of kindness towards Negroes were the only relief in the reality of a system which placed white masters in a position of absolute and total control over their slaves. Jews participated in every aspect and process of the exploitation of the defenseless blacks. The most extreme case on record was the murder of a slave by Joseph Cohen of Lynchburg, Virginia, in 1819, a crime for which he was indicted, tried and convicted—although of course the penalty for the murder of a Negro by a white was much less severe than the penalty for a trivial misdemeanor committed by a Negro.[23]

Crimes of violence against slaves by Jews were probably quite rare, since most of these occurred in rural areas where there were few Jews. But Jews in the towns and cities appear to have been quite content to abide by the excessively cruel punishments meted out to blacks who were caught by the law. These are a few examples of the testimony of Jews against Negroes taken from the Richmond court records. In 1798, Polly, a mulatto slave, was tried for taking a loaf of white sugar worth two dollars from Benjamin Solomon's home, and was sentenced to five lashes on her bare back and ordered to be branded on her left hand.[24] Two years later, Joseph Darmstadt had "a bag and lot of beeswax," valued at fifty shillings, stolen from his store by Daniel Clayton, a free Negro, and heard Clayton sentenced to thirty-nine lashes on the bare back.[25] Another free Negro was accused of stealing two silver watches valued at $32 from Myer Angel in 1832, and the culprit was

23. 2 Va 158–159, cited in *HTC*, I, 131. The records of the Lynchburg courts are so incomplete that it has not been possible to discover any details of Cohen's crime.
24. *EL*, 78.   25. *EL*, 79.

sentenced to five years imprisonment, six months of which was to be spent in solitary confinement.[26] Benjamin Wolfe's store was broken into in 1797, and $500 in merchandise was stolen. Three slaves were tried for the crime, but only one was convicted. He was sentenced to be hung.[27]

Not only did Jews bring slaves to court as private citizens, but they also participated as public officials in legal action against slaves. In 1792, for instance, Mordecai Sheftall of Georgia was responsible for issuing warrants for the arrest of runaway slaves in his district.[28] A large number of Charleston Jews held public positions which required their constant involvement in the apprehension and punishment of Negroes: Lewis Gomez was Turnkey of the Jail in 1802; Moses Solomon (1802), Nathan Hart (1821), and Solomon Moses (1822) were Constables; Samuel Hyams was Keeper of the Jail in 1822; Elisha Elizer (1802), Mark Marks (1822), and Solomon Moses, Jr. (1822) were City Deputy Sheriffs.[29] Moses Levy, also of Charleston, achieved a state-wide reputation as the most successful detective on the city's police force.[30] Moses N. Cardozo, who had a plantation near Richmond, was also the Jailer of Powhatan Courthouse. One of his responsibilities was the incarceration and disposition of runaway slaves.[31] J. S. Cohen was City Marshal of Mobile in 1841. In connection with ordinary bankruptcies, Cohen was required to supervise the sale of Negro slaves for the account of the creditors. In the *Mobile Daily Advertiser and Chronicle* of November 4, 1841, he offered ten Negroes for sale for immediate cash, including "a first rate mantua maker, and several good cooks, washers and ironers."

From testifying against Negroes in court, to apprehending a runaway slave, to inflicting punishment upon a convicted Negro, these Jews were thoroughly a part of their society.

V Business Dealings of Jews With Slaves and Free Negroes

Jewish merchants were probably more likely than others to have dealings with slaves and free Negroes, because large numbers of immigrant

26. EL, 91.   27. EL, 77–78.
28. MC, 63.   29. E, 142.
30. Jack Kenny Williams, *Vogues in Villainy, Crime and Retribution in Ante-Bellum South Carolina* (Columbia, S.C., 1939), 73.
31. Richmond *Enquirer*, May 21, 1805.

German Jews in the Southern states were marginal traders. Frederick Law Olmsted commented on the large numbers of Negroes who paraded the streets of Richmond on Sunday, wearing "the cast-off clothes of the white people . . . purchased of the Jews, whose shops show that there must be considerable importation of such articles, probably from the North." Olmsted was not, of course, an unbiased observer; he manifested a constant antipathy to Jews in all of his books. But there was probably some truth to his assertion that Jews in many Southern towns engaged in "an unlawful trade with the simple Negroes, which is found very profitable." [32]

Not all business dealings with Negroes were illegal. Slaves were frequently authorized to make purchases with their own small savings; sometimes they were sent on errands for their masters. Free Negroes, and even slaves who were permitted to hire themselves out for work, could transact business in stores where they were well-known. The difference between Jewish and non-Jewish merchants was probably this: that the Jewish traders displayed somewhat less reluctance to do business with Negroes. Such, at any rate, was the impression of those who wrote of the post-bellum transactions of Jewish merchants with former slaves.[33] There is no question that this observation applied to Lewis B. Levy of Richmond, a manufacturer and vendor of "Servants' Clothing," who publicly solicited the patronage of slave traders, and masters who were selling or hiring out their slaves.[34]

A number of law cases record difficulties which some Jews encountered in their business dealings with slaves. In 1836, Daniel Becker was convicted of illegal liquor sales to Negroes in South Carolina.[35] In 1843, Samuel F. Isaacs was convicted of selling a horse to a slave without permission, in the same state. But this case was based on a technicality which reveals the rigidity of laws relating to slaves: the overseer had given verbal consent to the slave and to Isaacs, but the law required written permission.[36] In 1859, Charlotte Levy of New Orleans leased a

32. Frederick Law Olmsted, *The Cotton Kingdom*, ed. Arthur M. Schlesinger (New York, 1953), 37, 196.

33. E. Merton Coulter, *The South During Reconstruction, 1865–1877* (Baton Rouge, 1947), 202–203.

34. Richmond *City Directory* for 1852, p. 27 of the advertising section.

35. Riley 155, cited in *HTC*, II, 361.　　36. 1 Spears 223, cited in *HTC*, II, 385.

house to a slave, and was hauled into court over the illegal transaction.[37]

All merchants had perennial troubles with the law over the question of Sunday sales, both to whites and to Negroes, but slaves were particularly involved because Sunday was generally their only shopping day. In 1806, when the Richmond officials conducted a special campaign against merchants who did business on Sunday, two of the thirty-one merchants who were prosecuted were Jews, Marcus Levi and Reuben Cantor.[38] Among many other subsequent cases, Walter Thalheimer was fined $20, in 1847, for selling goods to slaves on Sunday without the consent of their owners.[39]

But these business dealings with Negroes pale into insignificance compared to the major business involvement with slaves, namely slave-trading itself.

VI   Jews as Slave-Traders

Everyone who owned slaves participated in the barter of human beings. There were three classes of people so involved. The first group were those who purchased and sold slaves only in connection with their own personal needs. There was hardly a slave-owner who had never bought or sold a slave; only as an heir to a sizeable workforce could he fail to do so. But there were few who did not see fit at some time or other to dispose of a few superfluous slaves, or to increase their holdings through additional purchases. And even if one treated his slaves with the utmost of kindness, short of outright emancipation which was forbidden in most Southern states in the last two decades before the Civil War, no one could predict the fate of his slaves after his death. A particularly tragic case was that of "A Negro named Sam, about Eighty Years of age, diseased, and a Negro woman named Sylvie about Seventy five years of Age," who were sold for ninety dollars in 1852 by Benjamin D. Lazarus, as Executor of the estate of Dr. Jacob De La Motta.[40] This was the same Dr. De La Motta who gave directions in his will for kindly treatment to other slaves. Perhaps the estate required cash, and undoubtedly the slaves were too old for any useful

37. 15 La. An. 38, cited in *HTC*, III, 676.
38. *EL*, 82.   39. *EL*, 98.
40. Bill of sale, dated May 11, 1852, in the writer's collection.

purpose, but what future could they have at the hands of a purchaser who would be compelled somehow to regain his investment?

After Solomon Jacobs, Acting Mayor of Richmond in 1818–1819, died in 1827, his family composed a tombstone epitaph which described him in most sentimental fashion:

> Fond as a Husband.
> Indulgent as a Father.
> Kind as a Master . . .

If these were more than words, what would Jacobs have thought of his widow, Hetty, who in 1829 succeeded in having a special law passed by the Virginia House and Senate, allowing the sale of a number of female slaves and children because the "conduct of said slaves towards their mistress . . . was so very malevolent and very objectionable?" [41]

Thin though it may have been, there was still a line of demarcation between persons who bought or sold slaves as individuals, and those who dealt in slaves as part of their occupational pursuit. The second group of those who participated in the sale of Negroes were those merchants who dealt in many commodities, including slaves. Philip Sartorius of Louisiana and Mississippi, for instance, recalled the time in 1850 that his partner Sam Rothschild "gambled all our money off and sold [our trading] boat and stock to another flat boat man for a Negro girl, took her to New Orleans and traded her off for tobacco." [42] To Sam Rothschild, there was little difference between buying and selling a slave girl and any other kind of merchandise.

Sometimes Jewish store-keepers would take a flier at an investment in slaves for purely speculative purposes. An example of this activity was the purchase of three Negro slaves "named Joe, William and Friendly" for $4,500, in July, 1863, by Jacob Adler and Herman Cone of Jonesboro, Tennessee. Adler and Cone lost their investment, however; the Union victories deprived them of both capital and property. [43]

An outstanding example of this kind of speculator was Jacob Bar-

41. *EL*, 43, 298.   42. *MM*, II, 28.
43. Photostats of slave bills loaned to me by Ben Cone of Greensboro, N.C., Herman's grandson.

rett, an early merchant in Columbia, South Carolina, and later a resident of Charleston. Barrett was a characteristic store-keeper of the time, who carried a stock which included dry-goods, groceries, provisions, liquor, hardware, crockery, shoes, hats, saddles, horses, real estate, and when the opportunity presented itself, slaves as well. One of his clerks recalled the time when a gang of twenty Negroes was sent to him from Charleston; he promptly disposed of the slaves "at very large profits, keeping for his own use Armistead Booker, a goodlooking, active carriage driver and barber, who attended to his horses and in the store, and Aunt Nanny, a first rate cook." Barrett later married the daughter of his cousin, Jacob Ottolengui of Charleston, another speculator in Negroes, and claimed before the Civil War to have around a thousand slaves working his rice plantations near the Savannah River.[44]

Among this group of merchants were numerous Jewish auctioneers, commission merchants, and brokers. This was an avenue of commerce in which many Jews found their niche, because no stock of merchandise or investment of capital was required, at least at the beginning. As a merchant achieved a record in the community for sagacious advice, clever salesmanship, and financial reliability, he prospered, and then could build his own warehouses and auction rooms, and buy and sell for his own account as well as for his clients. Auctioneers were licensed by law in most communities; they were, in a sense, public officials. Even if they disliked the traffic in human flesh, therefore, they could not avoid it; they were expected by the public to deal in slaves as readily as in any other sort of merchandise. To all intents and purposes, they were slave-traders, but not exclusively. This is a list of Jewish auctioneers in various communities:

ATLANTA, GA., D. Mayer, Jacobs & Co.[45]
CHARLESTON, S. C., Jacob Cohen[46]

44. Edwin J. Scott, *Random Recollections of a Long Life* (Columbia, S.C., 1884), 82–85.
45. Advertisement in Knoxville (Tenn.), *Daily Register*, Apr. 30, 1863.
46. Advertisement in Charleston *Daily Courier*, Apr. 28, 1857. Though he auctioned other commodities, slaves were a very substantial part of his business. Frederic Bancroft, in his *Slave Trading in the Old South* (Baltimore, 1931), 190, states that Cohen was the tenth largest Charleston dealer in slaves, earning $2,500 in commissions on slave sales in 1860.

CHARLESTON, S.C., H. H. DeLeon[47]
Jacob Jacobs[48]
Myer Moses[49]
Jacob Ottolengui[50]
Ralph de Pass[51]
Abraham Mendes Seixas[52]
COLUMBIA, S. C., J. and L. T. Levin[53]
GEORGETOWN, S. C., Abraham Cohen[54]
KNOXVILLE, TENN., Isaac Joseph[55]
MOBILE, ALA., George Davis[56]
S. I. and I. I. Jones[57]
NATCHEZ, MISS., Jacob Soria[58]
NEW ORLEANS, LA., Jacob Levy and Lewis Florence[59]
E. J. Hart & Co.
Hemingway, Friedlander & Co.
Levy & Summers[60]
RICHMOND, VA., Benjamin Davis
David Judah[61]
Ash Levy
Samuel Reese[62]

47. Bancroft, *op. cit.*, 175.

48. Reference in his will in *AJA*, dated Nov. 20, 1797.

49. Advertisement in Charleston *Southern Patriot*, Aug. 14, 1815, cited in Morris U. Schappes, *A Documentary History of the Jews in the United States, 1654-1872* (New York, 1950), 612.

50. Advertisement in Charleston *Daily Courier*, Jan. 1, 1857.

51. *R*, 139.　　　　　　　　52. *RE*, 76.

53. Advertisements in Columbia *Daily South Carolinian*, Nov. 15, Dec. 2, Dec. 9, Dec. 17, and Dec. 29, 1852.

54. Arthur Hecht, "Abraham Cohen: Deputy Postmaster at Georgetown, South Carolina (1789-1800)," *PAJHS*, XLVIII, no. 3 (March, 1959), 178.

55. Advertisement in Knoxville *Daily Register*, Apr. 30, 1863.

56. Mobile *City Directories* for 1839 and 1842; article on Mobile Jewish History by Alfred G. Moses, Mobile *Register*, June 19, 1932.

57. Advertisement in Mobile *Daily Advertiser and Chronicle*, Feb. 6, 1841.

58. *Mississippi Free-Trader* and *Natchez Tri-Weekly Gazette*, September 29, 1836; Edwin Adams Davis and William Ransom Hogan (eds.), *William Johnson's Natchez: The Ante-Bellum Diary of a Free Negro* (Baton Rouge, 1951), 66, 175, 224, 366, *passim*. The Johnson diary contains frequent references to sales of various kinds of merchandise, including slaves, at the Soria auctions. Davis and Hogan, *The Barber of Natchez* (Baton Rouge, 1954), 31, 173.

59. New Orleans *City Directory* for 1832.

60. New Orleans *City Directory* for 1855.

61. *EL*, 44-54, 143.　　　　　　　　62. Bancroft, *op. cit.*, 97-98.

Advertisements of slave auction notices of two of these firms, J. and L. T. Levin of Columbia, and S. I. and I. I. Jones of Mobile, are reproduced in order to underscore the fact that these members of Jewish communities who were dealers in slaves were not scorned by their fellow Jews. Both Jacob Levin and Israel I. Jones occupied particularly prominent positions in the Jewish life of their towns.

Levin was the acting rabbi and recognized leader of the Jews of Columbia. For many years he gave the main address at the annual public meetings and examinations of the Columbia Hebrew Sunday School, of which his wife was directress. His speeches, which were deemed important enough to be reported and even quoted at length in Rabbi Isaac Leeser's Philadelphia monthly journal, *The Occident and American Jewish Advocate*, were high-minded appeals to Jewish adults as well as children to devote themselves to the traditional ideals of Judaism. Levin was also an early Secretary and Treasurer of the Hebrew Benevolent Society of Columbia. His non-Jewish neighbors held him in equally high esteem: he was elected Illustrious Grand Master of the Masonic Council.[63]

Israel Jones was an even more distinguished leader. One of the first of Mobile Jewish residents to cleave loyally to his faith, he was the President of the first congregation in Alabama, Congregation Shaarai Shomayim, from its founding in 1844 until 1873. During the few brief years of activity of the pioneering Board of Delegates of American Israelites, the first national Jewish organization for the purpose of national and international representation, Israel Jones was honored with the office of Vice-President. Jones took great pride in the fact that his daughter Emily married the talented Rabbi James K. Gutheim of New Orleans. Occupying a similar position of high repute in the general community, he was at various times a member of the City Council of Mobile, President of the Mobile Musical Association, and founder of Mobile's street car line.[64]

63. *OCC*, II (1844), 83–87, 147–50; IV (1846), 387–89; V (1847), 164; VI (1848), 153; VIII (1850), 145–58; IX (1851), 268–69; XII (1854), 326; Helen Kohn Hennig, *The Tree of Life . . .* (Columbia, S.C., 1945), 3–4.

64. Bertram Wallace Korn, "An Historical Excursus," in *1844–1944, Congregation Shaarai Shomayim, Mobile, Alabama* (Mobile, 1944); Mobile *City Directories* for 1839, iii, 24a; 1842, p. 64; 1850, p. 48; 1856, p. 57; Korn mss. files on Jones; letter, Myer S. Isaacs to Jones, Aug. 14, 1860, Board of Delegates Mss. Files, Library of the American Jewish Historical Society.

Slave-dealing obviously did not disqualify Jews from receiving the friendship and esteem of their co-religionists any more than it disqualified Christians; engaging in business transactions in Negro flesh was not regarded as incompatible with being a good Jew.[65]

Abraham Mendes Seixas was not a Jewish leader, but his brother was the famous rabbi of Colonial and early Federal New York and Philadelphia, Gershom Mendes Seixas. Abraham, like other auctioneers of slaves was neither ashamed of nor apologetic about his offerings of Negroes. He even burst into doggerel about his slave merchandise:

> ABRAHAM SEIXAS,
> All so gracious,
> Once again does offer
> His service pure
> For to secure
> Money in the coffer.
>
> He has for sale
> Some Negroes, male,
> Will suit full well grooms,
> He has likewise
> Some of their wives
> Can make clean, dirty rooms.
>
> For planting, too,
> He has a few
> To sell, all for the cash,
> Of various price,
> To work the rice
> Or bring them to the lash.
>
> The young ones true,
> If that will do,
> May some be had of him
> To learn your trade
> They may be made,
> Or bring them to your trim.
>
> The boatmen great,
> Will you elate

65. Nor, of course, did slave-owning seem to be offensive in a rabbi. Bertram Wallace Korn, *American Jewry and the Civil War* (Philadelphia, 1951), 29, gives data on the Rev. George Jacobs' hiring of a slave woman. A. J. Marks, acting Rabbi of New Orleans in the 1830s, listed eleven slaves in his household in the 1840 Census for New Orleans.

They are so brisk and free;
What e'er you say,
They will obey,
If you buy them of me.[66]

The third group of those who dealt in Negroes were, of course, the full-time slave-traders, whose sole income was derived from purchasing, transporting and selling slaves. None of the major slave-traders was Jewish, nor did Jews constitute a large proportion of traders in any particular community. Frederic Bancroft, who has made an exhaustive study of the business, attempted to classify all traders and auctioneers in the major Southern markets. In Richmond, according to his list, only three of seventy were Jews; in Charleston, four out of forty-four; in Memphis, only one of more than a dozen.[67] Other standard works limited to the investigation of the slave-trade in Kentucky and Mississippi list many dozens of slave-traders among whom not a single Jewish name appears.[68] Probably all of the Jewish slave-traders in all of the Southern cities and towns combined did not buy and sell as many slaves as did the firm of Franklin and Armfield, the largest Negro traders in the South.

These are the Jewish slave-traders whose identity we can establish:

ATLANTA and AUGUSTA, GA., Solomon Cohen[69]
CHARLESTON, S. C., B. Mordecai[70]

66. Quoted from the Charleston *South Carolina State Gazette*, Sept. 6, 1784, in E, 129–30.

67. Bancroft, *op. cit.*, 97–98, 175–77, 251–52.

68. J. Winston Coleman, *Slavery Times in Kentucky* (Chapel Hill, 1940); and Charles Sackett Sydnor, *Slavery in Mississippi* (New York, 1933).

69. Receipt for sale of slave "Warren," dated Augusta, Feb. 20, 1864, signed by Jacob Reese, for "S. Cohen, Dealer in Slaves, Elias Street, Augusta, Ga.," in the writer's collection; this Reese may have been related to Samuel Reese, a slave auctioneer of Richmond. *AJA* has a similar receipt, dated July 3, 1863, with an imprinted address in Atlanta which has been crossed out, with "Augusta" superimposed in handwriting. Cohen probably had offices in both cities. *AJA* also has receipts for three slaves purchased by Levi Cohen in various Georgia towns in 1862–1864; there is no indication whether these Cohen's were related.

70. Mordecai, an important mercantile power in Charleston is listed here, in spite of the fact that this was not his only source of income, because his slave-dealings were so extensive; his traffic in Negroes was so constant that he had his own slave-pens alongside his warehouses. In 1859 Mordecai purchased $12,000 worth of slaves in a single sale. 12 Richardson 547, cited in *HTC*, II, 325; Charleston *Mercury*, Jan. 10, 1859, cited in Bancroft, *op. cit.*, 183; Charleston *Courier*, Jan. 1, 1857.

LUMPKIN, GA., J. F. Moses[71]
MOBILE, ALA., Philip Goldsmith[72]
NATCHEZ, MISS., and NEW ORLEANS, LA., Benjamin and Jacob
Monsanto[73]
NEW ORLEANS, LA., Levy Jacobs[74]
PETERSBURG and RICHMOND, VA., Ansley, Benjamin, George,
and Solomon Davis[75]
RICHMOND, VA., Abraham Smith[76]

Slave-dealing was an extremely profitable business. Through natural increase, the upper South produced more slaves than its overworked soil required, while the lower South needed constant recruits for an ever-increasing labor force on its newly developed plantations. When the price of cotton was high, slave-traders could double their investment by leading long coffles of slaves from one section of the South to the other, despite the expenses of fattening up their wares and giving them medical attention.[77]

A simple example of the profit to be made in a slave sale is given in two bills of sale relating to transactions of B. Mordecai's firm in Charleston. Mordecai purchased a slave named Abram or Abraham,

71. Broadside, dated Nov. 14, 1859, reproduced in Charles F. Heartman, *Americana Catalogue No. 120* (1947), 145.

72. Mobile *City Directories* for 1850 and 1856.

73. The Monsanto brothers owned plantations at Natchez and dealt in slaves there and in New Orleans, where they also maintained a residence. There is good reason to believe that they were Dutch-born Marranos, and if so, they were probably the first residents of Jewish birth in Natchez and in New Orleans. *AJA* has photostats of documents relating to their transactions in slaves during 1787–1794, from the Office of Chancery, Natchez, and the files of the Louisiana Historical Society contain many references to the brothers and their wives. See also, *MC*, 456–57, and *Universal Jewish Encyclopedia* (New York, 1942), VII, 586, for additional references to the Monsanto brothers.

74. New Orleans *City Directories* for 1823, 1824, 1827, and 1835.

75. Bancroft, *op. cit.*, 93–94.

76. Interview with his granddaughter, Mrs. Hattie E. Genbrun, recorded by Louis Ginsburg, Petersburg, Aug. 29, 1958.

77. Every once in a while an unconscionable dealer would foist a sickly slave on an unwary customer. *HTC* gives instances of such occurrences which were brought to court: In June, 1821, a man named Samuel sold a slave woman ill of a venereal disease to a client named Minter; the woman died soon afterwards, and Minter went to court to regain the purchase price. 3 A. K. Marsh 480, cited in I, 296. In November, 1860, B. Cahn of New Orleans sued a slave-trader who had sold him a consumptive slave; the vender had to repay Cahn the money involved in the transaction. 15 La. An. 612, cited in III, 685.

about fifty years old, for $180, from an estate, on Dec. 3, 1851. The slave was sold about six weeks later for $250. The slave must have been fairly undesirable to bring such a small sum of money, but thirty-nine percent profit was a good return on a six weeks' investment.[78]

The largest Jewish slave-trading firm in the South seems to have been the Davis family of Petersburg and Richmond, including Ansley, Benjamin, George and Solomon.[79] They were the only Jews mentioned by Harriett Beecher Stowe in her little-known commentary, *A Key to Uncle Tom's Cabin.*[80] Mrs. Stowe quotes a letter by Dr. Gamaliel Bailey, referring to them: "The Davises, in Petersburg, are the great slave-traders. They are Jews, came to that place many years ago as poor peddlers . . . These men are always in the market, giving the highest price for slaves. During the summer and fall they buy them up at low prices, trim, shave, wash them, fatten them so that they may look sleek, and sell them to great profit." The Davis family traveled far and wide with their slave merchandise. We reproduce a bill of sale imprinted with Ansley Davis' name, produced for use in South Carolina, attesting to the receipt of $475 for "a female slave named Savry about 15 years of age warranted Sound and Healthy," from the purchaser, Abraham Tobias of Charleston, signed as witness by another Jew, M. Lopez, on Dec. 14, 1854.[81] The Davises were obviously well-prepared to do business in various Southern states, with legal forms already printed for their use. The family was also known in Georgia. Benjamin Davis advertised in the Columbus *Enquirer* of April 12, 1838, that he had for sale "Sixty Likely Virginia Negroes—House Servants, Field Hands, Blow boys, Cooks, Washers, Ironers, and three first-rate Seamstresses." Davis was remaining in Columbus, and assured the local folk that he would continue to receive shipments of additional bargains "by every arrival" for almost two more months.[82]

In these ways did Jews participate in the commercial components of the slave system.

78. Bills of sale in the writer's collection.
79. Data about these men is given in Ginsburg, *op. cit.*, 25, 31, 35–36, and *EL*, 143.
80. Boston, 1853, p. 151.
81. Photostat from the family papers of Thomas J. Tobias, Charleston.
82. Cited in Ralph Betts Flanders, *Plantation Slavery in Georgia* (Chapel Hill, 1933), 185.

VII   *Cases of Miscegenation Involving Jews*

Inter-racial cohabitation was quite common in the South, but there is little available documentary evidence which can be utilized to establish statistical indices, either for the general white population, or for any minor division thereof.

A search in the available records for Jewish names borne by Negroes encounters the inevitable difficulty of distinguishing Jewish from non-Jewish names. Many, like Aaron, Abrahams, Benjamin, David, Davis, Emanuel, Hart, Isaacs, Lyons, Marks, Moses, Myers, Noah, Samuels, Salomons, and Stein, can be Jewish or Gentile, as the case may be. Nor have we any notion of whether Northern Negroes with names like Hannah Adler, Perry Cohen, Isaac Farber, Richard Levy, Peter Levy, Benjamin Levy, Isaac Nathans, Abraham Stern, and thirteen Negro Tobias', went North before or after receiving their names. But it is likely that some of these Negroes did receive their names either from Jewish owners or Jewish fathers. This is probably also true of Sheldon Cohen of St. Peters Parish, South Carolina, Constance Herschell of New Orleans, Levy Jacobs of Fayetteville, North Carolina, George and Samuel Kauffman of King and Queen County, Virginia, Affey Levy of Charleston, Justine Moïse of New Orleans, Harry Mordecai of Frankfort, Kentucky, Betty Rosenberg of Charleston Neck, and Catherine Sasportes of Charleston.[83] Lists of Negroes active in Reconstruction days in South Carolina provide a few additional Jewish-sounding names: H. B. Da Costa, a well-regarded teacher; Philip E. Ezekiel, who was nominated for the positions of inspector general and adjutant on the Reform Republican ticket in 1872; Richard Moses, who was a leader in the South Carolina Conference of the Methodist Episcopal Church in 1870; Julius Mayer, a Representative from Barnwell District; T. K. Sasportas, a delegate and secretary of the 1867 organizational convention of the South Carolina Republican Party; Charles C. Levy and J. R. Levy, who were South Carolina delegates to National Republican Party Conventions in later days.[84]

83. Carter G. Woodson, *Free Negro Heads of Families in the United States in 1830* (Washington, 1925). Eight of these Negroes, incidentally, owned a total of thirty-nine slaves: Woodson, *Free Negro Owners of Slaves*, 4 ff.

84. John S. Reynolds, *Reconstruction in South Carolina, 1865–1877* (Columbia, 1905), 60–61; Alrutheus Ambush Taylor, *The Negro in South Carolina During the*

There are no available data to help us to ascertain whether these Negroes took their names from Jewish masters, or fathers, or neighbors, or benefactors, or, in certain cases, from the Bible. But there are situations where a relationship of friendship if not of parentage seems quite likely, as for instance, George Darmstadt, a free Negro of Richmond, who, with his wife Patty, was given permission in September, 1816, to live in the city in recognition of his "faithful services, honesty, and good demeanor." [85]

We do not even have the help of religious affiliation in our investigation of this question, since Jewish congregations would not accept Negro members. The Richmond congregation required that its members be free; and the Charleston Beth Elohim constitution of 1820 accepted proselytes only if "he, she, or they are not people of colour." [86] There is only one reference to a Jewish Negro in all of Southern Jewish records, "a free man of color" who was converted to Judaism by his master, and was accustomed to attending services at the Charleston synagogue in 1857, during the tenure of Rabbi Maurice Mayer.[87] The fact that Jewish masters, with this exception, did not educate their slaves in the Jewish faith, and that synagogues did not welcome Negro worshippers, would seem to negate the contention that present-day Negroes who regard themselves as Jews are descended from slave-converts of Jewish masters.

There are actually only five instances in which documentary evidence indicates cohabitation of Jews with Negro women, and it is important to note that in each case they were free Negroes. In the first, the only one to be brought in court, David Isaacs and Nancy West, a free mulatto woman, were indicted in 1826 by the grand jury of Al-

Reconstruction (Washington, 1929), 98, 116, 127, 207; "South Carolina Negro Delegates to Republican National Conventions," *JNH*, XII (1922).

85. *EL*, 86.

86. *ME*, II, 224; *E*, 153; *Constitution of the Hebrew Congregation Kaal Kodesh Beth-Elohim, or House of God. Charleston, 1820* (reprinted Charleston, 1904), 16.

87. *RE*, 78. Thomas J. Tobias of Charleston has directed my attention to two further references to the same person, "Old Billy," "a Jewish Negro, then about 70 years of age . . . gained his living carrying newspapers" (*Weekly Gleaner*, San Francisco, Jan. 16, 1857); the man died in 1860, as reported in the *Jewish Chronicle* (London), May 11, 1860, which stated that "for years he has been a faithful attendant at the Jewish Synagogue on the Day of Atonement, making his appearance on these occasions in a ruffled shirt."

bemarle County, Va., "for outraging the decency of society . . . by cohabiting together . . . as man and wife, without being lawfully married." A higher court reduced the serious charge of the indictment to the lesser charge of fornication.[88]

In our second case, the evidence is less positive. Samuel Simons, whose will was proved in Charleston on Feb. 13, 1824, left his entire estate to relatives and Jewish institutions in London, with the exception of an extensive bequest to his "House Keeper Maria Chapman a free woman of Colour." Simons left Maria "the Sum of fourteen hundred Dollars, two Negroes named Pompey and Peggy with the issue and increase of the females and also two Bedsteads bedding and six chairs." Negro concubines were frequently called "housekeepers," and Simons' bequest to Maria was extraordinarily large. The supposition would be that her employer had a much more personal relationship with Maria than would be mentioned in polite society.[89] This may also be true of other men whose generous bequests have already been noted, especially when the names of children are also mentioned.

The third instance is far more definite. The will of Moses Nunes of Savannah, who died on Sept. 6, 1797, acknowledges "Mulatta Rose" as his concubine, and recognizes her children, Robert, James, Alexander, and Frances (married to George Galphin), as his own progeny. He bequeathed certain tracts of land, his home, furniture and clothing, and thirteen Negro slaves, to Rose and his four children, in addition to "a full and perfect freedom from all Slavery and servitude in reward and as an acknowledgement of the faithful conduct and behaviour of the said Mulatta Rose towards me and my Children."[90] Moses Nunes' will became an important document in 1853 when it was exhumed in connection with a lawsuit which was carried through the courts during the next eleven years. The case concerned the legality of Moses' grandson, Joseph's, sale of five slave children, his own, by his Negro concubine, Patience. What was at stake was the question of Joseph's race, since his father, James Nunes, had passed for white, and had been married to a white woman. Many witnesses testified to their belief that both James and Joseph were of pure white ancestry. Unfortunately, however, the grandfather's will was strong evidence

88. *HTC*, I, 145, citing 5 Randolph 634.   89. Will in *AJA*.
90. Will in *AJA*.

of mixed blood. But Sherman's march through Georgia made the entire question an academic one before the final appeal was adjudicated.[91]

A less complicated example, in certain ways, was that of the Negro branch of the Cardozo family, which produced two leading figures in Reconstruction governments. It is a moot question whether their father was Jacob N. Cardozo, the famous Southern journalist and economist, or his lesser-known brother Isaac, who for twenty-four years was a weigher in the Charleston Custom House. Historical writers seem to have favored Jacob's name, while present-day members of the family believe that Isaac was their ancestor.[92]

Be that as it may, Francis Lewis Cardozo, Sr., was probably the most distinguished member of the Cardozo family between his father or uncle Jacob, and Supreme Court Justice Benjamin Nathan Cardozo. Francis was born in Charleston on Jan. 1, 1837, the son of Lydia Williams, a free mulatto of mixed Negro and Indian blood. He went to school from the ages of five to twelve, and probably received some private tutoring from Jacob Cardozo; he was apprenticed to a carpenter for five years, and then pursued the trade independently for a few more. At the age of twenty-one, with money which he had saved over the years, and possibly with some help from the family and from the American Missionary Association, he went to Scotland. He matriculated first at the University of Glasgow, where he won prizes in Latin and in Greek, and then at the theological seminary of Edinburgh. He later studied at the London School of Theology, was ordained, and then returned to the United States to become the minister of the Temple Street Congregational Church in New Haven, Conn. A year later, immediately after the conclusion of the Civil War, he was sent by the American Missionary Association to Charleston, where he founded the Avery Institute, a normal school. In the following years, he was president of the South Carolina State Council of Union Leagues, a member of the South Carolina Constitutional Convention of 1868, a member of the Board of Trustees of the University of South Carolina

91. 14 Ga. 185–207; 20 Ga. 480–512; 33 Ga. 11–29, as cited in *HTC*, III, 33, 50–51, 87–88.
92. For Jacob N. Cardozo, see Alexander Brody, "Jacob Newton Cardozo, American Economist," *Historia Judaica*, XV (1955), 135–66; for Isaac, see *E*, 161, 163–64, 204; and Barnett A. Elzas, *The Old Jewish Cemeteries at Charleston, S.C.* (Charleston, 1903), 12.

in 1869, Secretary of State in the Scott administration of 1868–72, and State Treasurer in the Moses and Chamberlain administrations, 1872–76. During the latter years he studied at the South Carolina College and received his LL.B. degree in 1876. Cardozo was described by those who knew him as a "handsome, well-groomed man, with cultivated manners," as "almost white in color," with a "tall, portly . . . figure and elaborate, urbane manners." He was removed from office during the upheavals of 1877, although there was virtually no evidence of corruption on his part. To the contrary, he had fought hard to keep the state's financial condition free of peculation. In this regard, he stands in strong contrast to Franklin Moses, Jr., the notorious Reconstruction Governor, also of Jewish parentage, though never a practicing Jew. Even the most vigorously pro-Bourbon historians have been hard-pressed to uncover any excuses for criticism of Cardozo's leadership and record.

This is, of course, not the proper place for an extensive evaluation of Cardozo's services to his people and to the state of South Carolina, or of his later career as an educator in the nation's capital, but it is vital to underscore his reputation both among whites and Negroes as one of the most brilliant and highly educated public servants in South Carolina. Governor Daniel H. Chamberlain, in the midst of great corruption and mismanagement, said of Cardozo, "I have never heard one word or seen one act of Mr. Cardozo's which did not confirm my confidence in his personal integrity and his political honor and zeal for the honest administration of the State Government. On every occasion and under all circumstances he has been against fraud and jobbery and in favor of good measures and good men."

I would not want to conclude this brief sketch of Cardozo without quoting an excerpt from the comments on school desegregation which he made during the debates of the Constitutional Convention of 1868: "The most natural method of removing race distinctions," he said, "would be to allow children, when five or six years of age, to mingle in school together . . . Under such training prejudices will eventually die out." How far we would have been in the solution of all of the problems of race relations, if Francis Lewis Cardozo, Sr., and other honorable Reconstruction leaders, had been given a genuine opportunity to erase the vestiges of slavery.[93]

The other member of the Cardozo family to occupy an important position in the Reconstruction period was Francis' brother, Thomas Y. Cardozo, who had a far less distinguished career in Mississippi political life. He came out of an obscure background which has not been recorded to any significant degree, to become a circuit court clerk in Warren County, Mississippi, following which he was elected Mississippi State Superintendent of Education, which office he held from 1874 to 1876. In the latter year he resigned under threat of impeachment. He seems to have been quite intelligent and well educated, for during 1875 he was editor of the Vicksburg *Plain Dealer*, and a man of natural capacity for leadership, in view of his founding the same year the Vicksburg branch of the Grand United Order of Odd Fellows of America. He was, however, accused of participation in certain corrupt bargains of the time, and there was seeming proof of his embezzlement of two thousand dollars from the funds of Tougaloo University. It has not been possible to learn any further details of his training, career, or activities after 1876.[94]

93. The literature on Cardozo and his participation in South Carolina political affairs is extensive. Works consulted include: William J. Simmons, *Men of Mark* (Cleveland, 1887), 428–31; W. E. B. Du Bois, *Black Reconstruction* (New York, 1935), 392–93, 395, 397–98, 402, 427, 617; John E. Farley, "Francis L. Cardozo" (Ms. senior thesis, Princeton University, April 13, 1949); Franklin, *op. cit.*, 201, 313–14; William Francis Guest, *South Carolina, Annals of Pride and Protest* (New York, 1960), 264–65; Ralph Selph Henry, *The Story of Reconstruction* (New York, 1938), 292, 314, 445; Daniel Walker Hollis, *University of South Carolina* (Columbia, 1956), II, 50, 70, 75; L. P. Jackson, "The Educational Efforts of the Freedmen's Bureau and the Freedmen's Aid Society in South Carolina, 1862–1872," *JNH*, VIII (1922), 39; James S. Pike, *The Prostrate State: South Carolina Under Negro Government* (New York, 1874), 75, 152 ff.; Reynolds, *op. cit.*, 77, 87, 123, 157, 224, 235, 247, 296, 307, 366, 462, 485; Francis Butler Simkins and Robert Hilliard Woody, *South Carolina During Reconstruction* (Chapel Hill, 1932), 55, 77, 92, 97, 116–17, 168, 203–204, 206, 437, 446, 448–49, 475, 516–23, 543, 546; Taylor, *op. cit.*, 87, 98, 103, 107, 127, 130, 132, 136, 138–39, 142–43, 156–57, 193, 206, 222–24, 258, 284–85; Mary Church Terrell, "History of the High School for Negroes in Washington," *JNH*, II (1917), 256–58. Additional data have been provided by Cardozo's grandson, W. Warrick Cardozo, M.D., of Washington, D.C.

94. Data about Thomas Cardozo are difficult to locate. The first appearance of his name, according to the records of the Mississippi State Department of Archives, is in the Warren County tax rolls for 1871. The following works supply the few available facts: James Wilford Garner, *Reconstruction in Mississippi* (New York, 1901), 293, 332, 336, 405–406; John R. Lynch, *The Facts of Reconstruction* (New York, 1913),

It is instructive to note that some historians of the Reconstruction are far more eager to dwell upon those political figures who were guilty of corruption than those who had an honorable and useful career. Both Claude G. Bowers and E. Merton Coulter take occasion to mention Thomas Y. Cardozo as an example of a corrupt, politically-oriented Negro office-holder, without even a bare mention of his more important, more talented, and more honorable brother Francis.[95]

Our final example of miscegenation concerns the family of Barnet A. Cohen, who was born in 1770 in Bristol, England, had plantations in King's Creek, South Carolina, and died there on March 23, 1839. The fortunate preservation of a batch of family papers enables us to comprehend, in a uniquely personal way, the difficult social and psychological problems which faced a free mulatto.[96]

By 1810, when the first of these papers was drawn up, Barnet A. Cohen had fathered two children, Barnet Owens Cohen and Benjamin Philip Owens Cohen, by a "free woman of Colour," Catherine Owens. A number of neighbors, including four Jews, signed a document attesting to the family relationship and the free status of the woman and her children. According to the second document, in March, 1822, Barnet A. Cohen, the father, as legal guardian for his son Benjamin, and on his behalf, purchased "a Negro wench named Sarah and her child Lina," the mother probably being bought as a concubine for Benjamin. The lot of a free Negro was far from simple; his choice of mates was extremely limited. Most frequently he had to buy his own women, and unless he could emancipate them, which was next to impossible, he was compelled also to own title to his own children.

74–75; *Journal of the State of Mississippi—Sitting as a Court of Impeachment, in the Trials of Adelbert Ames, Governor; Alexander K. Davis, Lieutenant-Governor; Thomas Y. Cardozo, Superintendent of Instruction* (Jackson, 1876); Vernon Lane Wharton, *The Negro in Mississippi, 1865–1890* (Chapel Hill, 1947), 164–272. Dr. W. W. Cardozo supplies these dates for his great-uncle's birth and death: Dec. 19, 1838, and April 13, 1881. There was a third brother, Reverend Henry W. Cardozo, born in 1831, who died on Feb. 21, 1886.

95. Claude G. Bowers, *The Tragic Era* (Cambridge, 1929), 414; Coulter, *op. cit.*, 322–23.

96. These papers, in the writer's collection, are dated April 4, 1810; March 30, 1822; Jan. 23, 1833, Nov. 13, 1837; May 2, 1840; April 8, 1844; n.d., 1850. Data about Barnet A. Cohen from *E*, 133, 144; Cecil Roth, *The Rise of Provincial Jewry* (London, 1950), 41; *R*, 24; Barnett A. Elzas, *The Old Jewish Cemeteries of Charleston* (Charleston, 1903), 5–6.

In 1832, with the approval of his father-guardian, Benjamin Cohen purchased a nine-month old Negro, "Alonzo," for $100. It would seem obvious that Alonzo must have been his own child by a slave woman whose owner refused to part with her; why else should he, or for that matter, anyone, buy a Negro infant?

In 1837, two years before his father's death, Benjamin purchased some land in Barnwell District, adjoining farms which belonged to his father and his mulatto brother, Barnet. By now, his white half-brother, Moses A. Cohen, was signing as his guardian. It is significant that the Negro and white members of this family lived in such close proximity and, apparently, harmony, as well. The father's white wife, Bella, died in 1836; and when the father died in 1839, there was no sign of strain in the family's feelings, at least on Barnet's tombstone, which commemorated "the virtues of a beloved parent . . . as a memorial of [his childrens'] love and veneration." What a shame that we have no way of telling whether Benjamin and Barnet had a hand in composing this epitaph!

From 1840 to 1850, Benjamin was worrying about the future of his slave family. He wanted to set them free, and thus assure their status after his own death, but he could not find the way. In 1840, he consulted an attorney who informed him that "no Slave can be Set free in this State except by Act of the Legislature on a Petition. But it is *almost impossible* to have such a Petition granted—The Legislature almost always refuses them." If it was "*almost impossible*" in 1840, it became altogether so, on December 17, 1841, when the South Carolina legislature passed "An Act to Prevent the Emancipation of Slaves," a copy of which Benjamin secured and kept among his papers. According to this law, any effort through "bequest, deed of trust, or conveyance," to send slaves out of the state for the purpose of emancipation, was declared null and void. The act also prohibited any stratagem whereby "slaves shall be held in nominal servitude." In 1844, Benjamin Cohen consulted another lawyer, and, after paying a fee of ten dollars, received the categorical advice that "a free coloured man can purchase a Slave, but he cannot give her her freedom—the Slave and her children will always remain Slaves."

In 1850, Benjamin Cohen, free man of color but without the freedom to do very much, by then about fifty years of age or perhaps older, was altogether anxious to do something for his family. So he drew up a draft of a will—one of the most pathetic wills I have ever been privileged to read. After the usual formalities, including a request for "Christian burial," he bequeaths all his property to his "esteemed patron and benefactor, Samuel Cohen," who must have been another white half-brother. Then, in an effort to forestall the effects of the law of 1841, he offers this declaration of loyalty and disclaimer of intention:

SECONDLY. I give and devise unto the aforesaid Samuel Cohen, the following Slaves, viz—Jane, John, Susan, Benjamin, Alonzo, Moses, Dani[e]l, Emma, Sarah, and Frances, and as most of them are my offspring, and Jane my wife, it may be thought that this devise is intended to avoid and defeat, the laws of this commonwealth, which affords me protection, and to which I defferentially bow, in gratitude. I therefore declare and Solemnly asseverate that I intend no such unlawful act. I know that by the law, they are slaves, and must remain so. Wherefore through the means of this my will I choose their Master, preferring him, for my heir at Law to any one else. Neither is there any understanding secret, or otherwise, that the above named Slaves are to be held in nominal servitude only.

Benjamin makes only one bequest—he provides for a gift of $100 to his niece Emily, the daughter of his deceased mulatto brother Barnet (or "Barney" as he calls him in this document). All other property is left to Samuel Cohen, "in consideration of my friendship and his many kindnesses to me." It was apparently no longer proper for a will to mention the familial relationship of Negroes and whites.

This is the final document which concerns Benjamin Philip Owens Cohen. A probated will cannot be discovered in the records of the Barnwell Court House. Only this rough draft has been preserved, together with his other papers, among the records of his half-brother Samuel, who lived into the 1870s and had a store in a town with one of the most remarkable names in the United States, Cohen's Bluff, South Carolina. But the fact that these papers relating to Benjamin were preserved by Samuel, without the inventories and other documents an executor would have needed to prepare, would seem to be convincing proof that the will was never executed in its present form. Perhaps Benjamin Philip Owens Cohen outlived the institution of slavery and was able to spend his last days with a family freed from involuntary servitude by the bloodshed which began a century ago this year. That at least is the hope and prayer of the present-day owner of the papers which record the tribulations of Benjamin Cohen.

VIII   Opinions of Jews About Slavery

This study has thus far traced a pattern of almost complete conformity to the slave society of the Old South on the part of its Jewish citizens. They participated in the buying, owning, and selling of slaves, and the exploitation of their labor, along with their neighbors. The behavior of Jews towards slaves seems to have been indistinguishable from that of their non-Jewish friends. This description also characterizes the opinions of Jews about slavery.

No Jewish political figure of the Old South ever expressed any reservations about the justice of slavery or the rightness of the Southern position. Men like David Levy Yulee of Florida and David S. Kaufman of Texas were typical exponents of Southern views on states' rights and the spread of slavery.[97] Judah P. Benjamin of Louisiana was regarded as one of the most eloquent defenders of the Southern way of life. Though far from a fanatic, he stood squarely with his Senatorial colleagues every inch of the way that led from Washington to Montgomery and then to Richmond. Benjamin did question the wisdom of entrusting Negro slaves with complicated agricultural machinery, and advised sugar planters to employ trained white mechanics, but he never admitted that this deterrent to progressive agriculture was an inevitable consequence of the slave economy. Despite his conservative views, however, he was the only notable Confederate leader who advocated the arming of slaves during the Civil War, and who urged that they be emancipated as reward for this effort. He seems to have been far ahead of most Southerners in his willingness to use any

97. *Speech of Hon. David S. Kaufman, of Texas, on The Slavery Question. Delivered in the House of Representatives, February 10, 1847* (Washington, 1847); *Speech of Hon. D. S. Kaufman, of Texas, on The Slavery Question and Its Adjustment. Delivered in the House of Representatives, Monday, June 10, 1850* (Washington, 1850); Hühner, *op. cit.*, 14, 20–22. Although Kaufman has generally been regarded as stemming from Jewish parents, there is no contemporary evidence for the assumption; all such testimony is of comparatively late date, as for instance, Henry Cohen *et al., One Hundred Years of Jewry in Texas* (Dallas, 1936), 8.

weapon for the deliverance of the Confederacy. "The true issue," he said, is "is it better for the Negro to fight for us or against us?" He urged the adoption of his policy as an answer to the ever-present man-power shortage, but he also believed that "the action of our people on this point will be of more value to us abroad than any diplomacy or treaty-making." But most Southerners would rather lose the war than weaken the slave system in any way.[98]

Benjamin's proposal was certainly not a repudiaton of slavery. Neither was the program which Judge Solomon Heydenfeldt of Alabama advocated in 1849 as an antidote to the problems created by the concentration of Alabama capital in slave property. Heydenfeldt first published his *Communication on the Subject of Slave Immigration, Addressed to Hon. Reuben Chapman, Governor of Alabama*, in the Huntsville *Democrat* on Jan. 31, 1849, and subsequently in pamphlet form. The jurist questioned the economic wisdom of unlimited slave immigration and protested that the state would become impoverished through the uncontrolled "dumping" of slaves in Alabama. But his arguments were renounced by fellow-Alabamians. One critic said, in the Wetumpka *Daily Stateguard* of February 12, 1849, that if Heydenfeldt's proposal were to be adopted, an artificial scarcity of slaves would be created, the prices of slaves would soar, and the rich would become richer, while the poor who hoped sometime to become slave-owners would be deprived of any expectation of economic advancement. Heydenfeldt was far from being the abolitionist some have imagined him to be.[99]

Long after the Civil War had been fought and lost by the South, Philip Phillips of Alabama, who for a time served in the House of Representatives and was perhaps the outstanding Jewish attorney of the ante-bellum South, said that he regarded emancipation as a new opportunity for the South. "So far as the loss of property in slaves was involved," he said, "I regard it as the greatest blessing . . . A new generation with self-reliant spirit will create a new South, and crown

---

98. Sitterson, *op. cit.*, 131, 154; Meade, *op. cit.*, 92, 100 ff.; Bell Irvin Wiley, *Southern Negroes, 1861–1865* (New Haven, 1938), 152, 154, 157; *Speech of Hon. J. P. Benjamin, of Louisiana. Delivered in the Senate of the United States, May 22, 1860* (Washington, 1860).

99. Schappes, *op. cit.*, 293–301, 643–44; James Benson Sellers, *Slavery in Alabama* (University, 1950), 188–90.

it by their energy and industry, with all that enriches and enobles a land." But he never criticized slavery as an enemy of self-reliance and creativity while it was the accepted economic and social foundation of his state and section.[100]

Nor was there anyone among the many Jewish journalists, writers, and publicists of the Old South who questioned the moral, political, or economic justice of slavery. Jacob De Cordova, the Texas real-estate promoter, newspaper editor and geographer, emphatically denied charges that he had given voice to "free-soil doctrines" during his 1858 lecture tour in the North, and "wish[ed] it distinctly understood that our feelings and education have always been proslavery." [101] Isaac Harby, the Charleston dramatist and political essayist, was writing in Charleston in opposition to "the abolitionist society, and its secret branches," as early as 1824.[102] Jacob N. Cardozo, the editor and political economist, asserted that slavery was defensible both economically and morally. In the former respect, he maintained that: "Slavery brought not only great wealth to the South, but to the slaves a greater share of its enjoyment than in many regions where the relation between employer and employee was based on wages." In regard to the ethical question, he placed the responsibility squarely on the Deity: "The reason the Almighty made the colored black is to prove their inferiority." After the Civil War, in his well-known *Reminiscences of Charleston*, Cardozo expressed his sympathy with the planters who were now suffering great privation: "The owner of two hundred to five hundred slaves, with a princely income, has not only to submit to the most degraded employments, but he frequently cannot obtain them. In some instances, he has to drive a cart, or attend a retail grocery, while he may have to obey the orders of an ignorant and coarse menial. There is something unnatural in this reverse of position—something revolting to my sense of propriety in this social degradation." [103]

100. *MM*, III, 149.

101. *Lecture on Texas Delivered by Mr. J. De Cordova, at Philadelphia, New York, Mount Holly, Brooklyn and Newark. Also a paper read by him before the New York Geographical Society, April 15th, 1858* (Philadelphia, 1858), 2, 24–25.

102. "Essays by Junius," in Henry L. Pinckney and Abraham Moïse, *A Section from the Miscellaneous Writings of the Late Isaac Harby, Esq.* (Charleston, 1829), I, 95, 135.

103. *Reminiscences of Charleston* (Charleston, 1866), 10; Brody, *op. cit.*, 150–51.

Edwin De Leon, the journalist and Confederate diplomat, devoted many pages of his reminiscences to an extended apologia for slavery.[104] His brother, Thomas Cooper De Leon, one of the most prolific Southern litterateurs of the second half of the nineteenth century, wrote many novels and other works in the Southern romantic style of which he was a major practitioner. In one of his most famous works, *Belles, Beaux and Brains of the Confederacy*, De Leon described all talk of cruelty in the slave system as propaganda and mythology; he underlined the fact that Harriett Beecher Stowe was compelled to ascribe a Yankee origin to her famous character, Simon Legree.[105] Samuel Mordecai, the bachelor journalist of Richmond, derived part of his income from his articles in Edmund Ruffin's *The Farmer's Register*, a journal devoted primarily to the interests of Southern employers of slave labor forces. Mordecai loved everything about old Virginia, and wrote tenderly of the old colored aristocracy, in his *Richmond in By-Gone Days*. He too regarded slavery as a natural and desirable condition of society.[106]

Even in the days of the secession crisis, and the subsequent prolongated war and eventual defeat, many Southern Jews believed slavery to be indispensable to their happiness and security. George W. Mordecai, born a Jew but now an Episcopalian banker, railroad executive, and plantation owner in North Carolina, wrote to a Northern Republican in Dec., 1860: "I would much sooner trust myself alone on my plantation surrounded by my slaves, than in one of your large manufacturing towns when your labourers are discharged from employment and crying aloud for bread for themselves and their little ones." [107] In 1864, Private Eugene Henry Levy of the Confederate Army objected to the radical suggestion that Negroes be utilized in the war effort and be freed for this assistance. "The slaves," he said,

---

104. *Thirty Years of My Life on Three Continents* (London, 1890), I, 13–36.

105. (New York, 1909), 15–16; see also his *Four Years in Rebel Capitals* (Mobile, 1890), 370.

106. "Writers of Anonymous Articles in *The Farmer's Register* by Edmund Ruffin," *Journal of Southern History*, XXIII (1957), 90–102; *Richmond in By-Gone Days* (Richmond, 1946), 354–55; letter, Samuel Mordecai to G. W. Mordecai, Dec. 17, 1860, Mordecai Mss., Duke University Library.

107. Quoted in Clement Eaton, *Freedom of Thought in the Old South* (Durham, 1940), 232.

"are in their proper sphere as they are at present situated within the boundaries of the Confederacy." [108]

After the war was over, some Southern Jews still believed that slavery had been a necessary foundation of human society. Eleanor H. Cohen, the daughter of Dr. Philip Melvin Cohen of Charleston, said in the innocent selfishness of young maidenhood: "I, who believe in the institution of slavery, regret deeply its being abolished. I am accustomed to have them wait on me, and I dislike white servants very much." [109] Perhaps no more concise and self-deceptive rationalization of slavery was ever written than the observations which were recorded by Solomon Cohen, the distinguished civic leader and merchant of Savannah, who had lost a son in the war, in a letter which he wrote to his sister-in-law, Emma Mordecai, shortly after the end of the war: "I believe that the institution of slavery was refining and civilizing to the whites—giving them an elevation of sentiment and ease and dignity of manners only attainable in societies under the restraining influence of a privileged class—and at the same time the only human institution that could elevate the Negro from barbarism and develop the small amount of intellect with which he is endowed." [110]

Such sentiments might well be expected of members of families long resident in the South and thoroughly acclimated to its habits and assumptions. The De Leon's, Mordecai's, and Cardozo's had lived with their neighbors long enough to share their ideas and attitudes. But what of the newly immigrant German Jews who came to the South in increasing numbers beginning in the 1840's? There is no evidence that they found it very difficult to adjust to the slave society of which they became a part. Julius Weis, of New Orleans, who came to the United States in 1845, recorded his shock at his first sight of a Negro "being whipped upon his bare back by an overseer. The sight of a human being punished in this manner was very repugnant to me, though living in the midst of a country where slavery existed. I afterwards got somewhat accustomed to it, but I always felt a pity for the poor slaves." But Weis' compassion seemed to be limited to this matter of punishment, for he owned several slaves during the period from 1853 to 1857,

108. *MM*, III, 308–309.   100. *MM*, III, 368.
110. Letter, dated Jan. 8, 1866, Mordecai Mss., Duke University Library.

and bought a Negro barber in 1862. He notes that " I never found it necessary to punish them in such a manner," but his feeling of pity never led him to adopt a critical attitude toward the entire system of slavery.[111]

Louis Stix of Cincinnati wrote of a German Jewish immigrant to the South who became violent in his pro-slavery opinions. They met at a Jewish boarding-house in New York City; at dinner one night this unidentified Southern Jew said that "Southerners could not live without slavery." "I replied to this," wrote Stix, "by a very uncalled-for remark not at all flattering to our race who were living in the South. The Southerner . . . drew his pistol to compel me to take back my words. I hope [he] has since learned to do without slaves, or has returned to the place from which he came, where he was almost a slave himself." [112] But such a direct application of logic from Jewish experience in Europe to the situation of the Negroes in the South could only stem from the mind of a Northern Jew; it was never, to my knowledge, expressed in such blunt terms by a Southern Jew. To the contrary, the average Southern Jew would probably have agreed with Aaron Hirsch, who came to the United States in 1847 and worked through Mississippi and Arkansas, and who said that "the institution of Slavery as it existed in the South was not so great a wrong as people believe. The Negroes were brought here in a savage state; they captured and ate each other in their African home. Here they were instructed to work, were civilized and got religion, and were perfectly happy." [113]

Some Southern Jews, however, did not deceive themselves into thinking that the Negro slaves were "perfectly happy." These sensitive spirits were appalled at human exploitation of the life and labor of other human beings. Most of them reacted in a purely personal way, by avoiding the owning of slaves or by helping slaves. Major Alfred Mordecai of the United States Army, reared in the South and brother to planters and defenders of slavery, purchased only one slave in his life, simply to emancipate her. He believed that slavery was "the greatest misfortune and curse that could have befallen us." Yet he would do nothing to oppose slavery, and when the lines were drawn, he re-

111. *MM*, I, 51, 56.   112. *MM*, I, 338.   113. *MM*, II, 138.

signed his commission rather than fight for the North, without being willing to take up arms for the South.[114] Judah Touro, the New Orleans merchant, is reported to have emancipated many slaves whom he purchased solely for that purpose, and is even said to have established some of them in business at his own expense.[115] Another such spirit was Lazarus Straus, immigrant store-keeper of Talbotton, Ga., who used to argue with local Protestant ministers about the Biblical grounds for the defense of slavery. According to his son, Oscar, hired slaves who worked for the Straus family would beg to be purchased by them. "As the result of such pleadings," Oscar said, "my father purchased household slaves one by one from their masters, although neither he nor my mother believed in slavery." [116] Probably many Jews as well as non-Jews were caught in the dilemma of purchasing slaves just because they did not believe in slavery; since emancipation was virtually impossible, all they could do was to become the most generous masters possible under the circumstances. But there is, of course, no way of telling what proportion of people who could not conscientiously condone slavery were included in the statistics of slave-owners.

The literature has preserved only one instance of Jewish participation in the dangerous game of taking a Negro slave to the North for clandestine emancipation. This was the risk taken by the Friedman brothers of Cincinnati, Ohio, and Tuscumbia, Alabama, who purchased Peter Still and conspired to take him North after he had earned enough money to refund his purchase price. This exciting story is told in Kate E. R. Packard's *The Kidnapped and the Ransomed.*[117] Joseph Friedman and his brother Isaac had been regarded by the townsmen with suspicion and dislike when they first came to Tuscumbia, but their behavior gradually overcame the local prejudices. Six or seven years later, Peter Still, beloved by his owners and by the community in general, prevailed on the Friedmans to hire him. After he felt certain that he could trust them, he confided to their ears his hope of obtaining freedom, so they purchased him from his owner. There was

114. Stanley L. Falk, "Divided Loyalties in 1861: The Decision of Major Alfred Mordecai," *PAJHS*, XLVIII, no. 3 (March, 1959), 149–50.
115. Leon Hühner, *The Life of Judah Touro* (Philadelphia, 1946), 69.
116. *MM*, II, 295–96.
117. First published in 1856, and reprinted in part in *AJAM*, IX (1957), 3–31, with notes and introduction by Maxwell Whiteman.

much criticism of the transaction in the town. People knew that the Friedmans had no use for a slave in their business, and that they maintained no home. The townsfolk therefore suspected that Joseph Friedman would ultimately sell Peter away from the community to some stranger who would mistreat him. Kate Packard quotes a child as saying, "Ma says he's a Jew, and she says *Jews will sell their own children for money*." The authoress highlights the contrast between the behavior of "the slandered Jew" who is Peter's friend, and "the gaudy hypocrisy of his traducers" who "had bought and sold, and beaten and oppressed the poor until their cry had gone up to heaven." The plot succeeds: Peter saves up enough money to repay Joseph Friedman; the brothers close up their store and return to Cincinnati, taking Peter with them so that he can be freed. But the brothers never return to Alabama, for eventually their duplicity is revealed. Peter's well-wishers are indignant that the slave has been emancipated: that was carrying friendship too far! Joseph and Isaac Friendman are worthy of remembrance as anti-slavery activists: though other Southern Jews may well have risked fortune and reputation to evade state laws which restricted the emancipation of slaves, theirs are the only names recorded as having taken part in this risky venture.

We should not be surprised to discover that there was not a single abolitionist among the Jews of the South, but at least one did stem from this background. He was Marx E. Lazarus, eccentric scion of two distinguished Southern Jewish families, who was attracted to various radical movements, including Fourierism, the North American Phalanx, Socialism, phrenology, spiritualism and homeopathy. In 1860, Lazarus contributed a number of articles and translations to Moncure D. Conway's radical journal, *The Dial*, which was published in Cincinnati. One of these was entitled "True Principles of Emancipation," and was signed, "A Native of North Carolina and a Citizen of the World." In this article, Lazarus reminded his readers that Negro slavery was only one aspect of "the manifold cruelties that labor elsewhere suffers at the hands of capital, classes or castes, from their social superiors." He warned idealists against the "conversion of chattel slavery into that of labor for wages, changing the form, but not the facts, of slavery and oppression." "This prolonged crucifixion of a martyr race," he said, "demands a resurrection more humane than the liberty of selling one-self by the day, the cut-throat competitions of labor for wages, the outrages sanctioned by prejudice against color, careworn indigence or paralyzed pauperism." Despite these advanced views, Lazarus, in con-trast to Major Mordecai, would not abandon the land of his birth-place; with the outbreak of war he returned home to enlist in the Confederate army as a private.[118]

But men like Marx Lazarus were outright anomalies. The South-ern intellectual scene in the main, was a drab, monochromatic land-scape of unquestioning adherence to the dominant Southern doctrine about slavery during the two decades before the Civil War. Jews not only accepted this doctrine; some of them helped to formulate and circulate it, although their role was by no means a significant one.

IX An Evaluation

This investigation has traced Jewish participation in various aspects of the "peculiar institution" of the Old South. Jewish opinions about and relationships to the system of slavery were in no appreciable de-gree different from those of their non-Jewish neighbors. If more Jews owned slaves in terms of their numerical proportion of the popula-tion, it was because larger percentages of Jews lived in the towns and cities; if more Jews were auctioneers of slaves, it was because they were also auctioneers of every kind of merchandise; if fewer Jews were large-scale planters, it was for understandable social and eco-nomic reasons.

The significant thing is that being Jewish did not play any dis-cernible role in the determination of the relationship of Jews to slav-ery. Except for the teachings of a very few rabbis like David Einhorn of Baltimore, Judaism in America had not yet adopted a "social jus-tice" view of the responsibility of Jews towards society. Ante-bellum Southern Jews were more likely to quote the Talmudic maxim that "the law of the land is the law [for Jews]," and to regard the institu-

118. Caroline Cohen, *Records of the Myers, Hays and Mordecai Families from 1707 to 1913* (Washington, 1913), 56; Moncure Daniel Conway, *Autobiography, Memories and Experiences* (Boston, 1904), I, 313–14; Eaton, *op. cit.*, 322; Frank Luther Mott, *A History of American Magazines, 1850–1865* (Cambridge, 1938), 535; letter, Marx E. Lazarus to George W. Mordecai, New York, March 24, 1846, Mordecai Mss., Southern Historical Collection, University of North Carolina Library; *Dial*, I (1860), 219–28.

tion of slavery as part of the law which they were bound to uphold and follow, than they were to evaluate the failings of slavery in the light of the prophetic ethic.

Their acceptance of slavery as a natural aspect of the life of their section should not be regarded as a deliberately contrived "protective coloration," in order that they might remain inconspicuous. There is no iota of evidence, no line in a letter, no stray remarks, which would lead us to believe that these Jews gave conscious support to the slave system out of fear of arousing anti-Jewish prejudice. Any such motivation for their behavior and attitudes, if it existed at all, was well hidden in the unconscious psyche.

It is true, however, that their small numbers militated against the creation of a distinctively Jewish approach to any political or social question other than anti-Semitism. Jews were only a fragment of the Southern population, thinly distributed throughout the area. Even in the largest cities, New Orleans, Charleston, Richmond, they were a tiny group. They would be entirely likely, therefore, to derive their opinions from discussions with non-Jewish neighbors, rather than with Jewish friends. This was especially true of the more prominent Jews, planters, attorneys, physicians, newspaper editors, merchants, whose associations with non-Jews were quite intimate.

Whatever prejudice there was in the South, before the Civil War aggravated every possible source of tension, was directed largely against the alien Jew, the immigrant peddler and petty store-keeper, the insecure newcomer, whose very survival was in the hands of his customers. He would, therefore, be inclined to adopt their opinions and attitudes, not because he was afraid to disagree with them, but because he wanted to succeed in his new home.

Slavery played an unacknowledged role in this question of Jewish status in the Old South, too. Although Southern society fostered a caste system which also applied to various classes of whites, and which distinguished the store-keeper from the wealthier merchant, the merchant in turn from the professional man, and the attorney and physician from the planter, the all-pervasive division was between the races. The Jews were white, and this very fact goes a long way towards accounting for the measurably higher social and political status achieved by Jews in the South than in the North. Foreign observers like Salomon de Rothschild and I. J. Benjamin were acutely aware of the sharp contrast between the South, where so many Jews were elected to high office, and the North, where Jews constituted a larger percentage of the population, yet had achieved fewer honors.[119] The Negroes acted as an escape-valve in Southern society. The Jews gained in status and security from the very presence of this large mass of defenseless victims who were compelled to absorb all of the prejudices which might otherwise have been expressed more frequently in anti-Jewish sentiment. As I. J. Benjamin said, "The white inhabitants felt themselves united with, and closer to, other whites—as opposed to the Negroes. Since the Israelite there did not do the humbler kinds of work which the Negro did, he was quickly received among the upper classes, and early rose to high political rank." Although this was too broad a generalization, and not all Jews were treated so generously, the road to social and economic advancement and acceptance for many Jews was smoothed by the ever-present race distinction which imputed superiority to all whites. And even the path of the poor, foreign Jew was made easier by the institution of slavery. Oscar Straus remembered that when his father was peddling through the rural areas of Georgia, he "was treated by the owners of the plantations with a spirit of equality that is hard to appreciate today. Then, too, the existence of slavery drew a distinct line of demarcation between the white and black races. This gave to the white [peddler] a status of equality that probably otherwise he would not have enjoyed to such a degree." [120]

Slavery, therefore, played a more significant role in the development of Jewish life in the Old South, than Jews themselves played in the establishment and maintenance of the institution. The history of slavery would not have differed one whit from historic reality if no single Jew had been resident in the South. Other whites would have owned slaves; other traders and auctioneers would have bought and sold slaves; other political and intellectual leaders would have propagandized in behalf of slavery; a few slaves might have fared better or worse at the hands of other masters, but their feelings were immate-

119. *MM*, III, 104; I. J. Benjamin, *Three Years in America* (Philadelphia, 1956), 76.
120. *MM*, II, 291.

rial details in the total story of the institution itself. But whether so many Jews would have achieved so high a level of social, political, economic and intellectual status and recognition, without the presence of the lowly and degraded slave, is indeed dubious. How ironic that the distinctions bestowed upon men like Judah P. Benjamin, Major Raphael J. Moses, and the Honorable Solomon Cohen were in some measure dependent upon the sufferings of the very Negro slaves they bought and sold with such equanimity.

Bertram Wallace Korn

American Judaeophobia:
Confederate Version

THE SAME psychological, social, economic, and political factors which brought latent prejudices against Jews into the open in the North were creating a similar pattern of scapegoatism in the Confederacy. Economic tensions, personal fears and frustrations, and mass passions required an outlet and a victim in the South just as in the North.

Additional social factors peculiar to life in the South tended to strengthen and heighten the reaction to Jews: a general dislike of all aliens and foreigners which, during the War, created the legend that the Union Army was a band of German and Irish hirelings and mercenaries, while the Confederate Army was said to be exclusively native;[1] a wide-spread suspicion of the merchant and storekeeper, typical

---

1. Ella Lonn wrote her fascinating study *Foreigners in the Confederacy* (Chapel Hill, 1940) to investigate and evaluate this legend. The evidence which she has marshaled from an exhaustive search of contemporary sources demonstrates that many thousands of foreigners were resident in the Confederacy, loyal to it, and active in its military campaigns.

Frank Moore cited an interesting example in Moore (ed.), *The Rebellion Record: A Diary of American Events, with Documents, Narratives, Illustrative Incidents, Poetry, etc. . . . * (12 vols.; New York, 1861–68), VI, 412, reprinted from the *Richmond Enquirer* of July 15, 1863, of the Confederate belief that all traitors were foreigners:

> Foreigners of every age and sex crowded the office of the provost-marshal, in Richmond, anxious to get passports to go North, by way of the blockade. The Jew, whose ample pockets were stuffed with confederate money; the Germans, with hands on pockets tightly pressed; Italians, with the silvery jargon; and the Irish woman, with "nine children and one at the breast," all beset the office and wanted passports to leave the country. . . . It is not fair that those who have drained the very life-blood of our people, should be let

of a society dominated by the plantation owner and farmer; a deeper commitment than existed in the North to fundamentalist "Bible" Christianity; the intensified emotional depression as the War dragged on from year to year and Confederate chances for victory became more slight with each passing month. Granted an original suspicion and dislike of the Jew before the War, the four-year-long travail of the Confederacy was certain to emphasize it.

Two examples have been preserved of discrimination against Jews in the military forces. Captain R. E. Park tells us that his Colonel was so prejudiced against Jews that he attempted to block the promotion of Captain Adolph Proskauer of Mobile, Ala. Proskauer insisted on taking an examination in military strategy and discipline so that he might be able to demonstrate his qualifications. The Colonel agreed, but, according to Captain Park, instructed the Committee of Examiners to make the test as difficult as they could. Let Captain Park continue his story:

During the day of the examination there was an unusual interest felt by the officers of the camp, and especially by the Colonel. Late in the afternoon, after an all-day examination had been concluded, one of the officers rode rapidly up to Col. Pickens' headquarters and in reply to an anxious inquiry, was told that the Committee had done all they could to defeat Capt. Proskauer, but that after an examination [in] squad drill, in company drill, in regimental drill, in brigade drill, in drill by echelon, and in the army movements as suggested in Jomini's tactics, Captain Proskauer did not fail to answer promptly and accurately every question. The General [chairman of the Examining Board] added, "he knows more about tactics than any of the Examining Committee, and we were forced to recommend his promotion.[2]

---

off thus quietly, and not made to shed the first, at least, if not the last, drop of blood for the Government which protected them in the collection of their hoarded pelf.

An illustration of the general suspicion in which foreigners were held in a newspaper poem clipped by the Rev. George Jacobs and preserved in his scrapbook, entitled "Ho! Profundum," of which this is one verse:

Tis noon—yet scarcely is begun
Up in the treasury the run,
Where Dutch and Yankee, Jew and Hun,
Meet in stock jobbery.

2. R. E. Park, *Sketch of the Twelfth Alabama Infantry* . . . (Richmond, 1906), 10.

When a Jewish Colonel was assigned to a Texas regiment, newly arrived in Virginia, the enlisted men did not attempt to hide their feelings. Two said in voices loud enough for all to hear: "What? What is it? Is it a man, a fish or a bird?" "Of course it is a man, don't you see his legs." The Colonel swallowed his pride. But when he found, the next day, that his horse's tail had been cut off, he threw up his hands at an impossible task and left forthwith. His departure was a signal for a regimental celebration.[3]

If a Jewish officer would have difficulty, what could a Jewish cabinet member expect? Judah P. Benjamin was a popular target all through the war, in the Confederacy as in the North. Those who disliked all Jews took especial pleasure in being able to blame him for all the problems of the Confederacy, its defeats in the military sphere while he was Secretary of War, and its failures in diplomacy while he was Secretary of State.[4] A citizen of North Carolina swore that "all the distresses of the people were owing to a Nero-like despotism, originating in the brain of Benjamin, the Jew." [5] A writer to the *Richmond Enquirer* believed it blasphemous for a Jew to hold so high an office as that of Secretary of State, and thought that the prayers of the Confederacy would have

3. N. A. Davis, *The Campaign from Texas to Maryland . . . with the Battle of Fredericksburg* (Richmond, 1863), 18–19.

4. See the authoritative biography by Robert D. Meade, *Judah P. Benjamin, Confederate Statesman* (New York, 1943), 218, 280. Although he never identified himself with Jewish causes or the Jewish communities of places in which he happened to reside, Benjamin always was pigeonholed as a Jew. When Sir William Howard Russell, the renowned British journalist, took a trip through the South at the outbreak of war, this was one of his comments about Louisiana:

> It is a strange country indeed; one of the evils which afflicts the Louisianians, they say, is the preponderance and influence of South Carolina Jews, and Jews generally, such as Moise, Mordecai, Josephs, and Judah Benjamin, and others. The subtlety and keenness of the Caucasian [*sic*] intellect give men a high place among a people who admire ability and dexterity, and are at the same time reckless of means and averse to labor. The Governor is supposed to be somewhat under the influence of the Hebrews.

William Howard Russell, *My Diary, North and South* (New York, 1863), entry for May 29, 1861. See Bertram Wallace Korn, "Judah P. Benjamin as a Jew," *Publications of the American Jewish Historical Society*, No. 38 (1949), for details of Benjamin's lack of interest in the Jewish community.

5. John Beauchamp Jones, *A Rebel War Clerk's Diary at the Confederate States Capital* (2 vols.; New York, 1935), I, 165–66.

more effect if Benjamin were dismissed from the cabinet.[6] A Confederate Brigadier General and member of the Provisional Congress, Thomas R. R. Cobb of Georgia, said of him: "A grander rascal than this Jew Benjamin does not exist in the Confederacy, and I am not particular in concealing my opinion of him." [7] A Tennessean denounced him as the "Judas Iscariot Benjamin" of the Confederacy.[8] A man from Virginia was heard to assail President Jefferson Davis in violent language, "and the sole offense alleged against him was that he had appointed one Jew a member of his cabinet." [9] These were only a few of the recorded denunciations of Benjamin in which his Jewish origin played a large role. Popular and Congressional disfavor seemed to pursue Benjamin more than any other Confederate official, and it was undoubtedly his Jewishness which made him so vulnerable. But it is to be counted to the everlasting credit of President Davis that he steadfastly refused to sacrifice Benjamin's administrative talent as a sop to prejudice, and that he retained his Jewish friend and confidant as a trusted lieutenant all through his service as the Confederate chief of government. It was inevitable, but nonetheless sad and disheartening, that under the stress of war the public should utterly forget Benjamin's record as a loyal servant of the South in state and national affairs.

Prejudice against Jews was revealed most frequently in connection with the economic life of the Confederacy, and here again Benjamin's Jewish origin was a feature of the attacks. Anti-Jewish mythology had always described the Jew as grasping, thievish, and unscrupulous in business practices; now, in a period of severe economic crisis, the old canard appeared with renewed vigor. A sizable number of references in contemporary diaries and memoirs, as well as in the columns of Con-

---

6. *New York Tribune*, Mar. 7, 1865. The editor of the *Tribune*, in reprinting this communication from the Richmond paper, took occasion to object to all attempts in the North to amend the U.S. Constitution for the purpose of recognizing Christianity as the official religion of the nation. This gave rise to a lively correspondence on the subject.

7. *Southern Historical Society Papers*, XXVIII, 290. See also Cobb's reference to Benjamin as "an eunuch" in letter to Mrs. Cobb, Jan. 15, 1862, in Thomas R. R. Cobb Collection, University of Georgia Library, Athens.

8. Max J. Kohler, "Judah P. Benjamin: Statesman and Jurist," *Publications of the American Jewish Historical Society*, No. 12 (1904), 79.

9. *Richmond Sentinel*, Jan. 25, 1864, clipping from the George Jacobs Scrapbook.

federate newspapers, attests to the widespread belief that Jews were the chief source of the Confederacy's economic troubles.[10] "Extortion" was the word commonly applied by citizens of the Southern states to the high prices charged by merchants and shopkeepers, and it was alleged that Jews were the chief "extortionists."

In the Confederate House of Representatives, during a heated debate on January 14, 1863, concerning the question of drafting foreigners into military service, Congressman Henry S. Foote of Tennessee made a major pronouncement on this subject. The Jews had flooded the country, he said, and controlled at least nine-tenths of the business of the land. They were engaging in all kinds of illegal trade with the enemy without any official hindrance. Why was this permitted to continue? Because, he said mysteriously, the Jews had been invited to come to the Confederacy "by official permission" and were under official protection. Here he was obviously alluding to Judah P. Benjamin, whose appointment to high office always irritated him. He was not yet prepared, he said, to make any specific charges, but would continue gathering evidence, and he hoped eventually to be in a position to expose the powerful influence which was transferring all of Southern commerce to the hands of "foreign Jews." He concluded by quoting a friend of his who had said that "if the present state of things were to

10. See Lonn, *op. cit.*, 335–38, 390–95, for the evidence which led Miss Lonn to conclude that "Jewish merchants had largely acquired possession of the stores" in all the larger cities except New Orleans. Most of the accounts she quotes are highly colored by prejudice and anti-foreignism, but can nonetheless be interpreted as tributes to Jewish enterprise and ingenuity. It depends upon one's point of view. She quotes the story, for instance, of a German Jew who had pitched a tent on the "sandy waste between San Antonio and Brownsville," far from the nearest town, to sell crackers, cheese, and whisky to the passing troops (p. 338). The anecdote had been directed as an attack against Jews by its original narrator, who finished by complaining that the Jew demanded Northern currency for the refreshments but accepted, under pressure, Confederate money. No word for the "rugged individualism" of that Jewish peddler?

When Frederick Law Olmsted wrote his *A Journey in the Seaboard Slave States* in 1856, he wrote, in the glib language of prejudice, that "a swarm of Jews, within the last ten years, has settled in nearly every southern town, many of them men of no character, opening cheap clothing and trinket shops; ruining, or driving out of business, many of the old retailers, and engaging in an unlawful trade with the simple negroes, which is found very profitable." Quoted in Burton Rascoe, *An American Reader* (New York, 1939), 226.

continue, the end of the war would probably find nearly all the property of the Confederacy in the hands of Jewish Shylocks." [11]

Foote never made good his threat to expose Benjamin, nor did he ever produce any statistics to bear out his contentions, but three months later he was still calling the attention of his fellow Congressmen and of the public to the deplorable condition of affairs. "Foreign Jews," he stated, "were scattered all over the country, under official protection, engaged in trade to the exclusion of our own citizens, undermining our currency." He predicted that "by the close of the war they would have the control of all the cotton and tobacco." [12]

Foote was not the only Confederate Congressman to speak of the Jews in such terms. On various occasions, Chilton of Alabama,[13] Miles of South Carolina,[14] and Hilton of Florida, voiced similar sentiments. Hilton said that the Jews swarmed all over the country, like locusts, eating up its resources and monopolizing its trade. The only way to control them was to draft them into the army. There was really no shortage of goods; demand had not created the high prices. It was "competition among buyers for the purpose of extortion," which was responsible for the rising cost of living! Hilton gave an example of Jewish persistence: a blockade-runner had landed on the Florida coast and its cargo was confiscated by the authorities, but somehow the Jews had heard about it and "at least one hundred" of them "flocked there, led even to this remote point by the scent of gain, and they had to be driven back actually at the point of the bayonet." [15]

John Beauchamps Jones, a clerk in the Confederate War Department, was another who attributed the inflation to Jewish extortioners and speculators. In his diary, which has become familiar to students of social and economic conditions in war-time Richmond, Jones indulged in almost daily tirades against the Jewish merchants. During a critical military campaign in 1862, for instance, he noted that the people of the

---

11. *Southern Historical Society Papers*, IX, 122. Foote feared Benjamin's influence on Davis so strongly that he said "he would never consent to the establishment of a supreme court of the Confederate States so long as Judah P. Benjamin shall continue to pollute the ears of majesty Davis with his insidious counsels." *Richmond Daily Examiner*, Dec. 17, 1863.

12. *Southern Historical Society Papers*, XI, 214; see also IX, 144, for another of Foote's outbursts against Southern Jewry.

13. *Ibid.*, X, 8–9.　　　14. *Ibid.*, 185.　　　15. *Ibid.*, IX, 122–23.

capital showed little interest in the course of events. The Jews were, as always, busy speculating on the street corners, he said; every once in a while there would be a loud burst of laughter, "when a Jew is asked what will be the price of his shoes, etc., tomorrow." Jones believed that the Jews did not care "which side gains the day, so they gain the profits." [16] Eight days later, he summarized his feelings about them:

The illicit trade with the United States has depleted the country of gold and placed us at the feet of the Jew extortioners. It still goes on. Mr. Seddon has granted passports to two agents of a Mr. Baumgartien—and how many others I know not. These Jews have the adroitness to carry their points. They have injured the cause more than the armies of Lincoln. Well, if we gain our independence, instead of being the vassals of the Yankees, we shall find all our wealth in the hands of the Jews.[17]

Foote's allegations against Jewish merchants in the arena of national politics had their counterpart in various local areas. In Thomasville, Ga., for instance, on August 30, 1862, a public meeting was called for the discussion of the "unpatriotic conduct" of Jewish merchants. Resolutions were passed in which "German Jews [were] denounced in unmeasured terms . . . prohibited from visiting the village, and banishing all those now resident in that place." [18] Unfortunately, there were no Jewish periodicals in the South; if there had been, they might have preserved further details of this episode. A Georgia Jew wrote, however, that denunciations of Jewish merchants were frequent in the area, and that the habit had spread from town to town throughout the state.[19] In Talbotton, the seat of Talbot County, a grand jury completed its session with a presentment referring to "the evil and unpatriotic conduct of the representatives of Jewish houses." [20] And in another Georgia town, according to a letter preserved in the Duke University Library, the wives of soldiers away with the army became so desperate that they raided Jewish stores and took whatever they wished at pistol point, accusing the Jewish merchants of speculating on the shortages and making fortunes while the men were fighting for

16. Jones, *op. cit.*, I, 213.   17. *Ibid.*, 221.
18. *Savannah Daily Morning News*, Sept. 16, 1862.
19. Memoirs of Isidor Straus (unpublished; American Jewish Historical Library), 16.
20. *Ibid.*

the life of the nation.[21] These examples indicate a trend which was characterisitic of many sections of the Confederacy—the Jews being held responsible for the inflation of prices and the shortages of goods— a pattern which bears a remarkable likeness to the background of the Grant Order.

That there was widespread acceptance of the alleged guilt of the Jews cannot be gainsaid. Diarists and letter-writers throughout the South attested to this. One correspondent wrote, "I should despise myself if in this time of our country's need I should do anything to put up the price of a single article of necessity. I leave that to the Jews and extortioners of whom there are unfortunately too many among us." [22] Another charged that cotton was "a favorite article with Jews, and the country swarms with them—and other speculators." [23] Frequent were the accusations that Jews were largely engaged in passing counterfeit money, running the blockade, aiding the inflation by charging outrageous prices, driving well-established "Anglo-Saxon" firms out of business by unfair competitive methods, and, in general, "batten[ing] and fatten[ing] upon speculation to the misery of the population." [24]

Natives of the South very quickly transmitted these opinions to visitors from other countries, particularly England. One writer, who called himself "An English Combatant," wrote:

The Israelites, as usual, far surpassed the Gentiles in shrewdness at the auspicious moment, and laid in stocks (procured on credit) which, in almost every instance, were retailed at rates from five hundred to one thousand

21. Letter from Huldah A. (Fain) Briant Papers, Apr. 14, 1863, Santa Lucah, Ga., in the Flowers Mss. Collection, Duke University Library, Durham, N.C. A similar incident occurred in Milledgeville, Ga., according to a report in the *Memphis Daily Bulletin*, Apr. 28, 1863.

22. Burckmyer Letters, March, 1863–June, 1865, p. 236.

23. Barnsley to Reid, March 26, 1863, in Barnsley Papers, University of Georgia Library.

24. See E. Merton Coulter, *The Confederate States of America, 1861–1865* (Baton Rouge, 1950), 223–29, for many such citations. The two preceding notes are derived from his references. Coulter, incidentally, is the first Civil War historian, dealing with either the North or the South, to give even passing attention to anti-Jewish prejudice as a social phenomenon of the war period. Coulter's entire picture of the inflationary process in the Confederacy offers ample evidence that the role of the Jews was minor at best, yet he himself appears not to understand fully the nature of anti-Jewish prejudice from a psychological point of view. The quotation itself is from Sallie A. Putnam, *Richmond During the War; Four Years of Personal Observation. By a Richmond Lady* (New York, 1867), 271.

per cent above ordinary prices; cash being always exacted. Many of these gentry proved unscrupulous knaves during the war; for having husbanded their goods for one or two years, and converted them into coin, if they did not decamp from the Confederacy altogether, they found a thousand and one excuses for not bearing arms. . . . This is true of Hollanders generally, and of Dutch Jews almost universally.[25]

"An English Merchant," speaking of Charleston as a center for blockade-run goods, marveled that there seemed to be "more Jews in Charleston than . . . in Jerusalem," so thoroughly had he been indoctrinated with prejudice.[26]

That these and other descriptions of the Jews of the South were the result of prejudice, and not of a realistic consideration of the actual facts, was recognized by many who tried to be fair minded. The editor of the *Richmond Sentinel*, for instance, acknowledged the fact that "intolerant and illiberal views and prejudices" against the Jews "prevail to some extent . . . in no wise affecting their [the Jews'] individual and personal merits and character." [27] A Missionary Chaplain to the Army wrote to the *Savannah Daily Morning News* that he was saddened by the "many unfair, and, to my mind, very unjust, as well as injudicious *flings* at this part, no unimportant part, of our fellow citizens." [28] A Jew who wrote a lengthy letter of defense to a Richmond paper began his plea with these words: "I have marked with sorrow and dismay the growing propensity in the Confederacy to denounce the Jew on all occasions and in all places. The press, the pulpit, and grave legislators, who have the destiny of a nation committed to their charge, all unite in this unholy and unjust denunciation." Then he continued: "That a man like Foote should habitually denounce the Jew is to be expected; he denounces everybody and every thing; his mouth is a "well spring"

25. *Battle-Fields of the South, From Bull Run to Fredericksburg, with Sketches of Confederate Commanders, and Gossip of the Camps. By an English Combatant . . .* (New York, 1864), 15. This paragraph demonstrates the true nature of prejudice. The "English Combatant" had undoubtedly been told this by someone who referred to Germans as "Dutchmen" and German Jews as "Dutch Jews." Knowing nothing of this Americanism, he solemnly libels Dutch and Dutch-Jewish immigrants, without realizing that there could only have been a handful of them in the Confederacy.

26. *Two Months in the Confederate States, Including a Visit to New Orleans under the Domination of General Butler. By an English Merchant,* 126, cited by Coulter, *op. cit.*, 227.

27. *Richmond Sentinel*, Jan. 25, 1864 [clipping from George Jacobs' Scrapbook].

28. *Savannah Daily Morning News*, Feb. 23, 1863.

of slander; and I should doubt the beauty of virtue, itself, should he chance to praise it. But that the whole press of your city (your paper excepted) should add fuel to these fires of persecutions, and should seek to direct public opinion in such foul channels, surpasses my comprehension." [29] A year after the war had ended in defeat for the Confederacy, the editor of the *Augusta* (Ga.) *Sentinel*, in commenting on North Carolina's refusal to abandon the religious test for public office, defended the Jews against "the charges which we have frequently heard made by our street-corner gossipers and windy patriots, that the Israelites of the South failed to perform their duty during the recent war." [30]

So frequent and bitter were the verbal attacks on the Jews that the Rev. Maxmilian J. Michelbacher, rabbi of Beth Ahabah Congregation of Richmond, delivered a public answer to them in a sermon which he preached at a Confederate Fast Day service in Fredericksburg in 1863 and which was printed in the daily papers and even found its way up North.[31] He said that accusations against Jewish merchants were so common that he could no longer keep silent. If the Jews were guilty, he said, they would find no defender in him, because he prided himself on the fact that "I always speak of your faults without fear, favor, or affection." He had investigated the conduct of Jewish merchants and was convinced that "the Israelites are not speculators nor extortioners." How could they be? The Jewish merchant specialized in rapid turnover sales, he said; the speculator made his fortune by hoarding. Besides, Jews did not deal at all in the basic commodities in which speculation was most common: "Flour, meal, wheat, corn, bacon, beef, coal and wood." For that matter, if the Jews actually were the extortioners, how could they stay in business? Wouldn't the trade go to non-Jews who were, by implication, free of all taint of profiteering? How, then, could one explain the uproar against the Jews? Michelbacher said he was pre-

29. *Richmond Sentinel*, Jan. 25, 1864 [clipping from George Jacobs' Scrapbook].

30. Quoted in *Occident*, XXIV, No. 6, p. 282–83, Sept., 1866. The Jews of the North were also under the impression that anti-Jewish feelings were as strong in the Confederacy as in the Union. Isaac Leeser said that a reading of Southern papers gave one the impression that Jews and disaffected citizens were synonymous, that all smuggling was done by Jews, and that Judah P. Benjamin would never have been retained in office if the war had ended favorably for the Confederacy. *Occident*, XXIII, No. 7, pp. 313–19, Oct. 1865.

31. The sermon was delivered on May 27, 1863, and reprinted in *Jewish Record*, II, No. 13, p. 1, June 5, 1863, as a curiosity.

pared to assert that the condemnation of the Jews was deliberately *instigated*—"cunningly devised after the most approved mode of villainy"—to shield the real extortioner and speculator, "who deals in the miseries, life and blood of our fellow citizens," from the pent-up indignation of the Confederate populace. The "monstrous and evil thing that draws its nourishment from the heart's blood of men, women and children" was blamed on the Jews so that those who were actually guilty could escape punishment!

Was Michelbacher defending the Jews because they were his people and he had to speak out in their behalf? Or was his contention that prejudice and profit were the roots of the accusation, valid and demonstrable?

Before we can attempt to assay the evidence, a clear picture of the Southern economy must be kept in mind. Although industrialization had proceeded farther than is commonly supposed, it is nevertheless true that the South was basically an agricultural society. Its entire life and conception of life were founded on a maintenance of the slave system and the plantation standard. The section had never produced anything approaching the equivalent of its consumption of manufactured goods; imports from Europe and the North were always required to supplement local production. This need for the importation of the products of modern industry gave rise to certain significant items in the South's brief against the North: resentment against the tariff system which protected Northern industry but penalized the South; and the widespread belief that the South was being exploited only for the benefit of the Northern industrialist empire.[32]

An obvious impasse was reached with the outbreak of the war. Supplies from the North were cut off. The blockade of Southern ports by the Union Navy prevented the importation of European products. Whatever trend there had been, before the war, towards increased industrialization was necessarily channeled into the production of war materiel. The result was, of course, an instantaneous shortage of all kinds of goods, and a rapid inflation of prices. Buying agents from the larger cities scoured the interior in search of stocks which might still be unsold in the rural stores; blockade runners earned fantastic prices

32. See Professor James G. Randall's first chapter, pp. 3–36, in *The Civil War and Reconstruction* (New York, 1937), for a discussion of these problems.

for cargoes taken on in the Caribbean area; illegal trade along the borders increased by leaps and bounds as smugglers risked life and liberty to get valuable merchandise across the lines.

The process of attrition had been an inevitable one. The only corrective would have been a completely authoritarian control of economic affairs by the Confederate government. Such a regime would have pegged prices, but there would still have been no safeguard against the development of a black market. Price controls could not have produced more goods.[33]

Everyone who produced or sold commodities was involved in the inflationary spiral: farmers, manufacturers, merchants, tradesmen, Jews and Gentiles, natives and foreigners, traitors and patriots. This was the way the *Macon Daily Telegraph* put it: "It is doubtful if any man in these times can pursue a speculative or money-making business consistently with his duty to his country." [34] Unless they changed their means of earning a livelihood, or entered military service, they had to participate in the economic system. Were they to blame, however, for the scarcity and the inflation? Should the responsibility not be ascribed to the fire-eaters who had assured their compatriots that the South could maintain itself militarily and industrially in peace *and in war*, that the slave system was not only an advantage to the Southern economy but that it was worth fighting for, that the South could live as an independent nation and had to fight for the right to do so? Far more guilty than the farmers and merchants were the men who led the South into secession and war without calculating fully the realistic problems of a war crisis, and the legislative and executive leaders of the Confederacy who failed to grapple with the serious economic struggle for survival on the home front.

It is not difficult to prove that, in at least a few cases, the accusations against Jews were motivated by a climate of prejudice rather than an

33. See Professor Charles W. Ramsdell's excellent study of the economic problems of the Confederacy during the war, in *Behind the Lines in the Southern Confederacy* (Baton Rouge, 1944), 14 ff. Professor Ramsdell comes to no conclusion as to the extent of unscrupulous practices (pp. 20–21); he does not even mention the accusations against Jews.

34. Cited in Coulter, *op. cit.*, 231. Even Southern clergymen were suspected of speculating! See the discussion on a bill to exempt ministers from conscription, Jan. 13, 1865, in *Journal of the Congress of the Confederate States of America, 1861–1865* (7 vols.; Washington, D.C., 1904–1905), VII, 455.

objective consideration of the facts. We are fortunate, for instance, in possessing the memoirs of a Talbotton Jew.[35] He was Isidor Straus who was later to become one of the outstanding merchant princes of the nation. In 1862 he was seventeen years old, living with his father and family: *they were the only Jewish family in Talbotton and theirs was the only Jewish store in the county*! Isidor recalled in after days how hurt and bewildered his father had been when he was informed of the grand jury's condemnation of Jewish merchants. Lazarus Straus had believed that he had earned the respect of the fellow-townsmen, that they were fond of him and his family. But how wrong he had been. So he immediately determined to move away from a town "which had cast such a reflection on him as the only Jew living in their midst." The reaction to the announcement of his imminent departure was bizarre: his fellow citizens waited upon him in large numbers, seeking to persuade him to remain; every member of the grand jury which had issued the pronouncement called upon him; every minister in town asked him to change his mind. They assured him that there had been no intention to reflect upon *his* business ethics or *his* faith—although they now saw that it was possible for their action to be so interpreted! Nevertheless, the Straus family moved on to Columbus, Ga. One is moved to pity and compassion for these folk who were so possessed by prejudice that they could not anticipate Lazarus Straus' reaction to their denunciation of his people.

Congressman Foote, on the other hand, does not deserve pity. It was generally known that he disliked Jews and took advantage of every opportunity to vent his hatred upon them, no matter how flimsy the evidence. On January 7, 1864, for instance, the *Daily Richmond Examiner* printed a rumor that an unnamed Congressman had obtained passports out of the Confederacy for three Jews.[36] According to the

35. Straus, *op. cit.*, 15-17. Young Straus later went to Europe as an agent for a firm attempting to organize a systematic blockade-running fleet to supply the Confederacy with scarce goods. A large portion of the memoirs deals with his experiences in this regard.

In 1852, just before the elder Straus came to the United States, there were five Jewish families in Talbotton, but only eight men, not enough for a religious service. They had organized a Hebrew Benevolent Society and presented a silver ornament for a Torah-scroll to a New York congregation, *Occident*, X, No. 8, p. 414, Nov., 1852. All eight men were probably peddlers, operating in the surrounding country. That was the way Lazarus Straus reached Talbotton.

36. *Richmond Daily Examiner*, Jan. 7, 1864.

report, he had been paid three thousand dollars for his helpfulness. That very morning, Foote jumped to the floor and demanded the appointment of a committee to investigate the charges and to bring the culprits to the bar of justice. He wished it understood in advance that he had no desire to become a member of the committee because, said a newspaper report, "many members thought him already too fond of ferreting out abuses and frauds." The resolution was adopted and the committee appointed forthwith.[37] Its members reported back to the House on January 25. They had found "nothing to sustain the charge." When they had asked the editor of the *Examiner* for evidence, he told them a long, involved story. The article had originally been written by one of his reporters, but when he asked the reporter for the evidence and became convinced by his silence that there was no truth to the story, he had forbidden its publication. Some slip-up had occurred, however, and the article found its way into print. He was still unable to furnish any proof, and said that he "knew nothing of the truth of it." [38]

The House had not been interested, of course, in investigating a story about three Jews; the purpose of the committee was to ascertain the truth of a report about a Representative's dishonesty. Foote never suggested that a committee be appointed to investigate any of his other charges against Jews, nor did the House ever trouble itself to do so. This was the only investigation which was ever ordered to track a rumor about Jews to its source—and it proved to be without foundation.

It is interesting to note in passing the contrasting tone of the Confederate loyalties of Congressman Foote and the Jew he disliked so deeply, Secretary Benjamin. The latter fled the Confederacy at the very last, after Lee's surrender and the transfer of the capital from Richmond, with the vow never to be taken alive by the Union forces. He made good his pledge and established a new life in England. Foote's political career reached its zenith on February 27, 1865, when he was

37. *Journal of the Congress of the Confederate States of America, 1861–1865*, VI, 598; *Richmond Daily Examiner*, Jan. 8, 1864. The same day the *Examiner* printed an unchallenged report that "very recently, two immensely wealthy Israelitish merchants on Broad Street, departed for the North leaving their wives and daughters to carry on the business of their stores."

38. *Richmond Daily Examiner*, Jan. 26, 1864.

expelled from the Confederate House of Representatives for deserting the Stars and Bars and crossing the lines to the Union.[39]

The appointment of the investigating committee, at Foote's behest, was grist for J. B. Jones' mill. It earned a typical flourish against the Jews in his diary.[40] But he did not feel it necessary to mention the committee's report which proved the *Examiner* article to be a fabrication. Jones could not, by any stretch of the imagination, be regarded as a detached observer when it came to Jews. He appears to have been driven by a psychopathic Judaeophobia. The word *Jew* appears in his diary more than forty times—each time part of an unfriendly reference to an individual Jew or to all Jews. Some psychological compulsion forced him to label Jews as though they were members of a curious species; if there was any uncertainty about a person's religion, he would hazard a guess to be on the safe side: (*Jew?*)[41] or (*Jew name*)[42] or *perhaps a Jew*[43] or (*another Jew, I suppose*).[44] So he assured himself that if it came to a test he could not be accused of missing a single one. Any testimony by Jones about J. P. Benjamin, or Quartermaster General Myers, or any or all Jews, ought to be accorded the credence which his hostility deserves.[45]

The reaction of the Jews to the public outcry against them was similar to that in the North: bewilderment, hurt pride, anger, rebellion.

39. *Journal of the Congress of the Confederate States of America, 1861–1865*, VII, 454, 458, 465, 466, 490, 659.

40. Jones, *op. cit.*, II, 126. 41. *Ibid.*, I, 304, 320. 42. *Ibid.*, II, 39.

43. *Ibid.*, I, 185. 44. *Ibid.*, II, 144.

45. It should be superfluous to comment that so unabashed a Judaeophobe as Jones ought not to be regarded as a fair witness in any discussion of the role of Jews in the Confederacy. The editor of the 1935 edition of the Jones *Diary* felt that the Grant order and the Jones comments were reliable evidence on the basis of the "where there's smoke, there's fire" theory of logic. "Certainly there is a strong presumption in the records of both sides," he states, "that fair-minded men felt the general charge of profiteering could be made against the whole class of Jewish merchants." (I, p. 289.) Grant in later days admitted his order was unfair; Jones cannot possibly be regarded as a "fair-minded witness." The above-mentioned editor cites only one other witness, Colonel Fremantle, who asserted that Matamoros (a town on the Mexican-Texas border!) was "infested with numbers of Jews whose industry spoils the trade of established merchants." Lt. Col. Arthur J. L. Fremantle, *Three Months in the Southern States: April–June 1863* (New York, 1864), 14. There is a great deal of difference between commercial success and profiteering. In fact one might almost be inclined to suppose that the "established merchants" were the real profiteers whose extortionist practices were mitigated by the "industry" of the Jews.

In Savannah, they held a public meeting, passed resolutions against the people of Thomasville who had banished Jews from their town, and urged their non-Jewish neighbors to repudiate the citizens of that place as "enemies of human liberty and freedom of conscience." [46]

In Richmond, the two congregations, Beth Ahabah and Beth Shalome, held consultations for the discussion of possible courses of action "to vindicate our character as Jews and good citizens, which has been repeatedly and grossly assailed in public prints, etc." The Board of Beth Ahabah suggested that the Jews raise a special fund to be distributed among the poor of the city, apparently in the belief that this would earn the gratitude of Richmond citizens. A meeting of Beth Shalome congregation was called to consider the project, and unanimously rejected it in the conviction that the poor were the responsibility of all denominations, not only of the Jews. The Beth Shalome members probably suspected that unilateral generosity would be regarded as an evidence of guilt, rather than of charity. In regard to the existing prejudice, they resolved: "That while this meeting denounces the unfounded aspersions made against the Israelites of this city, and feels satisfied that the acts of our co-religionists can well bear the test of comparison with those of any other denomination in this community for patriotism, charity, or freedom from selfishness; yet think the best and most dignified course to be adopted, will be to treat them with silent contempt, confident that the enlightened and unprejudiced do not join in this crusade against our people." [47]

Letters were written to the editors of newspapers,[48] and one Jew even challenged an editor to a duel. Colonel Adolphus H. Adler of

46. *Savannah Daily Morning News*, Sept. 16, 1862. One item in the resolution, condemning "all newspapers giving currency to this slander and intolerance" and asking Jews to withhold their support from such newspapers, received a justifiable rebuke from the editor of the *News*. A newspaper which printed news about such events was, in his opinion, not necessarily guilty of sharing the opinions voiced. An editor could not be held responsible for the accuracy of his statements, let alone for sentiments expressed by others. He had performed a service to the Savannah Jews, he believed, by printing the report from Thomasville.

47. Herbert T. Ezekiel and Gaston Lichtenstein, *The History of the Jews of Richmond from 1769 to 1917* (Richmond, 1917), 246–77. In 1865 the Rev. M. J. Michelbacher of Beth Ahabah was one of a number of distinguished Richmond citizens who signed a general appeal for an "adopt a soldier" plan in an effort to obtain more food for the military. Putnam, *op. cit.*, 252–55.

48. See, for example, *Richmond Sentinel*, Jan. 25, 1864 [clipping from George Jacobs Scrapbook].

the Confederate Army, a Hungarian who had served as an officer in Garibaldi's army, was so incensed at the editor of the *Richmond Examiner* for printing libelous statements about the Jews that he wanted to settle the matter with his sword. The editor is said to have made an apology in lieu of an appearance with seconds.[49] The answers of the Jews were the same as they have always been: Jews were individuals; many were fighting in the Confederate Army; some had given their lives in the conflict; Jews were as patriotic as their neighbors; blanket condemnations are unjust. These arguments would always be brought forward by a people hounded by slander.

In the Confederacy as in the Union, there were fair-minded non-Jews who were convinced that the generalized accusations were unjust, and that they were motivated by prejudice and dislike. The editor of the *Richmond Sentinel* felt that Jews, like all others, should be judged as individuals, and that the Confederacy ought to defend this principle of fair play especially at this time of crisis in the national epic. Loyal citizens should, he felt, be wary of spurning any support—no class of the population should be insulted and, perhaps, alienated, by prejudiced statements. "We consider it a duty to hail every good citizen as a brother. We ask him not where he was born or what his faith." The editor went on to question the loyalty of those who were activated by prejudice; they were espousing principles foreign to America, and though they were born in America, their identification with the nation might be judged by the Irishman's remark: "a man's being born in a stable doesn't make him a horse." [50]

49. *Israelite*, IX, No. 24, p. 188, Dec. 19, 1862. There is some doubt as to the authenticity of this report; the *Israelite* quoted no source. It might have been contained in a delayed message from the South or transmitted by a Jew coming North, but Col. Adler, so far as we know, was confined in a Richmond prison by Oct. 19, 1861, on charges of Northern sympathies, supposedly revealed by his bitter criticism of his superior officer's military talents. He attempted to commit suicide in Libby Prison but was unsuccessful. Nine months later he escaped to the North. That would be about June, 1862. He was, then, already in the North when the report appeared in the *Israelite*. Over a year later the same periodical was asking for information concerning Adler's whereabouts, since letters for him had been addressed to the editorial offices. The paper described him as "a Hungarian gentleman styling himself Colonel Adler, who was arrested in Cincinnati as an officer of the Confederate Army." Adler was indeed a soldier of fortune. William C. Harris, *Prison Life in the Tobacco Warehouse at Richmond* . . . (Philadelphia, 1862), 87, quoted in Lonn, *op. cit.*, 177–78; Moore, *op. cit.*, III, 51, citing *Richmond Enquirer*, Oct. 19, 1861; *Israelite*, X, No. 8, p. 59, Aug. 21, 1863.

50. *Richmond Sentinel*, Jan. 25, 1864 [clipping from George Jacobs' Scrapbook].

The missionary chaplain who wrote a letter of protest to the *Savannah Daily Morning News* had long wanted to reply to the complaints about Jews, he said, but his service with the military forces had consumed all his time. Now the formation by the Jews of Macon of a company for the defense of Savannah, had reactivated his interest in the question. He did not intend to be an apologist for the Jews. They needed none. But he wished it understood that he had concluded, from his own personal experience and contact with Jews, that they were "pretty largely represented" in the military, and that they made "good, enduring, hard-fighting soldiers." He had seen them in camp, in battle, on long marches, sharing all the privations and hardships of their fellows. In civilian life, he knew them to be "true patriots . . . giving as much towards supporting the Government, clothing the troops, administering comforts for the sick and wounded, &c., as any other class of citizens." [51]

An editorial in the *Augusta Sentinel*, in 1866, said that its editor had been in a position to observe Jewish conduct during the war, and that he was certain that the charges of Jewish disloyalty were "most gratuitous and unfounded slander upon that people." He gave examples of Jewish officers and soldiers who played outstanding roles in the front lines, and cited the names of young Augusta Jews who had served in the army.[52]

One of the fairest answers to the anti-Jewish libels came from the pen of the editor of the *Richmond Dispatch*. He would have no part in the campaign of propaganda against Jews. He agreed with the Rev. Michelbacher's assertion that, though Jews may have speculated in

51. *Savannah Daily Morning News*, Feb. 23, 1863, p. 1. This gentleman evidently prided himself upon his expert knowledge of Jewish religious practice. The bulk of his letter was an explanation that whole regiments of Jews could be organized if the War Department would permit them to handle their own commissary problems! If they could obtain the animals for slaughter, purchase their own utensils, and keep them ritually clean, "professional butchers of their own—educated men," would handle the rest. He asked the Macon Jews to organize the "first Israelite Battalion of the Confederate army. Let them take for the battle flag—'*The Lion of the tribe of Judah*,' and the God of Moses, Abraham, Isaac, and Jacob will fight their battles for them, and tread our enemies beneath His feet." This suggestion will be a cause for levity among those who are familiar with the consternation aroused in American Jewish circles during the early years of World War II when pro-Zionists sought to organize a Jewish Army (it was finally done, as a Jewish brigade of the British army) whose personnel would be made up of Palestinian and refugee Jews.

52. Quoted in *Occident*, XXIV, No. 6, pp. 282–83, Sept., 1866.

certain merchandise, they had not profiteered in flour, grain, or any other food products, in which category the most ruthless speculation was done. He suggested that the so-called Christians who were the leading speculators, "starving people to death by their horrible extortions in the staff of life," and who were "grieving their righteous souls over the audacity of Jews in speculating in jewels and other luxuries," should read their New Testaments somewhat more frequently. Jews were as good and as bad as non-Jews, and for every Jew who left the country with a fortune, there were many non-Jews guilty of the same thing. So far as he could tell, Jews had contributed money and support and blood to the Confederate cause in their correct proportion, and Christians had better look to the guilty in their own midst before criticising Jews. These were the opinions of a non-Jewish editor.[53]

Yet another eminently just comment on the outcry against the Jews came from the editor of the *Charleston Courier*:

We have said, and shall say, and urge our opinions against extortioners and bloodsuckers and prowling beastly bipeds of prey under whatever guise they come, but we protest earnestly and emphatically against any wholesale denunciation of Germans or Jews, or of German Jews. We have no more and no less opposition to an extortioner who happens to be a German and a Jew, than one who is an Englishman, or a Frenchman, or a Welchman, or a Yankee, and a so-called Christian. If there is such an animal as a Christian extortioner, we hate and abhor it, and would gladly exterminate it. Let the offenders and all who trouble our political Israel, and devour people, be rebuked, denounced, execrated, imprisoned, or expelled, if it can be done, but let us hear of no more abuse of a class as a class.[54]

In these impassioned phrases, the Charlestonian came to the crux of the problem, seeing clearly that it was a question of fanatical prejudice versus fair-mindedness.

Although the evidence relating to anti-Jewish propaganda in the Confederacy is less voluminous than that which has been gathered for the North, its total cumulative effect is equally damning. Continued

53. Quoted in *Jewish Record*, III, No. 23, p. 2, Feb. 26, 1864. The editor of the *Mobile Daily Advertiser and Register* (Nov. 5, 1863) had another answer: "If our fair friends will cease to patronize, instead of complain of the Jews, wear their old clothes, and give the money now spent in silks to thinly-clad and badly-shod soldiers, one source of speculation would soon dry up. . . . Try it, and dry goods will fall to rational prices within six months."

54. Quoted in *Richmond Daily Whig*, Oct. 16, 1862.

research in the periodical and journalistic literature of the Confederacy will undoubtedly uncover hosts of items which will offer further substantiation of the pattern of prejudice.

The North and the South, despite provincial and sectional loyalties and hostilities were, after all, part and parcel of the same country. The people who dwelt in Alabama were not so vastly different from those residing in Illinois or New Hampshire that they should be diametrically opposed in culture and thought patterns. This is especially true in regard to their conceptions of the Jewish people. It would actually be unaccountable if anti-Jewish prejudice had not appeared with equal virulence in both halves of the sundered nation.

The war was the key, the secret combination, which unleashed heretofore dormant prejudices. If there had been no leading public figures who were anti-Jewish, if all the Jews had been law-abiding patriots, the emotional, economic, and social frustrations of the war years would still, in all likelihood, have been directed against them. Society had to have scapegoats, in the South and in the North, for all its pent-up passion, frustration, anger, disappointment, fear, insecurity, anxiety, shame, jealousy. Lincoln was the outstanding scapegoat in the Union, while Davis occupied a similar position in the South; both suffered bitterly from the senseless slander which was directed against them. There were other scapegoats during the war, as well: Yankees who were caught in the South at the outbreak of the hostilities, German settlers in Texas, sincerely loyal Democrats in the North; but, apparently, the Jews were a more popular scapegoat in all areas than any of these.

There were no realistic causes, no justified reasons, no logical bases, for the war-time rise of prejudice—as there never have been—except the unconscious roots of hostility, transference, and anxiety which the psychiatrist uncovers, and the deliberate hate-promotion of men who hope to profit when a competitive group loses caste in the public eye. Many of the economic libels against Jews were undoubtedly set forth by men who stood to gain from the removal of Jewish business men. But for all, consciously or unconsciously, an escape-valve was necessary. General Sherman was telling more of the truth than he realized in a letter which he wrote to Grant about the smugglers, in 1862: "The great profit now made is converting everybody into rascals, and *it*

makes me ashamed of my own countrymen every time I have to ex-
amine a cotton or horse case. . . ." [55] Sherman's shame was wiped away
by imputing the major responsibility for smuggling to the Jews.

Consciously or unconsciously, citizens both North and South ab-
solved themselves of guilt and cleansed themselves of fear, and protected their anxiety, by blaming their scapegoats for all the evils of
American life and the dangers and hurts of war. A British visitor to
the Confederacy was saying this, perhaps without realizing it, when
she wrote: ". . . These extortioners were generally known to be
'Northern men with Southern sympathies' (for Southern dollars), or
German Jews. . . . No perquisites, no money-making contracts and
frauds were heard of in the South, but such as were traced to Jews or
Yankees. . . ." [56] Could she not have carried this thought to its logical
conclusion by saying: the average Southerner would have lost faith
in himself, his fellows, and his cause, were he to admit to himself that
the economic and social evils unleashed by the war were, in the final
analysis, his own responsibility; foisting the blame upon "traitorous"
Jews and Yankees saved him from the emotional agony of such realism.

If no Jews whatever had lived in the Union and Confederacy, some
other group—perhaps the Catholics, as in the recent days of Nativism—
would have served as a major escape-valve. The Jews were an insig-
nificant feature of the story. The fact that any scapegoat was necessary was an important commentary on the nature of the American
ethos in time of stress.

55. *The War of the Rebellion . . . Official Records of the Union and Confederate
Armies* (73 vols., 128 parts; Washington, 1880–1901) Ser. I, Vol. XVII, pt. II, 272–74.
56. Catherine C. Hopley [Sarah E. Jones, pseud.], *Life in the South; from The
Commencement of the War. By a Blockaded British Subject. Being a Social History
of Those who Took Part in the Battles, from a Personal Acquaintance with Them in
Their Homes. From the Spring of 1860 to August 1862* (2 vols.; London, 1863), II, 41,
188.

Section 2 Jews in the New South

From the end of the Civil War to the beginning of the First World War, the "New South" underwent enormous social and economic changes, as its residents struggled to reconstruct their lives. In the countryside farmers sought to eke out a living by planting the traditional staple crops of cotton and tobacco in their already exhausted soil. Immigrant Jewish peddlers traversed the rural areas and provided the poverty-stricken families with their basic needs. As historian Thomas D. Clark indicates, many of these peddlers became successful merchants by establishing dry goods and specialty stores in numerous southern towns. These businessmen did not create the ruinous agricultural system, but they nonetheless became identified with it in the minds of farmers because they accepted promissory notes and mortgages in lieu of cash payments. Thus the merchants gained more and more land while their customers went deeper into debt. In spite of this source of friction, Clark asserts: "It is a remarkable fact that large masses of Southerners were free of feelings of anti-Semitism."

In some areas, such as Charleston, South Carolina, long-established southerners ignored changing conditions and looked nostalgically to the golden pre–Civil War years. Jewish newcomers discovered a rigid society and they often lived in lonely isolation. Outside of the conservative enclaves, energetic southerners sought to bring industry to their region. Job opportunities in newly industrialized areas, the failure of crops, indebtedness, and the boredom of life on the farms brought thousands of southerners to growing cities like Memphis, Birmingham, and Atlanta. Harsh working conditions and squalid living accommodations blighted the promise of a bountiful life in the fledgling industrial communities. Yet rural conditions were even worse and few of the new urbanites wished to return to the farm. The strains of change and oppressive poverty led to increased numbers of lynchings and urban riots in the late nineteenth and early twentieth centuries.

From a Jewish point of view, the most outrageous injustice occurred in Atlanta, Georgia, in 1913, where growing urban tensions found some outlet in the Leo Frank case. Although economic conditions had improved since the 1890s, most of Georgia's workingmen and farmers still had inadequate incomes. Some of the impoverished malcontents blamed successful Jewish merchants and manufacturers and branded them as exploiters. Growing prejudices developed into flagrant antisemitism, especially after Leo Frank, a Jewish factory superintendent, was implicated in the horrible murder of a thirteen-year-old girl.

Life for Jews in the New South proved to be trying for many, perilous for some, and prosperous for others. The following selections indicate various features of that life.

Thomas D. Clark

The Post–Civil War
Economy in the South

THE CONFEDERATE soldier straggling home after Lee's surrender at Appomattox came home to ruin. Many Southern towns and all of the railroads were laid waste by the invading Union Army. Four years of conflict had taken a terrific toll of property and human life. More important even than this was the fact that Southern energy was depleted not only during the war but for many years to come in the future. No historian can ever estimate the price of total destruction in many parts of the South because much of this was in the form of loss of highly potential human leadership. Many a bright young Southerner went to a soldier's grave who in the years ahead might have given the South the necessary impetus to bring about changes.

Even though Southern economy was greatly disrupted and displaced it was not pushed out of the grooves of its old procedures. Unhappily the idea that cotton was king was so deeply impressed upon the Southern mind before 1860 that it became within itself a cause to be defended. Cotton was a prime commodity during the war in both domestic and foreign trade. Smugglers had slipped thousands of bales out of the region, farmers had hidden their crops from the invaders, and the United States Government held other hundreds of thousands of bales in warehouses. No one knew at the war's end how many bales of raw cotton were available. One thing, however, was clear—cotton was bringing a good price, and it seemed that Southern farmers could begin all over again devoting their attention to the production of this staple crop.

There was little actual choice for hosts of Southerners after 1865 but to become yeoman farmers. It is true, of course, that the plantation survived, but not in its old forms with its large labor force of slaves. A bigger difference was the fact that cotton farmers now had to find some way to finance production. They were faced actually with the primary challenge of making a subsistence living from the soil, but even this required some kind of a system of capitalization. Farmers had no capital, no seed, fertilizer, or equipment with which to farm. They had no organized market on which to sell their produce if they grew it.

In much of the region merchants suffered the same disaster as did their customers. They were without credit, and their store shelves stood barren of merchandise. Transportation facilities were so badly disrupted that shipment of goods was next to impossible. Goods themselves were difficult to obtain from Southern sources, thus it was necessary to turn to other sections for supplies. The booming Civil War economy had brought about the creation of great storehouses of goods in the North. There merchants and manufacturers were in search of new customers to take up the slack created by the coming of peace.

One of the most serious mercantile losses to come out of the war for the South was the disappearance of the factorage system. No longer could factors find customers who could promise to meet their obligations within a year, or ever as for that matter. No longer was this unique system of agricultural supply and credit able to survive, yet its passing created an enormous vacuum which stifled Southern agricultural economy. This old system had depended upon the plantation, slavery, and cotton. Two of these were gone.

In the factor's place there appeared the wholesale merchants in Louisville, St. Louis, Baltimore, Charleston, Cincinnati, New Orleans, and Mobile. Many of these houses were operated by Jewish merchants who had either survived the war or were quick to see the opportunity for trade on a new basis of merchandising in the post-war South. This was especially true of merchants in the Ohio and Mississippi valleys, and in Charleston. The challenge to these merchants lay not so much in the field of merchandising as in helping to devise systems of capitalization and distribution which would work in a bankrupt region. The

South was a rich potential market but it had no fluid security and no money.

No longer could wholesalers wait for customers to come to their doors. They now had to develop the trade themselves. It was necessary to send agents or "drummers" into the region to organize crossroads or furnishing stores geared to the floundering agricultural economy. These agents selected likely storekeepers, stocked their shelves with merchandise, and gave them some elementary instructions in the business of storekeeping. No one, in fact, knew much about operating the new credit system. For the most part drummers were Confederate veterans who spoke a common language from a common experience with their customers. They were highly successful both in the organization of new stores and in the sale of their employers' goods.

It is doubtful that there was ever organized anywhere on the globe a system of merchandising so thoroughly integrated with the economy of the daily lives of common everyday people as was the Southern general store. The country store was not confined solely to the South, nor to the post-war period. New Englanders were masterful storekeepers, and about their counters they developed much of the rich folklore associated with this rural trade. The general store existed everywhere. It went in lock-step across the continent with the great westward movement. It existed in mining towns, at cattle railheads, at county seats, and even in the fur trade centers. There were general stores to supply the trade wherever there were customers with money to buy merchandise. The Southern country store, however, differed from these in several aspects. First it was closely integrated with a staple crop agricultural system, its customers were dirt poor, seldom handling as much as ten dollars in cash in a year's time, the stores were centers of supply for vast lists of merchandise which ranged from Hoyt's Cologne to the coarsest sort of farm implements; they sold fertilizers, livestock, feed, fencing, and burial supplies. The merchants were postmasters, bankers, special agents for all sorts of businesses, undertakers, social correspondents, professional referees for the general local character, cotton buyers, news media, members of school boards, of church boards, and officials of the local lodges.

As cotton buyers the merchants served the much broader function enabling the staple crop agricultural system to function. On the other hand they were necessary agents of the highly speculative cotton trade. Without the furnishing merchant neither farmer nor cotton speculator could have survived. The merchant was the eyes and ears for both speculator and wholesale merchants. It was he who kept account of the conditions of crops, the growing seasons, the reliability of farmers, the validity of local integrity, and the capacity of his community to purchase a given amount of merchandise. These were truly little businessmen, but in the aggregate they were highly important.

In 1867 the General Assembly of Georgia enacted one of the first agricultural lien laws. This act was patterned after an earlier steamboat law which created a legal facility for securing and collecting debts contracted for productive purposes. Specifically the agricultural lien law permitted a moneyless and propertyless yeoman farmer to mortgage an unplanted crop for the purpose of securing supplies to sustain him in the growing season. Otherwise the little white farmer and the newly freed Negroes would have found themselves without means of supplying the meagerest subsistence while they produced a crop. In turn the lien contract permitted furnishing merchants to discount their paper to wholesale houses, and wholesale houses to banks, sometimes as far away as New York City.

By 1880 there was a furnishing or general store at almost every crossroad in the South. No village or town was without its large general stores. Back of these were many rich human stories in entrepreneurial activity. Suppliers tried to select bright young men who under other circumstances might have gone into one of the professions, but lacking funds and education the bright youths turned to storekeeping. At Dewey Rose, Georgia officials of the Louisville and Nashville Railroad Company persuaded J. T. Hewell to open a store, and when he demurred that he might go broke, he was asked if he had money. When he said, "No," the promotion agent asked, "How in hell can you go broke when you ain't got nothing?" This young Hewell had never pondered. At any rate such a philosophy evidently put the proposition in a new light, for soon a long-barreled house was serving a thriving trade as a store-cotton market and freight station.

Elsewhere plantation owners, army sutlers, adventurous ex-soldiers, Alsatian Jews and enterprising native yeoman sons opened stores. Sidney Andrews, a Northern newspaper reporter, saw Northern men coming south with their stocks of goods and letters of credit. They saw in the reconstruction South an opportunity to make their fortunes.

Many a Southern store had its beginnings in a humble peddler's pack. There was a close affinity between the peddler with all his worldly goods wrapped in a canvas bag, and the poor cotton farmers whose hopes for the future were wrapped up in a cotton lien note. The Alsatian Jew was a hero, and he has remained largely unnoted and unsung by the historians. He walked thousands of miles over dusty or muddy roads bearing on his back heavy packs of merchandise, or he bumped over impassable roads in one-horse wagons. One can only wonder what dreams or what frustrations these people had. One thing was clear they got a full concept of what the struggling South was like. Like the old Methodist circuit riders they had time in their travels to think through their problems, and no doubt to plan for future operations of stores.

The Jewish pack peddler replaced the old Yankee who had come south prior to the war selling nutmegs, clocks, tinware, and anything else that a backwoods customer could be tempted to buy. Like the Yankees, the Jews were of a humorous turn of mind. They understood the whimsical Southern rural nature and could joke with their customers. They might even have carried "budgets" of local news about with them. Unhappily many of them became the butts of rural country practical joking.

Few things brought the isolated rural family more excitement than the visitation of a pack peddler. A circle was cleared out before the fireplace, chairs and beds were pushed back, and the peddler was given a place of honor in the middle of the floor. With a flourish he undid his stout leather fastenings, and then rolled back the awning-striped cover of his pack to expose his wares. With subtlety of salesmanship he placed his bright colored cloths in the first bag to be opened. When his canvas roll was opened there came a rush of smells. Odors of sachets, cheap perfumes, soap, leather goods, and spices filled the room. It was like bringing a country store right up to the most isolated country hearth.

Jostling around the countryside, these peddlers dreamed of the day when at last they could back their wagons under the shed and turn their tired old horses out to graze. They searched for just the right spots to open stands, and when they located them, they emptied their packs onto store shelves and went into business in permanent locations.

Already the peddlers knew their trade. They had learned whom to trust and whom to watch. Old friends who had traded generously with them in their horse-and-wagon days were given advantages of lower prices and, frequently, little presents or lagniappes for old time's sake.

There is a long history of merchandising and personal relationships which remains unexplored in the location of Jewish merchants in Southern towns. Almost every town had one or more of these merchants who made modest beginnings and advanced his mercantile career as the South moved further away from the reconstruction years. Possibly a major portion of the dry goods and clothing sold in the southern small towns were sold by these merchants. A good example of such a business was that developed by David Ades in Lexington, Kentucky. He came to that town as a small merchant and developed the Lexington Dry Goods Company which sold yard goods to all of Eastern Kentucky. The smaller retailers really clothed the South either by the sale of cloth or ready-made clothing.

There was another side to this story, the local Jewish merchants in a great majority of cases became well-known citizens of the towns. They were members of the lodges, served on all sorts of boards and committees, were sources of advice, and oftentimes gave a sound leadership in the organization of banks. To a great extent they set the styles of their communities because they had the outside purchasing contacts from which they imported new goods and styles into their trade. Where stores evolved through the stages of general store to department store these merchants were to have a marked influence on the taste of their customers.

The Jewish population of the South after 1870 represented a facet in another phase of Southern history. Clearly the South needed an ingenious population if its resources were to be profitably exploited. There was deep animosity against the freed slave in some quarters, and serious doubts that he would be able to make a major contribution for a long time to come in improving regional economy. There were two sources which could supply the South with new blood: the foreign immigrant and the Yankee migrant. The Southern states joined in their efforts to attract immigrants to their region. Between 1870 and 1900 state-maintained immigration agencies produced hundreds of thousands of pamphlets, leaflets, handbooks, special reports, resource surveys, and land prospectuses. These were translated into several foreign languages and were widely distributed in countries which fed the large numbers of immigrants into the great stream flowing into North America.

The South was equally as solicitous in its attempts to attract Northerners to the region. It was felt that they would bring industry and ingenuity which would help to correct many economic failures. All sorts of seductive inducements were offered. The region offered up its rich lands, timber, and mineral resources as bait. Booklets proclaimed the virtues of Southern society, described the educational dreams of the region, boosted towns which they hoped would soon grow into cities, proclaimed cotton as king, and described the new railroads which in a short time would be in operation. Almost any sort of a promise was made to attract the flow of Northern population and capital into the South.

Generally speaking the campaigns to attract Yankees and European immigrants to the South were failures. Few European immigrants came into the region. They either failed to understand the promises of success there, or they wished to escape having to compete with the Negro. They no doubt were afraid they could not grow cotton and tobacco. In the case of the German immigrants they were rather well-informed about conditions in North America before they left home. German agents plodded through the South gathering detailed statistics, bits of economic information, notes on capital supply and industries, railroads, the nature of the towns, the position of the Negro, and southern politics. They produced ponderous reports which often compared the South unfavorably with the expanding agricultural belt in the Northwest.

Remarkably few European immigrants came to the South. A fair number of Jewish newcomers came below the Potomac. They were uninfluenced by the reports which favored agriculture. Their interests lay elsewhere, and the South offered opportunities which could not have appealed to other immigrants. Jewish farmers were fairly rare, and few engaged in businesses which brought them into competition with the Negro.

The Jewish newcomer to the South proved to be a good psychologist. He learned quickly to gauge the character of both poor whites and Negroes. Both native white and Negro may have laughed at the Jew's foreign accent, his physical appearance, and nervous mannerisms but they traded with him. Two character traits stood out: the Jewish merchants had infinite patience in dealing with simple people in small business affairs, and they were willing to bargain over prices. The Southerner, white and Negro, was a born trader.

It is a remarkable fact that large masses of Southerners were free of feelings of anti-Semitism. This was true for several reasons: they were so deeply prejudiced against Negroes and Catholics that they had little room to hate the Jews. Too, they were schooled in the Old Testament and much of their religious imagery was the same as the Jew's religious imagery. Jews were quiet and unobtrusive in the practice of their religion, and never offered competition to the rock-ribbed Protestant South. Economically the Jew seldom if ever competed directly with the Southerner in his main economic activities.

The Southern agricultural system underwent many crises before the great revolution began in 1920. Passionately Southern farmers attempted to reinstate cotton as the king of their staple crops. This, however, became less possible with the passage of years. The ruinous system of agricultural credits which had been established by the enactment of the lien laws made farmers poorer after each crop year. No agricultural system anywhere could have survived the handicaps which the Southern agrarian economy faced. Between 1870 and 1900 foreign cotton growers began to compete with those of the South. Prices dropped continuously until the late 1880s when they fell below the cost of production. Lands were exhausted by the eternal drive to meet the last year's expenses, and families were forced into a state of abject poverty or had to leave the South to make new beginnings of their lives. There were cotton farmers who, of course, succeeded in producing the staple, but they were few and far between. Cotton came to symbolize poverty for the man who grew it. Tobacco offered little more promise. In places farmers were thrown into open warfare by the drop in prices paid the producer.

Southern agriculture for almost a half century was the subject of bitter editorializing. All sorts of reformers begged for a change in agricultural procedures in the South. They assailed the cotton system, the merchants, the trusts, and the fertilizer and cotton distributors and buyers. So eloquent a critic as Henry W. Grady of the *Atlanta Constitution* published a bitter denunciation of the cotton system in 1881 in *Harper's Magazine*. M. B. Hammond of Columbia, South Carolina and Charles Otken of Mississippi upbraided the cotton system in highly intelligent books. Almost every country editor in the South scolded their subscribers for their failures to change their system of farming. Yet the South remained wedded to cotton, tobacco, sugar, and rice as staples until after 1920.

No one received more severe scoldings than did the furnishing merchants. They were charged with overpricing their goods, of selling cheap and shoddy merchandise, of charging exorbitant rates of interest, of discriminating among their customers, and generally of driving the Southern farmer into complete failure. Some of these charges in specific instances no doubt were true. The merchant, however, was caught up in the same unhappy bind as his customers. In the examination of literally hundreds of accounts this author is not convinced the discriminations were in quite the precise areas as charged by earlier critics. Staple agriculture and the lien laws were chief offenders.

An analysis of accounts made after extensive examination of general store records indicates the common failings of the lien laws and the furnishing stores. Both of these seem to involve land in their final settlement; and for most merchants, land, valued at low prices, was often the only safe security available. There was involved in land dealing, however, the exceedingly delicate question of foreclosure, and not even the hardest-hearted furnishing merchant relished the opprobrium which was likely to result from the public sale of chattel goods and land for debt. It was much simpler to secure the transfer of ownership of property in quiet private negotiations than to stand exposure to criticism by public sale. It was in this way that many furnishing merchants accumulated large tracts of land, and sometimes men who started out as merchants became larger farmers who gradually came to run their stores as adjuncts to their farming activities. Doubtless many merchants insured the future success of their stores by building up a controlled trade upon their private domains. So prevalent did the custom of giving land as security become that it was common practice in much of the South to speculate on the amount of mortgage every man had on his farm and as to the probable date on which he would have either to secure an abundance of providential assistance or be foreclosed.

Some merchants made money from their stores. Some of them were able to accumulate a considerable amount of cash savings. Others accumulated little money, but came to own large holdings of land. Most of them were able to build comparatively good homes, but it is doubtful that many of them grew rich in the business. When the boll weevil reduced the cotton crop, and when competition of cash stores developed an expansion of industry, the old line furnishing business went into eclipse in the South. Its end came only after merchants had committed countless sins against real Southern agricultural progress, and had been properly criticised for it in the newspaper and periodical press, and even in books. But the question remains, what part did the furnishing merchant play? Actually he was never an originator of anything. He was the most direct means by which the lien laws were made to work as a source of credit and banking for his community. His safe bulged with thousands of liens and mortgages. His store was both a source of supply and a market facility. He facilitated the one-crop system of agriculture, and as a special agent for the fertilizer companies he sold guano in April to be paid for at high November prices plus an exorbitant profit and interest charge. Also, he helped to channelize an enormous amount of extra-regional capital into the South.

There were Jewish country merchants who succeeded in the general merchandising business. At Lorman, Mississippi, the Cohn brothers developed an enormous rural trade, and their store became a rather highly specialized departmental business ranging from the sale of dry goods to the sale of farm implements, wagons, and carriages. Scattered over the South were other stores operated by merchants who had immigrated to the South. The major merchandising role of the Jewish businessman, however, was in the establishment of small town specialty stores, and in the organization of the large wholesale houses in the central towns which recovered from the losses of the Civil War. There is not a Southern city whose main business streets are not lined with department stores and wholesale houses which grew out of this era. Contrary to popular notion the Jewish merchant found the South almost as good a base of operation as the East.

The reputation of Bernard Baruch of Charleston, South Carolina, is too well known to be repeated here, but it was in the New South that this famous American first found his bearings. Two Jewish lads of Southern origin personify to a high degree the success of men who were cast in the hard years of Southern reconstruction. These were Samuel S. Fels who was born in the isolated backwoods community of Yanceyville, North Carolina. There in a great rambling general merchandising house he got his first taste of business. Perhaps the old store still stands unless progress or the ravages of time have not destroyed it. This imaginative young merchant moved away to Philadelphia to develop the Fels-Naphtha business which was of national importance. He was founder and benefactor of the Samuel S. Fels Fund, a non-profit philanthropic foundation established in 1935.

One of the most exciting personal histories of any Southerner was that of Adolph S. Ochs. Ochs was the son of German immigrants who came to America in the great rush of 1848. In 1877 this young man moved from Knoxville to Chattanooga to begin his newspaper career. He had worked in the *Knoxville Chronicle* office, and now at nineteen he was setting forth on an independent career. Out of his partnership with Franc M. Paul in ownership of the Chattanooga *Daily Dispatch* grew the Chattanooga *Times*, and subsequently the ownership of the New York *Times*. In 1880 Adolph Ochs brought his parents to Chattanooga where Julius Ochs became the first real lay Rabbi in that city. In time the influence of Ochs's Southern *Times* was to play a major role in helping to develop the South in the post–Civil War years.

The immigrant Jewish newcomer and the New South largely grew up together. The history of the people and of the region are inseparably linked. It would be impossible to consider Southern economic and social history with any degree of thoroughness without also considering the history of the Southern Jewish people.

Leonard Dinnerstein

Atlanta in the Progressive Era: A Dreyfus Affair in Georgia

FRUSTRATION and disillusionment with the rapid social changes caused by the industrial transformation at the end of the nineteenth century set off racial attacks in the United States and Europe. Alfred Dreyfus, Mendel Beiliss, the Haymarket anarchists, and Sacco and Vanzetti were all aliens victimized by societies undergoing rapid conversion. Jews, Italians, Germans, immigrants, anyone, in fact who deviated from the ethnic norm easily served as a scapegoat for the turmoil accompanying industrialism. Barbara Tuchman attributed anti-semitism in France to "building tensions between classes and among nations. Industrialization, imperialism, the growth of cities, the decline of the countryside, the power of money and the power of machines . . . churning like the bowels of a volcano about to erupt." To a considerable extent, many of these same forces—in greater or lesser degree—also applied in Kiev, Chicago, and Boston. In Russia, Maurice Samuel tells us, "the Beiliss case was mounted by men who hoped by means of it to strengthen the autocracy and to crush the liberal spirit that was reviving after the defeat of the 1905 revolution." In Chicago, fear of foreigners, social revolution, and labor ascendancy triggered the vigilante response to eight immigrant anarchists charged with the bomb-throwing incident in Haymarket Square. "A biased jury, a prejudiced judge, perjured evidence, extraordinary and indefensible theory of conspiracy, and the temper of Chicago led to the conviction. The evidence never proved the guilt." Sacco and Vanzetti, atheists, labor agitators, and "Reds" of Italian birth, were convicted of robbery and murder in Dedham, Massachusetts in 1920. The case made by the prosecution led many observers to believe in the innocence of the defendants, but the jury foreman allegedly concluded, "Damn them, they ought to hang anyway." [1]

Social bias played a crucial role in obtaining the convictions described above. The industrial transformation of society uprooted too many too quickly, and made those caught up in the whirlpool of change cling all the more tightly to their old ways. Situations that might have been tolerated or handled differently in more stable societies seemed like conspiratorial attempts to undermine civilization. Dreyfus, Beiliss, the Haymarket anarchists, and Sacco and Vanzetti symbolized unwelcome innovations. So, too, did Leo Frank, a Jew upon whom Atlantans would vent their unveiled, nervous tensions in 1913.

I

Atlanta was not spared the problems that industrialism brought to other cities. Indeed the traditions of southern culture intensified the burden of social change. Typical of most American cities during the Progressive era, Atlanta's population practically doubled between 1900 and 1913 (89,870 to 173,713). The population in other urban areas in the United States also increased at an impressive rate during the first decade of the twentieth century. In the South, though, of cities with populations over 100,000, only Birmingham outpaced Atlanta's population spurt between 1900 and 1910.[2] Newly established industrial en-

1. Barbara Tuchman, *The Proud Tower* (New York: Macmillan, 1966), 182; Maurice Samuel, *Blood Accusation* (New York: Alfred A. Knopf, 1966), 7; Henry David, *The History of the Haymarket Affair* (New York: Russell & Russell, 1936), 528, 535, 541; Louis Joughin and Edmund M. Morgan, *The Legacy of Sacco and Vanzetti* (Chicago: Quadrangle Books, 1964), 201–203.

2. A partial listing of growing American cities, and their population figures for 1900 and 1910, follows:

		Population	
State	City	*1900*	*1910*
Alabama	Birmingham	38,415	132,685
California	Los Angeles	102,479	319,198
	San Francisco	342,782	416,912
Colorado	Denver	133,859	213,381
Florida	Tampa	15,839	37,782
	Miami	1,681	5,471
Georgia	Atlanta	89,872	154,839

terprises offered jobs to all comers. Although urban conditions were better than rural squalor, the city fell far short of the industrialists' promise of the good life. Large groups of recently displaced Georgia crackers mingled uneasily with each other and with the foreign immigrants who wore strange costumes and spoke unintelligible tongues. In the concrete jungle, the newcomers worked together in the most menial jobs and congregated in the least desirable housing. Although foreigners comprised less than 3 percent of the city's residents,[3] the few Europeans loomed as a great menace to those many Southern-

		Population	
State	*City*	*1900*	*1910*
Illinois	Chicago	1,689,575	2,185,283
Indiana	Indianapolis	169,164	233,650
Kansas	Kansas City	51,418	82,331
Louisiana	New Orleans	287,104	339,075
Massachusetts	Boston	560,892	670,585
Michigan	Detroit	285,704	465,766
Minnesota	Minneapolis	202,718	301,408
Mississippi	Jackson	7,816	21,262
Missouri	Kansas City	163,752	248,381
Nevada	Reno	4,500	10,867
New Jersey	Newark	246,070	347,469
New Mexico	Albuquerque	6,238	11,020
New York	Buffalo	352,387	423,715
	New York	3,437,202	4,766,883
North Carolina	Charlotte	18,091	34,014
Ohio	Cleveland	381,768	560,663
	Youngstown	44,885	79,066
Oklahoma	Oklahoma City	32,452	64,205
	Tulsa	7,298	18,182
Oregon	Portland	90,426	207,214
South Dakota	Aberdeen	4,087	10,753
Tennessee	Memphis	102,320	131,105
	Nashville	80,865	110,364
Texas	Dallas	42,638	92,104
	Fort Worth	26,688	73,312
	San Antonio	53,321	96,614
Utah	Salt Lake City	53,531	92,777
Virginia	Norfolk	46,624	67,452
	Richmond	85,050	127,628
Washington	Seattle	80,671	237,195
	Tacoma	37,714	83,743
West Virginia	Charleston	11,099	22,966

Source: *Abstract of the Thirteenth Census of the United States, 1910,* pp. 65–75, *passim.*

3. *Atlanta Constitution,* Jan. 18, 1915, pp. 1, 2, cited hereinafter as *AC.*

ers who retained strong feelings about racial purity and community homogeneity.

Working conditions in Atlanta compared unfavorably with those in other parts of the country.[4] Despite a periodic shortage of workers, factory wages were low and hours long. The normal work week lasted sixty-six hours, and, except for Saturday, the working day generally extended from 6 A.M. to 6 P.M. with only a half hour for lunch.[5] In 1902, the average wage-earner took home less than $300 a year. Atlanta's Commissioner of Public Works commented that the prevailing wages did not enable the men in his department to provide even the minimum necessities for their families.[6] By 1912, when average earnings rose to $464[7] living costs had increased correspondingly and Atlanta's relief warden reported a record number of public assistance applications. "Even where women and children worked," he observed, "the money they receive is not enough for their support." There are too many people on the ragged edge of poverty and suffering," the warden concluded.[8] A year later, some children still earned 22 cents a week for their labor in the city.[9]

4. The cost of living in 1913 was the second highest in the nation (Boston was first), and wages lagged behind those paid in northern cities. *Atlanta Journal*, Sept. 17, 1913, p. 1, hereinafter cited as *AJ*. See also W. J. Cash, *The Mind of the South* (New York: Alfred A. Knopf, 1941), 247. C. Vann Woodward reported that in 1912 and 1913 hourly earnings in New England averaged 37 percent above those in the South, *Origins of the New South* (Baton Rouge: Louisiana State University Press, 1951), 420-21.

5. United States, *Report of the Industrial Commission*, 1901, VII, 56, 57. A few years later the U.S. Senate's *Report on Conditions of Woman and Child Wage-Earners in the United States*, 61st Cong., 2nd Sess., 1910, *Senate Document*, no. 645, Serial no. 5685, I, 261, noted that the average work week in Georgia cotton mills in 1908 was 64 hours, which was longer than that in Virginia, North Carolina, South Carolina, Alabama, and Mississippi. Of the thirty-one establishments the Commission investigated, sixteen had a sixty-six hour week; forty minutes was the average lunch time.

6. *Annual Reports of the Committees of Council, Officers and Departments of the City of Atlanta*, 1902-1903, pp. 96, 192. During the period 1900-1914, the average hourly wage in the United States was 20-21 cents an hour. For a sixty-hour week this would be about $12. The average annual earnings in manufacturing for the following years indicated: 1907, $522; 1908, $475; and two different estimates for 1909, $518 and $557. John R. Commons and Associates, *History of Labor in the United States*, 1896-1932 (New York: The Macmillan Co., 1935), 59-61.

7. Atlanta, *Comptroller's Report for 1913*, p. 57.

8. Quoted in *Journal of Labor*, November 7, 1913, p. 4.

9. "Dixie Conditions Stir Unionists—Description of Actual State of Atlanta Textile Workers Make Delegates Weep," *Textile Worker*, III (December, 1914), 21.

Atlanta's unplanned growth plagued officials and created problems similar to those in other cities at the time. Health hazards abounded, educational facilities were found wanting, and recreational outlets could not increase fast enough to service the burgeoning population. As late as 1912, for example, Atlanta provided no public swimming pools or parks for its Negro citizens. An overabundance of gambling dens, dope dives, and brothels, on the other hand, beckoned both whites and Negroes who sought to escape from factory drudgery and dingy tenements. On a number of occasions, in fact, the Mayor of Atlanta, James G. Woodward, "disgraced the city . . . by public drunkenness." His private conduct, however, proved no political liability. Woodward received a third renomination after being "found in a state of intoxication in the red light district of the city." [10]

Living conditions were no better than public facilities. In 1910, there were only 30,308 dwelling units for 35,813 families. Eighty-two miles, or more than half of the city's residential streets, existed without water mains and more than 50,000 people—over a third of the population—were forced to live in areas of the city not served by sewers. A continuous fog of soot and smoke irritated people's lungs and eyes, and an appalling number of urban dwellers suffered from ill health. Ninety percent of the city's prisoners in 1902 were syphilitic.[11] Wherever records were kept, the statistics indicated that the problems grew worse during the next decade, rather than better. A comparison of the number of residents afflicted by disease in 1904 and 1911, when the city's population had increased by only 64 percent, showed the following:

10. *AC*, March 4, 1907, p. 3; June 4, 1913, p. 2. Franklin M. Garrett, *Atlanta and Environs* (3 vols.; New York, 1954), II, 574; "Decency As An Issue," *Outlook*, 90 (December 19, 1908), 848; "An Advertising Campaign Against Segregated Vice," *The American City*, IX (July, 1913), 3, 4; *Annual Report of the Park Commissioner of the City of Atlanta for the Year Ending December 31, 1910*, p. 20. *Report . . . for the Year Ending December 31, 1913*, p. 32.

11. Atlanta Chamber of Commerce, *Annual Report for 1909*, p. 5; U.S. Bureau of the Census, *General Statistics of Cities: 1909*, pp. 88, 148; Atlanta, *Comptroller's Report for 1911*, p. 41; Atlanta, *Annual Reports*, 1902–1903, pp. 100–101; Herbert R. Sands, *Organization and Administration of the City Government of Atlanta, Georgia* (New York: New York Bureau of Municipal Research, November, 1912), 62.

Table I [12]

	1904	1911	% Increase
Diphtheria	114	396	347
Typhoid Fever	85	315	307
Tuberculosis	37	223	602

Atlanta also suffered an above average death rate. A United States census report for 1905 noted that of 388 cities in this country, only twelve had more deaths per thousand persons than Georgia's capital. In 1911, Atlanta's figures still exceeded the national average by almost 40 percent (13.9 to 18.75 per thousand). A year earlier, sixty-nine people had died from pellagra, a vitamin deficiency prevalent among the poor. This was more than triple the figure for any other city in the country. Birmingham and Charleston, S.C., the two cities that ranked second to the Georgian metropolis, reported only seventeen deaths from the illness in 1910. The situation did not improve much in succeeding years. In 1914 the United Textile Workers complained that far too many Atlanta children still fell victim to the disease. Although exact statistics for all ailments are difficult to obtain, industrialism provided its share of fatal illness. One Georgian official reported in 1912, "occupational diseases are much more common than is believed true. Lead, arsenic and phosphorous poisoning has caused much suffering and many deaths." [13]

The crime rate in Atlanta highlighted the stresses of the new urbanites. In 1905, Atlanta policemen arrested more children for disturbing the peace than did those in any other municipality in the United States. Two years later, only New York, Chicago, and Baltimore, cities with considerably larger populations, exceeded Atlanta's figure

12. *AC*, January 18, 1915, p. 1; U.S. Bureau of the Census, *Statistics of Cities Having a Population of Over 30,000: 1905*, p. 111. Atlanta's population in 1904 was 98,776; in 1911 it was 161,515; Atlanta, *Comptroller's Report*, 911, p. 19.
13. *Ibid.*, 20; *Annual Report of the Atlanta Chamber of Commerce*, 1909, p. 5; U.S. Bureau of the Census, *Historical Statistics of the United States: Colonial Times to 1957*, p. 27; U.S. Bureau of the Census, Bulletin, no. 109, *Mortality Statistics*, 1910, p. 31; "Dixie Conditions Stir Unionists . . . ," *The Textile Worker*, III, 21; *Preliminary Report of the Commissioner of Commerce and Labor, State of Georgia, for the Term Ending June 11, 1912*, p. 7.

for children arrested. That very year, the police booked 17,000 persons out of a total population of 102,702. The Mayor found the statistic "appalling." "It places Atlanta," he said, "at or near the top of the list of cities of this country in criminal statistics." [14]

The police force, another city institution overwhelmed by the population spurt, proved unable to grapple with the new problems thrust upon it. The major reasons for its incapacity were inadequate staffing and facilities. In 1912, the Mayor acknowledged that two hundred men were unable to protect the city, "and, as a result, the residential sections cannot be effectively policed." Atlanta, alone among American cities whose area exceeded twenty-five square miles, existed with only one police station and no substations.[15]

Besides the pathological conditions that menaced the growing city, the southern heritage also conditioned the Crackers'[16] reaction to the enormous differences in urban living. Of all the sections in the country, none has been so tied to the past as has the South. W. J. Cash characterized this southern revulsion to change as "the savage ideal— the patriotic will to hold rigidly to the ancient pattern, to repudiate innovation, in thought and behavior, whatever came from outside and was felt as belonging to Yankeedom or alien parts." [17]

The race riot that erupted in Atlanta in 1906 was an example of the periodic explosions of violence that occurred when transplanted rural dwellers rebelled against the drudgery and disruptiveness of their new urban existence. Rampaging white mobs attacked Negroes with abandon. Before the National Guard successfully quelled the rioters several days later, twelve people had been killed (two white and ten Negro) and seventy had been injured (ten white and sixty Negro).

14. U.S. Bureau of the Census, *Statistics of Cities Having a Population of Over 30,000: 1905*, p. 111; U.S. Bureau of the Census, *Statistics of Cities Having a Population of Over 30,000: 1907*, pp. 102, 107, 410; Inaugural Address of Mayor James G. Woodward, *Annual Report of Atlanta for 1905*, p. 27.

15. *Comptroller's Report*, 1911, p. 43; *Annual Report*, 1902–1903, p. 302; Sands, *Organization and Administration*, 36.

16. The term "cracker" connoted isolated, ignorant, backward frontiersman. Bevode C. McCall, "Georgia Town and Cracker Culture" (Ph.D. dissertation, University of Chicago, 1954), 105–106.

17. Cash, *Mind of the South*, 327. See also Stewart G. Cole, *The History of Fundamentalism* (New York: R. R. Smith Inc., 1931), 26; Josephine Pinckney, "Bulwarks Against Change," in *Culture in the South*, ed. W. T. Couch (Chapel Hill: University of North Carolina Press, 1935), 41.

The riot had been incited by sensational newspaper reports exaggerating Negro assaults upon white women. These incendiary statements were published a few weeks after Hoke Smith had whipped up popular passions in his racist campaign for the gubernatorial nomination. Subsequent explanations blamed the newspapers for the outburst, but the press could not be held responsible for the poverty and squalor of the new urban masses. One "educated negro" shrewdly noted that recently arrived rural whites resented the relative prosperity of Negro business people in the city. A national reporter spoke more bluntly in calling Atlanta "one of the very worst of American cities" filled with the "riff-raff that the mining towns of the West used to relieve us of." [18] In either case, the exacerbated race relations in Atlanta focused national attention upon the city. The upheaval was obviously an admission that discontent with city life had become unbearable for the erstwhile rural folk.[19]

The conservative nature of the dominant religious groups in the South compounded the difficulties of adjustment to urban life. No secular influence of any kind, C. Vann Woodward has attested, had the power to sway men's thoughts with as much vigor as did those who allegedly spoke with the authority of God.[20] Baptists and Methodists, the two largest denominations in the South since colonial times, have, for the most part, preached a Fundamentalist creed that opposed change, glorified the past, and uttered invectives against aliens of any stripe. During the nineteenth century, these sects "became centers of conservative political sentiment and of resistance both to the invasion of northern culture and to the doctrine of the New South." Their allegiance to the past and fundamental theological beliefs continued well into the twentieth century.[21]

The great bedrock of Fundamentalist support came from the rural

18. "Facts About the Atlanta Murders," *World's Work*, XIII (November, 1906), 8147.

19. Glen Weddington Rainey, "The Race Riot of 1906 in Atlanta" (M.A. thesis, Emory University, 1929), no pagination; Ray Stannard Baker, "Following the Color Line," *American Magazine*, LXIII (April, 1907), 569; Anon., "The Atlanta Massacre," *Independent*, 91 (October 4, 1906), 799–800.

20. Woodward, *Origins*, 448.

21. Joseph H. Fichter and George L. Maddox, "Religion in the South, Old and New," in *The South in Continuity and Change*, ed. John M. McKinney and Edgar T. Thompson (Durham: Duke University Press, 1965), 360, 364.

population. When these people moved into the towns and cities, they brought their ministers along with them. Many of the Fundamentalist preachers, who had earlier railed against urban wickedness, "continued to regard the great city centers as 'jungle areas' no less pagan than the Congo, and looked upon themselves as life-saving missionaries." [22] Southern ministers also eyed the new industrialists with great suspicion. Among Methodists, both "pulpit and press inveighed against corporate wealth for denying labor a living wage," [23] while Baptist objections "to industrialization arose from the fear that industry would lead to rapid urbanization which in turn would corrupt the morals of the people and hinder the spread of Christianity." [24]

The Fundamentalists stressed the godliness of maintaining the homely virtues and living a simple, agricultural life. They also believed in a literal obedience of God's word. In fact, they considered adherence to scriptural instruction as man's most sacred duty. Their preachers continually railed against modern innovations and warned parishioners that dancing, card-playing and theater-going undermined Christian teaching. The Fundamentalists also abhorred the alteration of woman's traditional role. She belonged in the home, they believed, and any changes in her position must invariably lead to a loosening of Christian morality.

The Fundamentalists hoped to stem the floodtide of progress by condemning social change as blasphemy against God's revealed word. This resistance, although unsuccessful, complicated and delayed adjustments to modern times. Anyone and anything that violated their own literal interpretation of the Bible became subject to assault. Violence frequently accompanied accusations. The self-righteous crusade to restore the simple, godly life often justified the use of weapons against those who dissented.

Southern Baptists also considered the influx of immigrants one of the great dangers of modern times. During the 1880s, southern Baptist periodicals expressed concern with the foreigners whom they

22. Carroll Edwin Harrington, "The Fundamentalist Movement in America, 1870–1920" (Ph.D. dissertation, University of California at Berkeley, 1959), 102.
23. Hunter Dickinson Farish, *The Circuit Rider Dismounts* (Richmond: The Dietz Press, 1938), 333–34.
24. Rufus B. Spain, "Attitudes and Reactions of Southern Baptists to Certain Problems of Society, 1865–1900" (Ph.D. dissertation, Vanderbilt University, 1961), 229.

regarded as "a threat to American customs and traditions." Many Baptist editors attributed the moral corruption of the nation to the newcomers and felt that national good demanded a cessation of our traditional open-door policy. One spokesman enunciated his anxieties at the Southern Baptist Convention in 1895: "Foreigners are accumulating in our cities, and hence our cities are the storm centers of the nation. But the great misfortunes of all of this is that these foreigners bring along with them their anarchy, their Romanism, and their want of morals." [25]

In his analysis of southern mores, W. J. Cash perceptively summarized the Fundamentalists' demands. They wanted "absolute conformity to the ancient pattern under the pains and penalties of the most rigid intolerance; the maintenance of the savage ideal, to the end of vindicating the old Southern will to cling fast to its historical way." [26]

Despite the pervasive influence of the Fundamentalist creeds and the inherent southern hostility toward innovation, the leaders of the new South—the railroad magnates and the owners of cotton mills and factories—endeavored to build an industrial community patterned after the North. To a considerable extent they succeeded and "by 1900 the industrialization of the South had become largely a case of capital seeking labor supply." Atlanta's *Journal* succinctly expressed the prevailing need: "The Southern States have reached a point in their industrial progress where the work necessary . . . can not be done by the present force of workers. . . . The South needs more folks—folks for the farm, folks for the factory." In Georgia, for example, it was said that without immigrant labor, the development of the iron and cotton mills and the building of the railroads would have to be halted.[27]

25. *Ibid.*, 230; Carl Dean English, "The Ethical Emphases of the Editors of Baptist Journals Published in the Southeastern Region of the United States, 1865–1915" (Th.D. dissertation, Southern Baptist Theological Seminary, 1948), 187.

26. Cash, *Mind of the South*, 347. The major sources of my commentaries on fundamentalism have been Norman F. Furniss, *The Fundamentalist Controversy, 1918–1931* (New Haven: Yale University Press, 1954), 35–44; Harrington, *Fundamentalist Movement*, vi–vii; Cash, *Mind of the South*, 341; Cole, *Fundamentalism*, 53, 322; and H. Richard Niebuhr, "Fundamentalism" in the *Encyclopaedia of the Social Sciences*, ed. Edwin R. A. Seligman (15 vols.; New York: The Macmillan Co., 1931), VI, 526–27.

27. Rupert B. Vance, *Human Geography of the South* (Chapel Hill: University of North Carolina Press, 1932), 279; *AJ*, December 23, 1906, as cited in *Congressional Record*, 59th Cong., 2nd Sess., 3018; Rowland T. Berthoff, "Southern Attitudes Toward Immigration," *Journal of Southern History*, XVII (August, 1951), 329.

The desperate plight of industry forced southern state governments to establish immigration bureaus in the hope of attracting suitable laborers. But most southerners were quite specific as to whom they would welcome. Senator Ben Tillman of South Carolina announced "We do not want European paupers to come to the South." Tennessee's Governor Ben Hooper expressed his opposition to receiving the "motley mass of humanity that is being dumped upon our shores. . . ." And Georgia's Federation of Labor "objected to 'flooding' the South and Georgia with a population composed of the scum of Europe. . . ." Atlanta's two major newspapers stated their preferences clearly. The *Journal* desired persons of Teutonic, Celtic, and Scandinavian origins, "peoples near akin to [our] own by blood, and capable of full assimilation. . . ." And *The Constitution* editorialized, "The German makes a splendid citizen." [28]

Unfortunately for both the South and the arriving immigrants, most of the newcomers were from eastern and southern Europe. They were treated, for the most part, with conspicuous inhospitality. In some sections, Italians, or " 'dagoes' were regarded as about on a par with 'niggers', and the treatment of them corresponded." [29] In 1891, eleven Italians were lynched in New Orleans after three of them had been acquitted of murdering the police chief. Five years later, three Italians suspected of homicide were strung up in Hahnville, Louisiana. In 1899, five Italians were lynched in Tallulah, Louisiana, after injuring a doctor in a quarrel over a goat. The twentieth century had hardly begun when three more Italians were mysteriously shot in Erwin, Mississippi. Czechs and Slovaks established a colony south of Petersburg, Virginia, in the nineteenth century, yet forty years after their arrival, the "natives" still resented their presence.[30]

In Atlanta, the single largest influx of immigrants was 1,342 Russian

28. *Congressional Record*, December 15, 1907, p. 3031; Berthoff, "Attitudes," XVII, 329; "Amendment of Immigration Laws," *Senate Document*, no. 251, 62nd Cong., 2nd Sess., 1912, Serial no. 6174, p. 5; *AJ*, December 23, 1906, December 30, 1906, as cited in *Congressional Record*, 59th Cong., 2nd Sess., 3018–19; *AC*, March 13, 1914, p. 4.

29. "Southern Peonage and Immigration," *Nation*, LXXXV (December 19, 1907), 557.

30. Berthoff, "Attitudes," XVII, 344.

Jews who comprised 25 percent of the city's foreign-born in 1910.[31] Although this group made up less than 1 per cent of the population, it was well-known that they ran a large percentage of the saloons, pawnshops, and restaurants catering to Negro trade. The Jews were viewed contemptuously by other whites. One reporter wrote, "as to the white foreigners who cater to negro [sic] trade and negro [sic] vice . . . it is left to the judgment of the reader which is of the higher grade in the social scale, the proprietors or their customers." Sensual pictures of nude white women allegedly decorated the walls of the saloons, and some people even thought that the liquor bottle labels aroused the Negroes' worst passions. Many Atlantans thought that the beer parlors "served as the gathering and hatching place of criminal negroes." When the patrons got drunk and caused social disturbances, the nearby whites blamed the saloon owners for the mischief. One analyst of the 1906 riot, for example, observed, "It was the low dives where mean whiskey was sold to Negroes by whites that bred the criminality which furnished an excuse for the outbreak of the mob; and it was from the doors of the saloon that the ruffians of the mob poured forth to do their deadly work on the innocent." [32]

Although Jews had been in the South since colonial times, they had never been accepted by the dominant Protestant community. To be sure, opportunities to assimilate existed, but those who desired to retain their faith suffered restrictions upon their political and religious liberties. Denial of the trinity, for example, had subjected Jews to imprisonment in Virginia and Maryland in the colonial era. Therefore, Jews did not settle in Maryland until after the American Revolution. Virginia, on the other hand, did not permit Jews to enter the colony without express permission. Georgia granted Jews political and religious equality in 1798, but not until 1826 were Jews allowed to vote in Maryland. Although John Locke's original Constitution for the Carolinas provided for toleration, both North and South Carolina deprived Jews

31. Solomon Sutker, "The Jews of Atlanta: Their Social Structure and Leadership Patterns" (Ph.D. dissertation, University of North Carolina, 1950), 74; *AC*, January 18, 1915, p. 1.
32. Thomas Gibson, "The Anti-Negro Riots in Atlanta," *Harper's Weekly*, L (October 13, 1906), 1457–58; "Results in Atlanta," *Independent*, LXII (January 3, 1907), 52; Rainey, *Race Riot*, Chap. 3; *Baltimore Morning Sun*, November 23, 1914, p. 3.

of their political rights. A South Carolina law of 1759 barred non-Protestants from holding office and the North Carolina Constitution of 1776 forbade them to vote. A Jew elected to the North Carolina Legislature in 1809 was challenged, upon taking his seat, but defended himself successfully. A Constitutional Convention, however, banned all Jews from holding office in the Tar Heel State in 1835, and the restriction remained in effect until 1868. In 1818, in a letter to the Jewish editor of a New York City newspaper, Thomas Jefferson acknowledged "the prejudice still scowling on your sect of our religion. . . ." [33]

Despite restrictions on office holding, concerted anti-Jewish prejudice did not occur in the South until the Civil War era. During this period, however, Jews did become scapegoats for Confederate frustrations. They were accused of being "merciless speculators, army slackers, and blockade-runners across the land frontiers to the North." One southern newspaper observed, "all that the Jew possesses is a plentiful lot of money together with the scorn of the world." [34]

Some Georgia towns specifically singled out the Jews as the cause of their woes. In 1862, 103 citizens of Thomasville resolved to banish all Jewish residents and a grand jury in Talbotton found the Jews guilty of " 'evil and unpatriotic conduct.' " Talbotton prejudices, in fact, forced the Lazarus Straus family—later to become famous for its de-

33. Miriam Kotler Freund, "Jewish Merchants in Colonial America" (Ph.D. dissertation, New York University, 1936), 96; Merle Curti, The Growth of American Thought (New York: Harper & Brothers, 1943), 51; Anson Phelps Stokes, Church and State in the United States (3 vols.; New York: Harper & Brothers, 1950), I, 854, 857; Jacob Rader Marcus, Early American Jewry: The Jews of Pennsylvania and the South, 1655–1790 (Philadelphia: Jewish Publication Society of America, 1953), 167, 228, 231, 333; Paul Masserman and Max Baker, The Jews Come to America (New York: Black Publishing Co., 1932), 88; Peter Wiernik, History of the Jews in America (New York: Jewish Publication Society of America, 1931), 127; Joseph L. Blau and Salo W. Baron (eds.), The Jews of the United States, 1790–1840 (3 vols.; New York: Columbia University Press, 1963), I, 17; Clement Eaton, Freedom of Thought in the Old South (New York: Peter Smith, 1951), 27; Thomas Jefferson to a New York Jewish editor, quoted in "Legislature of Maryland," Niles' Register, XV, Supplement (1819), 10. Although voting and office holding were generally restricted to Protestants in all of the American colonies, the restrictions upon Jews tended to last longer in some of the southern states. See, for example, Jacob Rader Marcus, Early American Jewry: The Jews of New York, New England and Canada, 1649–1794 (Philadelphia: Jewish Publication Society of America, 1951), 103, 116.

34. Eaton, Old South, 233; E. Merton Coulter, The Confederate States of America (Baton Rouge: Louisiana State University Press, 1950), 226; Rudolf Glanz, The Jew in the Old American Folklore (New York: Waldon Press, 1961), 54.

velopment of Macy's department store in New York City—to leave Georgia during the Civil War.[35]

The next major anti-Semitic eruption occurred in the 1890s. The Populist crusade, the severe economic depression of 1893, and the squalid living conditions in urban slums all helped to intensify hostility toward those who loomed, on the one hand, as the seeming monopolizers of material possessions, and on the other, as the manipulators who unfeelingly deprived the people of their purchasing power. In Georgia, for example, it was "quite the fashion to characterize the Jew as exacting his interest down to the last drachma." [36]

Accusations of financial manipulation gave rise to suspicion of a vast Jewish international conspiracy. One writer, in fact, concluded that the "Rothschild combination has proceeded in the last twenty years with marvellous rapidity to enslave the human race." In North Carolina, Elias Carr, Governor from 1893 to 1897, frequently reiterated his point that "Our Negro brethren, too, are being held in bondage by Rothschild." [37]

When rural southerners flocked to the cities at the end of the nineteenth century, their impressions of the Jew combined traditional stereotypes of financial wiliness with the time-worn southern prejudices. In 1906, Horace M. Kallen, the Jewish philosopher, observed that "there is already a very pretty Jewish problem in our South. . . ." William Robertson, author of *The Changing South*, later noted, "It was enough for Jews to prosper right under [southern] noses, without affording the added insult of being the descendants of the murderers of Christ." [38]

A lack of scholarly studies makes it risky to generalize about anti-semitism in the South or to suggest regional differences. The two most prominent historians who have investigated American attitudes towards

35. Rufus Learsi, *The Jews in America: A History* (Cleveland: The World Publishing Co., 1954), 103; Margaret Case Harriman, *And the Price is Right* (Cleveland: The World Publishing Co., 1958), 34.

36. Lucian Lamar Knight, *Reminiscences of Famous Georgians* (2 vols.; Atlanta: Franklin Turner Co., 1907), I, 512.

37. William M. Stewart, "The Great Slave Power," *Arena*, XIX (May, 1890), 580; Carr quoted in Harry Golden, *A Little Girl is Dead* (Cleveland: The World Publishing Co., 1965), 226.

38. Horace M. Kallen, "The Ethics of Zionism," *Maccabean*, XI (August, 1906), 69; William J. Robertson, *The Changing South* (New York: Boni and Liveright, 1927), 99.

Jews in the nineteenth and twentieth centuries—Oscar Handlin and John Higham—have found evidence supporting positive and negative judgments.[39] Both historians, however, dealt primarily with northern experiences and provided relatively few examples from southern states. Studies about alleged Populist antisemitism, moreover, have concentrated almost entirely on the expressions of northern and western agrarians.[40] There are no indications, for example, that Tom Watson, the Georgia leader, engaged in any antisemitic diatribes in his Populist heyday.

A significant clue to southern attitudes may be garnered, however, from Higham's findings. He noted that American antisemitism was deeply ingrained in the agrarian tradition—which was suspect of urban prosperity based upon the toil of others—and cropped up most frequently in times of crisis. "The prophets of anti-Semitism," Higham continued, "were alienated and often despairing critics of the power of money in American society," and frequently attributed their own woes to the "lords of finance and trade": banks, moneylenders, and bondholders. He discovered, moreover, that hostility toward Jews in this country was strongest in those sectors of the population where there were relatively few Jews and where "a particularly explosive combination of social discontent and nationalistic aggression prevailed." [41] Finally, he found nationalistic fervor "most widespread and in many

39. John Higham, "Social Discrimination Against Jews in America, 1830–1930," *Publications of the American Jewish Historical Society*, XLVII (1957), 1–33; Higham, "Anti-Semitism in the Gilded Age: A Reinterpretation," *Mississippi Valley Historical Review*, XLIII (March, 1957), 559–78; Oscar Handlin, "American Views of the Jew at the Opening of the Twentieth Century," *Publications of the American Jewish Historical Society*, XL (June, 1951), 323–44; John Higham, "American Anti-Semitism Historically Reconsidered," *Jews in the Mind of America*, ed. Charles Herbert Stember (New York: Basic Books, 1966).

40. No anti-Semitic remarks are attributed to any southern Populists *during the Populist era* in any of the following works: Richard Hofstadter, *The Age of Reform* (New York: Alfred A. Knopf, 1955); V. C. Ferkiss, "Populist Influences on American Fascism," *Western Political Quarterly*, X (1957); Norman Pollack, *The Populist Response to Industrial America* (Cambridge: Harvard University Press, 1962); W. T. K. Nugent, *The Tolerant Populists* (Chicago: University of Chicago Press, 1963); C. Vann Woodward, "The Populist Heritage and the Intellectual," *American Scholar*, XXI (Winter, 1959–60); Frederic Cople Jaher, *Doubters and Dissenters* (New York: The Free Press, 1964).

41. Higham, *Mississippi Valley Historical Review*, XLIII, 572.

ways most intense in the small town culture of the South and West." [42] The South was the least urbanized and most discontented region in the United States. Consequently, if Higham's conclusions are accurate, the South must figure as the most antisemitic area in the country.

Certain aspects of southern culture—aside from the squalor that existed in Atlanta and other fledgling urban areas—tended to make the natives react more violently to Jews than did residents of the North and West. Southerners were more inbred than were northerners and were, therefore, more concerned with the purity of their Anglo-Saxon heritage.[43] Religious fundamentalism, another force that encouraged antisemitism, was more widespread in the South than the North. According to William J. Robertson, most southern Methodists and Baptists were advised by their spiritual leaders that the Jews were "Christkillers." [44] Social instability accompanied by personal anxiety was the final factor that intensified regional hostility toward Jews. Throughout history, the position of the Jews has reflected the degree of security prevailing in a given society. They have frequently been blamed for defeats, depressions, and other disruptive crises.[45] Southerners, notoriously insecure and continually on the defensive, seized upon hatred for Jews as one outlet for the frustrations of their existence.

42. *Ibid.*, 559–78; Higham, *Publications of the American Jewish Historical Society*, 22, 47; Higham, *Jews in the Mind of America*, 248–49. Although Atlanta was not a small town after 1900, in part, it did have a "small-town culture."

43. Benjamin Kendrick, "The Study of the New South," *North Carolina Historical Review*, III (January, 1926), 10.

44. Robertson, *Changing South*, 99.

45. Elias Rivkin has written: "At every moment of economic or social crisis, especially since the 1890's, anti-Semitism has manifested itself [in the United States]. This antisemitism more and more linked the Jews with the sources of disintegration and decay and attempted to identify the Jews with the twin threat of international capitalism and international communism." Rivkin has also observed that "the position of the Jews in every society of the past has been as secure as the society itself. For every stress the Jews have been held essentially responsible; for every collapse they have been blamed." *Essays in American-Jewish History* (Cincinnati: American Jewish Archives, 1958), 60. In our own times, many southern Jews still feel defensive and hesitate to disrupt the status quo. Alfred O. Hero, Jr., a sociologist, has written that "small-town, Deep Southern Jews have feared especially that someone with a Jewish name would express controversial ideas and thus stimulate unfavorable reactions to Jews in general." *The Southerner and World Affairs* (Baton Rouge: Louisiana State University Press, 1965), 501. Hero's chapter, "Southern Jews," is the best historical discussion that I have seen on the subject.

The above mentioned factors existed, to some extent, in different parts of the North as well, and anti-Semitism appeared among different northern groups. But despite temporary interludes of cataclysm and depression, most northerners expected progress to improve the conditions of life. Many southerners, however, clung to fantasies of past heroics to compensate for a forbidding contemporary life, and looked upon change as subverting cherished values.

It is against this complex background of social change and the resistance it engendered that the murder of a thirteen-year-old girl, in 1913, triggered a violent reaction of mass aggression, hysteria, and prejudice. Leo M. Frank, the Jewish superintendent and part owner of the National Pencil Factory where the dead girl, Mary Phagan, had been employed, became the prime suspect. It was to be Frank's misfortune that he symbolized the alien institutions about which the South had always had the greatest apprehensions.

II

Mary Phagan had been found dead and disfigured in the basement of the National Pencil Factory by a Negro nightwatchman at 3 A.M. on April 27, 1913.[46] Near her body lay two notes, purportedly written by the girl while being slain. They read:

Mam that negro hire down here did this i went to make water and he push me down that hole a long tall negro black that hoo it wase long tall negro i wright while play with me.

he said he wood love me land down play like the night witch did it but that long tall black negro did but his slef.[47]

Georgia, and particularly Atlanta, newspapers milked every ounce of sensationalism that they could from the tragedy. One daily indicated that the "horrible mutilation of the body of Mary Phagan proves that the child was in the hands of a beast unspeakable," [48] while the editors of another added: "Homicide is bad enough. Criminal assault upon a woman is worse. When a mere child, a little girl in knee dresses, is the

46. *AC*, April 27, 1913, "extra," 1, 2.
47. Henry A. Alexander, *Some Facts About the Murder Notes in the Phagan Case* (privately published pamphlet, 1914), 5, 7.
48. *Augusta* (Ga.), *Chronicle*, May 2, 1913, 1.

victim of both, there are added elements of horror and degeneracy that defy the written word." [49]

An aroused public demanded vengeance. One of the victim's neighbors remarked to a reporter, "I wouldn't have liked to be held responsible for the fate of the murderer of little Mary Phagan if the men in this neighborhood got hold of him last night." The minister of Atlanta's Second Baptist Church thundered, "The very existence of God seems to demand that for the honor of the universe the murderer must be exposed." [50]

Atlanta's inadequate police force was under intense pressure to find the culprit. Aside from being understaffed, the force left much to be desired in terms of intelligent action. They had been accustomed to a slower pace and simpler life and their inability to handle the problems of an industrial metropolis made them rely increasingly on an irrational use of power. On one occasion, for example, when Atlanta had experienced a labor shortage, the police attempted to rectify the condition by arresting all able-bodied men found on one of the main streets. Employed and unemployed, black and white, were hauled into court, fined, and sentenced to the stockade without being given a chance to defend themselves. One man so punished had been in the city for only three days. Neither relatives nor employers were notified of the round-up or the sentencing.[51]

The police also had a poor record for solving crimes. A few years before Mary Phagan's death, a national periodical had revealed that only one murder in one hundred was ever punished in Georgia.[52] Atlanta policemen allegedly used brutality with those people who were picked up. In 1909, they were accused of beating one Negro to death and chaining a white girl to the wall until she frothed at the mouth. In 1910 a commission investigating prison conditions in the city uncovered "stories too horrible to be told in print." [53] During 1912–13, more

49. *AC*, April 29, 1913, p. 4.
50. *AC*, April 28, 1913, p. 3. *Atlanta Georgian*, May 4, 1913, p. 2, hereinafter cited as *AG*.
51. Philip Waltner, "Municipal and Misdemeanor Offenders," in *The Call of the New South*, ed. James E. McCulloch (Nashville, Southern Sociological Congress, 1912), 110–11.
52. Hugh C. Weir, "The Menace of the Police," *World To-Day* (January, 1910), 52.
53. *Ibid.*, March, 1910, p. 174.

than a dozen unsolved murders tried the public's patience.[54] Because these victims had been Negroes, there had been no great protestations over the constables' inefficiency. But Mary Phagan was, as a Georgian so characteristically put it, "our folks." [55] Failure this time would not be tolerated.

A great deal of action seemed to be taking place at the police station. Seven people were arrested, and although four were quickly released, three were still held on suspicion, including the Negro nightwatchman who had discovered the corpse. Of the trio, the one upon whom suspicion quickly fell was Leo Frank, the superintendent of the National Pencil Factory where Mary Phagan had been employed and where her body had been found.

When the police had first questioned Frank, he appeared quite nervous and overwrought. From him, they discovered that Mary Phagan had come to pick up her pay shortly after noon on April 26—Confederate Memorial Day. The superintendent admitted having been alone in his office, and having paid the girl her $1.20 in wages for the ten hours that she had worked that week. Mary had then left his office, and no one else ever admitted to having seen her alive again.[56]

The day after the corpse had been discovered, strands of hair "identified positively" [57] as Mary Phagan's, and blood stains, were found in a metal workroom opposite Frank's office. The night watch-

---

54. In regard to the conduct and competency of its policemen, Atlanta was typical of other American cities. "There is probably not a city in the South where the police do not make needless arrests." Waltner, "Offenders," *New South*, 107. Crime existed in every major city in the United States and the failure of police forces to control the widespread lawlessness evoked extensive comment. The Conference for Good City Government discussed the lack of competent policemen in 1906, 1909, and 1910. Delegates to these conventions argued that police reform could not be postponed. Better laws, better methods, and better men were essential to meet the needs of growing cities. In 1910 a national periodical ran a series of articles condemning police incompetence, inefficiency, and brutality. The author warned, "Gentlemen of the police, you are on trial." Edward M. Hartwell, "The Police Question," *Proceedings of the Atlantic City Conference for Good City Government*, 1906, p. 397. And see Augustus Raymond Hatton, "The Control of Police," *Proceedings of the Cincinnati Conference for Good City Government*, 1909, pp. 157–61; Leonhard Felix Field, "The Organization of Police Forces," *Proceedings*, 1910, p. 281; Weir, "Menace of the Police," 59.

55. Wytt E. Thompson, *A Short Review of the Frank Case* (Atlanta: n.n., 1914), 29.

56. *AC*, April 28, 1913, pp. 1, 2.

57. *AG*, April 28, 1913, p. 1. It was later made known that a microscopic test had not proven the hair to be Mary Phagan's.

man had also told the police that Frank had asked him to come in early on the day of the girl's death, but dismissed him when he arrived and ordered him to return at the normal time. Frank's uneasy behavior before the police and the pressure from an hysterical public led to his arrest.[58]

Leo Max Frank was the Jewish superintendent and part owner of his uncle's pencil factory. Although born in Texas, in 1884, he had been reared in Brooklyn and educated at Cornell University. His first position had been with a firm in a Boston suburb, and he did not settle in the South until 1907. Once in Atlanta, however, he planned to stay. He married Lucile Selig, daughter of one of the more prominent Jewish families in the city, and was popular enough to be elected president of the local chapter of the B'nai B'rith in 1912.[59]

The arrest of the northern, Jewish industrialist won the approval of Atlanta's citizenry. Rumors spread that the prison might be stormed and the prisoners, Frank and the Negro nightwatchman, Newt Lee, lynched.[60] Street talk had it that one of the two must be guilty and killing both would avenge the murder. The *Atlanta Constitution* cautioned its readers to "Keep An Open Mind." "Nothing can be more unjust nor more repugnant to the popular sense of justice," its editorial read, "than to convict even by hearsay an innocent man." [61] The advice went unheeded.

The furor that erupted after the murder can largely be attributed to the deed having rekindled the residents' awareness of the harshness of their lives; having reawakened traditional southern resentment toward outsiders who violated southern mores; and having, once again, dramatized the inherent iniquities of industrial life. "What was uppermost in the minds of those who were indignant," the *Outlook* reflected in 1915, "was the fact that the accused represented the employing class, while the victim was an employee." [62] And the Jew, more than

58. *AC*, April 28, 1913, pp. 1, 2; April 29, 1913, pp. 1, 2; April 30, 1913, pp. 1, 2.

59. *New York Times*, August 26, 1913, p. 18; February 18, 1914, p. 3; *AC*, June 1, 1915, p. 4; *AG*, May 13, 1913, p. 2. Interview with Alexander Brin, a Boston reporter who covered the later stages of the Frank case, in Boston, August 19, 1964. Mr. Brin now publishes the *Jewish Advocate*.

60. *Savannah Morning News*, May 2, 1913, p. 1.

61. *AC*, May 2, 1913, p. 4.

62. "The Frank Case," *Outlook*, CX (May 26, 1915), 167.

the Negro, provided a symbol for the grievances against industrial capitalism and its by-product, urbanism. The Baptist Minister of Mary Phagan's church made the conventional southern identification of Jewishness, evil, the stranger, and hated northern industrialism when he recalled: "[My] own feelings upon the arrest of the old Negro nightwatchman, were to the effect that this one old Negro would be poor atonement for the life of this innocent girl. But, when on the next day, the police arrested a Jew, and a Yankee Jew at that, all of the inborn prejudice against Jews rose up in a feeling of satisfaction, that here would be a victim worthy to pay for the crime." [63]

The employment of minors in factories particularly aroused the ire of Atlanta's residents. A spokesman for those crusading to restrict child labor viewed Mary Phagan's death as the inevitable consequence of industrial perfidy: "If social conditions, if factory conditions in Atlanta, were what they should be here, if children of tender years were not forced to work in shops, this frightful tragedy could not have been enacted." The antagonism and venom harbored toward the entrepreneurs and their characteristically inhumane attitudes found expression in Atlanta's *Journal of Labor*: "Mary Phagan is a martyr to the greed for gain which has grown up in our complex civilization, and which sees in the girls and children merely a source of exploitation in the shape of cheap labor. . . ." The *Southern Ruralist*, Atlanta's largest circulating periodical, also interpreted the slaying as the product of a heartless and cruel society. It branded "every Southern legislator" who thereafter refused to vote for laws prohibiting the employment of children in factories, "as a potential murderer." [64]

There were other reasons for resenting the factories. White females had always been placed on a pedestal, to be worshipped, exalted, and protected. To southerners they embodied the purity and nobility of the South itself. Considered a "queen worthy of honor [and] deserving protection from the contamination of a man's world," the white woman had to be zealously guarded from the evils of society. [65]

Industrialism, however, had inaugurated factory work for women.

63. L. O. Bricker, "A Great American Tragedy," *Shane Quarterly*, IV (April, 1943), 90.
64. *AG*, April 30, 1913, p. 1; *Journal of Labor*, XV (May 2, 1913), 4; "Accessory After the Fact," *Southern Ruralist*, XX (June 15, 1913), 13.
65. English, "Ethical Emphases," 219.

Since tradition dictated that women belonged in the home, southern society regarded the change as subversive of regional honor and family ties. Few white men accepted the alteration without qualms. They may have felt unmanned because they could not maintain their families without an additional income—a feeling particularly disturbing in a society that had always emphasized virility. Guilt was also aroused in the traditionalist southern conscience because the factory system forced wives and daughters to come in contact with strange men. The Southern Baptists, it is said, had an "abnormal fear of the intimate association of the sexes." [66] An Atlanta judge later elaborating upon this argument claimed: "No girl ever leaves home to go to work in a factory, but that the parents feel an inward fear that one of her bosses will take advantage of his position to mistreat her, especially if she repels his advances." [67] A factory owner expressed similar southern sentiments: "It was considered belittling—oh! very bad! It was considered that for a girl to go into a cotton factory was just a step toward the most vulgar things. They used to talk about the girls working in mills upcountry as if they were in places of grossest immorality. It was said to be the same as a bawdy house; to let a girl go into a cotton factory was to make a prostitute of her." [68]

Given the nature of southern prejudices, Atlantans were particularly receptive to the devastating indictments the authorities apparently unearthed against Leo Frank. One newspaper reported that pictures of Salome dancers "in scanty raiment" adorned the walls of the National Pencil Factory.[69] At the coroner's inquest, a thirteen-year-old friend of Mary Phagan's told his audience that the girl had confessed her fears of the superintendent's improper advances. Former factory employees recalled that Frank had flirted with the girls, that he had made indecent proposals, and that he had even put his hands on them.[70]

Regardless of the veracity of the accusations, other witnesses at the inquest corroborated Frank's statements as to his whereabouts on the

66. Spain, *Attitudes*, 299.
67. Arthur G. Powell, *I Can Go Home Again* (Chapel Hill: University of North Carolina Press, 1943), 287.
68. Broadus Mitchell, *The Rise of Cotton Mills in the South* (Baltimore: The Johns Hopkins Press, 1921), 195.
69. *AG*, April 29, 1913, p. 3.
70. *AC*, May 9, 1913, p. 2; *AG*, May 8, 1913, p. 2; May 9, 1913, pp. 1, 2; *Savannah Morning News*, May 9, 1913, p. 1.

day of the murder' which, if true, made it almost impossible for him to have been the culprit.[71] Nevertheless the coroner's jury ordered Frank held on suspicion of murder.

Subsequent police disclosures incriminated the factory manager even more in the eyes of many Georgians. A park policeman swore that he had seen Frank and a young girl behaving improperly in a secluded section of the woods a year earlier, while the proprietress of a bordello confessed that the superintendent had phoned her repeatedly on the day of the murder in an effort to obtain a room for himself and a young girl. Both statements were eventually repudiated but not before an impact had been made upon the public. At the time of the madam's affidavit, newspaper readers were informed that her remarks constituted "one of the most important bits of evidence" that the state had against the factory superintendent.[72]

The numerous suggestions dropped by newspapers and police gave rise to the wildest rumors, most of them concerned with the "lasciviousness" of the "notorious" Leo Frank. The Jewish faith, it was widely asserted, forbade violations of Jewesses but condoned similar actions with Gentiles. Frank had allegedly killed another wife in Brooklyn, had illegitimate offspring too numerous to count, drank heavily, was about to be divorced by his wife, and finally, was a pervert. One man said he knew that Frank was a "moral pervert" because he looked like one.[73] These tales, lacking any foundation in fact, suggest how concerned Atlantans were with the religious and social background of Mary Phagan's suspected slayer. Gossip magnified fears. The people, it seemed, wanted Frank to have the characteristics attributed to him.

III

The trial of Leo Frank for the murder of Mary Phagan opened on July 24, 1913, amidst great hullabaloo. It lasted until August 26. During the

---

71. *AJ*, June 2, 1913, p. 9.   72. *AC*, May 11, 1913, p. 1; May 23, 1913, p. 1.

73. *AG*, May 11, 1913, p. 2; *Augusta Chronicle*, May 5, 1919, p. 2; *Baltimore Morning Sun*, November 19, 1914, p. 3; A. B. MacDonald, "Has Georgia Condemned an Innocent Man to Die?" *Kansas City* (Mo.) *Star*, January 17, 1915, p. 1; C. Thompson, *Short Reviews*, 25; C. P. Connolly, *The Truth About the Frank Case* (New York, 1915), 14; Abraham Cahan, *Blätter Von Mein Leben* (5 vols.; New York: Forward Publishing Co., 1931), V, 494.

entire period, the temper of the crowd indicated the antipathy Atlantans felt toward the defendant. "The fact that Frank is under indictment today," one reporter explained the day before the trial began, "means to many minds that he is therefore guilty. . . ." [74]

The state's case rested primarily upon the testimony of Jim Conley, a Negro sweeper who had been employed in the National Pencil Factory. He charged Frank with having committed the murder and acknowledged that he had helped his employer remove the body to the factory basement.[75] There were no witnesses to corroborate any of the sweeper's statements.

The defense based its case primarily upon proving that Frank did not have the time to commit the murder. Witnesses were presented who corroborated the superintendent's account of his whereabouts on the fatal day. Frank maintained his innocence and characterized Conley's tale as "the vilest and most amazing pack of lies ever conceived in the perverted brain of a wicked human being." [76]

The jury needed less than four hours of deliberation before finding the defendant guilty. The judge sentenced Frank to hang. Atlantans were jubilant with the verdict. A crowd outside of the courthouse, estimated at between two and four thousand, screamed itself hoarse. As he stepped out of the courthouse, the prosecuting attorney was lifted to the shoulders of two husky men and carried to his office amidst huzzahs and cheers. After what was perhaps one of the wildest celebrations in Atlanta's history The *Marietta Journal and Courier* observed, "It seems to be the universal opinion that Frank was guilty and that he was the cause of the demonstration when the verdict was announced." [77]

Frank's lawyers appealed his case through the Georgia courts and ultimately to the United States Supreme Court. None of the tribunals ordered another trial. The Governor of Georgia re-evaluated the evidence in June, 1915, and commuted the death penalty to life imprison-

74. *AG*, July 27, 1913, p. 2.
75. *Frank vs. State, Brief of the Evidence*, 54–57.
76. Quoted in *AJ*, August 4, 1913, p. 1.
77. *AG*, August 25, 1913, p. 1; August 26, 1913, p. 1; *AC*, August 26, 1913, p. 4; *Greensboro* (Ga.) *Herald-Journal*, August 29, 1913, p. 4; *Marietta Journal and Courier*, August 29, 1913, p. 2.

ment. Two months later, in August, 1915, a band of men stormed the prison, kidnapped Frank, and lynched him.[78]

IV

The joyousness with which Frank's conviction was received revealed the people's desire for a scapegoat for their deeper resentments.[79] Georgia's Governor, John M. Slaton, explained the hostility toward Frank as "the prejudice of the employe against the employer. The fact that the head of a large factory is accused of attacking a girl, one of his employes, has been sufficient to give rise to this kind of prejudice." [80]

The antisemitism that erupted in Atlanta also suggested the need for a particular type of a villain. Manifestations of this sentiment are evident in the widespread acceptance of Negro Jim Conley's testimony; the numerous rumors that Frank's Jewish friends had collected a "fund of hundreds of thousands of dollars" to buy the jury; and tales to the effect that some defense witnesses had been bought with "jew money." In addition, Frank's lawyers had received anonymous phone calls with the cryptic message, "If they don't hang that Jew, we'll hang you." Crowds outside of the courtroom frequently hurled epithets like, "Lynch him!" and "Crack that Jew's neck!" The jury was also threatened with lynching if it did not "hang that 'damned sheeny'!" [81] This passionate hatred disclosed the Atlantans' intense yearning for some culprit upon whom they could fix blame for the frustrations of their barren lives. "People haunted by the purposelessness of their lives," Eric Hoffer has written, "try to find a new content not only by dedicating themselves to a holy cause but also by nursing a fanatical

---

78. *AC*, June 22, 1915, pp. 1, 2, 9; *New York Times*, August 18, 1915, pp. 13; August 19, 1915, pp. 1, 3; August 23, 1915, p. 5.

79. Daniel Bell has written: "Social groups that are dispossessed invariably seek targets on whom they can vent their resentments, targets whose power can serve to explain their dispossession." "The Dispossessed," in *The Radical Right*, ed. Daniel Bell (Garden City, N.Y.: Doubleday & Co., 1963), 2–3.

80. *New York Times*, November 28, 1914, p. 5.

81. *Greensboro* (Ga.) *Herald-Journal*, August 29, 1913; Thompson, *Short Review*, 9; Connolly, *The Truth*, 11; "Frank's Prophesy of Vindication Comes True 10 Years After Georgia Mob Hangs Him as Slayer," *Jewish Advocate*, XLII (October 18, 1923), 20; *Minutes* of the executive committee of the American Jewish Committee, November 8, 1913 (located in the American Jewish Committee Archives, New York City).

grievance." [82] This was especially true of the newly urbanized working classes in the South.[83]

Ignorant, frustrated, and frightened, the workers sought a devil to exorcise. Moreover, their severe tribulations and limited education made necessary a dogmatic oversimplification. In such a situation, Leo Frank could easily be visualized as the diabolical perpetrator of savage crimes against society.

Reinforcing these cultural and emotional sources of prejudice is the herd tendency in human nature. Widely shared personal opinions are difficult to sway. People tend to absorb the knowledge to which they are exposed through the refraction of their own emotional needs and experiences and through the evaluations prevalent among the groups with which they identify. Facts and opinions that differ from one's own or that are disturbing to convention are frequently not perceived. Psychologists have found a high correlation between belief and desire $(+.88)$ but a negative one in regard to belief and evidence $(-.03)$. In other words, factual information is insufficient to disturb established opinions.[84] Ellen Glasgow, the Virginia novelist, has noted that in the South for people "to think differently meant to be ostracized." [85]

Enthusiastic acceptance of Frank's conviction was further enhanced because people are conditioned to defer to those whom they have been trained to respect. Statements made by public officials are accepted as accurate unless there is some reason to suspect obfuscation.

82. Eric Hoffer, *The True Believer* (New York: New American Library, 1958), 92.

83. Alfred O. Hero, Jr. has written: "the newly urbanized Southern working class . . . seemed especially open to leadership by charismatic and authoritarian figures who would appeal to their anxieties and insecurities, with dogmatic, oversimplified 'solutions,'" *The Southerner and World Affairs*, 354.

84. Frederick Hansen Lund, "The Psychology of Belief," *Journal of Abnormal and Social Psychology*, XX (1925), 194–95; Gordon W. Allport and Leo Postman, *The Psychology of Rumor* (New York: Henry Holt & Co., 1947), 191; Melvin M. Tumin, *An Inventory and Appraisal of Research on American Anti-Semitism* (New York: Freedom Books, 1961), 115; Eunice Cooper and Marie Jahoda, "The Evasion of Propaganda: How Prejudiced People Respond to Anti-Prejudice Propaganda," *Journal of Psychology*, XXIII (1947), 15; Mahlon Brewster Smith, "Functional and Descriptive Analysis of Public Opinion" (Ph.D. dissertation, Harvard University, 1947), 500, 507; George Cornewall Lewis, *An Essay on the Influence of Authority in Matters of Opinion* (London: Longmans, Green & Co., 1875), 10.

85. Quoted in William H. Nicholls, *Southern Tradition and Regional Progress* (Chapel Hill: University of North Carolina Press, 1960), 135.

This was especially true in the South where the ruling classes "had extraordinary powers over the whole social body." [86] Hugh Dorsey, the Georgia-born prosecutor, had announced before the trial: "the possibility of a mistake having been made is very remote." [87] Southern Pinkerton and Burns detectives, who had conducted separate investigations, had also expressed their firm belief in the factory manager's guilt.[88] Why, then, should the masses have assumed that the alien Jew was telling the truth while their own leaders were not?

The members of the jury, a representative cross-section of Atlantans,[89] pleased their peers with the verdict. A spokesman for the jurors stated that they had all accepted the prosecution's arguments and conclusions.[90] To be sure, they may have been convinced of Frank's guilt on the basis of the evidence presented in court. But even if the material had been less persuasive, the opinion of the Atlanta crowds would certainly have influenced those who had to decide Frank's fate. What would have happened to their jobs, their social relationships, and the position of their families, for example, if the jurors had voted to acquit the man who most of Atlanta assumed had ravished the little girl? More than a year after the trial had ended, one juror confessed to a northern reporter that he was not sure of anything except that unless Frank was found guilty the jurors would never get home alive.[91]

V

A Boston newspaperman wrote in 1916 that had Frank been a native Georgian he would never have been convicted of Mary Phagan's death.[92] More likely, had he been a respected member of the gentile community, no southern prosecutor would have staked his case on a Negro's accusations. Moreover, had the people of Atlanta not found the cares of life so great a burden, there would have been less demand for a scapegoat to pay for their accumulated frustrations The coming of industrialism was not solely responsible for Frank's fate. But the

---

86. Cash, *Mind of the South*, 310.   87. Quoted in *AG*, July 27, 1913, p. 2.
88. *AC*, May 25, 1913, p. 1; May 27, 1913, pp. 1, 2.
89. One bank teller, one bookkeeper, one real estate agent, one manufacturer, one contractor, one optician, one railroad claim agent, one mailing clerk, two salesmen, and two machinists. Garrett, *Atlanta*, II, 622.
90. *AJ*, August 26, 1913, p. 1.   91. *New York Times*, February 23, 1915, p. 9.
92. Clipping from the morgue of the *Boston Herald-Traveller*, August 17, 1916.

technological changes in society, which uprooted people and set them down in strange, urban areas, aggravated whatever intolerance and anxiety the southern culture had already nurtured.

The murder of Mary Phagan stood out as a symbol of industrial iniquity. She was continually referred to as "the little factory girl" long after the focus of the case had shifted to Leo Frank. A newspaperman observed during the trial: "The little factory girl will be remembered as long as law exists in Atlanta." A Confederate War veteran contributed "a dollar for the erection of a monument to Mary Phagan, the little factory girl who recently laid down her life for her honor." And Georgia's patrician historian, L. L. Knight, narrating the events of the murder and the solution arrived upon, years later wrote, "Espousing the cause of the little factory girl, [Tom] Watson in a most dramatic vein of appeal, summoned the true manhood of the South to assert its chivalry in vindicating the child's honor." [93] The "little factory girl's" death, and the factory owner's responsibility for it, had at last provided an acceptable outlet for the discontented. Employment of minors, unconventional association of the sexes, and the evils of the factory system deeply disturbed a conservative society uneasily confronting the beginnings of industrialism. Most Atlantans, having uprooted themselves from rural origins, were alienated by their work in the factory and by life in the city. The murder of an innocent southern girl by a northern, Jewish factory superintendent evoked the hostility latent in their unsettled existence and directed this hostility to the symbol of their fears and grievances.

93. *AG*, August 5, 1913, p. 4; Dalton (Ga.) *North Georgia Citizen*, August 28, 1913, p. 4; Lucian Lamar Knight, *A Standard History of Georgia and Georgians* (6 vols.; Chicago: The Lewis Publishing Co., 1917), II, 1190.

Section 3 Southerners View the Jew

While other regions have been inundated and transformed by streams of immigrants and new settlers, the southern population has remained relatively homogeneous. The South has also been more heavily influenced by fundamentalist Baptist and Methodist teachings. Most importantly it has suffered more severely with economic problems. As a fairly insulated group, southerners have developed strong mores and folkways. Consequently strangers in their midst have often been objects of suspicion.

Through the years the southerner adopted stereotyped images of the Jew. These impressions accumulated because of fear and distrust of the outsider, through folk tales passed on from generation to generation, and from actual encounters as well. The ballad of "The Jew's Daughter," traditional in a number of states, conveys a feeling of apprehensiveness and hostility toward the Jew and his religious practices.

From time to time, eloquent pleas such as that written by Lucian Lamar Knight called for an end to discrimination. His tract appeared in

1907, when a fellow Georgian, Oscar Straus, received an appointment to the cabinet of President Theodore Roosevelt. Knight, a Protestant minister and archivist for the state of Georgia, praised the merits of Jews—although he saw them as stereotypes—and expressed the hope that America might set an example of tolerance toward these people that other countries would follow.

Thus not all of the fixed opinions about Jews have been unfavorable. The ensuing selections illustrate representative attitudes, in which the Jew is assigned certain "racial" or religious attributes and is therefore seen not as an individual, but as part of a group outside the mainstream of society.

Foster B. Gresham

"The Jew's Daughter": An Example of Ballad Variation

TWO NEW TEXTS of "Sir Hugh" or "The Jew's Daughter" (Child, 155) have come to light in a quite unexpected way. In the Matoaca Grammar School, Chesterfield County, Virginia, children of the second grade are allowed occasionally to present original programs arranged by their own committees and chairmen. One morning the chairman announced a song by a little girl, seven years old, who came to the front of the class and sang the traditional ballad "The Jew's Daughter." When asked where she had learned it, she replied, "My aunt learned it to my grandma's child, and she learned it to me." With the help of an older child acquainted with the family, the teacher, my sister, Miss Dorothy Gresham, was able to interpret the statement of family relationship and locate the aunt in the next county (Prince George). A visit to the aunt added a few more details to the line of transmission, for it was found that she had learned it from a cousin in Apex, Wake County, North Carolina, who in turn had learned it from her father.

When asked to sing the ballad, the aunt became self-conscious and refused. She agreed to recite the words and proceeded to give the first stanza. Her memory began to falter on the second, and by the time she had reached the third stanza she found that it was necessary to add music to her words to recall them at all. This necessity overcame her embarrassment, and she sang through the rest of the ballad. Then she was willing to sing it again and again until the collector could learn the tune well enough to take that down too. It is interesting to note that in reciting the words, she did not repeat the last line of the first and second stanzas; had she not turned to singing, the use of the last line of each stanza as a refrain would not have been indicated. The words she gave are as follows:[1]

> It rained a mist, it rained a mist,
>> It rained all over the town;
> Two little boys came out to play,
>> They tossed their ball around, around,
>> They tossed their ball around.
>
> They tossed the ball too high at first,
>> And then they tossed it too low;
> And then it fell in a Jewish yard
>> Where no one was allowed to go, to go,
>> Where no one was allowed to go.
>
> A pretty fine miss, she came to the door,
>> All dressed in silk so fine.
> "Come in, come in, my pretty little boy,
>> You shall have your ball again, again,
>> You shall have your ball again."
>
> "I won't come in, I won't come in,
>> Unless my playmate comes too;
> For they say when little boys go in,
>> They'll never come out again, again,
>> They'll never come out again."
>
> She showed him a rosy red apple
>> And then a blood red peach,
> And then she showed him a diamond ring
>> That urged his little heart in, oh in,
>> That urged his little heart in.
>
> She took him by his lily white hand,
>> And led him through the hall,
> She led him to her dining room,
>> Where no one could hear him call, oh call,
>> Where no one could hear him call.
>
> And then she took a red white towel
>> And tied it 'round his chin,
> And then she took a carving knife,

---

1. Sung by Mrs. Ruth Jones, Prince George County, Va., Feb. 23, 1933; title: "It Rained a Mist."

And cut his little heart in, oh in,
   And cut his little heart in.

"Oh, spare my life, oh, spare my life!"
   And then the little boy cried,
"If ever I should grow to be a man,
   My pleasure shall all be thine, oh thine,
   My pleasure shall all be thine.

"Oh, place a Bible at my head
   And a prayer book at my feet;
And ever my playmate call for me,
   Pray tell him that I am asleep, asleep,
   Pray tell him that I am asleep.

"Oh, place a prayer book at my feet
   And a Bible at my head;
And ever my mother call for me,
   Pray tell her that I am dead, oh dead,
   Pray tell her that I am dead."

With these words may be compared those noted down from the
singing of the little school girl: [2]

It rained a mist, it rained a mist,
   It rained all over the town.
The little boys came out to play;
   They tossed the ball.

They taught him the low and then
   They taught him the low high first,
And then he fell in a Jewish yard
   Where no one was allowed to go,
   Where no one was allowed to go.

There found a pretty maid came to the door,
   All dressed in nice fine silk.
She said, "Come in, my little pretty boy."
   "I won't come in unless my playmates come too,
   Unless my playmates come too."

She showed him a red apple and then
   She showed him a red bloody peach, and then
   She showed him a diamond ring.

2. Sung by Marie Caudle, second grade, Matoaca School, Chesterfield County,
Va., Feb. 4, 1933; title: "It Rained a Mist."

> It urge his little heart in, oh in,
>   It urge his little heart in.
>
> She took him by his little white hand,
>   She tolled him through the hall;
> She took him to her dining room,
>   Where no one could hear his call,
>   Where no one could hear his call.
>
> She took a red and white towel
>   And tied it around his chin,
> And then she took a carving knife
>   And cut his little heart in, oh in,
>   And cut his little heart in.
>
> "Oh spare my life, oh spare my life, oh spare my life,
>   Until I am dead;
> A pleasant at my feet and a Bible at my head.
>   If my playmates call for me,
>   Tell them that I am asleep.
>
> "A pleasant at my feet and
>   A Bible at my head;
> If my mother call for me,
>   Tell her that I am dead."

Here we have a text caught actually in the process of variation. With only one agent of transmission between the aunt and the child in school, the "grandma's child," aged eleven, we can note the beginnings of such differences as will probably produce in the course of a number of years of oral transmission a considerably different text from the aunt's. Occasionally the child has changed the thought by the use of rather unintelligible expressions, such as "they taught him the low high first" and "a pleasant at my feet"; and occasionally she has condensed into one stanza the details of two stanzas in the other text. Traces of her failure, or that of the grandma's child, to catch the right word as she learned the ballad are in evidence in such cases as the use of *little* for *lily* and *taught* for *tossed*; and there is the apparent failure to remember some lines and the subsequent substitution of some other line that seemed to fit in, as in the next to the last stanza: "Until I am dead" for "And then the little boy cried." Perhaps the conflations of stanzas and the use of some of the lengthy lines would not have occurred if the child had learned the tune accurately with the words. Her singing, however, was found a bit too complicated for one to note down the tune; there were variations for each stanza wherever her failure to remember the words correctly had caused a breaking down in the regular rhythm. The variations are apparently of her own composition; yet she has memorized them and seems to sing each stanza the same way each time. She did not learn the ballad for the special occasion of the school program; she said that she had known it for a "long, long time" and added that every time she reached the line "And cut his little heart in," her sister would cry because "it hurt her feelings."

These two texts show rather close resemblances to the F version of the ballad in A. K. Davis' *Traditional Ballads of Virginia*, which was also learned by its singer from a person in North Carolina (Guilford County). Another person reporting this version from North Carolina (Wilkes County) gave certain minor variations which compare with those in our texts. Very similar also is the text given in *The Journal of American Folk-Lore*, Vol. XV, p. 195, from a copy in *The New York Tribune* for August 17, 1902.

The tune sung by Mrs. Jones is as follows:

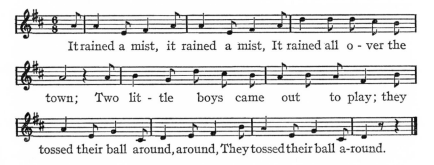

It rained a mist, it rained a mist, It rained all o-ver the town; Two lit-tle boys came out to play; they tossed their ball around, around, They tossed their ball a-round.

Lucian Lamar Knight
The Twentieth Century
and the Jews

THE INDEBTEDNESS of human society to the Hebrew race is by no means restricted to the creedal doctrines of the revealed religion. If the sheer truth must be told in Gath this inventory alone is sufficient to exhaust the assets and to mortgage the affections of the whole civilized world for all time to come. For it makes the Gentile debtor to the Israelite for larger supplies of richer manna than the Israelite himself ever gathered in the wilderness.

But the history of ancient Palestine contains only the first install-ment of the obligation. Besides autographing, transcribing and pre-serving the sacred Scriptures, under divine inspiration, furnishing the theater for the Biblical events and supplying the ancestral homesteads from which Judaism, Christianity and Mohammedanism have emerged, the Jews have galvanized the secular activities of all the four continents, set the pace for human progress in all the diversified arts and industries and multiplied the achievements of Joseph the Hebrew upon an hun-dred Egyptian thrones.

Whenever an extravagant statement is made or an ignorant opinion is entertained it is only necessary to address the custodian of the records in the primal command of the old Pentateuch: "Let there be light." To establish the truth of the proposition laid down, there files into the courtroom a host of dignified witnesses, each of which represents a sphere of activity whose belt is an equator. The world of politics pre-sents Benjamin Disraeli, the Earl of Beaconfield. The world of finance names Baron de Rothschild. The world of literature cites Israel Zang-

will. The world of music chants Mendelssohn. The world of philanthropy proclaims Montefiore and Hirsch.

But some one may demur that the names above presented are
exceptional, and do not lay the world under any tribute to the race at
large. The fact is admitted, but not the inference. Shakespeare and
Milton and Napoleon and Galileo and Kepler and Newton and Raphael
were also exceptions, but exceptions which portrayed the genius of
nations and embodied the spirit of epochs.

However, if the canvass is too large it is only necessary to localize
the area of discussion. The lowgrounds furnish quite as good a field
for the study of Hebrew character as the tops of the mountains; but
the change of venue may be prefaced with the statement that Jews are
seldom found in dead communities. Like the arteries of the human
body they move toward the vital centers. They are in no wise to be
identified with the insects, which multiply in putrefaction and fatten
upon decay; and, if they are to be classed among the insects at all, they
must be assigned to the coral builders which labor neither in stagnant
pools nor in noisome eddies, but which down in the ocean solitudes lay
secure beams and lift substantial fabrics amid the very fountains of the
troubled deep.

It is the surest sign of wholesome life in any community that it can
boast of at least one typical descendant of the thrifty Jacob. He regis-
ters the existence of the quickening pulse. But he comes to make the
money which his presence advertises; and, without invoking any
particular favor, he opens his workshop on the corner and soon begins
to flourish like the hillside cedars of his own forest of Lebanon. In the
hardest of times he has money to lend if not to burn and before he is
ready to execute his will he owns the grocery-store, the meat-market,
the grog-shop, the planing-mill, the newspaper, the hotel and the bank.

But the larger towns and cities serve better the purposes of illustration. In all the thorough-going centers the Jews are found in great
multitudes. They are moneymakers to such an extent that the roll-call
of the whole Hebrew population can be made from the tax-books.
They may be shrewd in driving bargains but they are open-handed in
sustaining public charities, in encouraging liberal arts, in cultivating
pure morals and in patronizing wholesome entertainments. The reason

why others do not compete with them in matters of trade is perhaps due less to instincts than to ideas.

It is quite the fashion to caricature the Jew as exacting his interest down to the last drachma. But the Jew is not the only money-lender on the modern Rialto who has demanded his pound of flesh; nor can it be said that the Shylocks of the present day have all sprung from the thrifty race which produced the Merchant of Venice. Some of the brethren whose names are not enrolled in the synagogues but whose pews are found in other places of worship have been known to exhibit qualities which the virtuous vampire would scorn to adopt and which would almost drive the honest leech to suicide.

Besides bearing considerably more than an average share of the burdens of government, it is an unvarnished statement of fact that no race of people on the globe are voluntarily more liberal than the Jews in supporting institutions of which they are not themselves the immediate beneficiaries. It is by no means unusual for them to contribute either to Christian hospitals or to Christian churches. Neither their orphans nor their indigents are wards upon the public except in the rarest instances. They furnish few inmates for the jails and penitentiaries and asylums, little business for the courts and little scandal for the newspapers. The women of Israel are proverbially chaste. They keep their households in order, their children in obedience and their husbands in respect. The observance of the Mosaic law has given the Jews remarkable immunity from bodily ailments and afflictions. They usually enjoy good health, cheerful spirits, hearty appetites and long lives.

Rascals are sometimes found among the Jews. But "the lost sheep of the House of Israel" are not more numerous than the errant waifs which have wandered from other folds. The Jew is not perfect; but neither was Adam who lived before Abraham and who has bequeathed the inheritance of original sin to the whole output of his loins, without any clause of reversion or entailment in favor of the Twelve Tribes. And while the Jews make no pretense of following the Nazarene they at least respect Him as a prophet and a teacher; and many of them are practically better Christians than some of blatant prayers and broad phylacteries, whose false discipleship is worse than nominal and whose deceitful lips even while framing the accents which profess the faith are printing the kisses which betray the Master.

Whether tested by the carpenter's tape line or the chemist's retort the claims of the Hebrew race to aristocratic distinction must be universally allowed. The tables of descent upon which the Jews rely for proof of remote antiquity reach back to the tables of stone which bore the Decalogue. Beside such an ancient scroll the most patrician documents which the Gentiles can boast become almost plebian. The New Englander is satisfied if he can trace his forefathers back to the Mayflower at Plymouth Rock; but the Jew in looking for ancestors on shipboard respects neither the Western Hemisphere nor the Christian centuries, but quietly follows his genealogical chart until it lands him at the door of the ark upon Ararat.

However, it is not antiquity alone which makes the household of the Jew illustrious. The heroes of Biblical story have all sprung from the seed of Abraham; and heading the long list which includes Moses and Elijah and David and Solomon and Daniel and Ezekiel and Isaiah and Paul and Stephen is the Man of Galilee whom christendom ranks above all the rest: the immaculate Hebrew, the Prince of the House of David, and the Lion of the Tribe of Judah.

The battle-field of Hastings laid the foundations and traced the patents of the British nobility in rubrics which were commonplace and paltry compared with the blood of the hierarchy of Israel. Nor have the life currents which ancestry has done so much to ennoble been contaminated by foreign admixtures. Senator Vance, of North Carolina, has not inaptly likened the Jews to the Gulf Stream, which journeys around the entire globe but never mingles with the ocean through which it moves. The average American is a conglomerate whose ancestors are distributed over the whole face of the earth and most of Europeans are tinctured with foreign infusions. But the Jew is still the Jew. Racially he has undergone no change whatever and the blood which ripples the veins of the modern Hebrew in America is substantially the blood of the ancient Hebrew in Israel. The candidate for social honors who is knocking at the door of the four hundred is sure to be admitted if he can show one single red corpuscle which has come from William the Conqueror, but the Jew without using the microscope requires only a needle to open a vein and out leaps the same blood which was bound to the altar on Mount Moriah.

The cynic who is still inclined to sneer at the Hebrew race will do well to recall the famous retort which Disraeli made in the House of Commons to the member who twitted him with being a Jew. "Sir," replied he, with the calm poise which truth only can give to resentment, "when your ancestors were tending swine on the plains of Scandinavia and drinking blood from the skulls of savage victims slain by savage victors, mine were priests and princes in Israel, worshiping God in the temple."

The anti-Semitism of France and Russia is by no means an expression of the sentiment of christendom toward the Jews. On the contrary it represents the death struggle of an old enmity which is slowly passing under the benign influences of twentieth century brotherhood into the fossil remains of medieval barbarism. The recognition of Oscar Straus by President Roosevelt indicates much more clearly the present drift of the great world currents. In this connection it is of some interest to observe that while the appointment of Mr. Straus to the portfolio of Commerce and Labor marks the first entry of the Hebrew citizen into the President's council-board at Washington, the event was anticipated under the Confederate government by the appointment of Judah P. Benjamin, first as attorney-general and afterwards as Secretary of State in the cabinet of President Davis. After the war, Mr. Benjamin took up his residence in England, where he became the queen's counsellor. Except as foreign ambassadors, it seldom happens that men can lay double claim to distinction by achievements in two hemispheres; but such was the dual accomplishment of Judah P. Benjamin.

Significant of the popular feeling in America toward the Hebrew race is the fact that among the national lawmakers in Washington at the present time there are four Congressmen of Jewish blood and one United States Senator. Nor is this recognition undeserved. The history of the country from the earliest colonial days will show that the Jews have been important factors in American affairs on the military as well as on the civil side. Indeed, antedating the discovery of the New World, it was from the coffers of the Jews of Spain that the money was obtained for the eventful voyage which brought Columbus to the Western Hemisphere. It was a Jew who prescribed for the exhausted crew; and a Jew who, sweeping the horizon from the breezy turrets of the rigging, first announced the sight of land and became the herald of the dawn of modern times. Though normally men of peace and inclined by instinct to trade rather than to arms, the muster-rolls of all the great conflicts will show that the Jews have been at the front whenever there was fighting to be done; and the men who have stood shoulder to shoulder with them on the fields of the Confederacy will attest that the descendants of Abraham espoused the cause of constitutional liberty with as little thought of surrender as if they were battling for the very Ark of the Covenant.

But while the appointment of Mr. Straus is pleasing to the country at large as an act of recognition justified by individual as well as by racial merit, it is specially gratifying to the people of Georgia. Years ago when the Straus family first emigrated to America it was toward this State that the pioneer movements of the household band were directed. Perhaps in the library of the old home in Rhenish Bavaria there were books on the shelves which told of how the Jews had prospered in the colony of Oglethorpe, some of them having landed on the bluffs of the Savannah river as early as 1733. In looking over the long list of distinguished Hebrews the eyes of the elder Straus must surely have lingered upon the Sheftalls and it may be that prophecy even suggested Hirsch and Moses and Elsas and Levy and Haas and Schlesinger and Eiseman and Jacobs. The philanthropic spirit was one of the strongly marked characteristics of the Straus family, and the humane enterprise in which the colony of Georgia originated could easily have supplied the emigrating impulse. At any rate the elder Straus gathered up his household effects and with Isadore, Nathan and Oscar he started to Georgia.

This was in 1854. Locating at Talbotton, Georgia, he straightway began to prosper. The two eldest boys as soon as they were old enough entered Collinsworth Institute; but Oscar appears to have been too young to have enjoyed the benefits of this excellent school at least for any length of time. He was only four years old when he left Bavaria, and before he was twelve the family moved to Columbus where they lived from 1862 to 1865. The war entailed heavy disasters upon Lazarus Straus, and dismayed by the prospect which the State presented after General Sherman's energetic torch had ceased traveling from Chattanooga to Savannah he decided to start in business in New York; and thereupon he moved to Gotham.

Organizing the firm of Lazarus Straus and Sons, his establishment soon became one of the largest concerns importing chinaware in the United States, and the foundations of the family fortune were laid. In 1887 Isadore and Nathan bought an interest in the great department house of R. H. Macy and Company, which eventually became the sole property of the two brothers whose able financiering has made it one of the largest mercantile establishments on the globe.

Soon after the family moved to New York Oscar entered Columbia College, from which institution he graduated with the highest honors. Ill health prevented him from enjoying the career which he had mapped out for himself at the bar, and he entered his father's firm, where his legal acquirements proved of immense advantage. But he was not prevented by his business engagements from taking an active part in politics; and he proved his capacity for public service to such an extent that President Cleveland appointed him as minister to Turkey. Although a Democrat, he was subsequently honored by President McKinley with the same appointment. Besides winning the approval of the home government, he also gained the friendship of the Sultan, who wished to decorate him, but the compliment he felt constrained to decline. However, Mrs. Straus was made the recipient of the royal favor to the extent of receiving the highest mark of respect ever paid by the Turkish sovereign to the gentler sex. It is by no means the least of the diplomatic distinctions achieved by Mr. Straus that through the Turkish Sultan he was largely instrumental in preventing the Mohammedans in the Philippines from joining Aguinaldo. He also rendered effective service to the cause of American missions.

An accomplished literary scholar, Mr. Straus has written numerous essays on political and economic subjects for the magazines and periodicals, among them the *Westminster Review*. He has received the degree of LL.D. in recognition of his ripe scholarship and diplomatic services to the government; and his selection, independent Democrat though he is, for portfolio honors in the cabinet of President Roosevelt is an appropriate sequel to the academic compliment.

The typical Jew of the medieval times was not the Shylock of Shakespeare, but the Isaac of Ivanhoe; and the typical Jew of the modern world is not the money-lender of Mortgage Lane, but the far-sighted and sagacious man of affairs who sits at President Roosevelt's cabinet-board: skillful, energetic, practical and patriotic; quick to detect points of advantage, prompt to seize opportune moments, faithful in performing executive trusts and modest in wearing well-earned distinctions.

America has set an example which France and Russia must follow. The Jew is entitled to the considerate esteem not only of all who call themselves Christians, but of all who profess to be well informed; for so thoroughly is the philosophy of Israel ingrained in the structure of the world's thoughts—rising from its roots and mingling with its sap—that the man who is inclined to decry the chosen people of God can not repudiate the debt which he owes to the Jews by rejecting the Biblical theory of the universe. Nor can he date the simplest letter with the current numerals of the Christian era without kneeling unconsciously at the manger-cradle of the Babe of Bethlehem.

Going the full length of the skeptical tether he may scorn the law, revile the prophets and eschew the gospels, but the obligation still attaches to the civilization which he enjoys and which is all the wiser for the proverbs of Solomon, all the sweeter for the anthems of David and all the holier for the beatitudes of Jesus. He may be an avowed enemy to oxygen, but the despised element keeps him alive, in the water which quenches his thirst—aye, in the breath which fills his nostrils. And if perchance the very name he bears in the ranks of unbelief is not enriched with the associations of the temple it still remains that the very air he breathes on the streets of Babylon is fragrant with the blooms of Galilee.

Section 4 Life in the Twentieth-Century South

In the twentieth century, sociologists, clerics, novelists, journalists, and political scientists have made numerous studies of southern Jewish groups. Although the investigations in this collection date back a decade or more, and conditions have undoubtedly changed somewhat in recent times, these essays do delineate the role and status of the southern Jew.

In many areas Jews have been economically successful but socially segregated. Journalists David and Adele Bernstein outline the barriers Jews have encountered in Richmond. Leonard Reissman provides a detailed sociological study of the New Orleans Jews, noting what he terms "a status ceiling" which prohibits them "from full public acceptance into the social élite." Both the Bernsteins and Reissman observe an increase in antisemitism during this century. Even though the lack of full social acceptance is berated by many Jews, Rabbi Sidney I. Goldstein fears that complete integration which results in intermarriage "poses a serious threat for the survival of Judaism." His conclusions derive from his study of a small southern Jewish settlement.

In contrast to these selections which describe particular communities, there are two essays that seek to make generalizations about the Jewish situation in the South. Alfred O. Hero, Jr., bases his work on numerous interviews, while political scientist Theodore Lowi derives his conclusions from observations of a typical middle-sized city in the Deep South.

In general these studies reveal that southern Jews have made every effort to adopt all of the regional folkways except conversion to Protestantism. They express great concern about their standing in the community. Most refuse to take public positions that would make them stand out in contrast to their Gentile neighbors. Their situation is admirably summed up by Lowi, who states that, "Southern Jewry is a special phenomenon both in the particular context of American Jewry and the general context of group relations."

Alfred O. Hero, Jr.
Southern Jews

JEWS CONSTITUTED in 1960 some 200,000 inhabitants of the South, omitting most of Texas, suburbs of the District of Columbia in Virginia, and southern Florida; this number comprises a little over one half of one percent of the population of the region.[1] Nevertheless, their interest and knowledge in world affairs, which are far above the average, their on the whole more cosmopolitan thinking on foreign policy, their economic and community standing, and their potential influence on local thought in foreign relations suggest special consideration.

Jews have made up such a small fraction of the Southern population that their replies to national surveys cannot be compared statistically with those of other Southern and Northern groups. The interviews for this study with slightly less than two hundred Jews in the sample communities and in several other locales were also too few for statistical analysis. Furthermore, the interviewers were unable to contact cross sections of Jews of varied backgrounds and roles in all the major types of Jewish communities in the region. Most of the observations to follow are, therefore, relatively speculative in nature, pending systematic study of a carefully drawn representative sample of Southern Jewry, which would necessarily number several thousand interviewees.

1. Estimate derived from *American Jewish Yearbook* (Philadelphia: The Jewish Publication Society of America [for the American Jewish Committee], 1961), 62–63.

Jews, Gentiles, and World Affairs

LESS INTERNATIONALLY THOUGHTFUL THAN NORTHERN JEWS   Since a comparable sample of Northern Jews was not interviewed, the speculations about differences in international outlook and actions between them and their Southern coreligionists are based on replies by Northern Jews to survey questions dealing with world affairs[2] and the author's impressions from contacts with Northern Jewry over the years.

The Jewish informants differed considerably among themselves in their international thinking. But as a group they seemed less well read, less intellectually alert, less cosmopolitan, and more conservative about international relations than their Northern coreligionists of similar status. Southern traditions about the Negro as well as other subjects seemed to have exerted significant effects on most of the Southern-born Jewish informants. According to national surveys, only a limited minority of Northern Jews have felt as did over half the Jewish interviewees for this study that the process of desegregation was proceeding too fast in the South. A considerable fraction of the Southern-born Jews interviewed made observations to the effect that they were emotionally ill at ease about integration even when they accepted it as inevitable and in the long run desirable. Moreover, the interviewers' confidential discussions of Jews' private attitudes about race relations undoubtedly resulted in considerably more equalitarian replies than their public postures in their communities, a phenomenon which will be examined shortly.

Replies of Northern Jews to national surveys indicated that disparity between Southern and Northern Jewish attitudes toward world affairs appeared most marked on issues related to Negro-white relations—such as sentiments about the Union of South Africa, Sir Roy Welensky and the protection of white interests against the African majority in the Central African Federation, the behavior of anticolonialist, neutralist leaders of newly independent African states in the U.N. and international affairs generally, and the rapid rate at which underdeveloped African societies have been accorded independence from European tutelage.

2. Typical surveys of NORC and AIPO until the end of the 1950s included 45 to 65 Jews. However, samples of AIPO starting in 1959 included as many as 3,500 interviewees, of which 110 to 150 have typically been Jews.

Interviewers for this study did not encounter Southern counterparts of the small Northern urban Jewish leftist or socialist minority. There were no unilateral disarmers among the interviewees, nor were there individuals who thought we should make much greater concession to the Soviets in order to achieve agreement on arms control or other issues. Only two former New Yorkers advocated United States acceptance of a disarmament agreement without effective inspection. Moreover, interviewers did not observe the anti-military overtones which have been evident among a number of Northern Jewish liberals. Knowledge that the author had attended Virginia Military Institute, graduated from West Point, and served for eight years in the Regular Army stimulated considerably more favorable comment than among most liberal Northern Jews of the author's acquaintance.

Leading rabbis in Richmond and Savannah and other influential Southern Jews were active during and shortly after World War II in developing local support for the American Council for Judaism and other movements critical of arguments favorable to the establishment of a Jewish state in Palestine.[3] The interviews for this study indicated that a considerable fraction of Southern Jews of established position and inherited wealth and prestige, particularly in older, more traditional Southern communities, have agreed to a significant extent with thinking opposed to Zionism, although only a minority of those of such standing have accepted the more extreme of such orientations critical of Israel. Given the strong pressures for acculturation and against being overtly different from Gentiles in much of the South, identification with Israel has probably been weaker there than in the rest of the country taken together.

However, such Jews of several generations of residence and influence in the South were by 1959 a limited minority, and most of the Jewish interviewees seemed relatively favorably inclined toward Israel and appeared to feel that it is useful to have a government which could complain about maltreatment of Jews abroad and that Arab countries have been intransigent and unreasonable and more guilty than the Is-

3. Harry Simonhoff, *Under Strange Skies* (New York: Philosophical Library, 1953), 250, 267; and Mrs. David J. Greenberg, *Through the Years: A Study of the Richmond Jewish Community* (Richmond: American Jewish Tercentenary Committee, 1654–1954, 1954), 47.

raelis in the disagreements between them. Most of the interviews for this study were completed before the hanging of Adolph Eichmann, but only about a fifth, largely Southern-born and in small communities or among the highly acculturated in the older cities, were much concerned about his abduction from Argentina and trial before an Israeli court, and some of these seemed more worried about criticism among Gentiles than about the procedure itself. Furthermore, it appears that contributions to philanthropies devoted to a considerable extent to programs in Israel have been approximately as large per individual Jew, in proportion to his income, in the South as elsewhere in the United States.

On the other hand, some of the genteel, upper-class interviewees felt that the methods used to raise money for programs in Israel had been "crass." Only a minuscule handful among the sample favored the view of strong Zionists that Jews should be encouraged to migrate to Israel even though they were not under heavy pressure or discrimination. A considerable minority of the Southern-born consultants apparently believed that the Israelis had not been candid on some of their policies and disagreements with the Arabs and that they had been partly responsible for border and other difficulties.

THE MOST COSMOPOLITAN SOUTHERN ETHNIC GROUP   However, Jewish traditions of learning and rational analysis, contacts with Jews from outside the South and with liberal Jewish organizations, identifications with coreligionists abroad, and other influences have continued to move many, and probably most, Southern Jews in varying degrees in the direction of cosmopolitans. Moreover, Jews throughout the South have been on the average much better off, better educated, more concentrated in elevated social and occupational groups, and more urban than Gentiles—all factors associated with greater interest, knowledge, and exposure to world affairs and with more cosmopolitan, multilateralist, international attitudes. But even when compared with Gentiles of similar education, occupation, and income in their own communities, Jews in the sample for this study were on the whole more internationally minded.

Approximately one out of seven of this predominantly middle- and upper-class Jewish group often read about world affairs in some critical publication such as the New York *Times* (Sunday edition), *The Atlantic*, or the *Christian Science Monitor*. Three fifths of the remainder read newsmagazines or their equivalents. Approximately three fifths tended to agree that our foreign aid budgets had not been excessive in recent years or that they should have been pared only relatively little. Although some of the Jewish respondents were in garment and textile manufacturing and other import-vulnerable industries, over half believed we should increase imports, another third would maintain them at approximately the then current level, and only one out of eight would decrease them. Less than one out of twenty felt that Portugal would be able to maintain her control of her African dependencies over the long term, although almost half of those venturing replies felt that independence had come to many African countries too rapidly for orderly development and stability. Only five out of almost two hundred wanted us to withdraw from the U.N. and not many more urged reorganizing it without the Soviet Union. No more than 3 percent would have us pull out of NATO or pursue policies likely to weaken that alliance system. Except for a handful of vociferous racists, hardly any Jews proposed reduction of international exchanges, even with the Communists, or opposed the Peace Corps, technical assistance, and sale of agricultural surpluses for local currencies. The proportion of Jews accepting isolationist or neo-isolationist thinking was roughly half that among Gentiles of similar education and occupation in the same communities.

These less conservative attitudes on world affairs were related to the fact that the great majority of the Jewish interviewees, even in smaller communities in the Black Belt, ranged from mild segregationists to integrationists.[4] The informants were more than twice as likely as the Southern Protestant white average in surveys to feel that desegregation is both inevitable and, in general, desirable in the long run, and only about one third as inclined as the latter to believe that Negroes are constitutionally inferior. Few Jews even in Mississippi and Alabama apparently voted for independent electors in 1960. Only a

4. For comparable findings in three dissimilar Southern cities, see Leonard Reissman, "The New Orleans Jewish Community," *Jewish Journal of Sociology*, IV (1962), 111; Joshua A. Fishman, "Southern City," *Midstream*, VII (1961), 39–50; and Manheim S. Shapiro, "The Southville Survey of Jewish Attitudes" (MS of American Jewish Committee, New York, 1959).

handful of Jews were actively racist beyond the conformity apparently required for maintaining their businesses or professional careers in strongly segregationist communities. The majority of the small number of Jews on the rolls of Citizens Councils and other racist groups were by and large rather inactive and probably joined primarily to appease their segregationist neighbors, clients, and customers, to help keep these organizations "respectable," and to prevent development of anti-Semitism which many feared might be latent in such groups.[5]

Moreover, even when Jews seemed relatively conservative about race relations, their racial attitudes typically had less apparent effect on their international views than was the case among most racist Gentiles. Perhaps a considerable fraction of the relatively cosmopolitan Jewish interviewees exaggerated their attachment to segregation since public liberalism on this issue would in many cases have entailed serious local pressures, whereas they could express their true thinking on most issues of foreign policy without energizing as unpleasant local reactions. Their racial attitudes had some influence in the expected directions on their world thinking, especially where Africa was an issue. But the greater interest in world affairs of Jews, their wider exposure to cosmopolitan ideas in mass media and Jewish religious and secular organizations, and the tradition of learning—albeit much attenuated among many Southern Jews—had significantly moderated the impact of their racial traditionalism upon their international opinions.

Furthermore, extended conversations with even the more conservative Jews in the more traditionalist, racist, Deep Southern settings usually uncovered important liberal exceptions to the international syndrome related to racism. Few Jews who still identified themselves as such were as consistently isolationist, unilateralist, military interventionist, and generally reactionary as their ultra-conservative Gentile colleagues. Jewish interviewees in each of the sample communities were asked who were the Jews most conservative on foreign aid, the U.N., trade, and world affairs generally. With some exceptions those named turned out to be less isolationist or reactionary than the most conservative Gentiles of their same social and economic standing. Even the word "reactionary" used by Jews to describe other Jews typically

5. Fear of anti-Semitism in these white supremacy groups probably also discouraged some segregationist Jews from joining.

referred to people whose views on world issues were comparable to those of the average self-made, successful Gentile businessman in the area. The spectrum of international and related attitudes among Jews was significantly less conservative than that among local Gentiles of like status.

It was noted earlier that even small Jewish manufacturers of clothing in competition with cheap imports who were not above using racism to prevent unionization of their plants were for the most part apologetic protectionists, noting that they understood that expanded trade is in our national interest, that we should not drive the Japanese into the arms of Peking, and so on. Moreover, whereas most Gentile protectionists in the sample would reduce sharply foreign economic assistance to underdeveloped countries, most Jewish ones would not.

An influential Jewish state politician in the Deep South was profoundly uncomfortable about "turmoil" in his state due to "leftist Northern agitators" sowing unrest among "maladjusted" and "misled" Southern Negroes. He had advised his coreligionists to "keep quiet" on race, since "there is no race problem here except when it is created from the outside." He helped pass the state right-to-work law, was worried about the size of the national debt, the erosion of "states' rights," "big government," "waste" abroad, trying to "buy friends" among the underdeveloped countries, and "kowtowing to opportunists who are making fools out of us" in Africa and Asia. However, he would increase technical assistance, both bilaterally and through the U.N., stress foreign languages more than currently even in grade school in his state, and encourage more Americans to take foreigners, including non-Negroid colored peoples, into their homes to "learn about their countries and how they think." Another prominent Jewish business leader, who was considered on the right on most issues (including world affairs) by the rest of the Jewish community in his city, became the president of a voluntary organization devoted to adult education in world affairs in his community—most of the speakers before this organization had been less conservative than he.

Even the most conservative, extreme free enterprise, anti-foreign spending, pro-military interventionist Jews among planters in the Delta were seldom as solidly so as their Gentile counterparts. Discussion with two brothers and an in-law who had considerably expanded the interests of their prosperous father in cotton plantations, a bank, and retail stores in the Delta indicated that they favored free trade, but as a part of free enterprise in general. Free foreign trade, they seemed to feel, could not operate with minimum wage and hours laws, monopolistic trade unions backed by the President of the United States, federal intervention in agriculture and business, and other domestic "socialism." They opposed intergovernmental aid abroad, especially to countries which refused to declare themselves against Communism; United States refusal to oppose emotional, anti-Western politicians in Africa and Asia; "desertion" of the interests of our "real allies" in Europe; and toleration of seizures of American private property in underdeveloped lands, particularly in Latin America. One launched out against "fuzzy dreamers and impractical idealists" running our foreign policy—at that time the Eisenhower administration. One of these individuals had encouraged Jews in his part of the state to join the Citizens Council and to refrain from criticizing the racial *status quo*. He had also tried to convince at least one national Jewish organization to moderate its publicized liberalism on race. James Eastland, a planter like themselves, was "one of the best men in Washington."

But they also liked their Congressman, one of the most liberal legislators on both international and domestic questions from the Deep South (since defeated by a racist-isolationist). They were supporting Senator Kennedy and were opposed to both Vice-President Nixon and the independent electors in the forthcoming election. They wanted to have our colleges make room for more competent foreign students by admitting fewer "trifling" Americans. They felt that we should assist in educating the Africans, although not by putting them into white Southern colleges. They were viewed by Negroes in the county as "very fine" people, true paternalist humanitarians and fair toward Negroes. They contributed to liberal Jewish organizations, including the B'nai B'rith and the Anti-Defamation League.

Diversity of Jewish World Views

Most of the variables related to international thought among Southern Gentiles apply to Jews as well. Those with the most advanced educations, particularly at the better universities and colleges, have been more favorable to international cooperation in nonmilitary fields than those who did not go to college; the same is true of Jews in the liberal professions as opposed to merchants, of urban rather than small-town and rural Jews, and so on. As among Gentiles, critical attitudes in world affairs have usually been part of a general intellectual alertness and interest in ideas. Although, as observed previously, conservative racial attitudes among Jews were on the whole less closely connected with their international thinking than among Gentiles, the direction of correlation was similar. In general, the more cosmopolitan the Gentile middle and upper classes, the more internationally thoughtful the local Jews in similar roles; in any given community, however, at least a somewhat larger fraction of Jews than non-Jews in the professional, proprietary and managerial classes were relatively well read, thoughtful, and favorable to liberal, or multilateral, foreign policies.

ASPECTS PARTICULARLY APPLICABLE TO JEWS   The smaller and more homogeneous the backgrounds of the local Jewish community, the more conservative its international attitudes. This variable is, of course, closely associated with the size and complexity of the general community—the small Jewish groups, most members of which were raised in Southern towns and villages, have tended to be in less populous, less dynamic places rather than in growing metropolitan areas where New South influences have been more marked. However, within cities of about the same size, opposition to foreign aid for underdeveloped neutralists, and particularly Communist Poland and Yugoslavia, and to repeal of the Connally Amendment as well as support of unilateral intervention against leftist, anti-United States regimes in Latin America were more widespread where the great majority of Jews were raised in the South.

Related to this observation is the degree to which Jews have taken on the coloration of and been assimilated into the Gentile majority. Where they have been living for several generations without substantial influx of new Jewish people from the North and Europe, rewards for adjustment to Gentile mores have been considerable and penalties for overt maintenance of divergent Jewish values and attitudes compelling. Growing tensions about race relations in the last decade have accentuated pressures against Jewish nonconformity, as will be discussed later. But most Jews outside the few Southern cities were long isolated from Jewish religion and culture until recent decades. Resident rabbis within easy access of small towns and rural sections are largely a recent phenomenon—since the advent of good highways and urbanization. National Jewish organizations had few members in these isolated locales until the last several decades. In many small communities there were only half a dozen or so Jewish families.[6] Their contacts with other Jews were limited to a few wandering peddlers and alms collectors and infrequent trips to New Orleans, Richmond, Charleston, and a handful of other cities.

Isolated in their local communities and profoundly dependent upon local good will and friendly relations with local white Gentiles, most of these Jews adapted themselves to prevailing values and habits. They played poker with the sheriff, fished with the county judge, hunted with the planters, and became leaders of the local Chamber of Commerce, Rotary, and other service groups. Evangelical ministers and laymen were often persistent, and, since the church was a social as well as a religious organization, a considerable fraction of Jews, or their children, joined the Presbyterian, Methodist, Episcopal, or other church which included influential members of the community. Having few Jewish choices, sons and daughters frequently married Gentiles. Even if they did not change their own religious affiliations, their children generally became Protestants.[7] In some cases a parent of Jewish tradition transferred some of his emphases on intellectual pursuits, identification with the underdog, and contact with cosmopolitan values. However, as the generations succeeded one another, more and more Southerners of Jewish ancestry became virtually indistinguishable in ideology from the rest of the local power structure of planters and merchants.

This assimilation was also apparent in attenuated form in the older cities. Much of the early Sephardic Jewish population of Charleston has disappeared into the genteel Episcopalian group. Some descendants of these early settlers were still affiliated with the Reform Temple in

6. See, for example, Roger W. Shugg, *Origins of Class Struggle in Louisiana* (Baton Rouge: Louisiana State University Press, 1939), 43.

7. In Opelousas, Louisiana, for instance, sixteen out of eighteen marriages of Jews during a thirty year period prior to 1955 were with Gentiles; none of the offspring of these mixed marriages was raised in the Jewish faith. See Benjamin Kaplan, *The Eternal Stranger* (New York: Bookman Associates, 1957), 96–98.

1960–61, but most of those citizens who identified themselves as Jewish arrived in the late antebellum period or after. And a considerable number of even third generation Jews in the South have also become Episcopalians, Presbyterians, Methodists, Unitarians, or otherwise disassociated from Jewish religious and secular organizations. Similarly, many offspring of Jewish families who have lived in New Orleans for several generations are no longer, for practical purposes, Jews in religion or ethnic identification. Even in much newer cities like Greensboro, third and later generations of families of high social and economic standing have included a significant fraction of individuals married to Gentiles whose children will be affiliated with high-status Christian churches.

Jews who married Gentiles but maintained their Jewish religion and affiliation with such Jewish organizations as the American Jewish Committee, the National Council of Jewish Women, the B'nai B'rith, and the Anti-Defamation League seemed in many more cases than not more liberal in international orientation than the majority of local Gentiles of similar status. Frequently, their Christian spouses were more conservative about Negroes, foreign aid, domestic "Communism," and other public issues. Those who became Unitarians seemed predominantly liberals or responsible conservatives on world affairs—they were often more thoughtful and better informed about foreign policy than most Jews.

However, a disproportionately large number of first-generation Gentiles among the middle and upper strata—Unitarians excepted—appeared strongly conservative on race and world affairs. The dynamics of this rejection of Jewish cosmopolitanism require more systematic research, but it is apparent that many such new converts have been even more careful to adopt the more conservative attitudes prevalent in the Gentile power structure than many who were born into the Episcopal or Presbyterian church. Many of these prosperous Jews married above their own social origins. Insecurity about acceptance among the Gentile elite is probably at work in a number of these cases.

Likewise, Jews who have had little interest in Judaism or Jewish affairs seemed to include a disproportionate number of opponents of foreign aid and Goldwater supporters on both domestic and foreign policy within the Jewish community. Four of the six Jewish ultraconservatives who were also favorable to Citizens Councils were little identified with Jewish thought and activities. Two were newly prosperous businessmen who had not been to college and a third was a planter who had not completed his higher education.

Prosperous, well-educated Jews of several generations of Southern ancestry who were very active in the Gentile community and who maintained only formal affiliations with Judaism included as well a number of quite conservative people on world affairs. Urban Jews who have been accepted socially by upper-class Gentiles, whose contacts outside the Jewish community continued after office hours and beyond business, professional, and formal organizational relationships, who belonged to esteemed Gentile clubs rather than to the Jewish country club, and so on, have been mostly individuals of several generations of inherited wealth and social position in the South. Most of these have been relatively inactive in Jewish organizations, confining any memberships to paying dues and perhaps participation in a large, formal meeting now and then. The Jewish groups were frequented and run largely by "newer," more "Jewish" folk.[8]

Thus, in Charleston the minority of Jews who agreed with much of the foreign policy proposed by the two local newspapers, by the presidents of the two local colleges, by Senator Strom Thurmond and Congressman L. Mendel Rivers, and by the Goldwater wing of the Republican party (at the time of interviews, 1960–61) was composed primarily of those whose social contacts and organizational memberships were more with Gentiles than with Jews and Jewish agencies. They were among those most assimilated into prominent Gentile circles, the majority of whose members were racial paternalists, social standpatters, Old South traditionalists, and strong conservatives on foreign policy.

However, the Jewish aristocracy has also produced a disproportionately large fraction of the most intellectually sophisticated, internationally concerned minority of their communities—a much larger proportion of them than of upper-class Gentiles in the sample communities were well-read cosmopolitans of responsible internationalist per-

8. Fishman, *Midstream*, VII (1961); Leonard Reissman, *Jewish Journal of Sociology*, IV (1962), 117–18; and John C. Rosen, "A Study of Leadership in the New Orleans Jewish Community" (M.A. thesis, Tulane University, 1960).

suasion. Nor should one assume that assimilationists among these old Jewish families, largely of Sephardic, German, French, and other West European origins, have necessarily been neo-isolationists or otherwise strongly conservative in world affairs. Among the sample, of the twelve college-educated anti-Zionists (including three affiliated with the American Council for Judaism), seven approved of foreign aid at approximately the then current or higher levels, all favored active collaboration in the U.N. and its specialized agencies, ten felt international trade (including imports) should be expanded, and several were active in internationally oriented organizations like the Foreign Relations Association of New Orleans, the AAUW, and the League of Women Voters.

The most sophisticated cosmopolitans among those urban Jews who were active in Jewish secular organizations—typically people of newer prosperity and often more recent Northern or foreign antecedents[9]—were on relatively intimate terms and were in rapport primarily with other Jews of similar background and Jewishness, with a handful of the most intellectually oriented members of the Jewish upper class, and with the comparable small cosmopolitan and liberal Gentile minority. Their relationships with more typical middle- and upper-class non-Jews tended to be confined to business and professional contacts and activities within formal organizations like Rotaries, Chambers of Commerce, United Funds, hospital boards, and school committees.

Only a small fraction of middle-class Jews active in Jewish groups could be considered sophisticated and well read on world affairs by national standards. However, with but few exceptions Jewish organizations and rabbis have been relatively liberal on world matters, and even when rank-and-file members have not been particularly thoughtful or well informed, this internationalism has exerted significant effects on their thinking. Some Jews in agrarian sections who were active members of the B'nai B'rith, the Anti-Defamation League, and a Reform Temple and its affiliated societies were segregationists and otherwise conservative on public questions, including world affairs, because of the atmosphere in which they lived and worked. But, such persons

9. Rosen, "A Study of Leadership in the New Orleans Jewish Community."

who would greatly reduce foreign aid or intervene militarily in Cuba against the opposition of a majority of Latin American governments seemed a small minority in cities.

Many Northern Jews moved South, like many Southern Gentiles raised in the North, were probably among the less intellectually oriented, socially conscious, cosmopolitan, and more conservative of Northern Jewry before migrating. A number of Jews also undoubtedly moved South to take advantage of cheap labor, right-to-work laws, inexpensive Negro servants, and other Southern "advantages." But a recent study of Memphis Jews, only 28 percent of whom had two American-born parents, determined that 70 percent felt that "members of all races have the same basic capacities for education and training"; 60 percent felt that the destruction of Israel would entail a very deep personal loss for them; and 90 percent commented that it would be a personal loss to some extent.[10] The sample for the author's study was too small for definitive generalizations, but the impression was that Northern Jews who have moved South temporarily with corporations or other organizations have been more liberal about world affairs than those who came South to go into business themselves and spend the rest of their lives in the region. Nevertheless, many in this former category have been thoughtful internationalists as well. Perhaps crucial are the education and degree of attachment of the former Northerner with Jewish organizations; college graduates who have been active in Jewish bodies, as noted above, have tended to identify with active international cooperation in diplomatic, economic, and cultural as well as military affairs.

URBAN JEWRY   Thus, international thinking among Jews has varied from one city to the next and within the same community, depending on the relative prevalence of the characteristics mentioned above. Jews of Birmingham have appeared considerably less cosmopolitan in their interests and knowledge and less liberal in their international opinions than those of Atlanta, Jews in Shreveport and Charleston less than their counterparts in New Orleans. But the same comparative generaliza-

10. Shapiro, "The Southville Survey of Jewish Attitudes."

tions would apply to Gentiles of similar social standing, education, and occupation in these cities.

The Jewish community of Greensboro was among the more internationally liberal. Located in the North Carolina Piedmont where there has been little plantation experience, high (for the South) industrialization, relatively few Negroes, and relatively little racial tension, Greensboro has several colleges, one of them among the best in the South, and an educational tradition. The county in which it is located is the center of Southern Quaker population, and the only Quaker college in the region is located there. Although the textile industry was in 1961 strong and protectionist, the scientifically oriented and forward looking point of view of the Burlington Industries was influential. Other major textile industries in the area were divisions of Cone Mills, locally controlled by a prominent Jewish family. The two Greensboro newspapers were among the most internationally liberal in the region, even on international trade. Consequently, although the general community included a number of strongly conservative people, some of them of considerable influence, countervailing forces were potent.

Approximately half the members of the Reform Temple were raised outside the South, compared with nine out of ten in the Conservative Temple. The upper class of Southern origins, as elsewhere in the South, was concentrated in the former. They, as in the South generally, were the ones who belonged to the most esteemed country club, were members of law firms and other enterprises with Gentiles, and circulated socially with the local Gentile elite. There has been in recent years virtually no Jewish working class in Greensboro, or elsewhere in the South;[11] most of the salesmen, proprietors of smaller stores, and less prestigous professional people were in the Conservative Temple—there was little Conservative Judaism in the South before the Northern "invasion."

Perhaps as many as a third of Jewish adults in Greensboro read some of the international coverage in either the New York *Times* (Sunday edition) or other periodicals of comparable sophistication.

11. *Ibid.*; Fishman, *Midstream*, VII (1961); and Reissman, *Jewish Journal of Sociology*, IV (1962), 112.

There may have been a few Jews in Greensboro in 1961 who would send the Marines into Cuba, drastically reduce aid to India, withdraw from the U.N. if Communist China were admitted as a member, shift most of our foreign policy out of the U.N. on account of the influence of colored neutralists and underdeveloped states, support the arguments of the conservative *colons* in Africa and of the semifeudal white land-owners in the underdeveloped world, and terminate negotiations for the reduction of armaments and other sources of tension. But the Jewish interviewees for this study, including the rabbis, did not know of any among those individuals who still considered themselves Jews. No more than three or four out of approximately fifteen hundred were known to have supported the strongly segregationist candidate for governor I. Beverly Lake in the recent election, and only a small minority would assist those who wished to obstruct gradual desegregation. A few wealthy Jews agreed more or less with Senator Goldwater on domestic economic policy, but on world affairs almost all who had views seemed to agree with most of the general international orientations of the "modern" Republicans or the moderate or liberal Democrats. These generalizations applied to the manufacturers of textiles, although they wanted more protection from imports in their fields.

Charleston is a very different society from Greensboro and other New South communities, and its Jewish community differs as well.[12] It includes one of the oldest settlements in America. Sephardic Jews arrived in the late 1600s and by the mid-1700s a number of them were among the leading citizens of Charleston.[13] In 1800 the town had the largest, most prosperous, and probably most cultivated and intellectually sophisticated Jewish community in the New World;[14] in 1818 one

12. Richmond Jewry seemed to have much in common with its coreligionists in Charleston, except that influences from outside the Old South have exerted considerably more influence in Richmond. See Greenberg, *Through the Years*.

13. Elzas, *The Jews of South Carolina* (Philadelphia: J. B. Lippincott Co., 1905), 19–22; and Thomas J. Tobias, "Joseph Tobias of Charleston: 'Linguister,'" *Publications of the American Jewish Historical Society*, XLIX (1959), 33–38.

14. Elzas, *The Jews of South Carolina*, 120–30; Simonhoff, *Under Strange Skies*, 252; Tobias, *Publications of the American Jewish Historical Society*, XLIX (1959), 44–62; Charles Reznikoff and Uriah Z. Engelman, *The Jews of Charleston* (Philadelphia: Jewish Publication Society of America, 1950), 67; and Thomas J. Tobias, *The Hebrew Orphan Society of Charleston, S.C.* (Charleston: Published by the Society, 1957), v and 1.

third of the Jews in the United States resided in the low country.[15] By 1951, 41.5 percent of the Jews in Charleston were born there, 12 percent had been there for three or more generations, and well over half were natives of the South.[16]

Many Charleston Jews, particularly among the old established families, have a keen interest in their historic heritage and genealogies and, as is true of most Gentiles of like backgrounds, they would not live anywhere else.[17] As one cosmopolitan gentleman—whose family had been leaders in both the Jewish and general Charleston communities since the middle of the eighteenth century—explained, he walked over the same protruding bricks in the same sidewalks and listened to the birds in the trees in the same gardens when coming home to lunch as his ancestors had. He had grown up with most of the people with whom he associated, and he knew a great deal about each of them and their forebears. He loved his genteel society of politeness, warm interpersonal relations, and lack of needless rush, although he disagreed with prevailing ideas about many issues, including race relations, foreign aid, the U.N., Africa, and so on.[18]

Thoughtful Charlestonians, Jewish and otherwise, complained that the more vigorous critical minds who had a serious interest in world affairs usually did not return after college, or, if they did, tended not to remain. Charleston Jewry did seem considerably more conservative than the Jews of Greensboro on foreign policy.

Nevertheless, not more than 2 percent of Charleston Jewry were more outspoken segregationists in 1960–61 than their careers would require, and probably only about one out of four agreed privately with local white supremacists. A considerable proportion had been influenced to some extent by local criticisms of foreign aid—that it had in-

15. Elzas, *The Jews of South Carolina*, 132.
16. Uriah Z. Engelman, "The Jewish Population of Charleston," *Jewish Social Studies*, XIII (1951), 202.
17. *Ibid.*, 195–212; Reznikoff and Engelman, *The Jews of Charleston*, 243; Elzas, *The Jews of South Carolina*, 132, 289.
18. Louis Rubin, Jr., *The Golden Weather* (New York: Atheneum, 1961), describes the values of the Jewish gentry of Charleston as a youngster growing up within it. He notes that he learned as a child that he was "no kike with thick lips and a hook nose; I was a member of one of the Fine Old Jewish Families." (p. 263) His Jewish peers thought of themselves more as part of upper-class Charleston than as Jews; they minimized their differences in religion and ethnic traditions from the rest of the aristocracy. Pp. 81 ff.

volved much waste, had not prevented drift of underdeveloped countries toward the left and anti-Americanism, had been siphoned off by the corrupt leadership and landed elite groups, and so on—and of other aspects of our foreign policy as well. However, no more than 10–15 percent in 1960–61 seemed to agree with the extreme anti-foreign aid, anti-U.N., colonialist, and otherwise arch-conservative editorials of the local papers and the similar views of Congressman Rivers and Senator Thurmond. Perhaps as many as two thirds of the Gentiles of similar status—professional, managerial, and proprietory—agreed with the general tone of those opinions, if not with the details. Very few Jews were members of neo-isolationist and military interventionist groups like the Charleston Alert and the John Birch Society, and virtually none were active members. Those Jews who did agree with their Gentile peers, as elsewhere in the South, tended to be more "Southern," more "standpat" about local racial and other social change, and to be concentrated among those who associated socially primarily with conservative Gentiles and participated little in Jewish organizations.

New Orleans Jewry, like its general population, incorporates some of the attributes of Charleston and some of Greensboro Jews as well as other characteristics which are unique. Some New Orleanians can trace their forebears to Jews who settled in the city almost 250 years ago;[19] a large proportion of even antebellum Jewish migrants to the community came from well-established Southern communities like Charleston rather than from abroad.[20] Even in 1958, 41 percent of New Orleans Jews had been born in the city, another 24 percent had lived there for thirty or more years, an additional 24 percent had resided locally for at least a decade, and only 11 percent had been present for less than ten years.[21] Relatively few Jews have originated from Eastern Europe until quite recently. Prosperous Jews mixed on relatively intimate terms with Gentiles of like status prior to the Civil

19. Leo Shpall, *The Jews in Louisiana* (New Orleans: Steeg Publishing Co., 1936), 18 ff.
20. Bertram Wallace Korn, "Jews and Negro Slavery in the Old South, 1789–1865," *Publications of the American Jewish Historical Society*, L (1961), 157.
21. Reissman, *Jewish Journal of Sociology*, IV (1962), 113. For earlier examinations of New Orleans Jewry, see Julian B. Feibelman, *A Social and Economic Study of the New Orleans Jewish Community* (Philadelphia: The Jewish Publication Society of America, 1941); and Benjamin Goldman, *The Jewish Population of New Orleans, 1953* (New York: Council of Jewish Federations and Welfare Funds, 1953).

War.[22] Charleston-raised and Yale-educated Judah P. Benjamin of New Orleans and nearby Belle Chasse Plantation married into an old Creole family, was sent to the U.S. Senate by the state legislature, and subsequently became Attorney General, Secretary of War, and Secretary of State in Jefferson Davis' Cabinet.[23] Louis Solomon was the first king of the Mardi Gras, Rex, in 1872.[24]

The New Orleans Jewish community in 1960 was considerably more "Southern" than that of Greensboro or Atlanta, but less so than that of Charleston and Antebellum Town. A recent survey found that over 90 percent agreed that "insofar as possible, Jewish people should try to fit in with the community where they live rather than trying to keep themselves separate in any way." [25] Few have been active Zionists, and those who have been have tended to have lesser social prestige. As in other old Jewish communities, social status was clear-cut and relationships between the aristocracy of inherited money and "newer" people were largely limited to relatively formal situations. The exceptions were primarily cosmopolitans of the upper class who associated with equally sophisticated people of lesser social standing. Likewise, college-educated "successful" Jews who have migrated from elsewhere or have risen from more lowly local origins circulated little with Gentiles after office hours and beyond formal organizations, except for the cosmopolitans of both groups.

But more than in Charleston, dynamic, thoughtful Jews have returned from Harvard, Yale, and other stimulating national colleges to New Orleans, where they could find a considerably larger number of other sophisticated people and where the spheres of action open to them were, by comparison, greater. Although a relatively large number of New Orleanians who identify themselves as Jews have been paternalist segregationists by preference and uncomfortable with changing race relations in their city, virtually none have agreed publicly with

22. See, for instance, Leo Shpall, "Early Jewish Philanthropy in New Orleans," *Jewish Forum*, XXXVIII (1955), 14.

23. Korn, *Publications of the American Jewish Historical Society*, L (1961), 153; and Harry Simonhoff, *Jewish Participants in the Civil War* (New York: Arco Publishing Co., 1963), 161–71.

24. Robert Tallant, *The Romantic New Orleanians* (New York: E. P. Dutton & Co., Inc., 1950), 130.

25. Leonard Reissman, "Profile of a Community: A Sociological Study of the New Orleans Jewish Community" (MS at Jewish Federation of New Orleans, 1958), 118.

the intransigent position of the Citizens Council. Many have been seriously affected by the general local apathy about intellectual matters and the emphasis on warm human relationships, "not rocking the boat," and relaxed enjoyment of life and have, therefore, been relatively indifferent to, poorly informed about, and rather conservative on world affairs. However, neo-isolationist, anti-U.N., anti-aid to India Jews in the early sixties were a small minority. Discussions Unlimited, the local upper and upper-middle class organization which expressed that international posture, had virtually no active Jewish participation.

SMALL TOWNS AND OPEN COUNTRY There were no Jews in many Southern counties in 1960, including some with towns comprising as many as five thousand inhabitants. Jews did not settle where little prosperity and few potential customers for merchants were to be found, and, when the boll weevil or other economic misfortune struck, many of them left. In other counties or towns many of their descendants became Protestants and disappeared as Jews. Unless the community had access over the years to a resident or nearby rabbi, or was in contact with urban Jewish organizations, or attracted "new" Jews from outside within the last two generations, it usually had few or no inhabitants who considered themselves Jewish by 1960.[26]

All the factors mentioned so far applied to Jews in rural market towns and other small communities; those in the Deep South, particularly in heavily Negro areas, were the most conservative about world affairs and the most hesitant about expressing views diverging from local norms; the better educated, particularly at national colleges, were the most informed, interested, and internationalist; those most active in Jewish organizations were least inclined to be neo-isolationists; and so on. But these variables were compounded and reinforced by others in smaller places.

There was one Jewish lawyer and one rabbi in both Deltatown and Antebellum Town—otherwise there were no Jewish professional men in the eight communities of less than thirty thousand population in which interviews were conducted. Young Jews who received sophis-

26. For a description of the disappearance of Jews in small Louisiana towns, see Kaplan, *The Eternal Stranger.*

ticated higher educations and became interested and thoughtful about world issues were even more inclined to migrate to big cities and college communities than were equally cosmopolitan Gentiles. Moreover, sons and daughters of prosperous small-town Jews have been considerably more apt to go to excellent colleges outside the South than have offspring of Gentiles, an experience closely connected with migration out of small Southern cities and towns. In many cases these analytically inclined youngsters have sold the family business or real estate or left it to the supervision of their less intellectual siblings or in-laws. Others returned from college or married into these merchant families, but "couldn't stand it" and left for further graduate education and a city or university community. Small-town and rural Southern Jewry in 1960 was therefore composed largely of merchants, small manufacturers of soft goods, bankers, a few planters, and other non-professional folk, many of whom did not have college degrees. Most of these were regarded as "dull," "uncultivated," or "bourgeois," by the Jewish professional class in the cities. They were also, of course, highly vulnerable economically and socially to local opinion.

In fact, few well-informed, internationally sophisticated Jews lived outside of cities and university towns in 1959–62. Now and then a thoughtful cosmopolitan returned from college with his subscriptions to serious national periodicals, or a relatively unsophisticated son of a merchant brought in a bride who was considerably more interested in ideas than he, including world affairs. But the inducements toward conformity to parochial thinking were usually compelling for these Jews—there was little stimulation to discuss world affairs in a cause and effect fashion; few local people were interested in talking about this field; business contacts were usually relatively uninterested and uninformed about foreign policy; virtually no sophisticates in international relations came to town; the race issue inhibited discussion of controversial issues; and making a living was time-consuming. The result typically was that the returnee, like his cosmopolitan Gentile counterparts, gradually tapered off in his critical thinking and reading, lost much of his former ability to discuss world issues critically, and conformed more and more in his international concepts to local norms.

It was difficult to assess the private attitudes of small-town Jews. Many were obviously little interested in this field and had only rather vague inclinations. Increased racial tension and related pressures had caused many of them to project a more conservative public image of their international thinking than their true opinions warranted. On the other hand, many of them seemed to offer more internationalist or liberal views to interviewers from universities and research agencies than they were known for locally—and perhaps than their true thinking. The proportion of neo-isolationist Jews, or Jews who accepted many of the international attitudes associated with racism, was considerably greater outside cities and their suburbs. Most of their international thinking seemed to diverge less from that of local Gentile businessmen than was the case in metropolitan areas.

But the small-town Jews interviewed were privately at least somewhat more internationally inclined and less conservative than comparable local Gentiles in the same places. If there were as many as half a dozen Jewish families in a community, at least one Jew read the international content in one or more critical, relatively internationalist, periodicals. The more Jews in towns of comparable size, the larger the circulations of the New York *Times, Harper's, The Atlantic,* and the like. Causation is difficult to determine—perhaps Jews have gone to or stayed in towns where there were more Gentiles of cosmopolitan bent; existence of a few thoughtful Gentiles may stimulate more Jews to interest themselves in world matters; or the presence of internationally concerned and informed Jews may encourage more of the college educated Gentiles to be so. Probably a combination of these and other factors has operated in most cases. Only a minority of small-town Jews read such material frequently, but Jews were considerably more likely to do so than comparable Gentile elites in the same towns. Most Jews who did not read more analytical publications read *Newsweek,* or even *Time,* although many of them criticized the latter as unfairly biased against the South. *U.S. News and World Report* was more popular with small-town Southern Jews than with their urban coreligionists, but the former tended to be at least somewhat less enamored of its international views than were local Gentile merchants and planters. Moreover, a considerable number of Gentiles subscribed to periodicals like the New York *Times* (Sunday edition) to see what the "enemy" is saying, or to keep up with drama, literature, fashions, or other fields and ignored or read in fundamental disagreement the in-

ternational coverage. Few Jews seem to read these for "ammunition," and although these publications were more liberal on world
affairs than most of their small-town Jewish readers, Jews typically
were less hostile to the international interpretations therein than were
a considerable minority of Gentile readers.

Impacts on the General Community

As among Gentiles, the public position of cosmopolitan Jews before
less internationally interested, informed, and thoughtful colleagues has
depended on their own sense of self-assurance both in the subject matter of international relations and in their communities; their economic,
social, and emotional vulnerability to local pressures; the degree of
difference between their own thinking on foreign relations and that
among their prospective local audiences; the local level of tension over
the race question; personality factors; and the encouragement they
may receive from persons and organizations of similar persuasion both
within and without their locales. But the interviewees indicated that
cosmopolitan Jews with relatively liberal or responsibly conservative
international views have in recent years been considerably less inclined than Gentiles of similar knowledge and ideology to express
themselves before fellow Southerners of markedly more conservative
international opinion; Jewish cosmopolitans have been anxious about
calling attention to Jewish divergence from local thinking on controversial issues.

INCREASING FEAR OF ANTI-SEMITISM   Concern that expression of liberal opinion may stimulate negative reactions by conservative Gentiles
against themselves and Jews in general has been particularly apparent
since the Supreme Court decision of May 17, 1954. Growing insecurity has tended to silence many thoughtful Jews, particularly on the
race issue and national and international questions with racial overtones, but also indirectly in other controversial fields as well.

For generations Southern Jews and Gentiles have been saying that
there is less anti-Semitism in the South than elsewhere in the United
States and have taken pride in the rapport between Jews and Gentiles
in the region. Virtually no Jews in the South were publicly critical of

slavery during the antebellum period; although there were relatively few Jewish planters, concentration of Jews in the commercial class in the towns resulted in a probably larger fraction of Jews than white Gentiles owning some slaves.[27] Florida as well as Louisiana sent a Jew to the U.S. Senate before the war.[28] Most Jews in the region were pro-Dixie and they fought actively against the North in the Civil War.[29] In addition to Benjamin, the Quartermaster General, the Surgeon General, several Congressmen, and other high public and military officers of the Confederacy were Jewish,[30] although Jews were but a minuscule proportion of the Southern population.[31] The number of Jews in 1962 even in Southern cities has been small, and a larger proportion of them than of their Northern coreligionists have been there for several generations and have integrated local accents, mores, and thought patterns into their personalities. It has been pointed out that Southern Protestantism emphasized the Old Testament, as does Judaism, that Jews have long socialized with Gentiles in small Southern towns, and that Southern prejudices and aggressions have been focused on the Negro and the "Yankee meddler." Although there have been several unfortunate bombings of synagogues and other anti-Semitic incidents in the region since 1954, the incidence of such acts has been less in the South than in the rest of the country.[32] The smallest number of incidents occurred in states which had by 1960 engaged in no desegregation at all; the largest number of incidents took place in Southern states which had undergone some token integration.[33] These few incidents in the South were concentrated in the handful of larger cities.[34]

27. Korn, *Publications of the American Jewish Historical Society*, L (1961), 153–57.
28. Bertram Wallace Korn, *American Jewry and the Civil War* (Philadelphia: Jewish Publication Society of America, 1951), 3.
29. Simonhoff, *Jewish Participants in the Civil War*, xiii, xv, xvi, 161–71, 183–285, 310; Korn, *Publications of the American Jewish Historical Society*, L (1961), 191–98; James A. Wax, "The Jews of Memphis, 1860–1865," *Papers of the West Tennessee Historical Society*, no. 3 (1949), 84–88; Louis Ginsberg, *History of the Jews of Petersburg* (Petersburg, Va.: privately published, 1954), 42–43; Korn, *American Jewry and the Civil War*, ix, 49 ff.
30. Simonhoff, *Jewish Participants in the Civil War*, xv, xvi, 310 ff.; and Oscar Cohen, "Public Opinion and Anti-Jewish Prejudice in the South" (MS of the Anti-Defamation League, New York, 1959).
31. Korn, *Publications of the American Jewish Historical Society*, L (1961), 199.
32. David Caplovitz and Candace Rogers, *Swastika 1960: The Epidemic of Anti-Semitic Vandalism in America* (New York: Anti-Defamation League, 1961), 22.
33. *Ibid.*, 27.   34. *Ibid.*, 46–47.

The few surveys of attitudes toward Jews have been equivocal on prejudices among Southern as compared with Northern Gentiles, depending on the sphere of relationships examined. Thus, the proportion of Southerners, as of Northerners, who said they had heard any "criticism or talk against Jews in the last six months" declined considerably between 1945 and 1959; in the latter year 8 percent in the South as compared with 13 percent in the North answered in the affirmative.[35] This interregional difference was understandable, considering the few Jews that have existed in many Southern locales. White Southerners were about as apt as white Northerners in the late 1930s and 1940s to feel that we should allow a larger number of Jewish refugees from Nazism to enter this country,[36] contrary to the general tendency of Southerners to be more unfavorable to immigration than Northerners. Immediately after the war, Southern whites were distinctly less likely than Northern ones to think that Jews had "too much influence in the business world"; only in the South did less than half the population feel this way.[37] Questions that asked about the desirability of Jews as neighbors showed little difference between the South and the rest of the nation.[38]

But 35 percent of Southern whites as compared with 29 percent of Northern whites felt in 1959 that Jewish businessmen are "shrewd and tricky." [39] When a national survey asked in 1959, "If your party nominated a generally well-qualified person for President and he happened to be a Jew, would you vote for him?" 33 percent in the South, 11 percent in the Northeast, 22 percent in the West, and 25 percent in the Midwest said they would not.[40] However, a number of Jews have been elected to public office in the South; one encounters Southerners who voted for Mr. Levy down the street but want no part of "Yankee Jewish radicals."

In fact, most Southern Jews have been so quiet on controversial

35. Summary of previous surveys in an unpublished study by the American Jewish Committee, "The Nationwide Poll of March, 1959," Appendix D.
36. AIPO 139, 11/22/38 (3,131), and NORC 231, December, 1944 (2,471).
37. NORC 239, November, 1945 (2,540).
38. American Jewish Committee, "The Nationwide Poll of March, 1959," Table D-6.
39. Ibid.
40. AIPO 622, 12/18/59 (4,077). See also AIPO 604, 9/8/58 (1,522).

issues, including race, in the South that Southern Gentiles have greatly underestimated their real divergence from Protestant thinking on public and social questions. In 1959 only one percent of white Gentiles in the region felt that Jews were the group which had "done the most to stir up trouble over the (race) issue in those Southern communities where a serious dispute exists over the Supreme Court decision." When the public was asked, "In your community, which of the following groups of people do you feel are in favor of, or opposed to, integrating the public schools in the South?" only 15 percent said Jews favored integration, 10 percent said they opposed integration, 8 percent said they were neutral, and 67 percent said they did not know. Southern non-Jews tended to believe Catholics to be more liberal on race than Jews, contrary to the facts.[41]

However, surveys of communities under pressure for desegregation have found significantly higher incidence of anti-Semitic feelings among white segregationists than in the region generally;[42] in a period of mounting local racial tension, anti-Semitism apparently does rise considerably. And even when relatively cosmopolitan Jews in small Deep Southern communities said there had been little overt anti-Semitism, they usually admitted that they feared it would develop as racial disputes became central in local thinking, particularly if local Jews disagreed overtly with the attitudes of the white majority. They were anxious that expression of ideas less conservative than the prevailing thought on social and public questions, especially but not exclusively racial ones, would result in many Gentiles turning on them and the Jewish minority generally. The more intense the race issue in the community, the more insecure the local Jews have felt about expressing critical views on virtually any controversial issue. Thus, the discomfort among many Southern Jews over support of desegregation and racial equality by national Jewish organizations, like the Anti-Defamation League, the American Jewish Committee, the American Jewish Congress, and the National Council of Jewish Women, is understandable, as

41. American Jewish Committee, "The Nationwide Poll of March, 1959," pp. 47–50; and Cohen, "Public Opinion and Anti-Jewish Prejudice in the South."
42. Cohen, "Public Opinion and Anti-Jewish Prejudice in the South."

is their sensitivity to any Jewish prominence in liberal movements, especially racially oriented ones.[43]

CITY, TOWN, AND COUNTRY The larger the Jewish community and the less racially conservative the local white Gentiles, the more articulate Jews have been on such issues as independence of colonial territories, foreign aid, the U.N., domestic "anti-Communism," and other issues of foreign affairs.

For instance, the rabbis in Greensboro had not experienced any pressures from their coreligionists to tone down their liberal public positions on public questions, including race and foreign policy. Few Jews there felt much inhibited about expressing their views—more liberal and internationalist than those of the general community for the most part—on international relations, although most were reticent on race. Greensboro Jewry was in 1961 greatly overrepresented among participants in and supporters of such declared internationalist groups as the World Affairs Council, the League of Women Voters, the AAUW, college forums and lectures, and UNESCO-sponsored discussions.

Likewise, in New Orleans cosmopolitan Jews have with few exceptions felt free to express their opinions on foreign policy. If it had not been for their funds and energies in the early sixties, the relatively few agencies and groups offering or encouraging critical thought about foreign relations would either not have existed or would have experienced much greater difficulties than was actually the case. Although Jews have not been particularly numerous among the formal leaders on organizational letterheads, they have typically been major financial contributors and active workers. As elsewhere in the region, many Jews, as well as thoughtful Gentiles, have played down the proportion of Jews in liberal or internationally sophisticated organizations, because

43. Many Southern Jews seemed to manifest an ambivalence toward these liberal Jewish organizations. While wanting to separate themselves in the local Gentile mind from them and their equalitarian pronouncements and accusing them of generating anti-Semitism among segregationists, they have wanted the support of these agencies in case of anti-Semitic developments in the region. And many who have objected to the public statements favoring interracial justice by these agencies probably privately agreed with them. See also Fishman, *Midstream*, VII (1961), 50.

they have feared that too "Jewish" an image would seriously limit their effectiveness among the general public.

However, Jews of relatively liberal international bent in traditionalist Charleston have been much more hesitant about criticizing prevailing international thinking among their Gentile peers. Not only the most intellectually alert and cosmopolitan but also the most activist and articulate among the internationally thoughtful have left Charleston in disproportionately large numbers after college. Those who have remained have been primarily those willing to keep their peace when confronted by viewpoints very different from their own on controversial international matters, like aid to Africa and United States policy toward Moise Tshombe in 1961. Many, perhaps most, cosmopolitans who stayed tended to have abandoned much hope of changing the thinking of their arch-conservative associates; there were hardly any "crusaders" or "martyrs" among Jewish readers of *The Reporter*, *The Atlantic*, and the New York *Times*.

Even strongly conservative regular associates of Jews who favored most of the foreign policy of the Kennedy administration and disagreed with many of the international opinions of the local press, Congressman Rivers, and Senator Thurmond tended to feel the views of these privately liberal Jews were roughly the same as their own on world problems. One prominent Jewish businessman noted that public knowledge of his criticisms of the thinking current in Charleston on such issues as the supposed domestic Communist menace, Katanga versus the U.N. in the Congo (1961), economic assistance to Poland and foreign aid generally, and possible admission of Communist China into the U.N., would not only alienate many of his customers, but would probably also make it difficult for him to borrow money at banks run by "British Empire Loyalist" and "white man's burden" types. Lawyers and physicians believed that they would do damage to their practices by openly expressing their views. Jewish cosmopolitans who wanted to continue to live and prosper in Charleston seemed even more cautious about speaking out in opposition to the thinking of the *News and Courier* than were Gentiles of like mind. Conversations about world affairs were limited largely to a small circle of internationally thoughtful and relatively liberal intimates, but even then one feared "leaks" to the general community and social, if not economic, repercussions. Only individuals who were economically invulnerable to local pressures—a slender fraction of cosmopolitans indeed—felt free to criticize prevailing viewpoints, but even most of them did not wish to isolate themselves from relatives and friends.

The discouraging pressures operating on Deep Southern small-town and rural Gentile cosmopolitans have usually been even more compelling for Jews. A rabbi who had retired because of illness to Antebellum Town and who read widely and was generally cosmopolitan remarked that he had tended to voice disagreement with views expressed in face-to-face conversations when he first returned there. However, the shift to the right on foreign policy had been so acute, the local racial feelings so sensitized and emotionalized, and his previous efforts to advance responsible views so unsuccessful that he had given up trying to change people's thinking. When someone next to him at a Chamber of Commerce or other meeting expressed irresponsible neo-isolationist views, by 1961 he either let him "rave on" or changed the subject.

A Jewish merchant in Deltatown who had majored in political science, obtained a law degree at a major Midwestern university, married a cosmopolitan Northerner, and worked for an internationalist Jewish organization in the North, returned home to take over his sick father's business. A good customer came in to collect Citizens Council dues after the 1954 decision, and, having heard of loss of trade among merchants who did not join, the former lawyer became a member, though an inactive one. He commented that he felt like he was talking to himself much of the time and that his critical reading of serious periodicals had dropped off because of lack of opportunities to do anything with his knowledge. His sensibilities and his ability to express himself, he felt, had become dulled. He still managed to participate in thoughtful discussions with several other Jewish and Gentile cosmopolitans who also read the New York *Times* (Sunday edition), *The Atlantic,* or other thoughtful publications, but he remained "quiet" before most anti-foreign aid, anti-U.N. people. He noted that it was one thing for Judge X, descendant of several esteemed families of the region, leader in the Episcopal church, and relative of the socially prominent in the Deep South, to write critical letters to the arch-conservative papers in the state, chair the discussion groups in the library on public issues, and inform all and sundry of his views on world affairs—people merely said he was getting old and was just another genteel eccentric. A Jew who did likewise needed considerably more courage or less sensitivity to probable public reactions. The whole Jewish community might become a target for antagonism—other Jews would fear that one was risking the status of the entire ethnic group, and many local Jews felt that no one had any right to upset the delicate balance whereby Jews had been treated well and accepted generally as fellow Southerners.

A Jewish businessman in a conservative Deep Southern community of less than thirty thousand people who had an excellent education kept copies of *U.S. News and World Report* and the ultra-conservative daily paper of a nearby city in his office waiting room. His study at home, however, contained perhaps the best private library in town, including the *New Republic, The Economist*, and the New York *Times*. His favorite columnists on world affairs were James Reston and Walter Lippmann. He said he read this material as an indirect way of attacking local thinking, "instead of taking action," and as an escape from the ever present realities. Action in conformity with his real views would mean "bankruptcy." If it were not for contact with responsible thinking in such publications and frequent "buying" trips to New York, "I would go nuts." Reading and visiting cosmopolitans in cities seemed to serve this purpose for a number of such undercover "egg-heads"—as another thoughtful Jew noted, "If the local bunch thought I was an 'intellectual,' that would be my finish."

Southern Jews have been more inclined than Northern ones to be affiliated with and active in synagogues, as part of the general Southern involvement in organized religion; according to expert estimates by rabbis and Jewish organizations in the South, perhaps as many as 90 percent were members of synagogues in 1960.[44] Moreover, the rabbi has been a more central figure in most Southern Jewish communities than in most Reform groups in the North. At least until recently members of predominantly small congregations probably tended more than in the North to listen carefully to the rabbi's views. Although most

44. For example, some 80 percent of New Orleans Jews were synagogue affiliated in the late 1950's; this is above the Northern urban average. See Reissman, *Jewish Journal of Sociology*, IV (1962), 123.

Reform rabbis who have held pulpits in smaller Southern communities have not been among the more intellectually vigorous, and such congregations have in a number of cases called relatively conservative spiritual leaders, most rabbis in the region in the early sixties were considerably better informed and more favorable to multilateral commitments in world affairs than their average members. Conservative Jews have wanted rabbis to limit themselves to rituals and ceremonies and to remain silent on social and political questions. Nevertheless, most rabbis seemed to continue to inform their congregations of their views on world affairs as on other public issues, including race.

But Southern Jews tend to judge their rabbis in terms of their popularity in the white Gentile community. Even when many members of a congregation have more or less agreed privately with their rabbi's views, they have felt anxious about his image with non-Jewish segregationists. As one intellectually alert and articulate rabbi in a very conservative Deep Southern community noted, his rapport with members of his temple and security as their rabbi were closely related to their fears about Gentiles hearing of his liberal thoughts. They were particularly anxious about the reactions of the local racist press to his behavior. Another rabbi whose liberal ideas did become known to the general community left town for several weeks to find upon returning that the leaders of his temple had been warned by representatives of a potent white supremacist and otherwise ultra-conservative organization that Jews might suffer undescribed reprisals if the rabbi did not depart permanently.[45] Consequently, most rabbis have presented considerably more conservative, or noncommittal, positions to non-Jews than to their own people and have had relatively little direct impact on international attitudes beyond their congregations.

Similar depressants to active cosmopolitanism vis-à-vis the Gentile community have been exerted as well on Jewish laymen by their coreligionists; small-town, Deep Southern Jews have feared especially that someone with a Jewish name would express controversial ideas and

45. This incident was the climax of increasing pressures against this cosmopolitan rabbi. Although it was finally agreed that the rabbi would be more cautious in his public expressions and that he would remain as spiritual leader, further difficulties with the Gentile community developed and he finally departed for a temple outside the Deep South after interviews for this study were completed.

thus stimulate unfavorable reactions to Jews in general. There have been subtle pressures to keep quiet on such matters with the result that Jews in some communities have been willing to declare themselves against irresponsible views only when under direct attack themselves—they have been afraid even to criticize overt anti-Semitism by racists.

For instance, a graduate of the University of North Carolina, an institution regarded as ultraliberal in the Black Belt, married into a merchant family in a Deep Southern town. The word was gradually transmitted to him by asides and other subtle means that he should keep his ideas to himself and not "spout off" any "Frank Graham socialism" and the like if he wished to prosper and keep friends. He was informed that the rest of the Jewish community would not appreciate an "eager beaver" Goldberg (pseudonym) antagonizing the local conservatives. Since his father-in-law controlled the money and the family business in which he was employed, he "behaved." Another example was a local Jewish merchant who, when called upon by a regional representative (born and raised in Virginia) of a sophisticated national Jewish agency, grilled him about his background for fear he was "another one of those obnoxious, radical New York Jews." A recent study in a Black Belt city of 120,000 determined that liberal Jews who had indicated publicly their disagreement with local conservative thinking, particularly on race, had been informed that they had become a source of embarrassment to other Jews.[46]

Moreover, in small Deep Southern communities, cosmopolitan Jews seemed even fearful of expressing their true thinking before one another. In one such town the author met with several Jewish couples in a Jewish home for discussion of their international views. The initial half hour was spent in interrogating the interviewer—where was he born and raised, where did he go to college, what was he doing in the North, why did he want to know their opinions, was he not really the representative of some "leftist" or integrationist organization? Opinions expressed on foreign policy ranged from very conservative by national standards to what would be responsibly conservative in Boston. Views were particularly conservative on international questions related to race, and even more so on race in the South. Later questioning of several of them individually indicated that their private opinions were

46. Fishman, *Midstream*, VII (1961), 51.

considerably less conservative than those they voiced before their local Jewish colleagues. Each thought that each of the others was more opposed to foreign aid, long-term commitments to economic assistance, entry of Communist China into the U.N., domestic "Communism," and, particularly, school desegregation than was actually the case. One said before his colleagues that he would never send his children to school with Negroes and that he could understand people who would meet Negroes with loaded shotguns should they try to "force themselves" on whites. Later, he commented privately that he could not understand why the local Negroes were so "docile" and that they might achieve some of their "rights" if they were more activist. Another volunteered that he had to live with his Jewish colleagues and that one's criticisms of local thinking would be known to "everybody" in a town like his within a week.

Nevertheless, more than in cities, the small-town and few rural Jews have long circulated with local Gentiles in the proprietory, managerial, and professional classes after as well as during the work day. Some of their divergent thinking on world affairs—on cooperation with colored nations in the U.N. and in economic development, for example—has rubbed off on at least the less extreme opponents of foreign aid and has moderated somewhat the latter's opinions. And one or more internationally thoughtful Jews from even communities with a dozen or less families have usually discussed international matters at least now and then with the handful of local Gentiles of like inclinations. In the few communities where there have been organized groups interested, *inter alia*, in world affairs, such as a library or American Heritage discussion group, or in some towns of larger population a small League of Women Voters, several Jews have typically been active therein. The presence of a few Jewish families has helped to limit the natural provincialism and ignorance of ideas from outside of many Southern towns and to make life more tolerable for the few Gentiles of similarly broad horizons.

On the whole, however, Jews in Deltatown, Antebellum Town, and other small Deep Southern communities offer in the short run only very limited vehicles for communicating broader international thinking to the general population. Racial tension and Gentile hostility to gradual desegregation must lessen before cosmopolitan Jews in greatly increased numbers will express their more liberal (or less conservative) international ideas. As one noted, Jews could not be "fooled" by relatively liberal Quakers and Unitarians associated with cosmopolitan activities any more—the publicly declared cosmopolitans must be "big" Episcopalians, Presbyterians, Methodists, and Baptists for Jews to participate and express their support for active international cooperation in the U.N., in Africa, and in other touchy fields. In many Southern settings internationally thoughtful Jews will probably be the last to state their views publicly, after prominent Protestant leaders in considerable numbers have already spoken out in similar vein.

David and Adele Bernstein

Slow Revolution in Richmond, Va.:
A New Pattern in the Making

SOCIAL CHANGE is seeping through Richmond, Virginia, as quietly and pervasively as the aroma of tobacco from the mills down near the James River. Old-established patterns are reshaping themselves in a kind of middle-class revolution—an altogether respectable revolution, however, with an "r" so faint as to be almost indiscernible. The war brought new industries, new labor markets, new wealth, as well as new human experiences and values to the whole South. Du Pont has put up a huge new cellophane plant just outside Richmond, and there is an unlovely but lucrative factory district spreading along the farther reaches of Broad Street. The riverfront mills turn out more than sixty billion cigarettes a year, one in every six smoked in America. Since people smoke most when they worry most, this is one of the few American cities stable enough to ride out a possible depression.

Altogether, Richmond's standard of living is higher now than ever before. The Bureau of Labor Statistics recently chose three cities, Richmond, Washington, and Manchester (New Hampshire), for a study of annual savings by middle-income families: Richmond's average was $260, Washington's $36, and Manchester had an average deficit of $148.

A breeze of liberalism has poked into the musty corners of local politics. Last year, for the first time in Richmond's history, a Negro, Oliver Hill, was elected to the City Council; it took more white than Negro votes to put him there. For the past two years, Negroes have been on the municipal police force. In the gubernatorial primaries last summer, a mildly liberal politician named Francis Pickens Miller lost to the candidate of the ancient Byrd machine; but the protest vote was larger than ever.

The city has changed. Its drabness is not less drab, nor its little eddies of antiquarian loveliness less lovely. But the business district bustles as never before. On the streets people look, if not fashionably, at least solidly well dressed. Department stores now emphasize "gracious living"—a term taken very seriously here—for everyone. The old families, with their fixed, inherited wealth, still dominate local affairs, but without the old assurance. Society leadership still is theirs, but not in the way it used to be before the war, when they also controlled the city's politics, dominated the civic and welfare activities, and set the social tone. Today the recently rich nudge them with social aspirations of their own; and a newly emerging Richmond of Negroes who vote, of factory workers who join unions, and of a secure white-collar group, is seeking a voice in its own affairs.

Nowhere—except perhaps among the Negro third of Richmond—are all these signs of change so marked as among the Jews in the city, who number something less than eight thousand in a population of nearly a quarter of a million. For nearly two centuries their history has woven itself into the Richmond story; their roots are deep, and all the myths and shibboleths of this stronghold of Southern romanticism are theirs. There were Jewish slave-holders, and Jewish warriors in the Confederate cause, and Jews who suffered during the Reconstruction years. These were the old Jewish families, and it was quite natural that they should have dominated the Jewish community—as old families dominated the entire community—until the new Southern revolution began.

For fifty years past, Jewish newcomers have been absorbed by Richmond, not in the sense that they were accepted by the old families with open arms, but in the sense that they themselves willingly accepted a subordinate, if not submerged, status in the structure of the community. In Virginia, where only 2 per cent of the population is foreign-born, all newcomers are strangers for a very long time. And the inexorable, though slow, tempo of integration might have continued undisturbed along the lanes rutted by time, had it not been for a double impact—first, of the explosive changes in the South itself, and second, of the even more explosive effect on the Richmond Jews of events in the outside world.

The Jewish tragedy in Europe, the arrival of refugees, the re-surgence of Jewish consciousness, the widespread Zionist agitation, reached Richmond later than most other American cities. Roving speakers, fund-raising campaigns, and the local headlines created a new Jewish-consciousness here as in the rest of the country. In Richmond, however, there had been no preparation. The visiting speakers found audiences apathetic; the appeals for funds were only meagerly met; and the headlines were being offset by accounts of the numerous activities of Dr. Edward N. Calisch, for half a century the leading Jewish citizen and rabbi of the most fashionable congregation in the city.

Because this is an atmosphere where change is greeted grudgingly, and only when there is no well-mannered way of resisting it, even the emotional impact of events abroad was slow to stir the Richmond Jews. In the end, however, it was to change their whole communal way of life.

The weight of the past hangs heavy over Richmond—the memory of the great, gay days before the War Between the States, when Poe walked its streets, his head full of morbid ratiocination; when its society counted among the most elegant in the country, and Thackeray, visiting on a lecture tour in the 1850's, called it "the merriest and most picturesque place in America." And the memory, of course, of the desperately romantic days of the Confederacy, when Richmond was the political headquarters of the violent struggle which pitted states' rights, plantations, and slavery against the irresistible industrial revolution.

The past is real here, and until a few years ago it almost overshadowed the present. The WPA guide to Virginia solemnly relates: "The city's social season, from late fall to Ash Wednesday, retains its old ritual, with the Monday germans as highlights. Tea in darkened drawing rooms, dinners served by tradition-trained butlers, frosted mint juleps in ancient goblets, and Smithfield hams and beaten biscuits, are part of the ceremonial that has continued with no deviation. It is still proper in old Richmond to refer to a guest as So-and-So's granddaughter, or the descendant of a founding father."

At least one Jewish family in ten can trace its local ancestry back to the 1850's or earlier. In Richmond, this is synonymous with aristocracy. Until recently the bridge between them and the other nine-tenths was narrow and rarely crossed. In a community where "visiting" is the principal recreation, the two groups exchanged little hospitality; nor, certainly, did they belong to the same societies or share in social diversions. The scions of the old families inherited the first positions in the Jewish community along with their names and wealth—positions which involved communal as well as social leadership. They retained exclusive possession of their synagogue, Beth Ahabah, and of their rabbi, Dr. Calisch.

It is not altogether possible to understand what has happened to the Jews of Richmond without knowing something about Rabbi Calisch, who came to Richmond in 1891, at twenty-six, from a briefly held Reform pulpit in Peoria, Illinois, and spent his life creating an image of the assimilated Richmond Jew.

He was handsome and robust, something of a scholar, an eloquent speaker, and a sophisticated but enthusiastic participant in civic affairs. He exchanged pulpits with Protestant clergymen; he delivered patriotic speeches during both World Wars; he lunched with President Taft at the White House and with Lord Reading at the vice-regal palace in India; he was treasurer of the English Speaking Union, president of the Richmond Peace Council, and president of the Richmond alumni chapter of Phi Beta Kappa; in 1939 the Richmond *Times-Dispatch* put his name on its Roll of Honor as one of the ten outstanding men of Virginia.

He was equally active in Jewish affairs: he was on the executive committee of the local B'nai B'rith lodge; he lectured for the Jewish Chautauqua; he was president of the Central Conference of American Rabbis. In his maiden sermon at Beth Ahabah, Rabbi Calisch had said: "I shall endeavor to expound a religion that shall not flinch before the light of science nor cower beneath the flash of research, yet shall be loyal to the core to the grand old mother, Judaism." He instituted the practice of uncovered heads at worship; and on the rare occasions when he visited an Orthodox synagogue, he refused to don a skull cap. He modernized the Beth Ahabah ritual in accord with his Reform philosophy, revised the prayer book, and wrote a *Child's Bible*. He introduced progressive education techniques in his Children's Religious School, with arts and crafts classes, a dramatics class, a stamp club, and a photography club. Thirty years ago, at the height of the rabbi's prestige, the president of his congregation made some notes on "old-time observances" that were now "hardly known by any of the present generation." The list was long: "Wearing the *tallis*; separation of the sexes in the synagogue; fasting on Tisha-b'Av as well as on Yom Kippur; a strictly kept *shabbes*; unleavened meals on Passover; laying *tefillim*; a Kosher household; Sabbath blessing on Friday evening."

In his relations with Christian neighbors, the rabbi created in himself the most ingratiating of Jewish stereotypes—the man completely unaware of any personal problem as a Jew, at ease and unselfconscious, articulate but not argumentative, intelligent but not arrogant, worldly but not cynical. In 1907 he addressed a joint session of the House of Bishops and House of Clerical and Lay Deputies of the General Convention of the Protestant Episcopal Church, and the next day a Richmond paper exclaimed editorially: "His lofty, dignified, and graceful address was in every way worthy of the man, of the great race he represented, and the illustrious conclave that listened with respect to his words. For ourselves, we know not which most to admire, the spirit that moved the House to invite the address, or the manner in which that address was delivered. Both were admirable."

The accolades continued, in the press and pulpits and at civic gatherings, whenever he made a public appearance through the years that followed. Yet, shortly before his death, Calisch appears to have had some doubts about his career. "One thing in which I have failed was in developing a following among Jews such as I have among Christians," he told a friend.

"By the late 1930's and until his retirement," a Beth Ahabah member recalls, "Rabbi Calisch would deliver his sermons on Saturday mornings—on the philosophy of Spinoza, or the ethics of Judaism, or some other subject like that—and there would be scarcely a dozen of us in that big, dim synagogue. I hardly know why—unless it was that somehow I don't think Calisch was loved by the Jews here, or even greatly respected, during the last years of his life. It was a tragedy, in a way, and many of us wondered whether he was such a great success after all."

Calisch was, on occasion, invited to visit the darkened drawing rooms of the First Families of Virginia. He was asked to address the annual breakfast of the Hunt Club. Through him, and through its respect for him, all of Richmond that "counted" showed how much it thought of the Richmond Jews. But neither Rabbi Calisch nor any other Jew was invited to join the Hunt Club. Indeed, social exclusion —the only tangible kind of anti-Semitism in the city, aside from a few recent cases of restrictive covenants—seems, if anything, to have increased during his half-century there. A hundred and fifty years ago, when as much as one-sixth of Richmond's white population was Jewish, there was a good deal more social intercourse (with its inevitable result, intermarriage) and more active participation in municipal affairs than in recent times. When the most fashionable city club, the Westmoreland, was organized in the 1870's, its membership included several Jews, and once it elected a Jewish president. Today the club excludes Jews, as do the Commonwealth Club, the Country Club of Virginia, the Hermitage Country Club, the Junior League, and the most fashionable women's groups.

"The philosophy of the old Jewish families," a Richmonder explained, "was that they ought to be as quiet and unostentatious as possible. They would not dream of making a fuss about the fact that they received no invitation to join a club or to attend a party, no matter how much they would have wanted to go. If they were invited to join an important civic or welfare committee of some kind, they accepted graciously and worked hard. But they did not think it proper to volunteer their services. They hardly ever ran for public office, for example, and frowned on other Jews who did. They just didn't think a Jew should put himself forward."

In any event, the well-born Jews did receive the outward forms of acceptance. But they would have been less than human if they did not, however unostentatiously, yearn for full social acceptance in the very circles which treated them civilly but distantly—and if they did not, in turn, practice a polite but firm form of exclusion on Jews whose ancestry was not so deeply rooted in the Old Dominion.

The structure of the Jewish community lent itself easily to such stratification. The synagogues were—and still are—the very core of Richmond Jewish life. Beth Ahabah is the oldest; it was established in the early 1840's by German Jewish immigrants who were either excluded from or uncomfortable in the Sephardic synagogue they found on their arrival. In time, the energetic new group absorbed the diminishing

Sephardic families, and with them assumed unchallenged communal leadership.

Meanwhile, Polish Jews trickled into Richmond in the 1850's, followed thirty years later by Russian Jews in larger numbers. The Poles, who had founded an Orthodox synagogue of their own, were a little snobbish toward the newer wave, and a second Orthodox synagogue came into being.

To the Beth Ahabah aristocrats, there seemed to be little difference between these two foreign-accented groups; and a basic, rigid, and none too friendly pattern of nobleman and commoner lasted well into the 20th century. By the 1930's, however, some of the Polish Jewish families had reached the point where even Beth Ahabah was prepared to accept them; while the children and grandchildren of the wave of the 1880's were ready to strike out on their own.

These groups—English-speaking, native-born, increasingly prosperous, uncomfortable with both Orthodoxy and Reform Judaism—created a new Conservative temple, Congregation Beth-El. This turned out to be the first real challenge to Beth Ahabah, or, more accurately, to the Calisch mentality.

The timing is significant. Beth-El began as the depression years were ending. Its members were the second generation of Eastern European Jews, businessmen and professionals who were beginning to feel a sense of communal responsibility—in a community which did not encourage them to assume responsibility. They enjoyed increasing economic security, but a decreasing Jewish security, principally because of the news from Europe. Unable to escape into identification with Richmond's past, they made a virtue of the necessity to be Jewish.

It was not long before they became the stronghold of Zionist feeling and activity in the community, with a large, resourceful membership that included an unprecedented number of young people. Unwittingly, perhaps, they had provided Richmond's Jews with a station midway between Beth Ahabah and Orthodoxy. In doing so, they remade the social map of the community and provided the impulses which have changed Beth Ahabah itself.

To the Beth-El group, Beth Ahabah was not quite Jewish. It was "assimilationist," in the unpleasant meaning of the word; it was cowardly; it was frightened; it was anti-Zionist. And as the Beth-El middle class increased in economic strength, as well as in numbers, their sentiments could no longer be laughed off. Beth-El and what it symbolized thus brought to Richmond the fermentation process that had taken place, many years earlier, in most other Jewish communities throughout the country.

If Richmond had lagged behind the rest of the country, there were valid reasons.

First of these was the unusual size, wealth, and deep-rootedness of the old families. Indeed, it is hard to think of any American city, other than San Francisco, where so many Jewish families are so intimately identified with the earliest local history; and the evolution of the Jewish community in San Francisco is not unlike that of Richmond.

Secondly, the economic tempo in Richmond has been slower than in Northern cities. Tobacco kept Richmond fairly well off in hard times, but until recent years there were few opportunities for new enterprises to develop on an ambitious scale. In New York, Eastern European Jews were beginning to make fortunes forty years ago, and even to engulf the older families. In Richmond there are only a few such early success stories. On the other hand, this is a Jewish community without a working class, and without serious poverty (which means that there is little incentive toward a proletarian rebelliousness). The local Jewish welfare agency carries a maximum yearly case load of twenty, several of which are transients. A few years ago, the Orthodox congregation did boast of one impoverished member, an unemployable painter who worshiped regularly without paying membership dues. During the war, when prosperous congregants clamored for tickets for the High Holidays, the painter was asked to give up his regular seat and move down a few rows so that a large family could sit together. "I am the only poor Jew in Richmond," he protested. "I deserve more respect."

The third reason for the time-lag was Richmond itself. Nearly all its people, Christian and Jewish, tend to resist change; and the newest arrivals learn very quickly how pleasant it can be to put on the brakes.

With the war, however, the South as a whole began to emerge from its colonial economic status, and new opportunities for money-making came to Richmond. As it turned out, this Southern revolution began to stir almost exactly at the same time that outside influences affected the Richmond Jews. As the immigrant families began to build up their bank accounts, as the little tailor shop became the chromium-plated, neon-lit dress shop, as the young Jewish doctors developed large and lucrative practices, the papers were filled with daily stories of the Nazi persecution.

For the old families, this was a matter for polite if heartfelt horror. They could not possibly feel the personal involvement of the first or second generation Jew who realized that only a few years and miraculous good luck separated him from the possibility of the concentration camp and the gas chamber. The sixth generation Jew was more likely to feel the kind of sympathy felt by his Christian fellow-Southerners (for he dwelt in a region that was ardently anti-German and interventionist long before Pearl Harbor). But he was disturbed, too, by the fear that constant newspaper repetition of the unhappy events in Europe would have a harmful impact locally, that it would call attention to his Jewishness and give him a vulnerability that he thought had been buried with his ancestors. His reaction, in sum, was not unnatural in the circumstances: resentment, irritation, a certain embarrassment.

For the more recently arrived Jews, there was a different but equally human reaction—deeper, more emotional, more outspoken, and perhaps more masochistic. They sought an outlet for their revulsion; if they could do little to stop Hitler by themselves, they demanded the minimum satisfaction of strong language—the kind of language which the minority, the leading old families, considered "bad public relations." It was inevitable that the rising Jewish middle class should, at this point, begin to question the old leadership. By the time the war ended, it was possible to translate all their anxieties and resentments and guilt feelings into positive action. The remnants of Europe's Jews were in the DP camps, desperately awaiting aid. The drive to build a Jewish state in Palestine took on a new, dramatic urgency.

Rabbi Calisch had sensed all this even as the war was going on, and, as one of his last activities, he helped found the anti-Zionist American Council for Judaism. With him, most of the old families tended to see in Zionism a threat to their own status in Richmond, and perhaps even to their hope that one day they would achieve full social equality. The concept of any form of Jewish nationalism was alien to their whole way of life. It was hardly surprising that they should have made of Richmond a stronghold of Jewish anti-Zionism.

But the emotional stirrings among the newcomers were too vital to accept all this. The newly wealthy, the newly successful, the newly confident, could not be impressed with arguments that raising large sums of money for the United Jewish Appeal, for example, would antagonize their Christian neighbors. Having both money and energy, they began to assert their own leadership.

Before the war, a Jewish Community Council had been established under Beth Ahabah leadership to raise money in a modest way for various charitable causes. Now it was taken over as the vehicle for the high-pressure fund-raising so familiar in other cities. There was an immediate response. In 1945, the Council collected $118,000; in 1946 the collections jumped to $309,000; last year the Council raised $431,-000, with at least eighty-five per cent of all Jewish families contributing. These totals may not match other communities of equal size and wealth, which have had a psychological head-start; but it is the rate of increase that is significant. For this rate of increase stands in direct proportion to the shift in power from the old and settled families to the new and aggressive ones.

Several years ago the B'nai B'rith lodge (once a virtual Beth Ahabah stronghold, now no longer so) sponsored the creation of a Jewish Community Center, over the violent opposition of the old families, who considered the idea to reek of separatism. After much controversy, a small building was taken over, but it burned down recently. This year the Community Council is raising almost fifty thousand dollars for a new one; the Center and the "Jewish activities" planned for it are regarded by the new leadership as a victory over "the old way of thinking."

What is actually happening now, however, is that the two forces, the one stable and rooted and conservative, the other aggressive and new and emotionally involved, have begun to find a common meeting ground. The Council itself is no longer run by a tight little board of aristocrats; it now has twenty-eight members, from all segments of the community, who probably emerge from their wrangling with a close approximation of what the Richmond Jews as a whole would wish.

Nor do these wishes mean the disavowal of everything associated with the past. It is apparently possible to be a Zionist and at the same time to accept Richmond's belief that, while everyone presumably has ancestors, only the privileged have ancestors who lived in Richmond. Both old and new families have so far resisted the arguments of the earnest young social worker who believes that the Ladies Hebrew Benevolent Association ought to change its name to something less redolent of 19th-century charity. The Ladies Hebrew Benevolent Association, after all, succored Confederate wounded in the War Between the States. If the name was good enough for those heroes, it is good enough for the leading Richmond Jewish social agency in our own prosaic time.

So the new trend is having its effect on the relative newcomers as well as on the old-timers. The old-timers are not at all as anti-Zionist as they used to be; they have learned that no one in town will cut them dead if they contribute handsomely to the UJA; and they have learned to respect the drive and common sense of many of the new leaders. As for the latter, they have mellowed a little in their resentment against the cautious ideology of the artisocracy. Their Zionism, certainly, is by no means so melodramatic as in many other communities. Their attitude toward Israel is far more likely to involve disinterested and genuine symapthy than passionate devotion. The question of dual loyalty, which disturbs some people in other cities, would be ridiculous here. Both the old Jewish families and the new ones have, during the war and in the peace, played leading roles in city-wide and philanthropic activities, from war bond drives to community chest campaigns.

Curiously enough, the oldest old-timers and the newest newcomers among Richmond's Jews seem to hold identical standoffish attitudes toward the Negroes, though for utterly different reasons. The old families have tended to adopt the classical-romantic posture of mammy-nursed paternalism toward "the colored element." Among the newcomers, mostly small shopkeepers, there often exists the tradesman's contempt for the Negro customer who is considered less trustworthy than the white; and the feeling is reciprocated by many Negroes, who waste no love on such contacts with the white world. But these are the extremes. Between the two, most Richmond Jews fall into what is now clearly an American Jewish pattern of liberal behavior as far as Negroes are concerned. The most striking case of tangible advancement in Negro-white employment practices is being conducted quietly and effectively by a Jewish merchant (who feels that its value would be vitiated by public discussion in the present experimental stage). And about one-third of the money contributed locally to organizations aiming to further Negro rights comes from Jews—an amount obviously out of proportion to the Jewish population.

The synagogues remain the key to Richmond's Jews. Beth Ahabah's membership has swelled tremendously in the five years since Dr. Calisch's death. Nearly every old Jewish family can still be counted among the six hundred or so that belong to it, but an increasing number are those who ten years ago would have been excluded on genealogical grounds. Conservative Beth-El, next in size, this year dedicated a new temple, an uncompromisingly modern structure of which its members are extremely proud. The Orthodox Beth Israel combines the remnants of the old synagogues of Polish and Russian Jews, and is now the smallest of the three leading congregations.

(There is a fourth, a little *shul* named Aitz Chaim, where a few old folks pray without benefit of rabbis holding theological doctorates or of sermons on current events of a Sunday morning. Aitz Chaim has no great significance in the social scheme; the young folks are not attracted to it, and its dwindling membership is content to be left alone with the old-time religion. Besides, everyone in town knows that sooner or later Aitz Chaim will be absorbed by Beth Israel.)

The three synagogues are what count. Their combined membership probably runs as high as sixteen hundred families, a larger percentage of the total Jewish population than is usual in Northern cities. Services are generally well attended. The rabbis of all three are young and ambitious, with smooth faces and a remarkable similarity in sonorous pulpit diction.

By and large, you can still identify nearly any Jew in Richmond by his synagogal affiliation. It is not entirely an economic yardstick, for there are frayed aristocrats who show themselves at Beth Ahabah to hear the Sunday sermon, just as there are wealthy Russian-born Jews who attend Friday evening services at Beth Israel. The scale is social, and, therefore, still genealogical: Beth Israel harbors most Jews born in Eastern Europe, and many of their children; Beth-El is predominantly second and third generation; and Beth Ahabah consists mostly of people whose grandparents, at least, were born in the United States.

Like all human relationships, of course, these distinctions are too flexible and fluid to be quite as simple as this. In a single family, you may find members of two different synagogues (though rarely of three); and indeed there are a few Richmond Jews who, for reasons of their own, hold membership in two congregations. More significantly, there are many families in which the parents belong to one congregation, while the children, having grown up and established families, belong to another.

As for the young people who are not yet settled enough to think in terms of social barriers and hesitations, they are the purest evidence of the revolution that has taken Richmond. In school and college, and during the war, they mixed easily with people from other backgrounds, ignoring the old constricting patterns. The rate of intermarriage with Christians, as well as of intermarriage among Jews from differing social backgrounds inside Richmond, has in consequence been high in the past five or six years.

These intermarriages are, in most people's opinion, usually successful. The city absorbs nearly any new development having to do with marriage and family and children, for these bespeak stability and continuity. The city also keeps a firm hold on most Jewish young people, whether intermarried or not; for the changing social pattern has been accepted by them as a matter of course, and the prospect of business and professional opportunity in Richmond is altogether attractive (more so, apparently, than for many ambitious young non-Jews who go north to seek their fortunes).

Nevertheless, for the community as a whole, the three synagogues are steps in the social ladder, progressing from Orthodox Beth Israel to Conservative Beth-El to Reform Beth Ahabah. Since the barriers to Beth Ahabah have been lowered, the congregation has become the largest in the community. Similarly, the Jefferson Lakeside Country Club, once a Beth Ahabah stronghold, has opened its doors to relative newcomers—hampered only by lack of space to absorb the flood of membership applications.

The new content of Richmond's Jewishness thus lies almost wholly in synagogue membership for social purposes, and in the giving of funds for humanitarian purposes. The ghost of Rabbi Calisch may shudder at the implication of social climbing, or at the uses to which these funds are put. But the change has come, and no one could stop it now. Neither does anyone know where it will end. If Rabbi Calisch, as has been claimed, did not succeed in giving his coreligionists the "inner Jewish content" with which to cope with the calamities and the ideologies of the past ten years, neither have the new communal leaders so far provided Richmond's Jews with anything newer than a crisis psychology which is stale by now.

This, perhaps, is why no new Jewish image has emerged for the Richmond Christians. The whole South is changing; Richmond is changing; and the Richmond Jews are changing too. But the changes are still so fluid that Richmond, with its adherence to the past, prefers to adhere to the recognizable symbols.

"Dr. Calisch continues to represent the Jew for most of us," said Virginius Dabney, the distinguished editor of the Richmond *Times Dispatch*. "Everyone admired him. He was a fine man."

"But Dr. Calisch is no longer alive. What has replaced him as the symbol of the Jew in Richmond?"

"Well," said Mr. Dabney, "after all, it has been only a few years since Rabbi Calisch died."

Who will wear the mantle in the new Richmond of the generation ahead?

Theodore Lowi

Southern Jews:
The Two Communities

Introduction

AN ATTEMPT was recently made by Peter Rose to add
another piece to the puzzle of the life and ways of American Jews.[1]
One can only agree with Dr. Rose that the image of Jewish life portrayed by life in the eastern metropolis is incomplete indeed. Not all
the conditions of life in the big city extend to non-metropolitan en-
vironments where many Jews live. Thus, Rose argues, "Critical examination of Jewish life in the small community would seem to be
a logical extension of research in the study of American Judaism and
the nature of Jewish-Gentile relations."[2]

Rose's survey of two small towns in upstate New York adds, as he
hoped, a few pieces to the puzzle, but its limitations are as suggestive
as its contributions. First of all, he is dealing with a very small segment
of American Jewry, and he is leaving out a large slice of life in the
larger but non-metropolitan towns and cities, particularly in areas outside the Northeast. Second, in many aspects the small-town rural New
York Jews are really very special cases in comparison with all *but* the
metropolitan Jews of the Eastern seaboard. By Rose's own count, over
90 per cent of the Jews in his two rural towns were fairly recent im-

1. Peter I. Rose, "Small-Town Jews and their Neighbours in the United States,"
Jewish Journal of Sociology, III (no. 2, December, 1962). My thanks to Professors
Nelson W. Polsby, E. H. Mizruchi, L. A. Froman, and Lieut. Bertram H. Lowi, USN,
for careful reading and criticism of earlier drafts.
2. *Ibid.*, 1.

migrants from other parts of the eastern United States and abroad. Only 4 per cent were locally born and bred; over 60 per cent hailed from other American cities; and 30 per cent were refugees from Nazi-dominated European countries. Beyond the fact that so many were newcomers, identification with and commitment to the town were quite weak; many in all age groups displayed strong aspirations for residence elsewhere. Rose has an interesting subject and some significant findings, but his base for generalization is limited. At least it leaves one wondering whether truly non-metropolitan Jews, particularly in groupings sufficiently large to constitute sub-communities, are in any way significantly different.

The study offered here is not meant to be a description of all Southern Jews. This would hardly be possible. It is, rather, a participant-observation inquiry into some of the peculiar consequences of the adaptation of Jews in the South. The case involves the entire community of Jews in a middle-size Southern city. The issue was perceived by all the participants as one of the few vital issues ever faced by them as Jews; their behaviour confirmed their assessment that the stakes were high and the outcome a matter of intense interest. Given this degree of importance attributed to the issue by the participants themselves, I became convinced that the case was sufficient to reveal some of the basic attitudes of the Jewish community as well as to suggest some of the major attributes of its social structure.

Conditions in Southern towns are in many respects quite special. They are clearly unlike conditions in all American metropolitan centres, and are probably equally dissimilar from those of towns of the same size outside the South. And in these towns the Jewish community, while always a fairly small unit, is a substantial one both in numerical and economic terms. Many of the Jewish families have been located in the South for two, three, even four generations. Along with them are Jewish families much more recently Southern. They live together in a common social and usually identical institutional milieu. Yet they also live apart from one another, sufficiently apart to be thought of as constituting not one but two communities; and there is a clear pattern in this living apart. What is the basis of the two-community pattern and what are its causes and its consequences? What is its significance for our notions about Jewish life in particular and ethnic and other types of identification in general?

THE SETTING   Iron City[3] is a steel, rubber, and textile town of some 60,000 people. Located in the hilly north of one of the Deep South states, Iron City is blessed with many natural resources but not with much new investment in the past decade. Its population has for some time been stable both in number and composition. The white community is homogeneous, particularly in comparison with non-Southern and Southern seaboard cities. Jews and Catholics are recognized as white minorities. However, their minority status is seldom a problem, the reason perhaps being that Negroes constitute about 30 per cent of the population. Until quite recently even relations between Negroes and whites were stable. Except for some labour violence in the distant past, Iron City has little in its past to cast doubt upon the civic boasts of the civic boosters.

THE CASE   Early in 1958 on a quiet Saturday night the city of Birmingham, Alabama, was shaken by a blast which tore off a wing of its largest synagogue. Most of the residents of Iron City reacted with mild shock and short-lived indignation. But the Jews of Iron City were deeply disturbed by the bombing, the first such desecration close to home in any of their recollections. All felt strongly that something ought to be done, but there was little agreement among them as to what should be done. After many weeks of informal discussion, the entire congregation—for all Jews in Iron City were members of one congregation—was crystallized around a proposal made by two brothers, the Kahns, owners of a prosperous retail store. The Kahns sponsored a motion to make a contribution, in the name of the synagogue, to the Birmingham reward-fund, which by that time had accumulated many thousands of dollars. The Kahns got their motion on the agenda of the third regular monthly meeting of 1958 and were quietly campaigning in its favour.

3. The names of the town and the participants in the case have been changed to avoid embarrassing my friends on both sides of the issue. Otherwise the events and data are as accurate as possible.

Practically every member of the congregation of fifty to sixty families attended the meeting. Fully aware that the congregation treasury was almost empty, owing to recent expenditure on redecoration, the Kahns proposed to give the sum of $250 to the treasury on condition that it be sent to Birmingham in the name of the Iron City synagogue. As the Kahns' proposal would cost the congregation or an unwilling member not so much as a dollar, there would seem hardly to have been any issue at all. But every Iron City Jew knew that there was a most important issue to be settled, and that issue came through as simply and clearly as if it had been so stated in the motion: Resolved [in effect], that the Jews of Iron City identify themselves as Jews and as a congregation of Jews with the Jews of Birmingham and elsewhere outside Iron City. Aye or Nay?

The debate opened with a short but impassioned speech by Kahn the elder. It was essentially a for-whom-the-bell-tolls speech, stating firmly that to maintain the respect of the Gentile community as well as their own self-respect, they must all take their stand as Jews. The opposition, even more impassioned, was voiced first by the owner of the largest retail clothing store in town and then by the wife of the owner of the third largest retail clothing store in town. They were self-appointed spokesmen, for there was no opposition caucus prior to the meeting but only a strong awareness of consensus in the majority. The opposition recalled the Ku Klux Klan horse-whippings of some Jews and Catholics in the 1920s and stressed a well-enough-alone philosophy, which at the time of the debate was very well indeed. The proponents argued that German Jews had suffered because of their lack of identity as Jews. The opposition answered, with equal conviction, that for years they had been "treated all right"; in fact, relations with non-Jews would suffer to the extent that Jews identified with other Jews rather than with their home town as home-towners. The opposition cited such matters as equal treatment in the country club, the high school football teams, and other matters of social significance.

The case for the motion was altogether remote, academic, hypothetical; that against was immediate, concrete, compelling. The question was not called; a vote was never taken. At a point close to violence the brothers Kahn withdrew their motion. The meeting was gavelled

to a close amidst considerable shouting. As it was strictly a civil cere-
mony, the rabbi did not attend the meeting.

Not unlike the United States Senate, the congregation was seated
strictly along party lines, the opposition on the right well beyond the
centre, the proponents in the remaining seats to the left. As there was
no aisle of separation, the demarcation line was made by two almost
unbroken columns of husbands running elbow to elbow from the Chair
backwards to the rear of the room. For debate, this is a natural arrangement; however, it is made noteworthy by the fact that the columns of
husbands also separated the "old" Jews from the "new" Jews. As far as
could be determined during the meeting and for days thereafter, there
were no exceptions. The new Jews favoured the motion and sat on the
left; the old Jews without exception opposed the motion and sat to
the right and centre. Here were the two communities in congregation
assembled.

As the analysis proceeds, I hope to show, first, that there are two
separate social structures among the Iron City Jews and that the separate social structures both reflect and maintain some quite profound
differences in what it means to be a Jew. Second, I hope to show that
these differences exist within an even stronger set of identifications
common to all Jews. Both propositions and the fragmentary support
to follow should provide a basis for hypotheses about Southern Jews
in particular, and American Jews, minority relations, and value systems in general.

Some Features of Social Structure: Home, Club, and Campus

The distinction between old and new is not an easy one for an outsider to draw, but although it is implicit, the Iron City Jews appear to
understand it well enough and to behave accordingly. Roughly, there
are two dimensions in the distinction, one of time and one of place, and
both are vague, shifting, *ad hoc*, fortuitous. Not all the old Jews have
been residents of Iron City for over a generation; and many of the new
Jews can at least claim to have seen the Depression come and go in their
present businesses. In composite form, an old Jew is one whose family
has lived somewhere in the *South* for as far back as memory serves and
whose family has been at least self-supporting and free of bankruptcy

for a generation (perhaps longer, for one does hear of stories about such-and-such an old Jew whose father or grandfather was a "four-flusher"). The new Jew, in contrast, is one who himself came to town from "the North." (Very few in the past forty years or so came to town directly from Europe, except for three young German refugee men in the early 1940s who stayed for only a short time and were considered arrogant and rather zany.) The new Jew and his family may claim twenty-five years or more of respectable residence in the town, but he came directly from some metropolitan centre outside the South, his speech is not so colourful with local drawl and patois, and he has hosts of relatives in New York, Chicago, and the like. Jews of Eastern European ancestry are more likely than not to be of the community of new Jews, but this is not an important factor distinguishing the communities. The basic distinction is in degree of Southernness. By virtue of immigration patterns, most of the Jews in both communities are of German origin with a few of Iberian ancestry among the old Jews and a few of Eastern European ancestry on both sides, according to degree of Southernness. There is, then, a middle group, perhaps Eastern European but definitely Yankee, who at least were born in the South, probably around the First World War or after. They are acceptable as old Jews if they are in acceptable businesses and are thought not to be too "pushy" or too "kikey". (One of the most prominent Jews in town, for example, was of German origin with strong Southern ties, but had lived in New York, had strong business ties to New York textile interests, was involved in some union trouble, and was owner of an incorporated business. He was an old Jew but one towards whom other old Jews were always strongly ambivalent.)

It may be difficult for the outsider to understand how two communities could be based upon so superficial a distinction as degree of Southernness. But I think it should be clear from the reward-fund debate, or it should become clear presently, that over the years many quite profound differences were related to the quality of Southernness or actually developed as a consequence of Southernness. The separation into two communities probably arose out of superficial differences of culture and personality traits (a direct connotation of the term "Southernness"), and the separation is maintained by the friendship patterns that arose as a consequence. And, as the separate friendship patterns emerged, largely owing to the resistance if not outright hostility of the established old Jews, they acted in the manner of a self-fulfilling prophecy to maintain the differences. Over the years the differences have congealed.

Only a superficial acquaintance with Iron City Jews is necessary to detect two separate communities in ordinary social activities. The most reliable index is the frequency of exchange of social calls among and between old and new Jews. It is difficult to find cases of frequent exchanges of social calls between an old and a new Jewish household. There must certainly be numerous instances, but they are clearly exceptional. An old Jew will often identify the name of a new Jew (when presented to him in conversation) as that of a friend; but, when pushed, he can seldom recall the last time their families gathered in each other's living rooms. If one could draw a flow chart between old and new Jewish families, shaded and sized in terms of frequency of exchanges of social calls, the arrows between sets of new Jewish families would be wide and dark, between old Jewish families the same, and thin and wan across community lines. The arrows would converge from both sides on a scant two or three families, one by virtue of the personality of a wife in an old Jewish household and the other families probably by virtue of an "intermarriage" of an old and new family. If these particular households are channels of amity and communication, they are not the sources of leadership. Each community has its spokesmen for issues such as choice of rabbi, teaching of Hebrew, etc., and the congregation presidency tends to alternate between the two, although this office is often filled on a "most available" basis.

Since there is only one country club in town, many Jews are members; a few are actually charter members. Thus, one possible manifestation of separateness is hidden. However, there was an attempt some years ago to start a Jewish country club which failed after several unsuccessful attempts to enlist the support of a number of the old Jews. Many said they could not afford to be members of both clubs and were unwilling to give up their stake in the non-sectarian one. On the other hand, in one of the larger Deep South cities there is but one Christian country club and two Jewish clubs whose membership is divided along the lines of "old" and "new". Years ago, so the story goes, one of the "pushier kikes" was blackballed from the established Jewish club. Being a man of some means, he started another. In those Southern towns large enough to support more than one synagogue, the difference in composition of membership tends to be "old" versus "new."

Differences in the marital patterns of the two communities are more difficult to discern because they become submerged in extremely strong family solidarity and hidden from the observer. However, a few things are known. There are more marriages outside the faith among children of the old families, but the greater significance here lies in their small numbers and the reaction of the old Jews to such marriages. More will be said on the latter presently. The gulf between the two communities is best indicated in this respect by the rarity of marriages that connect old Jewish families *of Iron City* with new Jewish families *of Iron City*. When a marriage does take place between children of old and new Jews, one of the partners is almost without exception an "import."

Families in both communities have many connexions in other Southern towns, some far beyond their home base. When they visit another Southern town, the Jews of Iron City are expected to stay with or to look up and spend some time with an Aunt Sophie or a Cousin Abe or some friend-called-cousin. Wherever they go in the South, particularly the old Jews whose roots in the South are so deep, they almost never really leave the family. Thus, not only do there appear to be two communities in town after town, but this phenomenon is extended beyond to create a *dual Southern Jewish society*.

Besides family ties beyond Iron City, there are certain institutions that have helped maintain a dual Southern Jewish society. For example, such annual events as the Falcon Picnic in Montgomery, the Jubilee in Birmingham, and other events of the same sort in Atlanta and New Orleans were supported precisely for the purpose of having nice boy meet nice girl, usually by arrangement among families of old Jews. These were most often intensive four-day affairs over the Fourth of July, Labour Day and other holiday weekends. And gala and elaborate affairs they were, with tea dances, formal dances, garden parties, and the like, involving the country club (of the old Jews) and the finest Jewish houses. For many of the new Jews—but far from all of them—the elaborate Bar Mitzvah has performed the same function.

That the annual "picnic" has declined in importance is probably due to the more efficient functioning of the college fraternity through which the two communities maintain and extend their separateness. Zeta Beta Tau and Phi Epsilon Pi were always sought after and pledged by sons of the old Jews from Houston to Savannah. It is significant that these two fraternities are rarely found on the same Southern campus competing for the same types of boys. Note on the chart that among States of the Confederacy there has been only one campus where chapters of both fraternities co-existed, and Phi Epsilon Pi abandoned that campus in 1958. (It had probably been on the decline for some years before 1958.) It is only in the Border States that the specialization of campuses does not appear. (Note that even in the case of Florida, the fraternities co-exist only on the northernized campus. At the University of Florida, in the northern, therefore "southernmost", campus, only one of the fraternities has a chapter.) The trustees of both fraternities are from similar backgrounds and, apparently, have had no will to compete for the same types of boys, much less the incentive to recruit *all* Jewish students on the campus

There is another order of fraternities for the sons of new Jews. These have been, among others, Tau Epsilon Phi and Alpha Epsilon Pi, houses for the new Jews and what was in times past referred to by sons of the old Jews as the "new money" or the just plain "kike Yankees". Perhaps in the middle somewhere one finds an occasional Sigma Alpha Mu or Pi Lambda Phi chapter with some "nice Southern boys and the better class of Yankees." Friendship and dating patterns as well as prejudices towards the "others" are passed along these channels. Girls tend to be known as and identify as "ZBT" girls or "TEP" girls. (Similar distinctions can be found among Jewish fraternities on Northern campuses, but, in the guise of animosity toward New York, the distinction has a much stronger flavour of Western versus Eastern European ancestry.) Admittedly the system was never rigidly adhered to, but the differences are sufficiently distinct to contribute to the maintenance of the dual society and the two communities.

Zeta Beta Tau and Phi Epsilon Pi Fraternities:
Specialization among Southern Campuses

States of the Old Confederacy

State	Campus	Zeta Beta Tau	Phi Epsilon Pi
Alabama	U. of Ala.	1916	—
Arkansas	Auburn	—	1916
	U. of Ark.	—	1932 [1]
Georgia	U. of Ga.	—	1915
	Ga. Tech.	—	1916
Kentucky	U. of Ky.	1942	—
Louisiana	Tulane	1909	—
	LSU	1911	1933 [2]
Mississippi	U. of Miss.	—	1935
North Carolina	U. of N.C.	1927	—
	N.C. State	—	1949
	Duke	1935	—
South Carolina	U. of S.C.	—	1928
Tennessee	U. of Tenn.	1942	—
	Memphis St.	—	1949
	Vanderbilt	1918	—

Border States

State	Campus	Zeta Beta Tau	Phi Epsilon Pi
Florida	U. of Fla.	—	1960
	Miami U.	1946	1929
Maryland	U. of Md.	1948	1959 or 1960
	Johns Hopkins	1958	1920
Texas	Houston	—	1956
Virginia	U. of Va.	1915	1915
	W. and L.	1920	1920

1. Discontinued 1941.   2. Discontinued 1958.

Two Ideologies

The Jews of Iron City are politically unimportant. They do not live in one part of town, they do not constitute a majority in any district, and they are not thought of politically as a distinguishable unit. No individual Jew speaks politically as a Jew, and there is no single—or double—voice for Iron City Jews as a group. And there is no sign of change. To illustrate the point, practically all Jewish sons and daughters (old and new) of Iron City go to college, *but in a generation not a single one has studied for the law.* In fact, there are no Jewish lawyers at all in Iron City; the one Jewish holder of the LL.B. is an "import" who by marriage is owner of the *second* largest retail clothing store in town. A check in several other small towns in the area revealed that an occasional Jew does go to law school, but his practice is found to be in Birmingham, Atlanta, or some other large metropolitan centre. The Jews of Iron City have thus avoided the one profession which typically becomes charged with controversy—not only political controversy but controversy over estates, divorces, and the like that can be so noticeable and divisive in small towns. No Jews have ever sought or held public office in Iron City or beyond, and it is rare to find Jews publicly committed to a candidate in a wide-open election. Candidates seek their support, and they are often contributors to campaigns, but quietly.

The Jews of Iron City are politically silent. Many hold strong opinions, and many enjoy positions of informal opinion leadership without regard to religious affiliation. But they are silent. And for much the same reasons they are conservative. Iron City is a "redneck town." A large part of its population, attracted by jobs in the textile, steel, and rubber mills, migrated completely unequipped from nearby farms not more than thirty years ago. Local prohibition and a hundred neon-crossed tabernacles bear witness to their fundamentalist majority. As they are virtually all merchants, the Jews of Iron City are especially susceptible to reprisal by informal conspiracy, and they justifiably fear the unpopular view. But the same would be true of the Christian with liberal tendencies.

If all the Jews of Iron City displayed considerable anxiety about politics and open controversy, it would still be too easy to overdramatize the "dilemma of the Southern Jews." Practically all Jews in Iron City are publicly conservative, but easily a majority are privately conservative as well. Thus, it is difficult to gather firm evidence for assessing the differences in ideology between the two communities that both reflect and maintain the spirit of two communities. The old Jews probably enjoy higher status in the social structure of Iron City proper, but there are no gross economic disparities between old and new Jews that would invite jealousy and continuous conflict. More important, the manifest values of Jews, as suggested above, are homogenized under the pressure of Southern consensus on the most important political and social issue of all. One must, then, look for differences in propensities and predispositions, the distributions of which are always matters of scholarly controversy. With these problems in mind, let us look at some rough indices of difference.

On matters of partisan politics, the Jews of Iron City reflect the Southern tradition. Almost all of them are Democrats, and both communities are predominantly liberal on economic questions. Further in harmony with recent Southern trends is a growing Republican sentiment among the younger fathers, particularly in old Jewish families. The development was cut short in 1962 because the entire Jewish community of Iron City was repelled by a Republican state-wide candidate of that year. This home-grown product had paid the bail for the juvenile bomber of Iron City's own synagogue in 1960, and his campaign was intensely racist. Less rabid Republican candidacies in the future could, however, restore the trend among many of the young educated old Jews.

The best indices of contrasting ideology, however, can be found in the rare instances of conflict among Jews themselves. Probably the only such conflicts before the 1958 reward-fund debate were those over Zionism from time to time before and during the struggle for Israel. Internal cleavage then was the same as in 1958 and for precisely the same reason: all of these controversies involved the question of the nature and meaning of identification with Judaism. Even more than the reward-fund contribution, Zionism *would define the Jew by his ethnicity*. To support a Jewish homeland or to react with uncommon sympathy to a remote synagogue bombing is virtually to expose the fact (or, to the old Jew, *create the spectacle*) of the Jew as somehow separate from home town and local traditions. Deep in the idiom of the intelligent old Jew is the distinction "Judaism is a religion, not a nationality." Zionism has become a dead issue with the founding and success of Israel. But the meaning of Judaism, or Jewishness, still divides. Perhaps here is the whole mystery of the two communities in a nutshell. Certainly it shapes ideology, propensity, and predisposition.

As all of this should suggest, the new Jew reveals the greater capacity to identify with Judaism as such, to define himself as "minority" and to generalize, however incompletely, about "minority". As a consequence, the new Jew has the more liberal tendencies on a variety of issues. On the question of segregation the political sentiments of the two communities differ, although again it would be too easy to over-dramatize and misrepresent it. Since the passing of Zionism, it is here that the old Jew most willingly shows his hierarchy of identifications, as Southerner first, Jew second, and "minority" or "ethnic group" last (if such a concession is made at all). Typically, the new Jew can be pushed to concede the inevitability of desegregation; the old Jew can only be pushed to anger. Not a man on either side would join or otherwise condone a White Citizens Council (knowingly referred to as the "Klan in the Gray Flannel Suit"). But an old Jew, regardless of age, will use the rhetoric of states' rights, of Plessy v. Ferguson, and, if pushed, of race superiority and biblical sanction. The new Jew will not. The old Jew either bears no sense of guilt on the matter, or he deeply represses it. The new Jew is distinguished by a concern with and an only poorly repressed sense of guilt about Negro problems. The old Jews will make the inevitable adjustment to integration more easily and more quickly than their white Christian brethren, but they will verbally support segregation to the end. New Jews are less likely to give verbal support to segregation but will never openly support integration. However, private expressions of guilt or concern for an underprivileged minority serve still further to separate the two communities.

One Identification

It seems to me, therefore, that there is enough evidence to suggest the existence of two communities or subcommunities of Jews in Iron City and probably in other non-metropolitan Southern cities. Further, it appears that the phenomenon has important consequences in ideology or predisposition which, in turn, support the dual structure. Impressions suggest further differences in customs, aspirations, and general life-style, but to elaborate them would call for more systematic study.

However, it must be added immediately that there is at least as much to suggest that above and beyond the two communities is a set of identifications strongly held and shared by all. Factors in this phenomenon are as significant for theories of value maintenance and minority adjustment as was the earlier section for theories of American Jewry. What is significant is not that the new Jews maintain certain identifications but that the old Jews do as well. It is for this reason that the present section emphasizes most particularly the patterns of identification among the old Jews.

If the reward-fund debate or any related indices were interpreted as a case of strong versus weak identification, it would be totally misrepresented. New Jews may favour more strongly the teaching of Hebrew, the observance of a larger number of holidays annually, the contribution to the Birmingham reward-fund. They may have a slightly better record of attendance at Friday night services. They definitely appreciate Yiddish and old country humour more than the old Jews. But much vital evidence suggests that old and new Jews differ only slightly, if at all, in strength of identification. The difference between them—and the crux of the argument of the last section—*lies in what the identification means*. The one is no less a Jew than the other.

That there is great strength of identification in both communities can be seen clearly in marital and related patterns. There are more marriages outside the faith among old Jewish families, but the greater significance lies in their rarity and in the reaction of old Jewish heads of family to such marriages. While one seldom finds any concerted opposition by old or new Jewish parents to a mixed marriage of son or daughter, both communities seem to require some later act of identification—for example, sending the children to Sunday school. (Rarely does one find Saturday schools in non-metropolitan Southern cities.) Old Jews as well as new are capable of "losing touch" with youngsters who prefer a Unitarian or Episcopal life, and, at the risk of overemphasis, strong if unspoken hostility can be permanent. No members of either community ever seem to forget who the Jews are no matter how long ago the conversion took place. There is at least one instance in which the third generation, descended from converted and intermarried old Jews, were still regarded as Jews although few if any Gentiles were aware of the ancestry. In two other cases, Jewish men married Christian girls and allowed their children to be brought up as Christians. On High Holidays one of them comes alone to services, sits alone, and leaves alone. Both have had cordial business relations with other Jews; one, in fact, could not have started his business in Iron City without the substantial support of an old Jewish merchant. But neither was ever truly a friend of any other Iron City Jew.

There is a real workaday permissiveness in the Iron City majority toward white religious minorities. The fundamentalism of the lower class Christian sects is convertible into antisemitism, and theologically there is little tolerance among them for the Jews' not accepting the Gospel. Yet few local Jews can recall any overt expression of community antisemitism in Iron City. This is why the 1960 bombing attempt on the Iron City synagogue came as such a shock, especially among the younger generation of old Jews to whom antisemitism as well as dietary laws and observances was something in history books. Yet the old Jews are no less Jews. Iron City and other Southern cities are receptive to conversion, and there are sufficient examples of acceptance as a non-Jew to encourage conversion. This only emphasizes how rare indeed are instances of old (and certainly new) Jews discarding their identification. The arm's length at which old Jews hold new Jews is not a rejection of Judaism or Jewishness. To cite an extreme example, there is one very small town in Mississippi where, although there is only a single Jewish family (dating back into the mid-nineteenth century), there is a small synagogue which has been used for the High Holidays, weddings, and funerals. In the past a rabbinical student or young rabbi was imported for these occasions, and they were attended by the few other Jewish families from nearby smaller towns and the open country. Even here the one conversion, now over a generation past, is remembered; figuratively there remains a sign upon the doorpost of the Christianized descendants.

Old Jews are on the average more active and prominent in the noncontroversial civic and philanthropic affairs of Iron City, but this is merely a function of their greater average length of residence. Furthermore, the fact of their Jewish identification is never hidden; old Jews do not use the civic group as a channel of assimilation (in the pejorative sense). And, while old Jews exchange house calls with Christian families more frequently than do the new Jews, neither is this assimilative (in the pejorative sense) if the Christian families know them as Jews. If the old Jew is free to assimilate, he chooses not to do so, or else the possibility never occurs to him. Liberal Christians more readily accept Judaism as a religion that can be changed than do the old Jews themselves.

Conclusions

Southern Jewry is a special phenomenon both in the particular context of American Jewry and the general context of group relations. The old Jews are cut off from the mainstreams of Jewish culture by more than two generations. They live in relatively small numbers dispersed throughout city and open country in a social milieu which is hostile to Judaism but not to Jews or to conversion. And they are deprived through isolation, disuse and, in many cases, rejection of all but the most superficial of the rituals and ceremonies. Yet the old Jew maintains much of his Jewishness and his Jewish identification.

Here we have a situation of strong identification in the absence of many of those factors presumably necessary to its maintenance. Most conspicuous and interesting in its absence is ritual—the repetition of symbolic acts. The proposition, a negative one, that most immediately springs to mind is that *ritual functions as a value- or identification-maintaining force only where it has functioned in that manner for some time.* In fact, ritual may be important for value maintenance only where treatment of the minority is severe.

Identification can obviously be maintained and reinforced in many ways. Ritual is an institutional force usually attached to a church as a manifest function of a church. The fact that ritual and church have not constituted an important reinforcement for old Jews in Iron City suggests, then, a second proposition: *where the reinforcement of identification is institutionalized or is otherwise made a manifest function of some structure, group identification may come to depend upon the institution.* Since no such pattern of reinforcement is found in this particular case and identification remains strong, we must look to other, informal or latent factors. In the case of the old Jews, the family seems to be the reinforcing factor. Commitments among old Jews to "being different" were made when their ancestors were newcomers in the nineteenth century and were passed down as part of the family structure. In many respects, the function of family among old Jews is probably not dissimilar from that of the ancient Jewish family before the latent function of family was replaced by the manifest function of synagogue and ritual. This latent function of the old Southern Jewish family, the maintenance of identification, is probably also one of the underlying conditions of its solidarity. Institutions, from churches to big city machines and trade unions, gain solidarity as they add functions, and conversely.

The identification of Southern old Jews turns out in reality to be an ethnic rather than a religious experience. Old Jews display virtually every feature of ethnicity save its acceptance. Ironically, the old Jew is a living refutation of his own argument that "Judaism is a religion, not a nationality." Religion is quite superficial to him, but Jewry is not.

The phenomenon of the two communities is the more significant because it does not arise out of rejection of Jewry or Jewishness by the old Jews. In fact, the debate and all of the related materials present a fairly clear picture of a social system characterized at one and the same time by *strong identification and low solidarity*. The differences arise over what the identification means; the difference between old and new Jews lies not in the direction or focus of the identification but in the *substance* of the identification. The general proposition suggested by this is that *identification and solidarity (or cohesion) are independent factors which may be closely related under some conditions and entirely unrelated under others.*

It is commonly assumed in political sociology that the cohesion of groups is based upon shared attitudes and common goals. Professor David B. Truman, for one, has gone so far as to define *group* as a bundle of shared attitudes.[4] Karl Mannheim in *Ideology and Utopia* hypothesizes that as groups lose homogeneity they also lose solidarity, which gives rise to more vigorous theorizing towards the rediscovery of common goals.[5] Certainly there are many cases to support these hypotheses, but there are also many contradictory cases. The best type of case is the group based upon "log-rolling" relations. Here the members have absolutely nothing in common; in fact, the very basis of their solidarity is the dissimilarity of ultimate aims (identification). The "farm bloc" in the United States, highly cohesive in the 1920s and 1930s, was essentially a series of corn-cotton-wheat "log rolls". The

4. David B. Truman, *The Governmental Process* (New York, 1951), 24 and Chap. 2.
5. Karl Mannheim, *Ideology and Utopia* (New York, 1955), 131.

Southern Democratic-Conservative Republican coalition is an even better example of strong solidarity made possible by the fact that the Southerners have cared little about the economic aims of the mid-West and the mid-West has cared little about the social aims of the South. In contrast, many groups based upon shared attitudes or identifications display real pathologies in organization. This was clearly true of the Jews of Iron City.

An awareness of the different consequences of identification and variations in the bases of group formation opens up many new avenues of theory about group life and group solidarity. It also opens up new possibilities for refining the predictors of public opinion. For, while group membership and identification are functionally related to opinions, the connexion is not nearly so simple or straightforward as opinion studies have assumed. When ethnic group or trade union members are found to be concentrated 70 per cent or 80 per cent on one side of an issue, many important questions are avoided by stressing only the dominant characteristic. The 20 per cent or 30 per cent "deviant" cases may or may not be "cross-pressured"; they may be reading the symbols of identification differently.

Epilogue

About two years after the Birmingham attack, the synagogue in Iron City was victim of a bombing attempt. It was a spectacular attempt. For the first time, the attack occurred while Friday night services were taking place. Moreover, it was a dedication service for the new wing. The Mayor, the City Commission, many Protestant ministers, and Christian friends were in attendance. After the bombing attempt failed the young madman stood across the street and beseiged the place with an automatic rifle before driving away. The younger Kahn and one of the old Jews were shot as they ran out enraged to respond. The injured old Jew, speaking afterwards for the entire congregation, insisted that there be no pictures, no wide press coverage ("Magazine interference has already done the South enough harm."), and, once the bomber was captured, no special grand jury. The arguments of the Kahn brothers had been fully vindicated in the attack, and the entire Jewish community suddenly became aware of its unity. But four years later, the two communities remain.

Sidney I. Goldstein
Mixed Marriages
in the Deep South

THE PROBLEM of mixed marriage still has high priority on the agenda of American Jewry. True, we know very little about the actual rate of its incidence, in spite of recent studies. Many a rabbi will often be heard to say that some of his best members are non-Jews. But the truth of the matter is that the problem still awaits a first-rate study.

With a view to shedding light on this problem as it affects the life of a small Jewish community in the Deep South, the following study may prove to be of some value.

Much Intermarriage

The community in question comprises a list of approximately 100 names—family units, with or without children, widows, widowers, and unmarried adults. Of these, 60 are families. More than one-fourth of these, or 16 to be specific, are mixed marriages contracted in the Post-World War II period. In every instance, the wife is an unconverted non-Jewess. Four of these mixed-marriage families send their children to the religious school of the Reform congregation, which has the only Jewish educational program. Ten of the mixed families send their children to the Sunday schools of the various Protestant churches, although the Jewish father is a member of the Reform Temple and the mother participates in Temple activities on occasion. In a word, these families support "two churches," to use a good Southern phrase.

It must appear rather obvious that the fact of mixed marriage poses a serious threat for the survival of Judaism. Not that the individuals involved may not be happy human beings. Their personal feelings with regard to their marital relationships are an individual matter. But as far as the future of Judaism is concerned, there is no gainsaying the fact that mixed marriage causes a hemorrhage for Judaism and the Jewish people.

Lest one assume this community to be atypical, let it be said that a high incidence of mixed marriage exists in many small congregations in the Deep South. To be sure, the same or perhaps even a higher percentage of mixed marriage may be found in larger communities, but the large concentration of Jewish persons in an urban setting blunts the threat which this phenomenon poses for the continuity of Judaism.

The People Involved

Not alone are numbers important. The persons involved are a matter to be considered. In the case at hand, they are long-time residents of the community whose families have been identified with the congregation for several generations. They serve as officers, trustees, and leaders of both the Reform congregation and the community. In this respect, their very leadership serves to compromise the ideal of Judaism as taught in the Temple. How can a man be a leader of an institution which insists that a good Jew provide a Jewish education for his children, when he himself permits his children to be reared in a Christian church? Not alone is the image of the Temple blurred. Its program must needs suffer as well.

An oft-repeated cliché insists that mixed marriages occur more often among the Orthodox than among the Reform. This study would not give substance to that statement. The men who have involved themselves in mixed marriages were reared in Reform Jewish families, both of whose parents were Jewish. They grew up within the shadow of the Reform Temple, attending its religious school and participating in its holiday celebrations. If they married out it is not so much because they wanted to identify with the Christian community nor because they sought to escape their Judaism. Indeed, these may have been unconscious or subconscious factors. But the fact of propinquity coupled with the feeling that personal love overrides loyalty to Judaism and the Jewish people seem to be the decisive factors in explaining these out-group marriages. It is true that in every instance the men in question are formally identified with the Reform Temple as members. But this fact of formal affiliation cannot be construed as a willingness to perpetuate Judaism by rearing their children as Jews.

Half and Half

Even the children of the four mixed-marriage families who attend the Temple religious school may be said to be in a compromising position vis-à-vis Judaism. Their Christian parent and Christian relatives often cause them to challenge the option for Judaism which has been made for them. One father put it this way: "I celebrate Hanukkah with David. He gets a gift every night and Marge (the wife) buys him gifts for Christmas." The youngster once summed up his dilemma by saying: "I'm half Hanukkah and half Christmas."

Many a discussion of mixed-marriage problems confuses the issues involved with the question of rabbinical officiation at these marriages. In the case of the community under study, no rabbi officiated at any of the mixed marriages, although almost all the couples asked a rabbi to officiate. Rebuffed by the rabbi, the couples were married by Christian clergymen or Justices of the Peace. It should be noted, however, that despite the refusal of the rabbi to officiate, the couples were neither deterred from marrying nor hindered in their desire to affiliate with the Temple, nor (in the case of four couples) to send their children to the Temple religious school. If all of them wanted a rabbi to officiate at the wedding, it was out of a desire to appease parents and relatives, and to seek sanction for a relationship which they hoped Judaism could approve.

Rabbinical Officiation

There is a tendency in some quarters to confuse the question of rabbinical officiation with the factors making for mixed marriage. Thus in 1909, the Central Conference of American Rabbis discussed the problem of mixed marriage with a view to finding the mind of the Reform rabbinate on this matter. Rabbis Samuel Schulman and William Rosenau proposed a resolution "that a rabbi ought not to officiate at a marriage between a Jew or Jewess and a person professing a religion other than Judaism, inasmuch as such mixed marriage is prohibited by the Jewish religion and would tend to disintegrate the religion of Israel." I take it they felt that a strongly worded resolution would reduce the incidence of mixed marriage. The Conference chose to follow a more moderate course and declared "that mixed marriages are contrary to the tradition of the Jewish religion and should therefore be discouraged by the American rabbinate."

There is of course no way of knowing whether the resolution favored by Rabbis Schulman and Rosenau would have decreased the number of mixed marriages as against the one adopted by the Conference. But if the case history of a small Southern community can shed some light on the issue, it would seem that the factors making for mixed marriages and the question of rabbinical officiation are two separate matters.

Positive Approach

There is no question, then, that the problem of mixed marriage needs more study and documentation. This should be undertaken in different kinds of communities in various parts of the country to determine the many facets of the mixed-marriage problem. From the evidence before us, it would appear that mixed marriages in America will increase. The very nature of our open society makes this inevitable. But how mixed marriages threaten the survival of Judaism is a matter that will vary with the size and nature of the Jewish community.

Certainly the adverse effects of mixed marriage as it relates to Judaism are patent from this description of a small Southern community. But aside from study and discussion of the problem, a positive effort to deter mixed marriage can be made by way of our religious youth movements. The fact that the Southern Federation of Temple Youth brings young people together from communities as large as Memphis and New Orleans and as small as Hattiesburg, Mississippi, and Helena, Arkansas, bodes well as an attempt to stimulate in-group association.

But joined to the effect to stimulate in-group relationships is the need to reevaluate the role of the rabbi in the mixed-marriage situation. It would seem that a blanket refusal on the part of the rabbi to officiate at mixed marriages does little for those involved and less for Judaism. Might the Jewish religion not gain if the rabbi were to attempt to orient the non-Jewish person toward Judaism and seek to win the children for the Jewish faith? The insistence on conversion prior to marriage often ends in refusal because the non-Jew is uncertain about Judaism and what it would mean to be a Jew. This is where an orientation course in Judaism together with a promise to rear the children in the Jewish faith would at least steer the mixed marriage in the direction of Judaism. Granted that the children might grow up in a family where one parent had not fully embraced Judaism, a mixed marriage is by its nature a compromise situation in which an attempt should be made to persuade those involved to opt for Judaism. An attempt of this kind is certainly preferable to a situation where the children of the mix-married end up in Christian churches or are left to drift.

Leonard Reissman

The New Orleans Jewish Community

THE JEWISH community in New Orleans differs from most others in the United States and especially those outside the South.[1] By its variance, however, it exposes some interesting features of community organization that are worth considering. For here is a Jewish community that seems to stand so close to the larger community in which it is located that there is danger of its being overwhelmed. More so perhaps than in most other American–Jewish communities, New Orleans appears to give substance to the fears of benign assimilation that have always dominated Jewish history. Yet, in fact, the community has survived and has flourished for well over two centuries.[2]

The impression of social fragility comes with the recognition that the usual community supports are absent from New Orleans. For one thing, there are no solidly Jewish neighbourhoods, no self-created ghettoes that bolster community consciousness by the dense presence of Jews living together. Although more than half of the 10,000 Jews in New Orleans live in an area circumscribed by not more than a three-

1. The statistical data used in this analysis are taken from my study, *Profile of a Community*, prepared for and published by the Jewish Federation of New Orleans in 1958. I wish especially to stress that the views presented here are my own and should not be interpreted as necessarily those of the Federation. Data were obtained by interviewing a 10-percent probability sample of all known Jewish households in the city obtained from a master list of organization membership or otherwise known to the Federation.

2. One estimate is that the Jewish community is almost 250 years old, which is quite old by American standards. Leo Shpall, *The Jews in Louisiana* (New Orleans: Steeg Printing and Publishing Co., 1936), 18.

mile radius, so do most other white, middle-class families. But there is no appreciable ecological massing of Jews within the area.

Neither is there a heavy proportion of Orthodox Jews to create a sense of sharp separation by religious behaviour, language, and diet. On the contrary, over half of the community belongs to the three Reform temples in the city and only one-quarter to the three Orthodox synagogues. This prevailing Reform atmosphere, so different from other American cities,[3] reflects the history of the community that was settled by Sephardic and then by German Jews. Here was the genesis of the Reform tradition in the city, old and well established by the twentieth century. Furthermore, the Eastern European immigration that overwhelmed most other cities early in this century had relatively little effect on New Orleans. The unchallenged dominance of a Reform tradition means, in this context, the appearance of few uniquely Jewish practices that would have separated the Jew from the rest of the New Orleans community. The practices of Orthodoxy, the secular Jewish culture, the political radicalism, and the culture of the *shtetl* that were the special baggage of Eastern European immigrants made relatively little impact on New Orleans.

Another feature that makes the Jewish community somewhat unique among most American cities is its long continuity. Some 40 per cent of the current population were born in New Orleans, with a large proportion of third and fourth generation New Orleans families. This has meant a significant time spread separating today's community from its immigrant origins. American values in general, and those of New Orleans in particular, are the accepted victors over the immigrant traditions for most of the population and the battle is long since over.

3. Compare, for example, the congregational preferences of New Orleans with those of Riverton, an eastern United States community reported on by M. Sklare and S. Vosk in *The Riverton Study* (American Jewish Committee, 1957), 16.

Congregational Preference	New Orleans 1958	Riverton 1957
	%	%
Reform	60.6	30
Conservative	11.0	43
Orthodox	24.8	16
None	3.2	4
No Answer	0.4	7
Totals	100.0	100

The Jewish community has had a long time, as these things go, to adjust itself to New Orleans and to establish the grounds for its own acceptance by the larger community.

The regional culture of the South is yet another unique feature of this community. It has played some part in shaping the character of the Jewish community but the effect is difficult to establish precisely. To be sure, some typically Southern values have been assimilated by Jewish families who have lived as Southerners for generations. It could not really be otherwise. Hence, one encounters a loyalty to the city and the region that is hardly the mark of a *luftmensch*. Or again, attitudes towards race are not unrestrainedly equalitarian but sometimes are hedged by some of the elaborate rationale that Southerners of conscience have evolved to justify segregation. Regional values, especially those of a Southern aristocracy, have affected the Jew in his striving for upward social mobility and in his stance towards a society divided by race. But the Southern tradition has been tempered by a Jewish tradition which has prevented a complete acceptance of that strange orientation mystically called 'the Southern way of life'. The Jew is not an average white Southerner in his general attitudes towards race, aristocracy, or the Civil War. It is difficult to disentangle the separate strands involved here, but I shall have more to say about it because the South is a significant part of the texture of Jewish life in New Orleans.

All in all, these brief clues document a different, perhaps a unique, type among American-Jewish communities. Where others are now moving painfully from an older Orthodoxy to a newer Conservatism, New Orleans began virtually as Reform and stayed that way, thus avoiding some of the turmoil involved in a religious transition.[4] Where other communities are seeking to expand religious identification, New Orleans has a majority already affiliated with a synagogue as part of its traditional pattern.[5] Where other communities are feeling the re-

4. Not entirely painless, however. For the last few years the attempt by a majority of one Orthodox congregation to institute mixed seating has led to strife and legal action by the other side which insists upon observing the original charter. One related consequence has been the formation of a new Conservative congregation, making it the seventh synagogue in the city.
5. I realize that membership and identification are not the same thing. Nonetheless, the fact that about 80 per cent of the community does belong to a synagogue cannot be dismissed as only a paper membership.

awakening of Jewish consciousness among the native-born, in line with Herberg's well-known thesis that this is the first generation secure enough in the American environment to do so, New Orleans has long since passed that generational bench-mark. Where other communities are reforming their relationships to the larger community, New Orleans has achieved a stable level of integration that only now is being threatened, but in dimensions and with consequences quite different from those encountered by other communities. Before moving on to that part of the analysis, however, a brief sketch of the community's demography will help to provide perspective.

Demographic Characteristics

Differences though there are between the Jewish community in New Orleans and in other cities, they are similar in at least the one major respect of their middle-class character. On each of the usually accepted indices the community emerges as strongly middle class. About 25 per cent are in professional occupations, another 40 per cent in managerial and proprietary, and 18 per cent in clerical and sales. The rest hold occupations lower in the prestige hierarchy. The median family income in 1958 was over $10,000 a year, a figure twice that for the U.S. as a whole. Over 60 per cent are home-owners. About half of the population have been to college, and half of them either have graduated or gone on for post-graduate study. These are striking accomplishments, and the more so in a community in which wealth and opportunity have never been, nor were expected to be, distributed with equality. On each of the above measures, the city's general population is dramatically below the level of the Jewish average. In tastes, consumption patterns, and social orientation, the community resembles the general American middle class even though here, as elsewhere, there are finer social gradations within that stratum. Wealth, position, and the length of time one's family has lived in New Orleans combine to develop significant class worlds within this broadly middle-class Jewish community. From the inside, the community is quite heterogeneous, and in its own way fragmented by its own criteria of acceptability.

The Jewish population numbered about 9,500 in 1958 and from earlier data it was estimated to be growing at a rate of from one to two per cent a year.[6] Migration has been partly responsible for the growth, but since 1953 there has also been an increase in the birthrate[7] as in the U.S. generally. A rise in births and the immigration of young families have lowered the median age of the community from 39.8 years in 1953 to 34.6 years in 1958. Jews comprised about 1.2 per cent of the total estimated population for the New Orleans metropolitan area in 1958 (800,000), and about 2 per cent of the white population (466,-000). This small proportion, even if only the white population is considered, was among the very lowest reported for twelve other American cities.[8] It may well be that the relatively small proportion of Jews has eased the adjustment to the larger community, leaving aside for the moment the many other complex factors that are involved. A group that constitutes little more than one per cent of the total population is hardly large enough to cause discernible pressures, especially if it chooses to adjust as smoothly as possible.

Since 1947 the Jewish population has grown by immigration from other states, within as well as outside the South. The university, particularly its medical school, and commercial opportunities have provided the major attractions. In 1958 the population could be divided as follows: 41 per cent born in the city, 24 per cent resident for 30 years or more, 24 per cent resident from 10 to 30 years, and 11 per cent less than 10 years. The composition of the migration has been significant for the Jewish community. It is my impression that this last group, about 1,000 persons, consists strongly of Northern-born, young, middle-class adults whose Jewish origins stem from Eastern Europe. This is a sharp contrast to the existing tradition in New Orleans. There is some indication that the two traditions make a difference for the membership

6. The figure of 10,000 used above is fairly close to the estimated present size in 1962. Earlier studies used in making the estimate were: Julian B. Feibelman, *A Social and Economic Study of the New Orleans Jewish Community* (Philadelphia, 1941), reporting on a 1938 survey; also Benjamin Goldman, *The Jewish Population of New Orleans, 1953* (New York: Council of Jewish Federations and Welfare Funds, 1953).

7. The fertility ratio—the proportion of children under five years to women aged 20–44 per 1,000 population—was 496.5 in 1953. Five years later this ratio had risen to 509.9. During the same period, the average family size increased from 2.83 to 3.20. Of course, these figures include the effects of families, usually with young children, who immigrated to New Orleans during the period.

8. Ben B. Seligman and A. Antonovsky, "Some Aspects of Jewish Demography," in M. Sklare (ed.), *The Jews: Social Patterns of an American Group* (Glencoe: The Free Press, 1958), 51.

of organizations in the community and in its leadership, but I cannot gauge how deeply these conflicting orientations go or, indeed, if they are in fact a basis for conflict. At some points, it is true, the newer leadership encounters the older and by now hereditary leadership, but this has not produced any serious or lasting fissures. Whatever the community's composition may have been in the past, it is certainly no longer homogeneous today.

These demographic facts invite a deeper analysis of the dynamic social features that are, in effect, the real community. For that purpose I have divided the features into two categories: the first, those which pertain principally to the Jewish community itself, and the second, those which originate from outside.

Within the Jewish Community

The character of Jewish identification and the structure of Jewish leadership have been selected as the best features to convey the social dynamics at work within the community. Both of these are obviously critical supports for the continuity of any community, perhaps even more so for the Jewish community. In the case of identification we must consider a social psychological quality that is vital for community life, ephemeral as it may appear to be. It is the willingness of the Jew to be conscious of and to recognize himself as a Jew among Jews. It is also the intensity with which he holds that consciousness and how far he feels bound to carry it in his behaviour and attitudes. Does he, in other words, stop at the lowest minimal recognition of himself as a Jew, or does he cultivate that sentiment to the point where it effectively directs what he does and what he thinks? Obviously, these are enormously complex dimensions and I do not claim to have probed them deeply in this study. Yet, the approach and the analysis that was followed have a logic and plausibility that make the conclusions reasonable.

The people who were interviewed in this survey were asked the following question: 'If you were able to emphasize just *one* thing as being most important for the upbringing of Jewish children today, which one of these would you say it would be?' [9] The alternatives

9. I know of no directly comparable data from Jewish surveys in other cities to allow some external assessment of the New Orleans reactions. I believe that the pattern of the responses in New Orleans is a valid reflection of the identification held by

from which they could choose and the distribution of their responses were these:

(1) Learning and becoming identified with the Jewish religion   34.2%

(2) Learning to appreciate the culture of the Jews such as literature, etc.   15.0

(3) Learning an appreciation of the State of Israel   0.4

(4) Learning an appreciation for the civic activities, welfare concerns, and social justice of Jewish people   11.8

(5) Not emphasizing Jewishness so much as teaching him to get along with other people in the community   30.1

(6) No answer or other answer given   8.5

Because such 'cafeteria-type' questions can be ambiguously interpreted by the respondent as well as by the analyst if taken just as they are, our respondents were also asked to give the reasons for their choice. The added comment provided the means for checking the alternative that had been selected and, it is presumed, for reducing a good deal of the possible ambiguity. Perhaps an illustrative verbatim comment for each of the four most popular alternatives would serve the same purpose here. A most typical comment for choosing religion, the first alternative above, was given by a young woman: "Religion is the most important because it's easy to lose the sense of Jewishness in a community like this; and not to know the religion will eventually be very unsatisfactory for the individual."

The second alternative, Jewish secular culture, has much less meaning in New Orleans than, I suspect, it now has elsewhere. Against New Orleans tradition, it is a somewhat alien concept. This choice represents one significant focus for identification, meant to include the products of Jewish culture as that term is popularly understood, such as literature, history, Yiddish and Hebrew, and the fine arts. Within this more restricted meaning, religion would not be included, or at most only as subject matter for what is essentially a secular endeavour.

---

the population and I would urge some application of the same question to other populations to check its validity further.

It was not possible to determine just how broadly this conception of secular culture was understood, but those who did select it as the most important thing a Jewish child should learn also seemed to understand the secular emphasis that was intended. For example, a relatively indicative response was this one: "Jewish people are *born* Jewish. They can't avoid it and they should learn about their culture to appreciate it. But, they must also know how to live in a world with all people." Or, as another respondent put it: "Because there is so much to be proud of and if you learned about the culture no one could make you ashamed of what you are."

Civic and welfare activities were considered as cohesive forces in the community and a basis upon which Jewish identification could be developed in the young, as this somewhat syllogistic response indicates: "There's a place in any community for Jewish civic activities. They would fit in more with the Jewish people. If Jewish people fit in with their community and civic activities, they will gain more respect from other religions."

Finally, the fifth alternative in the above list which can be called 'social adjustment', seemed to be most clearly intended in the meaning that one respondent expressed: "Over-identification brings the Jew his own ghetto. I appreciate my country. Judaism is my religion, but first and foremost I am an American." Those who selected this alternative intended the same thing as the sample comment just quoted, stressing the need to "get along with people", to "learn to live with non-Jews", and to recognize that "we are Americans and must live like Americans".

The next step was to discover what kinds of people chose which alternatives, and the subsequent analysis revealed some interesting and understandable relationships that pointed up the patterns of Jewish identification in the city. In a real sense the alternatives contain the spectrum of Jewish identification, and the alternative chosen reflects a valid disposition related to the individual's background. Let us consider only the three most popular responses in order to simplify the presentation: religion, social adjustment, and secular culture.

As might perhaps have been expected, Orthodox Jews chose religion predominantly (41.9 per cent) over any other single alternative. Reform Jews, however, divided almost equally between religion (32.9

per cent) and social adjustment (35.1 per cent) as the most important thing for a child to learn. In fact, the reaction by Reform Jews was quite similar to that by persons without any denominational affiliation (26.9 per cent and 38.5 per cent respectively). Culture was most often (19.2 per cent) chosen by the last group although even for them it was third in preference.

Cutting the analysis from another direction, we find that the age of the respondent made a difference for his choice.[10] Older people believed religion was the most important thing for a child to learn (44.8 per cent) and the proportion progressively decreased with each younger age group. Younger people, on the contrary, gave first priority to social adjustment (34.1 per cent), second to religion (25.7 per cent) and third to culture (19.5 per cent). Those in the middle age group generally expressed a scale of preferences between the old and the young, giving religion the strongest emphasis (34.9 per cent) and secondary emphasis to social adjustment (24.5 per cent).

The educational background of respondents in relation to their choice of what is important is given below. It will be seen that those who had never been to high school, generally the older persons, overwhelmingly chose religion above all other alternatives presented to them. College graduates, at the other extreme, divided almost evenly

"Most Important Thing for a Child to Learn,"
by Education of Respondent

| | Educational Level | | | |
Response Given	*No formal or grammar school*	*High school*	*Some College*	*College Graduate*
Religion	67.8	33.8	33.3	20.3
Culture	9.7	13.9	15.8	18.8
Civic activities	3.2	12.8	10.5	14.5
Social adjustment	16.1	34.9	31.6	29.0
Other answer	—	2.3	8.8	11.6
No answer	3.2	2.3	—	5.8
Totals	100.0	100.0	100.0	100.0

10. Age, education, occupation, and income were found to be related to denominational affiliation, and it is this relationship that is partly threaded throughout the patterns of choice on this question of Jewish identificaton.

between all the alternatives, but with slightly more stress on the importance of social adjustment. Generally, the higher the individual's educational attainment the less he emphasized religion as the focus for his identification and the more likely he was to choose social adjustment or Jewish culture instead.

Occupation and income were both related to the choices made. Those in high-prestige occupations tended to give less stress to religion than did other occupational groups. Hence, professionals thought religion was important (31.1 per cent), but not quite to the same extent as those in clerical or sales occupations (38.6) per cent). Among professionals, Jewish culture was considered more important (24.6 per cent) than in any other occupational group; 14.4 per cent of the managerial and 11.4 per cent of the clerical occupations gave it first priority. Social adjustment, on the contrary, was least important to professionals (19.7 per cent), yet much more so to proprietors (32.2 per cent) and clerical people (36.4 per cent). Analysis by income, shown in the table below, showed a similar pattern, in large measure because of the correlation between occupation and income. The greater his income, the more likely was a person's choice to be social adjustment or culture rather than religion. Religion was much more frequently chosen by those with lower incomes.

"Most Important Thing for a Child to Learn,"
by Annual Income of Respondent

| | Income Level | | | |
Response Given	Under $5000	5000– 10,999	11,000– 24,999	25,000 and over
Religion	55.2	45.3	20.3	18.9
Culture	6.9	13.3	18.6	24.3
Civic activities	10.3	6.7	20.3	8.1
Social adjustment	20.7	26.7	32.3	35.2
Other answer	6.9	6.7	6.8	8.1
No answer	—	1.3	1.7	5.4
Totals	100.0	100.0	100.0	100.0

A final dimension of this analysis can be mentioned. The level of the person's activity in Jewish as compared with non-Jewish organizations was related to his choice. Those who said they were more active in Jewish organizations most frequently selected religion (40.0 per cent) as the principal focus for their identification. Those more active in non-Jewish organizations, on the other hand, emphasized social adjustment (42.8 per cent) most of all.

In summary then, the young, the economically successful, and the educated segments of the community generally phrased their identification around the need to adjust to the larger community as much as around a special Jewish feature, such as religion or secular culture. Their view expressed itself in the fact that they were as much or more active in non-Jewish organizations, in their emphasis upon social adjustment, and in their generally Reform affiliation. At times, the recognition of a Jewish secular culture also played some part in their identification. Religion as a focus for identification found its greatest acceptance among the older and less successful people in the community. Separateness, not adjustment, lay at the core of their sentiments expressed in their greater activity in Jewish rather than non-Jewish organizations, and in their Orthodox affiliation.

A second perspective from which to assess the dynamics within the Jewish community is its structure of leadership.[11] Perhaps the most significant feature of that structure is its primary division into those who are recognized only within the Jewish community and those whose recognition extends more generally into the New Orleans community. One cannot help but consider this division as one more facet of the bifurcation that characterizes this community as I have described it in other contexts above. The division is one between the orientation that sees the Jewish community as a separate entity and the orientation that places the Jewish community always within the larger social context of the surrounding community.

Four groups of leaders were identified, two basing their support on the New Orleans community and two more evidently located within the Jewish community alone. Within the first was one group consisting

11. The description given here is based upon a study by John C. Rosen, "A Study of Leadership in the New Orleans Jewish Community" (M.A. thesis, Tulane University, 1960), which I directed. Rosen interviewed those persons who were most frequently mentioned as leaders by those in institutional posts such as rabbis and executive directors of the Federation and similar Jewish organizations.

predominantly of older, usually wealthy, but all long-time residents. These leaders once controlled the high-prestige Jewish organizations in the city by their positions on their boards. With age, however, they have become less active and their positions have been taken by a younger generation within the same élite level. It was from this older group that persons were picked by non-Jews for boards and committees that required community-wide representation. In some cases the reputation earned by individuals within this group was national, as evidenced by entries in *Who's Who* or in similar compendia.

A younger generation, but generally from the same background, formed a second leadership group. Some had already succeeded to the leadership posts left vacant by the retirement of an older leader, but at the least all members of this group were being prepared for succession. This process of succession seemed to be orderly and institutionalized as it is in a well-managed élite situation. Although there is something of the aristocratic and hereditary element at work here, it should not be considered as rigid and final for there is the possibility of deviation from the principle as I have described it.

Both old and young leaders tended to consider themselves as living in both the Jewish and the non-Jewish communities. They certainly did not aim at assimilating the Jewish community into the larger community, but neither did they build barriers to separate the two.

The other two groups of leaders were divided from those just described on two counts. First, there was the difference in their relative newness to the city. Second, there was the difference in orientation towards the Jewish community itself. Faced with a somewhat aristocratic barrier, one segment of this group has turned entirely inward towards the Jewish community and has sought its legitimation from within that social boundary. The other segment appeared to be in an ambivalent situation; these people desire the wider recognition of the New Orleans community but at present must be content with a more narrow recognition. Whether or not they will be able to translate their reputation in the Jewish community into one more generally recognized will depend as much on getting accepted in the Jewish élite group as on anything else.

The division of leadership into these multiple groups has not created any serious tears in the fabric of the community. On the contrary, it might even be presumed to function beneficially for the Jewish community as a whole by making a variety of opportunities available. There is room to support and to satisfy the differing orientations that are present in the community. For leadership, like identification, needs several alternative choices if there is, as in New Orleans, more than one kind of Jewish consciousness and orientation present.

Jews and the New Orleans Community

There is no doubt that the Jewish community has made a successful adjustment within the institutional structure of New Orleans. Its members generally have achieved a striking degree of upward mobility that has rewarded them with relatively high levels of material goods and satisfactions. Although there is ground for dissatisfaction, the community has maintained its Jewish identity and has functioned as a coherent and cohesive social entity. In large measure, these attainments, economic and social, have been effected by a successful community and its leadership. Yet in some ways the Southern setting has had its effect, too, and it is this aspect that now needs discussion.

The sociologically relevant facts about New Orleans can be very briefly given, but the consequences they contain strike deeply into the city's structure and into the Jewish community. The population of New Orleans is about one-half Catholic, about one-third Negro, and constantly alive to its Southern aristocratic traditions. What probably saves the city from the social stagnation and decay to which some of its history might condemn it is its place as the third largest port in the U.S. I do not mean that the economic ties with Central and South America automatically confer a cosmopolitan character upon the city, although they certainly help. Rather, the recognition of the world beyond the city limits that is forced by such trade does help to shape the orientation of the population. The Mississippi River and the Gulf of Mexico are seen by most people in the city as gateways rather than as barriers, and this impression is reinforced again and again by the mass media. It is the conception that New Orleans wants very much to have of itself. This self-image helps to give New Orleans an economic and social, if not a political, vitality that saves it from the possible erosion of *ante-bellum* Southern romanticism.

Yet the tradition of a Southern aristocracy dies hard. It has been curiously heightened in the hundred years since the Civil War and continues to play a significant role in the social structure of the city. The provincialism of that tradition becomes intermingled with the cosmopolitanism that the city's economy demands. The Jewish community shares in the latter, but the consequences of provincialism have had significant effect as well. In effect, Jews have encountered a status ceiling preventing them from full public acceptance into the social élite because they cannot share in the aristocratic tradition. On all other grounds they possess the necessary qualifications. There are wealthy Jewish families in New Orleans that possess a measure of economic power that is commensurate with their economic position. Similarly, some Jews are active in both local and national politics and no doubt they exert a significant political influence in the city. Some families can also trace their New Orleans ancestry back a respectable distance into the past. In spite of these economic, political, and genealogical qualifications, however, full membership in the status and ruling élite is not open to them.

The barrier is raised by the Catholic character of the city, reaching its clearest expression in the organization of Mardi Gras and the 'krewes' or associations that stage the festival. Mardi Gras was intended to be the last day of revelry before the solemnity of Lent. I am not concerned here that the festival has become commercialized as a major tourist attraction or that its original religious function has by now been rather generally shunted aside. Mardi Gras involves the entire city in festivities and its importance for the city stems from reasons other than income alone. Mardi Gras marks the peak of the social season for the status élite and for the status pretenders. In the weeks between Twelfth Night and Ash Wednesday those groups organize a costly and almost continuous series of social occasions for the début of their daughters and for defining élite participation. These functions and their timing are organized according to a tight status hierarchy, generally recognized in the city. For example, many krewes parade once during this period and end the parade in an elaborately staged and expensive ball held in the city's only auditorium adequate for the event. The closer a krewe can arrange its celebration to Mardi Gras, the higher is its standing. But the dates are allocated in strict accordance to the status of the krewe, at least in the last days before Mardi Gras. Without any doubt, member-ship of one of the top three krewes is at once a prerequisite for entry into the élite as well as a recognition of one's élite status.

There is no question that some Jews belong to Mardi Gras krewes, although there is ground to question whether they belong to those with highest status. Whether they do or not, the Catholic complexion of Mardi Gras prevents a Jewish member from making his claim. The Jewish family of means, therefore, generally is disqualified from trans-lating its class position into a commensurate status position. Some families, it is said, leave the city during Mardi Gras, perhaps to avoid what may seem to them an unpleasant confrontation.

The same kind of barrier or ceiling also exists for membership in the élite clubs, which intermesh with the status structure of the krewes. One of the two highest-ranking clubs, it has been said, has claimed that no Jew has ever got beyond the foyer in the building it occupies. Whether apocryphal or true, the statement is indicative of a generally accepted point of view. Given these characteristics about both krewes and clubs, the Jew gains but little status honour even if he does manage to gain membership, for it brings him doubtful honour in his own community and no publicity in the larger community. If he wishes to maintain his Jewish identification, therefore, he must also come to accept the status ceiling.

I do not wish to give the impression that this situation produces intolerable frustration in the Jewish community, because I believe that it does not really affect the large majority. If anything, the ceiling has worked to set minimum limits for Jewish identification.

Another effect that can be traced to Southern aristocratic traditions, if not perhaps to the status ceiling as well, is the status stratification within the Jewish community itself. As with other minority groups in other places, the Jews in New Orleans have tended to adopt the criteria accepted by the larger community as their own. Hence, one's genealogy tends to be as important as the usual criteria of wealth and position in determining the composition of the Jewish élite group. I have no definite information on this point, but it is my impression that entry into the Jewish élite is as jealously controlled as that into any élite.

A final aspect of the place of Jews in this Southern city needs to be mentioned, one that promises to become severely critical for the Jewish community in a short time. The Jews, as has been noted, are a small proportion of a multi-racial and multi-religious population in New Orleans. It seems to me that in the past antisemitism has been relatively weak, at least compared with Northern cities. To be sure, there does exist the antisemitism expressed by the status ceiling but there has not been much evidence of more aggressive antisemitic actions. A reasonable explanation for the absence of such prejudice can be said to lie in the large proportion of Negroes in the city and their inferior social position as enforced by Southern traditions. It is as if the Negro has been continuously available to take the brunt of prejudice, whether it was expressed in the more genteel manner of the upper-class master towards a slave-become-servant, or in the more violent eruptions of the lower classes generated by their own frustrations and failures. The Jew thereby has avoided a good deal of social conflict. The frustrated lower-class person always has had the Negro, lower yet in the hierarchy, upon whom he could vent his anger in an institutionalized and legitimate form. The upper-class person has never been really threatened by the Jew to whom he could deny access to his own élite level by the irrational expedient of the status ceiling. Nor has the Jew in New Orleans challenged the tradition as much as he has been willing to accept it.

The Supreme Court's decision in the school integration case in 1954 and in subsequent decisions has set into motion a heavy and obvious process of change in the existing patterns of race relations and race etiquette. These repercussions have been felt throughout the South, the Jewish community included. The Southerner feels his status threatened as well as other supports he has depended upon. His reaction in turning to the extreme right politically, for example, can be explained in terms of the status threat that is becoming more real each day. The Jewish community has been forced to take a position during this period of racial conflict because it is impossible for any person, let alone a group, to remain uncommitted in the South. The commitment has not been forced by moral or ethical reasons alone. Just as important has been the insistence by segregation leaders that people in the community be counted, and not just once but as many times as the occasion demands. The spectrum of race attitudes that was once possible has quickly been condensed into only two choices: either one is aggressively and publicly for segregation, or it tends to follow that one must be for integration. The fine differences and shadings between those extremes, once possible, are no longer tolerated. Caught in a crossfire deliberately planned by segregation leaders acting to make the most political capital out of this period of change, the Jew has come to experience the first signs of open antisemitism. Racial segregation, extreme right-wing conservatism, and now antisemitism are all part of the same pattern, and Southern leaders of this growing movement have relied upon the resources and experience of antisemitic demagogues in other parts of the country.[12] Whatever the private attitude of the Jew may be towards segregation, he finds himself more and more cast into what the Southern extremist thinks of as an integrationist and therefore an enemy. The Jews' sense of morality, of justice, and of equality tends to push them in the direction of integration even though this is not always their wish.

How these events will treat the Jewish community in New Orleans is impossible now to predict because there are many variables involved. One thing, however, is certain: the Jewish community faces change in its relationship to the larger community as surely as the South faces changes in its accepted traditions. The pattern of adjustment that was successful in the past will have to be altered to meet the demands of the present. Given the differences that have been described within the Jewish community, it is also certain that there is no unanimous future course of adjustment that can be set. Different sectors of the community have different degrees of Jewish identification and different degrees of loyalty and attachment to the city. It is possible that the Jewish community can emerge stronger and more unified than ever before; that its sense of identification willy-nilly will be forged by the events forced upon them to produce a newer alloy of greater strength and durability.

12. During the spring of 1961, for example, at the time of the Eichmann trial, there were leaflets and license plates in evidence with the phrase "I like Eich" (a reference to former President Eisenhower's campaign slogan, "I like Ike"). I have seen more antisemitic literature distributed in the last two years than in all of my eight previous years in New Orleans. Additionally, there have been public accusations against the B'nai B'rith and its Anti-Defamation League. These, too, are of recent origin. A good deal of the literature distributed is published in New Jersey and California, which indicates some cooperation between the antisemitic leadership in New Orleans and that outside the state and region.

Section 5 Jews and Desegregation

The controversial Supreme Court decision of 1954 has profoundly affected southern Jewish communities. As writer Albert Vorspan declares: "The segregation crisis has shaken Southern Jews more severely than any national event since the Civil War." Southern bigots have accused Jews of supporting integration, and extremists have even bombed synagogues in Mississippi, Tennessee, Florida, Georgia, and Alabama.

The following selections show that there are southern Jews who protest segregation, but fear of reprisal has silenced many of them. In contrast, northern and western Jews have usually been in the vanguard of battles for civil rights. On occasion individual southern Jews, laymen and rabbis alike, have spoken out boldly on the injustices of segregation, but they constitute a small minority of southern Jewry.

The articles in this section are all written by keen observers of human relations. Joshua A. Fishman, who worked in Alabama, Murray Friedman, who has studied Jewish communities in Virginia, and civil rights lawyer Marvin Braiterman, who lived for a short time in Mississippi, ably describe the mounting tension. While most authors agree that liberal Jews do not feel secure enough to voice their opinions, some express concern over the acquiescence of the southern Jewish community. Rabbi Allen Krause in his investigation concludes: "From a Jewish viewpoint the verdict can be put without froth or frills: the Southern rabbi has done a good deal, but he could do so much more." Counter to the more pessimistic standards made by the Bernsteins and Reissman in previous selections, Albert Vorspan proclaims antisemitism to be on the wane and warns that Jews must not be needlessly frightened into silence.

Whatever their faults, the southern Jews have faced many difficulties, as these essays clearly depict.

Joshua A. Fishman
Southern City

SOUTHERN CITY is closer to the southern stereotype so frequently fostered by our mass communication media than are most other southern cities its size. A large percentage of its roughly 120,000 inhabitants (about 40 to 45 percent of whom are Negro) are recent arrivals from rural districts marked by their backwardness, their poverty, and their high Negro population density. It is quite common to find children of elementary school age walking about barefoot in the heart of the business district, in stores and restaurants, and even in the state Capitol building. Although the population of the city has grown and the city itself has expanded, the pattern of life has not changed dramatically from that of earlier days. This is primarily a result of the fact that there has been very little industrial expansion of the city's economic foundations. As a result, wealth, social prestige and civic leadership have—with only a few exceptions—remained in the hands of the same mercantile, banking, and farm-holding families for several generations.

Southern City's major source of sustenance is the government—state and federal. As the state capital, it requires the services of thousands of lower echelon civil service employees as clerks, accountants, typists and assistants in various state agencies and bureaus. In addition, the presence of two federal Air Force bases (both of them racially integrated) in the immediate environs of the city has attracted another large contingent of civilian employees, many of whom have come from other sections of the country as well as from other parts of the state. The military and civilian personnel at these bases have provided the major stimuli to local retail trade and real estate development for nearly two decades. Recent estimates have shown that total agricultural receipts in Southern City (derived from the sale of produce brought in from the surrounding farm lands) amounted to $16 million while total receipts from military personnel were in the neighborhood of $90 million. If we add to this the amounts derived from employees of the state government, it becomes abundantly clear why Southern City is not nearly as dependent upon industrial development for its well-being as most other cities its size. Most people seem to share a general expectation that life will flow along quite uneventfully with neither "booms" nor "busts" to disturb it. Many people evince a quiet detachment from many of the concerns of the more industrialized neighboring cities, not to mention those of more distant cities, and a reluctance to change the comfortable status quo.

Southern City gives every appearance of being quiet and relaxed. In taxis, restaurants and stores, the people I met were friendly, helpful, and, although quite talkative, unconcerned with the nature of my business or my views on desegregation. Taxi drivers never reacted noticeably to the Negro addresses to which I directed or summoned them. (Nevertheless, I cautiously—or over-cautiously—always specified the nearest intersection rather than the specific address to which I was going.) Southern City may never be a particularly lively place, but it seemed to be especially quiet in mid-August, 1959.

Jews in Southern City are proud of the fact that theirs is an old and distinguished community. Jews were among the founders of the city (the first Jewish settler arrived in 1789) and a small number of Jews have always figured among the wealthy, prominent, civic and social tone-givers and pacesetters. Originally, these were all German-Jewish families and members of what is now the Reform congregation. More recently a few Jews of Eastern European and Sephardi backgrounds have also gained wealth, influence in city affairs, and, to a lesser extent, social prominence. The corporation lawyers, bankers, brokers, and businessmen who are descended from the old German-Jewish families are still looked up to by all others as the advisors of the Jewish community and as men of long-standing influence with the "best Christian families." Some of these have intermarried but their Jewish past is still far from forgotten or ignored by either Jewish or non-Jewish "society." In a few cases other Jews have married into these families and have come to share their prominence in Jewish as well as in citywide (civic-club and service-society) affairs. On the other hand, a number of Jewish businessmen and professionals of Eastern European and Sephardi backgrounds have also become quite wealthy in recent years. A few of these have attained influence in Democratic party politics, established new banks, built large shopping centers, office buildings and suburban housing developments. Others have established legal or medical practices that have gained citywide and even regional prominence. They live extremely well but have not yet gained the civic or social recognition that seems to come only with long inherited wealth and status. There are also many Jews who are owners of small shops and businesses while others are specialists of one sort or another at either of the two Air Force bases. The latter are by and large from the North (as are also many of the Jewish physicians) and they are beginning to find acceptance into the social life of the community on the basis of their intellectual and personal merits.

A young member of a distinguished Jewish family in Southern City summed up the social stratification of the Jewish community as follows: "Southern City Jewry is divided into three parts: *Diehls* [*i.e.*, the respected and wealthy old German-Jewish families, one of which carries this family name], *wheels* [*i.e.*, the Eastern European and Sephardi families who have achieved wealth and prominence, if not respect, in more recent years as a result of their own exertions] and *shlemiels* [*i.e.*, those who have not been able to achieve either prominence or wealth]."

Those members of the "top" Jewish group with whom I spoke impressed me with their emphasis on (a) their civic contributions and the recognition given to them for their leadership in this area (organization and leadership of the community-wide charities drive, of mental and other health programs, of the USO—which here is entirely dependent on Jewish subventions—and their devotion to the Rotary, the Kiwanis, the Scouts and various prominent business and civic-service organizations which have often elected them to office or given them public recognition) and (b) their intimate friendships with leading Christian families as evidenced by reciprocal invitations both at the adult and child levels. As a result of both of these areas of activity, they believed that they had gained much respect, recognition and friendship in important circles for the entire Jewish community. This is not to imply that they engaged in these activities solely or even primarily for the sake of such benefits but merely that they were considered to be important by-products. They felt that their acceptance by the non-Jewish community leadership was genuine and complete—at least "classically" so, *i.e.* until the recent appearance upon the scene of new developments. The only "social distinctions" which they admitted were (a) their non-eligibility for membership in the Christian country clubs (to which they are regularly invited to play golf and to attend parties and other functions) and (b) their non-eligibility for membership in the "mystic" societies (to whose annual dances and functions they are also regularly invited).

All other Jewish and non-Jewish informants with whom I spoke corroborated the above account of Jewish prominence in the civic and service activities of the town. On the other hand, Jews from the middle and lowest rungs in the status ladder were not nearly so unanimous about the social acceptance of the "top" Jewish families in non-Jewish circles. Thus, one informant felt that "they get invited to the homes and to the parties of only five out of every hundred Christians from whom they would like to get invitations." Another put it this way: "When the Diehls get an invitation from a Christian friend, *they make sure to go* whether or not they have a headache or a previous engagement!" Comments of this type imply both a lesser degree of social acceptance as well as a greater insecurity with respect to such acceptance as exists on the part of leading Christian families for the top level Jewish families. Nevertheless, such evaluations may also be biased by the unsatisfied status cravings of those who reported them to me. However, whatever internal jealousies may exist within the Jewish community, I found no one who questioned that the "top families" were depended upon for guidance and for policy decisions with respect to relations with the Gentile world.

The best available estimate sets the current Jewish population of Southern City at 1800. Jews thus constitute about 2.5 percent of the total *white* population of the city. The following Jewish organizations were reported to be currently functioning in Southern City:

a. The Reform Congregation, about 150 families, with its women's group and Sunday School. (This congregation is 107 years old. Its rabbi has served it for 27 years. He is senior in term of association with Southern City to every other minister in town.)

b. The Conservative Congregation, about 170 families, with its men's group, women's group and Sunday School. (This congregation is about to welcome a new rabbi who is Orthodox. It has had Orthodox rabbis in the past. Nevertheless, the tenor of the observances and sympathies of most of its members are far from strict Orthodoxy.)

c. The Sephardi Congregation, about 60-70 families, currently has no rabbi of its own. (Most of its members are descended from parents or grandparents who came from Rhodes and Cyprus. Many of them also hold membership in the Reform Congregation and send their children to the Reform Sunday School.)

d. The *B'nai B'rith* lodge is the only active men's organization. It has some 200 members from all three congregations, although for a long time it was primarily controlled by the Reform element. More recently, Conservative congregants have been among its most active members.

e. *Hadassah* and the *Council of Jewish Women* are the two active women's organizations. Most women are members of both organizations. However, the leaders of the former are primarily members of the Conservative and Sephardi congregations whereas the leaders of the latter are primarily members of the Reform congregation.

f. The *Jewish Federation of Southern City* consists of representatives of the other Jewish organizations. It coordinates the major fundraising and spending activities of the Jewish community and is concerned with community-wide policy issues. The Federation is *not* a member of the National Community Relations Advisory Council; this may be an indication both of the junior status of Southern City in the world of American Jewish communal leadership as well as of the desire of the local leadership to be independent of "foreign entanglements."

g. The *Standard Club* is the Jewish country club.

In addition to these organized groups, some national Jewish organizations have members in Southern City, although not in sufficient numbers to establish formal chapters or lodges. The local members of one of these national organizations have, from time to time, invited speakers representing the national organization to come to Southern City.

Most Jews seem to belong to some organization, even if only in the most perfunctory and inactive sense. A sizable number belong to more than one and the women's groups are generally more active than the men's groups. The B'nai B'rith lodge recently celebrated its one hundredth anniversary. In recent years it has been plagued by membership resignations and protests over the desegregationist pronouncements and activities with which it and its Anti-Defamation League, have been identified.

The social, economic and organizational position of Jews in Southern City may stand out more clearly if we consider briefly some of the other groups which constitute the bulk of the local population. The widespread quip that many southern cities are "owned by the Jews, run by the Catholics, and enjoyed by the Baptists" is even less applicable to Southern City than it is to most—if only because of the minute size of the Catholic population, which is estimated at 2500 (including a few hundred Negro Catholics) and is almost entirely unrepresented in the top city government or business-banking society circles. There are two Catholic hospitals in Southern City (the largest in the town), three Catholic parochial schools, and four Catholic churches. (The schools and hospitals are segregated; one of the hospitals, St. Luke's, receives federal support under the Hill-Burton Act and, therefore, accepts both white and Negro patients in segregated wards. This, too, is the only hospital in Southern City in which Negro physicians may practice. The Catholic churches are normally segregated except that a visiting Negro may on rare occasions attend mass in an all-white Catholic church.) The Catholic impact upon Southern City is much weaker than in some neighboring cities where there are many Catholics in the labor force or where old Spanish Catholic and French Catholic influences are still much in evidence. Most of the better educated and financially secure Catholics are at one of the two Air Force bases in either a civilian or military capacity. These have, by and large, come from other sections of the country and, although many of them have had long terms of duty here (5 to 10 years), they are still strangers to the social and cultural life of Southern City—both as "outsiders" and as Catholics. Like the Jews, Catholics are practically unknown outside of the few larger cities in the state. There are still approximately 20 counties (out

of a total of 60 in the entire state) where the Mass has never been celebrated. Even in Southern City, Catholics were almost unknown until
the Second World War when so many were stationed at the nearby
bases that they could not be accommodated for Mass at the on-base
chapels. As a result, truck loads of Catholic servicemen were trans-
ported to Southern City every Sunday in order to attend Mass there.
Even so, the smallness of the Catholic churches in Southern City forced
hundreds of servicemen to stand in line for hours every Sunday before
they could be admitted to Mass. It was under these circumstances that
most residents realized for the first time that there were "that many
Catholics." Nevertheless, although Catholics are somewhat more numerous than Jews, both their recency and their generally middle and
lower-middle-class concentration combine to make them generally far
less prominent than the Jews in the awareness of the average white Protestant resident of the city.

The majority of white residents are Baptists or Methodists—although there are quite a few Presbyterians and Episcopalians among
the "better" families. Other Protestant denominations are also represented in the white population of Southern City (Christian Scientists,
Jehovah's Witnesses, Mormons, Lutherans, Seventh Day Adventists)—
there is even a Greek Orthodox Church. However, none of these small
groups has significant influence. Negroes in Southern City—as elsewhere in the South—are preponderantly Baptists, although the number
of Negro Methodists is also large. Finally, as in most southern cities,
there are no white ethnic minorities.

Religion plays an active role in Southern City. Many churches have
daily activities for their members and the statements and doings of lay
and clerical religious leaders are widely publicized. The rabbi of the
Reform Congregation is widely known and respected. He is frequently
invited to speak at Christian services and at inter-faith meetings. Most
Jews consider him a valuable asset in maintaining good relations with
the Gentile community.

Most of my informants, Jewish and non-Jewish alike, agreed that their
picture of quiet, mutually respectful existence began to fade with the
Supreme Court's school desegregation decision. Even then, no serious
trouble was expected because the leading families could be depended

upon to be moderate and rational with respect to Negro civil rights and because their patriarchal influence could be counted on to control Negroes and "rednecks" (poor, ignorant and violence-prone whites). Some trouble was anticipated in nearby industrial centers ("where folks are just naturally fiercer") and in some of the rural districts (where the Negro population density is highest and a tradition of poor-white lawlessness has never been fully overcome). Perhaps this certainty that there was "no need to worry" was partially responsible for the paucity of authoritative local statements by religious or secular leaders in support of the Supreme Court's decision, or at least in support of the supremacy of the law and legal processes in our national life. Although local Jewish leaders felt uncomfortable about the support by national Jewish organizations for the Supreme Court's decision, there seemed to be nothing concrete to worry about: the White Citizens' Council remained a small and ineffective group and the Klan was (as it had been for over a generation) totally discredited in polite society. Moderate opinion, though unorganized, was felt to be dominant. Individuals freely admitted to each other that the Negro "deserves his rights" although there was no certainty as to how and when he was to get them.

While moderate opinion remained thus diffuse and in the absence of strong moral national leadership, the expression of extreme segregationist views began to mount. This is a general southern phenomenon of our times and would have to come to pass in Southern City even if the local Negroes had not had the temerity to demand decent treatment in public transportation. When moderate leadership did not come forward to support the reasonable and negligible Negro demands, more and more extremist voices were heard. The action of the Negroes was made to appear as a *precedent* of importance beyond the issues under dispute and, as a result, the White Citizens' Council underwent a phenomenal growth. Today, many of the major political leaders (including the mayor and the chief of police) are WCC members, as are many of the business leaders. Although the WCC is locally considered to be "more respectable" than the Klan (and many have rationalized their joining it on the basis of wanting to "keep it respectable"), the Klan, too, has become an active force. Its support is openly solicited by political candidates and its emblems are openly displayed together with those of other "civic clubs" on the highways approaching Southern

City. In addition to the anti-Negro bias which it shares with the WCC, the Klan has voiced anti-Catholic and anti-Jewish views. Finally, the local spokesmen of the nationwide anti-Semitic and fascist movements have also gained an appreciable following. All of these factors have combined to produce great interracial tension, the erosion of any moderate public position, disintegration of the few channels of communication that existed between white and Negro leadership and a constant witch-hunt against those "soft on the nigger issue." As the "decent citizenry" tumbled over each other to join the WCC, a number of prominent Jewish businessmen—primarily from the second status level—also joined. The newspaper editor, whose father had once won a Pulitzer prize for exposing the Klan and who himself had early identified the WCC as the Klan's modern counterpart, now declared that the WCC and the Klan were poles apart. The WCC began a door-to-door membership drive threatening to publish the names of all those who refused to join and the City Commission closed all of the city parks rather than have them used by Negroes and passed ordinances banning interracial social contacts of any kind. Local religious and educational groups dissociated themselves from the desegregationist views of their national organizations; the PTA's of local schools renounced their affiliations with the national PTA and formed their own PTO (Parents and Teachers Organization). The identification of dissidents from "the southern way of life" led to harassment and threats by "rednecks" and ostracism and criticism by family and friends. It was in this atmosphere that the incident cryptically referred to as "the meeting at St. Luke's" transpired.

A handful of women—white and Negro, Christian and Jewish—calling themselves the Fellowship of the Concerned, had been meeting irregularly for three years. After other meeting places had been denied to them, they began to meet in a room in St. Luke's Hospital. Their meetings were concerned with the interests of women in child-rearing, religious emphases in family life, etc. An "account" of what proved to be their last meeting (held in September, 1958, and devoted to the role of women in various countries) was published in a November issue of the weekly *Southern City Family News*, a rabidly anti-Semitic sheet which had little readership except among the lunatic fringe. Not only did it report the meeting as a conspiratorial cabal of racial mongrelizers and Communist agents, it published the names, addresses, telephone numbers and places of employment of all whose cars were said to have been parked outside of the meeting place. These individuals were immediately exposed to a campaign of abuse, vilification and threats. Many names were apparently listed in error and those so listed bought advertising space in the "respectable dailies" to declare their innocence. Others publicly dissociated themselves from relatives who had attended the meeting. The issue in which the meeting was reported quickly sold out and additional thousands of copies were printed and distributed free of charge throughout the city. When a small group of members met in a private home to discuss how they might best cope with this situation, flash-bulb photos were taken of all those leaving the meeting. This group has never met again and the *Southern City Family News* has continued with an assured audience of several thousand paid subscribers and many more readers who receive it free of charge.

Although it was not previously identified with him, the *Family News* has become the organ of John G. Biggot since the St. Luke's affair. Biggot is a member of an old and wealthy Southern City family. During the Second World War he gained a distinguished war record but became infected with the fanatical conviction that a secret Jewish-Communist conspiracy threatened America and the Christian world. He is considered to be a sincere and dedicated man by those who know him. He seems to have ample finances (there are rumors that he is supported by the millionaire Hunt of Texas who sponsored *Facts Forum* during the McCarthy days, the Arab League, the *American Mercury*, etc.) and he enters every local and state-wide election in order to bring his views to the public. Although he also attacks fluoridation of water and mental health as aspects of the Jewish-Communist conspiracy, his major ammunition has been the *Protocols of the Elders of Zion* and the statements issued by Jewish national organizations on behalf of school desegregation and Negro civil rights. He quotes these statements and brandishes copies of the Jewish publications in which they have appeared at every public address. In earlier senatorial and gubernatorial races he received a small fraction of the total vote. However, in the 1959 mayoralty campaign he received 10 percent of the total primary vote—an all-time high. Since it is unlikely that he received

any Jewish, Negro or Catholic votes, his following among white Protestant voters is actually somewhat higher than 10 percent. Liberals in
Southern City feel that Biggot can no longer be "written off" as a
lunatic. Some feel that he is part of an organized Fascist movement and
that his appeal to religious and class biases may become increasingly
dangerous and lead the "rednecks" toward more violent behavior. Jewish leaders are deeply concerned as to whether their "silent treatment"
of his charges is the most effective approach and whether their reliance
on public authorities to cope with Biggot in a crisis is well-placed.
Many feel that any public reply to him will dignify his charges, give
them additional publicity and single out the Jewish citizens as in some
way separate from the total white community, from which they do
not wish to be distinguished in any way other than on the point of
religious difference. Although there is some Jewish sentiment in favor
of answering Biggot, the leadership is still following the "silent treatment" advice of national Jewish organizations. Nevertheless, it is
greatly incensed that some of those organizations are providing Biggot
with "grist for his mill" by their desegregationist efforts.

The activities of the WCC, the Klan and Biggot have engendered
a great deal of fear in the Jewish community. Jewish leaders are extremely sensitive to any Jewish prominence in the entire desegregation
area. (I believe that this was the reason for the reluctance of several
prominent men to be interviewed by me.) During the week of my
stay in Southern City, the Klan and Biggot sought to embarrass the
Governor (whose election the Klan had previously supported) on the
grounds of his Jewish and Catholic connections. (Lehmann Brothers
in New York had bought a recent issue of state bonds and the Governor had made friendly statements concerning Kennedy's presidential
aspirations.) Thus, once more, a "Jewish issue" came before the public in an unfavorable light. Some Jewish leaders spoke to me of a
"paradise lost." "It used to be so quiet, the Jewish community used to
be so respected, Jewish leaders used to be welcomed in the best
society."

I conducted a total of 27 interviews in Southern City (some with both
husbands and wives or parents and their adult children). These interviews were distributed across the following categories:

Jews. 14 interviews. Included in this sample are the rabbi of the Reform synagogue; three individuals in the top "policy leadership" echelons, two from old and prominent families and one who had married into such a family; a very prominent physician of Sephardi background; a member of a very successful business family of Eastern European derivation with WCC ties; the current chairman of a Jewish fraternal organization; two families that had been very active in desegregationist efforts—one of whom represents a branch of an old and highly influential family; and five individuals of lesser prestige, two of whom are related to respected old families.

Because of severe time pressures, I was unable to schedule appointments with two additional members of the "policy leadership" group, two prominent businessman with WCC ties, and two leading members of the Sephardi congregation. Although these additional six individuals would certainly have contributed to my general understanding of the Jewish aspects of the segregation problem in Southern City, it was my opinion and that of others that their views would largely duplicate those I had already obtained.

Negroes. 4 interviews. Included in this sample are the leading minister and ideological tone-setter of the Negro community; a long-time NAACP officer and leader of working-class elements; the president of a Negro institution of higher education and a professor at this same institution.

White non-Jews. 9 interviews. Included in this sample are an officer of a major bank; two women active in church groups and in the state Council on Human Relations; a Methodist minister devoted to the educational work of his church; the vice-president of the state AFL-CIO; two families at the fore of desegregationist thought in Southern City and two long-term civilian employees at the Air Force base, both involved in educational research activities, one of whom is an expert on local Catholic affairs.

All informants, Jewish, non-Jewish white and Negro alike, had resided in the deep South for many years. *On the average,* the Jewish informants had been in Southern City longer. This is a reflection of the influx of Negro and white non-Jewish residents during recent years which has not been similarly paralleled among the Jewish population.

Although three of my Jewish informants had come from the North, even they had been in Southern City for eight or more years.

I believe that most of those interviewed were well-informed, intelligent individuals who were particularly well-informed about segregation-desegregation problems in Southern City. Their personal views (not necessarily representative of those current in Southern City at large) varied from mild segregationism to the uncompromisingly desegregationist position.

The following are summaries of the views expressed in response to my questions:

> What do people consider to be some of the major social problems in Southern City? (*What* people; are the problems any different now than four or five years ago; are the *Jewish* problems any different than those of white Protestants, Catholics, Negroes, other minorities?)

The segregation-desegregation struggle was uniformly mentioned first. It is the foremost social problem in everyone's awareness and even such other problems as anti-Semitism, education, housing and industrial development are directly related to it. All Jewish and white non-Jewish respondents felt that the tensions caused by the Supreme Court decision, the transportation strike and other desegregation pressures were in some ways more strongly felt by the Jewish community. This was usually attributed to Mr. Biggot's activities and to the Klan, which often singles out Jews as targets and has raised the suspicion of a "Jewish issue" in many minds. Many remarked on a steady deterioration in Gentile-Jewish relations over the past few years. Most Jewish informants felt that the Jewish problem was differentiated from that of the "rest of the white community" as a result of the publicized statements condemning segregation made by Jewish national organizations. This opinion was not shared by those Jews who had "exposed" themselves as being in favor of desegregation and by a few of the less prominent non-Jews who themselves held moderate or liberal views that had not been publicized. The latter felt that Jews faced a more serious problem which they interpreted as "Jewish insecurity," "Jewish fearfulness," "greater concern for business and social reprisals," "their exposed sensitivity for any kind of community unrest," etc. Most white non-Jewish respondents shared the Jewish concern over Biggot's activities but tended to view the Jewish problem as more "self-induced" than "reality related." Two white non-Jewish informants (women in church and state Council on Human Relations work) saw no particular Jewish problem at all, while one, a psychologist at a federal Air Force base, felt strongly that the anti-Semitic dangers could not be exaggerated. The Negro respondents lumped Biggot with the rest of the opposition and felt that Jewish fears merely classed them with most moderates who could not be counted on when the chips were down.

Neither Catholics nor organized labor were felt to be in any particularly embarrassing position, as locally they had taken no position and were not strongly identified in local popular awareness with their national bodies. Catholics have recently been headlined as part of the Klan's anti-Kennedy blasts but have otherwise not figured prominently in local events related to the segregation issue. Organized labor consists largely of office workers, which are not strongly identified with the labor movement. Among industrial workers a few extremists have been active. On the whole, union labor is an inconspicuous and organizationally weak group.

Local Methodist laymen have repudiated the desegregationist efforts of their national bodies, although there is a small local Methodist desegregationist group. Most Methodist ministers have not spoken out, however, and the group, as such, is not in the limelight.

The intrenched anti-Semitic apparatus has had almost no *local* Jewish desegregationist sympathy to point to. My impression is that a very few wealthy Jews who have achieved recent acceptance by the Gentiles are concerned that their genuinely segregationist views are under doubt (and that their newly won positions are, therefore, threatened). A slightly larger number of Jews are concerned about Jews being singled out from the general white community, in any way, during stressful times. My Jewish informants believed that most Jews hold moderate or liberal views but that the combination of Biggot, the Klan and the WCC has frightened them. Very few Jews possess both desegregationist views and a readiness to express them in words and action. Generally, my non-Jewish informants vacillated between the view that Jews felt and behaved no differently than others and the view that Jews were more frightened and more cautious than others—as well as privately more moderate. Both the Jewish historical experiences with discrimination as well as such group and individual advantages as better education, greater opportunities for travel, intellectual interests and community service orientation were offered as the reasons for the greater Jewish liberalism in this area.

> Have local Jewish organizations expressed any position with respect to the desegregation issue? (which have and in what way [public or "off the record"]; which have not, and why not; is it desirable for Jewish organizations to do so as *Jewish* organizations, is there a Jewish angle to this issue?)

No local Jewish organization in Southern City has made any public statement in connection with either the transportation issue or the general desegregation struggle. Not only have there been no statements sympathetic to desegregation, there have also been none espousing the "southern way of life" or dissociating the local Jewish community or its organizations from the statements and activities of national organizations. Only two Jewish informants attributed this to a realization that the Jewish national organizations were really acting on behalf of justice, democracy, and, ultimately, Jewish security as well. More generally, however, the absence of such dissociative statements (which some Protestant, labor and other groups *have* made) is related to the same policy which prompts the "top policy leadership" to advise that no reply be made to Biggot's charges. In part, this policy is supported locally out of the compelling desire to call no attention to Jews as such. In part, it is motivated by "strategic" considerations. No Jewish informants seriously supported a more aggressive policy. None questioned the policy of no *local* statements being made re segregation-desegregation in the name of the Jewish community or any of its organizations.

> Does the position taken by local Jewish organizations re desegregation differ from that taken by other organizations in town (particularly organizations of other minority groups)? If so, why? What do Jewish laymen think of the local Jewish organizational leadership?

There have been no statements of any kind from local Catholic leaders—either lay or clerical. There have been strong segregationist statements by some local Baptist and Methodist laymen's groups as well as by some schismatic labor groups. The Jewish leadership feels that the Baptist and Methodist leadership can argue publicly with their national organizations because they are a secure majority in the local white population. Jews, however, are such a small minority that they "cannot afford" to call attention to the desegregationist views of their national organizations. I found no Jewish informants who questioned this approach, although a few regretted and opposed the private protests of the local Jewish leadership to the national Jewish organizations. Nevertheless, the "top policy leadership" is accepted as such by virtually everyone within the Jewish community and their hegemony was recognized by most non-Jews with whom I spoke.

> Have national Jewish organizations adopted any positions in connection with segregation that are embarrassing or helpful to the Jewish population or to the desegregation movement here? (What organizations, what positions, in what way embarrassing [helpful], what publicity given?)

The "top policy leadership" informants argue that the statements by Jewish national organizations not only harm Jews locally but also harm the desegregationist cause which they seek to support. By linking Jews to Negroes, the Negro cause becomes the object of anti-Semitic attack in addition to WCC and Klan attack. One Negro leader, however, felt that the Negro cause was advanced by anti-Semitic attacks because these demonstrated that anti-Negro activities would, if uncurtailed, branch out to include segments of the white community as well. If this were realized, whites might withhold support from anti-Negro organizations.

Local Jewish leaders have protested vigorously to The American Jewish Committee, The American Jewish Congress, The National Council of Jewish Women and The Anti-Defamation League about their public statements on behalf of Negro civil rights. Some of these organizations have promised to be more careful about activities that might embarrass or harm their southern members. The American Jewish Congress currently seems to be considered the most militantly desegregationist of Jewish national organizations as it has apparently not retreated in the face of local protests.

Generally, only Biggott and the *Family News* have drawn attention to the desegregationist statements and activities of national Jewish organizations. The local "respectable press" (both the morning and the evening paper are owned by the same corporation) inconspicuously places press releases mentioning Jewish as well as non-Jewish national organizations but has never featured or editorialized upon the activities of Jewish national organizations.

> What role should national Jewish organizations play in the future? (What public role, what unofficial role, what services to local chapters, what services to individuals who may or may not be members?)

The rabbi, the "top policy leadership" and the Jewish businessman with WCC connections were all united in their views that Jewish national organizations should never have gotten into "the nigger issue" in the first place and that they should get out of it now and stay out. Their rationale is that Jewish organizations were organized for the purpose of "helping the Jews." It was on this basis that these organizations requested and received support from Jewish individuals and communities throughout the nation. Their entry into the desegregation issue, it is argued, is not only a misdirection of their energies but also a breach of faith with their constituencies. Only one individual in this group distinguished between public and official actions and unofficial or "off the record" actions. Realizing that Jewish national organizations could not very well campaign for full civil rights for Jews without also favoring them for Negroes, he nevertheless insisted that their exertions on behalf of Negroes be "kept quiet."

It did not seem to me that any of my other informants had given much thought to the question of how national organizations of *any* sort could help those whites who were committed to desegregation. Only a few Jewish informants felt that Jewish national organizations should continue to issue "statements" and "briefs" and even some of these suggested that this only be done in concert with the national organizations of other religious groups. My query as to what could be done on a more concrete level was regarded as "the sixty-four dollar question." The most frequent suggestion was the provision of financial support for those who suffer economic reprisals by "going out on a limb." Some suggested the establishment of a foundation or fund to which application could be made. Another suggestion was that a clearing house be established that would solicit and direct business opportunities for the firms which employ or are managed by "exposed" individuals. Some complained that northern firms don't realize their problems, and an unofficial directory of "businesses and professional services that need to be supported" was, therefore, suggested. It was also felt that "exposed" individuals should be given assurances of removal to the North when their physical and financial position in the South became unusually precarious.

Other suggestions were more vague. One Jewish informant suggested that the national organizations strengthen the "Jewish consciousness" of their Southern members. Also suggested were more intensive Jewish education for children and adults: more speakers and programs on "positive Jewish topics" to change the current emphasis on financial success and social recognition in the Gentile world. Somewhat akin to this approach was the suggestion that Jewish theological seminaries specifically prepare their graduates for moral leadership in southern pulpits and the related suggestion of annual leadership training seminars. These seminars could be held in a border state or in an "advanced city" like Atlanta or Miami Beach and should be devoted to topics not directly labelled as desegregation or civil rights. Local organizational leaders should be urged to attend and their expenses paid where necessary. This last (paying of expenses) was particularly underscored, because the "top policy leadership" does have funds available for attending meetings of national organizations. On the other hand, no similar funds are available for liberals to meet and exchange ideas with others.

The situation in Southern City is currently "too difficult" to make direct "services" to local chapters or to individuals (published materials, speakers, or funds) seem feasible or desirable. Perhaps such approaches will become more appropriate as the situation eases.

The spiritual isolation of the few "exposed" Jewish individuals seemed clear—particularly where their ideological strength did not have personal security to accompany it. Rabbi Mantinband of Hattiesburg and Rabbi Rothschild of Atlanta were the only *Jewish* sources of spiritual comfort and support mentioned to me. On the other hand, my Methodist, Episcopal and labor informants seemed to feel far less alone and far less isolated by the "opposition" within their own local groups. Perhaps a national committee of correspondents with "exposed" Southern Jews would be of some help.

> Are there any Jews who as *individuals* are particularly active *proponents* or *opponents* of segregation? (If so, what is their Jewish affiliational status, occupation, education and economic position; how long have they been in the community? etc.) Why aren't there more such individuals?

There are very few Jews who have taken active stands on either side of this issue. Most prominent by far are the few who have widely advertised their WCC affiliations. These are individuals of Eastern European parentage who have, in recent years, come into great wealth and influence with local political leaders. They have been attacked by Biggot because of their political influence. Since their financial success has been so flaunted and since in some cases it has been effected via competition with locally eminent Jewish and non-Jewish firms, their meteoric rise has not been accompanied by any great social acceptance in the select circle of "best families." They have also not been admitted into the "top policy leadership" group. No pressure was reported to have been exerted upon them by either this leadership or by their own congregation in connection with their WCC activities or openly segregationist statements. Nevertheless, the fact that some of them have felt the need to justify their WCC membership to fellow-Jews (on the grounds of trying to keep the WCC from becoming anti-Semitic) would imply that such membership is not generally favored among Southern City Jews.

On the other hand, the very few active desegregationists among Jews in Southern City have definitely been informed that their activities are a source of embarrassment and danger to the Jewish community. These few activists are all members of the Reform congregation. Although none of them is wealthy, they are—on one or both sides of each family—related to wealthy or prominent Jewish families. As such, they and their families have lived in Southern City or in other southern communities many years. They are college-educated individuals with broad intellectual and political interests as compared with the WCC members who are not college-trained and who are genuinely or defensively anti-intellectual. Neither group is particularly interested in Judaism or in Jewish organizational or cultural affairs. The intellectual group, however, seems to be freer from the social snobbishness and the success aspirations of most Jews and non-Jews in Southern City. Their strength seems to come directly from their ability to be "fringers" and "loners" and only indirectly, if at all, from Jewish commitments. In one case, there is a history of liberal or radical political interests.

The "exposed" non-Jewish individuals also have the strength to be unpopular—perhaps even the satisfaction of unpopularity. A few of these individuals possess exceptional intellectual talents and have held important federal government posts in earlier years. Some have a completely religious orientation to life from which they derive their inner strength. Others are "unchurched" or even anti-church. All of these individuals seem to feel their isolation less than do their Jewish counterparts.

> What are the reactions to such "exposed" individuals? (What are the reactions of non-Jews to them [socially, in business, etc.]; what are the reactions of Jews to them? How much actual censorship and intimidation vs. feared or rumored repercussions?) Have WCC leaders or publications commented on Jewish desegregationists? How does the local Jewish citizenry react to such comments?

Exposed individuals all report threats and abuse by mail and phone. No physical violence has actually been visited upon any of them, although one instance of malicious property damage was reported. All have been threatened with financial reprisals, but the effectiveness of such threats varies with the economic position of the individual as well as with his personal characteristics. One Jewish and one non-Jewish activist reported no serious impairment to their businesses: lost accounts had been replaced by new accounts. One informant stated that southern representatives of northern firms were more frightened of dealing with "controversial" individuals than were southern firms.

These informants stressed their view that the fear of economic reprisal was greatly exaggerated. On the other hand, two other informants had suffered great hardship. They were both professionals who were directly or indirectly financially dependent on local or state institutions (or their officials). It may well be that such individuals are in a much more precarious position than owners of businesses, particularly if the latter deal in a commodity or service not easily obtainable elsewhere and are not entirely dependent on a local market.

All of the "exposed" informants reported loss of friends—even intimate friends of long standing. Several also reported family pressures and dissociations. Only the Jewish informants reported requests from Jewish organizational affiliations to discontinue their desegregationist activities. The unchurched non-Jewish desegregationists seem to have had no organizational ties that could be used against them. They are actually the most prominent of the entire "exposed" group—much more prominent than the Jewish activists, who may actually be prominent in Jewish eyes only. With the exception of the St. Luke's meeting, neither the WCC, the Klan, nor Biggot have ever publicized the views of the local Jewish desegregationists.

> Are the reactions to Jews who are active proponents or opponents of segregation any different than the reactions to outspoken Catholics (or other minority group members)? Has there been any growth of anti-Semitism during the past few years in connection with the opposition to desegregation?

No local white Catholic or other white non-Protestant desegregationists have been publicized. Nevertheless, Biggot's activities have resulted in a greater awareness of a "Jewish angle" in the general desegregation conflict. This awareness may be greater among Jews than among non-Jews. The purported growth in local anti-Semitism is evidenced by Biggot's 10 percent share of the 1959 mayoralty primary votes. Neverthless, as there has been no noticeable increase in anti-Semitic acts or comments from the general population, it is possible that the high Biggot vote has political overtones other than anti-Semitism. His family name and war record alone may have attracted some uneducated votes and he may have gained the stature of a reliable protest candidate among those that are "against" many facets of modern life. The recently completed American Jewish Committee-ADL poll on anti-Semitism in the South notes no rise in the South as a whole during the last five years. This study reports that most non-Jewish southerners (67 percent) have no clear impression of where Jews stand on school desegregation, although of the 25 percent who *do* have an opinion on this matter, 15 percent tend to believe that Jews "favor integration." This may be an indication of an anti-Semitic potential in the South in conjunction with the desegregation issue. On the other hand, there has always been some anti-Semitism in the South, as elsewhere, regardless of the position of Jews on desegregation or other local issues. That it has *not* increased thus far on any stable, region-wide basis is certainly an important fact for both local and national Jewish bodies to realize.

> Have any outspoken Jewish proponents of desegregation continued their activities notwithstanding the opposition to them? (Contrast with Catholics, various Protestant groups, others, etc.) What has enabled them to do so whereas others have been silenced?

No desegregationist "activities" of any kind are now in progress within the white community. The only avenues of interracial contact that I was able to discover were: (a) The regular meetings of the state Council on Human Relations which are normally attended by about 20–30 individuals out of a total membership of some 70–80. These meetings are primarily devoted to an exchange of news concerning past events and future plans of groups within the Negro and white communities. The meetings of this group do not seem to be under attack, although some of the white lay members have received telephone calls and threats of economic reprisals. These meetings are never announced to the general public and even members receive reminders that cryptically state that the next meeting will be held "at the usual place." The Council on Human Relations has always had to meet in Negro institutions. (b) The Women's International League for Peace, a small group of some 20 members which meets twice yearly in private homes and receives and discusses reports from the national headquarters in Philadelphia. (c) Union council meetings attended by representatives of Southern City union locals. Some of the locals themselves are segregated but the council meetings are not. These meetings take place in a state building where committees for charity drives and sub-professional groups have traditionally met. (d) An informal inter-denominational ministerial group (of which the former rabbi of the Conservative congregation was a member) meets at monthly inter-vals—except during the summer—as a demonstration of good will and to plan whatever steps the Negro and white churches can take to improve race relations. These steps have mostly been limited to in-vitations to white ministers to give sermons in Negro churches. Simi-lar invitations to Negro ministers by white churches have not been extended.

All of the above groups are small in number, and, with the ex-ception of the labor council, their membership tends to overlap con-siderably. Another small group worth mentioning is the Forum Club consisting largely of businessmen. Although not interracial, it regu-larly debates topics of interest. Both segregationist and desegregation-ist views have been aired at its meetings.

It should also be mentioned that no large segregationist meetings have recently been held in Southern City. One informant was of the opinion that public "displays" of segregationism had begun to meet with an apathetic response because more and more individuals were "getting fed up with that sort of thing." Although moderate views are still not being publicly expressed, a school crisis might provide an op-portunity for such views to be heard.

> Do Negroes look upon Jews in Southern City any differently
> than upon other whites (expectations, attitudes, behaviors)?
> Has there been any *change* in this connection in recent years?

Most white and Negro informants were not aware of any Negro attitudes toward Jews which differed from those held toward other whites. One Jewish informant reported a recent anti-Semitic remark by a Negro that another Negro had reported to him. One Negro informant believed that there was much ambivalence toward Jews among Negro servants and employees, as well as among Negro pa-trons of Jewish-owned businesses. On the one hand, Negroes expect to receive and often feel they do receive kindlier and more respectful treatment from Jews. Negroes suspect that Jews are secretly more sympathetic toward them even when Jews publicly deny this. However, Negroes do not expect Jews to publicly "come out for them" because (a) Jews are white and (b) Jews are a minority themselves. Finally, Negroes at times express feelings of being exploited or cheated by Jewish employers and merchants who have a reputation for being "sharp" and likely to take advantage of the unsuspecting. None of this seems to be particularly intense or clearly formulated and no changes in this connection have been noted in recent years.

> Do Jews here feel any differently than other whites about Reverend Pastor and the transportation protest? (Why or why not, what were the dominant attitudes during the strike, what are they now?)

None of the Jews whom I interviewed had ever met with Reverend Pastor. On the whole, their attitudes toward him were entirely consistent with their more general desegregation attitudes. The "top policy group" and the prominent businessman with WCC connections considered him to be a trouble-maker and an opportunist. One informant characterized Pastor as "a victim of circumstances" which he proceeded to explain in terms of the large group of Negro intellectuals that nearby Negro educational institutions purportedly supplied to guide his actions.* The silent moderates—Jews and non-Jews—seemed to be curious about Pastor but had never seen him and hardly any had read his writings. The "exposed" informants were the only ones who expressed admiration for him. However, even some of these doubted whether Pastor had sufficient skill or following to forcefully press for desegregation over a long period of time.

Pastor himself vaguely remembered meeting only one Jewish resident of Southern City. This individual had made a substantial contribution to one aspect of Pastor's activities and had privately admitted that "segregation was unjustifiable." Since this individual's death Pas-

---

* This seems to be a widespread but erroneous view among pro-segregationists in Southern City. My key Negro informants assure me that none of the Negro educational institutions in or near Southern City made much of a contribution to the local situation—if for no other reason than their dependence on state subsidies and grants.

tor has had no contact at all with local Jewry. He does not seem to consider this any more unusual than the fact that he normally has no contacts with any other segment of Southern City's white population.

The school crisis was on everyone's mind during my stay in Southern City. The Negroes were expected to initiate some action in school desegregation in the near future. Wealthier white informants were already sending their children to private schools or were planning to do so in schools whose organization was underway. Most churches were expanding their educational facilities in preparation for the day when the public schools would close. Those individuals who could not afford the luxury of a private school were quite concerned The overwhelming consensus was that the public schools would close and that no initial storm of protest would develop to save them. Nevertheless, the "exposed" informants were hopeful that the schools would re-open on a token-integration basis, after being closed for a while, in accordance with the pattern established in other southern cities. Two Negro informants were far less sanguine in this connection. One felt that the coming school crisis would lead to such excesses on the part of the WCC and the Klan that they would finally be discredited by their own violence. Another felt that ways would be found of continuing "public" education for most white children while discontinuing it for Negro children. It seemed clear that all were girding themselves for the inevitable storm.

The Negro leaders, notwithstanding their personal rivalries and programmatic differences, felt certain of ultimate success in the civil rights arena. The "exposed" as well as the cautious moderates among my white informants also felt that "it was coming." The former tended to think in terms of possible federal actions as well as in terms of pressures from the Negro community and from an increasingly awakening white southern community. The latter placed greater faith in the gradual erosion of segregation in the face of economic development, increased education, travel, mass media, etc. Even a few of the Jewish leaders admitted that desegregation was inevitable. Only two Jewish informants—one a member of the "top policy leadership" and the other a successful businessman—claimed to be convinced that "the southern way of life would never alter."

At the moment, the greatest detriment to progress would seem to be the lack of communication both *between* the races as well as *within* each of the racial communities. The remaining channels of interracial contact are pitifully weak and few in number. Similarly, there is hardly any within-group discussion, debate, or exchange of views on alternative policies and rationales. The closing-off of discussion and the sealing-off of boundaries represent the greatest success of extremists thus far. As a result, the tremendous reservoir of moderate feeling remains unexpressed and, possibly, unaware of its own dimensions. This may change if an appropriate focus of moderate views can be attained— either in terms of an issue or a symbol. Many seem to be waiting, as if perched on a volcano, for "something to happen" that would mobilize the moderate forces.

Meanwhile all of the obvious debits and none of the possible assets of Jewish group membership seem to be operative. Without inner security from an independent source—and, of course, this is always difficult for a minority group to attain and to safeguard—self-concepts, status needs, and role aspirations are all derived from the environment. There are very few Jews (or non-Jews either, for that matter) who feel sufficiently secure to "buck the system" which surrounds them. However, there are probably very few southern Jews who do not realize that this system is at variance with Jewish ethics and, ultimately, with Jewish security. The specifically *Jewish* insecurity derives from the need to repress this awareness for the sake of the more immediate short-term personal advantages of identification with the Christian community. Fear of loss of *social* standing seems to be much greater than fear of loss of *economic* standing, for the former is even more dependent upon Christian favor than the latter. Throughout the country—but particularly in the South—the favors of the status-givers have always been hard to win and the social rewards dispensed by them have been uncertain at best—particularly for "eternal strangers."

However, there is also another side to the total Jewish picture in Southern City. Many intelligent Jews and non-Jews remember that during the stirring and difficult days of the early New Deal, two Jews became "saints" of the region's liberal and labor movements. One gave

up his university professorship to help organize steel workers of a
nearby industrial center. The other was a rabbi whose weekly Friday-
evening sermons on the social problems of the South and of the nation
and whose activities on behalf of liberal causes attracted Jewish and
non-Jewish audiences from far and wide. Both of these men were
martyrs to their convictions. The first was assaulted by hired thugs and
never fully recovered from his physical wounds or from the deeper
psychological wounds inflicted by his family and friends who feared
to come to his side. The second was forced to leave his pulpit due to
the displeasure which he incurred among leading parishioners. I had
not known of either of these men before coming to Southern City. Ini-
tially I discounted their importance but ultimately I came to recognize
that they both function as *symbols* to many people of good will in
Southern City. The ethical ideals and the devotion to social justice of
these two figures out of the recent past still urge some men on to act
and think for themselves, but, the price which each paid serves as a
reminder of how cruel the South can be.

In a time when Americans generally are proving themselves extremely loathe to mount barricades on behalf of causes of any kind,
it is probably not realistic to expect the minute Jewish minority to act
otherwise. One can only hope that Jews will have no greater reason
to look back with shame on these times of hatred and strife than will
most others.

Albert Vorspan

The Dilemma
of the Southern Jew

IN THE tragic drama which is unfolding in the South, the Southern Jew has been, until recently a minor actor, a bit player unsure of his lines, standing uncomfortably in the wings and hoping against hope that his cue would never come. But, suddenly, the script was changed and the bit player was shoved to the center of the stage to play a new role at a climactic moment in the performance. Synagogue bombings have focused public attention on the role of Southern Jews.

Crisis of Segregation

The segregation crisis has shaken Southern Jews more severely than any national event since the Civil War. They are torn by a painful dilemma. The Jewish community, comprising less than half of one percent of the population of the South, is largely composed of merchants dependent on the good-will of the community. The Jew is therefore the man in the middle, subject to pressures from the White Citizens Council crowd on the one hand, his Negro customers on the other. Most Southern Jews privately disapprove of racial segregation, realize the rightness of the Supreme Court decision, and are disturbed by the indignities heaped on the Negro. Many feel that segregation goes against the grain of their democratic beliefs and their religious faith. But there are few Southern Jews who will articulate this point of view publicly—and fewer yet will act upon this conviction in the current atmosphere. To do so, they fear, will jeopardize their economic status.

Perhaps even more persuasive is their desperate fear of losing their carefully-nurtured and still-fragile acceptance by the Christians. Many Southern Jews are assimilated and they balk at anything that will make them "stick out as Jews," different from their neighbors. And so the Southern Jew is divided against himself, haunted by guilt.

Southern Jews try to resolve this dilemma in various ways. Much depends on the section of the South in which they reside. The lone Jew in a xenophobic Mississippi Delta town lives in a different world from his Jewish friend in cosmopolitan Atlanta or New Orleans. Some Jews have joined White Citizens Councils; in some cases for sheer economic survival, in a few cases out of conviction. A few Jews in Mississippi actually toyed with the idea of forming a Jewish White Citizens Council until the rabbis of the state angrily threatened to publicly repudiate them from their pulpits. But, it is significant that the few Jews who are members of White Citizens Councils are held in universal contempt by their fellow Jews.

Driven by inner conflict, some Southern Jews have resorted to what has become a popular indoor sport: baiting their rabbis and national Jewish organizations. Many do not wish to appear to be different from their Southern Gentile neighbors and feel threatened by anybody who seeks to identify the Jew with the Negro. Pressures have been exerted by Southern constituents against their national Jewish organizations, (all of whom are clearly on record in support of the Supreme Court decisions) including reduced contributions, threats of secession from various organizations, and fiery denunciations on the floor of national conventions. The oft-repeated refrain is: You Northerners don't understand our situation, you act as if we were expendable, and you harm us by statements about segregation in the public press. One Alabama Jewish leader went so far as to say to a representative of a national Jewish agency: "You're like Hitler. You stir up anti-Semitism against us."

The Rabbi's Position

Southern rabbis have borne the brunt of this kind of distorted fear. Those who believe that racial segregation is a profanation of Judaism have sought to find a path between the pulls of conscience and the real and exaggerated fears of their congregants. In some synagogues there have been attempts to curb the freedom of the pulpit. As in some Christian churches, a few of these attempts have been successful. One congregation is considering a resolution that "no paid employee may speak out on controversial matters without prior approval by the Board of the Temple." That means the rabbi.

A president of a congregation said: "I don't know where you get the idea our rabbi doesn't have freedom of the pulpit. We give him freedom of the pulpit—we just don't let him exercise it." These are exceptions. Most rabbis will not stand for a controlled pulpit. Yet, since most Southern rabbis sincerely feel that it is the Christian churches of the South who must lead in this issue, they avoid publicizing their racial views, stay away from the NAACP (which is anathema to most Southerners), and do what they can quietly within Ministerial Associations (in those Southern cities where they are permitted by the Christian clergy to belong).

What caused the bombings? Are they related to Jewish stands on integration? Not directly. The attacks on Southern Jewish institutions reveal a crazy-quilt pattern. A rabbi deep in Mississippi publicly blasted segregation and riled the citizenry with the blunt statement that race relations in the Magnolia state "stink." There were a few brickbats but no bombs and no threats. But a synagogue in Jacksonville, Florida, in which there had never even been a discussion of the segregation issue, was ripped by a bomb. In Miami an Orthodox school which takes no position on any social issue was attacked. In North Carolina, two synagogues which played no role in the integration problem were the recipients of bombs. In Nashville, Tennessee, Rabbi William Silverman had taken a firm public position in support of integration. It wasn't his temple but a Jewish Community Center in the same city which was assaulted.

The Bombings

Although there is a tendency among some Jews to attribute the bombings to Jewish "outspokenness" on integration, there is much evidence that such expression—or lack of it—is irrelevant. Anti-Semites proceed on the basis of stereotypes and fantasies, not facts. In their unreal world, the Jews, Supreme Court, NAACP, and the Communists are interchangeable and all are plotting together to "mongrelize" the South.

If all the Jews of the South embraced Governor Faubus and Senator Byrd, it would not make one whit of difference to John Kasper and his ilk. Jew-hatred has a momentum and a twisted logic of its own.

While the bombings are not directly related to integration, they are, without any question, related to the climate of defiance of law, which, inevitably, breeds violence. One of the most searching comments on the Atlanta bombing came from Atlanta's Mayor William B. Hartsfield who said: "Whether they like it or not, every rabble-rousing politician is the godfather of the cross-burners and the dynamiters who are giving the South a bad name." He summoned the "decent people of the South to rise up and put an end to the preachers of hate and chaos." In the wake of the Atlanta bombing, and in the surcharged atmosphere of hatred and lawlessness, a pattern of terror by telephone and letter spread against synagogues and rabbis throughout the South.

The bombers did more than destroy a few buildings; they did their cause infinitely more harm than they did to these structures. Violence is the worst weapon the racists can lay hold of; it unites the community against them. The bombings aroused the President of the United States; they provoked action by the FBI which, previously, had pleaded non-jurisdiction in similar cases; they awakened a slumbering religious conscience throughout the South. And, it may very well be that the bombers blew up, also, some of the illusions which have beguiled Southern Jewry. One of these was that they could find refuge in silent neutrality. But the explosions have shattered the illusion that silence guarantees safety and security for the Jew. The message of the bombs is that hatred is indivisible. The Jew is caught up in the storm of the South whether he likes it or not, and there is no place to hide.

Some communal leaders have long been urging Southern Jews to stand up and be counted in the greatest moral issue of our time.

Atlanta

When eighty Protestant ministers in Atlanta, a year ago, issued an historic statement on the moral crisis of integration, Rabbi Jacob Rothschild of that city associated himself clearly with the forthright position of his Christian colleagues. His statement was published in full in the *Atlanta Journal and Constitution*. There are those who believe that

Rabbi Rothschild's record of sincere faithfulness to his religious conscience, and his vigorous participation in community affairs, contributed to the magnificent response of the entire Atlanta community when the disaster struck his temple.

The response of the city of Atlanta—from the Mayor down to humble laborers who sent gifts for the rebuilding of the temple—was overwhelming. So was the response of the Jews of Atlanta to the crisis which descended upon them unexpectedly. Following the calm lead of their rabbi, who declared from the rubble that he had complete confidence in the goodwill of the government and the people of Atlanta, the members of the congregation went about their business with dignity and without panic. The synagogue program proceeded with little interruption. On the first Friday evening after the bombing, more than one thousand people came to services, and heard a sermon entitled "And None Shall Make Them Afraid." By their presence, they affirmed that they would not be intimidated.

Southern Re-appraisal

The bombs are forcing an "agonizing re-appraisal" upon the Southern Jews. Strong voices like those of Rabbi William Silverman of Nashville and Rabbi Emmet Frank of Alexandria, Virginia, have appealed to Southern Jews to join in the struggle for integration. In a Yom Kippur sermon entitled "Byrdliness vs Godliness," Rabbi Frank blistered Virginia's political leaders for the campaign of "massive resistance" and urged Virginia Jews to rally to the cause of Negro rights: "The Jew cannot remain silent to social injustice against anyone. The fresh wounds of Hitlerism, the ghettos of Europe . . . these are the results of silence. . . . Speak out forcibly and you will be a social outcast and suffer economic reprisals for a while; but remain silent, fortify these satanic hate peddlers and let them be victorious, and they will march against every minority."

The Southern Jew is not seeking martyrdom, but acceptance. Like most other "nice" people, he has no great relish for social ostracism and economic reprisals. It is already evident that some Jews are taking great pains to dissociate the bombings of synagogues from the assaults on Negro churches and Negro homes, or on integrated schools in Clinton and Nashville. Frequently, they rationalize this detachment by repeating the prevailing Southern legends about the NAACP and the readiness of the Negro for equality. But, Southern Jews are coming more and more to the realization that the destiny of the Jew is linked with the fate of the Negro and all minorities, and that Jews can flourish only in an atmosphere of equality and respect for human rights.

Negro–Jewish Relationships

In their anxiety to maintain their "excellent relations with the white Christian community," (one wonders what all the anxiety is about if these relationships are truly excellent) Jews in the South frequently ignore the question of Negro-Jewish relationships. But in the new South, which is emerging, the Negro community cannot be ignored. There are already evidences of some Negro disenchantment with the ambivalent attitude of Southern Jewish communities. Rev. Martin Luther King has commented upon the virtual absence of Jewish support for Negro rights in Alabama. Another Negro minister, Rev. Shuttlesworth of Birmingham, angrily accused Southern Jewry of turning its back on the Negro community: "Why are you silent in our great hour of need, when we stand in a sea of troubles, besieged by hate and terror? It is there we need Jewish support—and it is there the Jews are silent." In New York City, Adam Clayton Powell denounced President Eisenhower for his speedy response to the bombings of synagogues after repeated failures on the President's part to react to attacks on Negro churches and homes. That there is bitterness, sometimes tinged with anti-Semitism, in the Negro community is a significant factor which must be reckoned with.

The present situation will require calm and clear-headedness on the part of American Jewry. It is possible to whip up emotion and to scare Jews into thinking that an ominous wave of anti-Semitism is sweeping the country, that we are on the threshold of American pogroms. In fact, despite the bombings, anti-Semitism is at a low ebb in this country. The heavy increase in hate literature does not necessarily mean there has been an increase in anti-Semitism. It may merely be that the handful of persons who always circulate this stuff have found some additional funds and, more important, have discovered an effective handle in the integration crisis. There is no evidence that this literature persuades anybody but the already anti-Semitic; and there is evidence that it arouses many decent citizens to action. The task of leadership for Jewish organizations will be to keep their eyes on the main target—which is the menace to all Americans in the breakdown of law and order—and not to yield to pressure for hasty legislation, which, while intended to harass anti-Semitic groups, might infringe upon basic American liberties of free speech, free press and freedom of assembly.

The Jew has often been the barometer of the moral health of a society. The bombers have again unwittingly rendered to the Jew this tribute. The years ahead will demonstrate whether American Jewry will be worthy of this compliment.

It may yet turn out that lasting good may be forged out of the horror of Atlanta. And the Jew may help all Americans to understand the relevance of the Talmudic passage: "A man who retires to his house and says, 'What have I to do with the burden of the community . . . why should I listen to their voices? . . . Peace to thee, O my soul!'—such a man destroys the world."

Murray Friedman

Virginia Jewry in the School Crisis: Anti-Semitism and Desegregation

A YOUNG Jewish attorney in a small city in central Virginia was discussing school desegregation with a non-Jewish friend. "I hear that the president of the NAACP is Jewish," remarked the latter. Within twenty-four hours almost everyone in the Jewish community had heard the story, and next day a Jewish defense agency was phoned for information. When the Virginians learned that Arthur B. Spingarn of New York, the NAACP's president, was indeed Jewish, there was grim silence at their end of the line. The knowledge that a Northern Jew was head of the leading organization for Negro rights had shaken the security of this Virginia Jewish community.

The incident illustrates the special problem Southern Jews face today, at a time when American Jewry generally is enjoying an unparalleled prosperity, and discrimination against Jews is being steadily reduced. The Southern Jews' problem stems from the possible consequences of the struggle over desegregation, the region's most severe crisis since Reconstruction. Many Virginia Jews feel "caught in the middle," fearful that any action they may take in the public school controversy will lead to an increase in anti-Semitism. For the Old Dominion is currently a major battleground in the Southern effort to nullify the Supreme Court school decisions. "Massive resistance" was first decreed by Senator Harry Byrd's long-entrenched political machine in 1956. A powerful, organized segregationist movement soon sprang up to mobilize that resistance. Now Virginia's laws have collided with the rulings of Federal courts. Nine public schools in Warren County, Charlottesville, and Norfolk have been closed under state legislation which demands shutdowns when Negro children are enrolled. Early this year, Arlington and Alexandria faced similar battles. Although hastily organized private schools and tutorial systems have been seeking to provide a temporary and makeshift education, almost 13,000 youngsters are presently receiving inadequate schooling or none at all.

There has been considerable opposition to school closings in Virginia, especially in Norfolk, but the position of the state authorities has not changed. In a speech to the Virginia Education Association in Richmond on October 30, Governor J. Lindsay Almond, Jr., said: "The question becomes one of surrender or continued exercise of every legal and honorable means at our command to resist. I shall never willingly witness or become a party to the destruction of education by the mixing of the races in the classrooms of Virginia."

The Virginia Jewish community numbers about 30,000 and is located primarily in Richmond, in the central part of the state, and in the Tidewater cities of Norfolk, Portsmouth, and Newport News. Richmond and Norfolk have 8,000 and 7,500 Jews respectively, while smaller towns such as Charlottesville have less than 100 each.

The first Jewish settler in Richmond, Isaiah Isaacs, arrived there before the Revolutionary War, and served on the original Common Council with John Marshall. Early Jewish settlers soon identified themselves with Virginia ideals and traditions. Lewis L. Strauss, former chairman of the Atomic Energy Commission and now Secretary of Commerce, is a worthy representative of Virginia's older Jewish families, with their tradition of public service and largely conservative attitudes. But their patterns have been modified since the Eastern European migrations, and particularly since World War II, which brought many second-generation Jews of East European descent to Virginia.

In the larger cities, Jews are active in all the businesses and professions; in the smaller ones, they generally own small businesses. In this well-to-do community, Jewish life is vigorous; in almost every town where Jews have settled, a temple, religious school, or community center is either being built or was recently completed. Until now anti-Semitism has scarcely figured as a problem, and Virginia's Jewish leaders regularly take their turns on planning commissions, in city councils, and as members and presidents of civic organizations.

Despite all these manifestations of security, the Virginia Jew is more keenly aware of the special character his Jewishness gives him than is his co-religionist in the North. He is, of course, far more isolated. Jews in New York, Chicago, or Boston live among a host of religious, ethnic, and racial groups, none of which can claim majority status. But the eighty Jewish families of Danville, Virginia, for example, are an obvious minority in an otherwise homogeneous white Protestant society. Their contacts with Christians are cordial, but rarely extend beyond business hours or community-service efforts.[1]

These factors help shape Virginia Jews' contradictory attitudes on the race question. Most Jews feel a natural sympathy for the aspirations of the Negroes, whom they see as a minority group now journeying down something like the same road they had to travel. But they are unwilling to set themselves off from the dominant white majority, to which they have made such strenuous efforts to belong. So they generally keep their views to themselves—which causes further uneasiness. As Rudolph M. Lowenstein says in *Christians and Jews*, "as much guilt is felt for unrealized intentions as for deeds actually committed." Because the thoughts they harbor on the race issue differ from those of the majority of their white neighbors, they feel "disloyal" to Southern attitudes and institutions.

Nevertheless, though Virginia Jews accept the idea of desegregation in principle, in practice their viewpoint is not far different from that of the general white population. The Jew frequently owns a grocery, appliance store, dress shop, or other business in the Negro section of town or where the Negro trades. He sees at first hand the poverty, disease, and lower cultural standards that are the lot of the poor Negro. While he understands their causes and acknowledges the responsibility of the white man in creating and perpetuating such conditions, he does not want the sins of the past visited on his own children. As one Norfolk Jewish businessman told me, "When integration comes, you know, our kids won't be going to school with Ralph Bunche's." There is also a small group of Jews who earnestly

1. See Harry Golden, "Jew and Gentile in the New South," *Commentary* (November 1955).

fear the dangers of "mongrelization" and the encroachments of the Federal government on states rights. But, unlike such states of the Deep South as Mississippi, there is not, to my knowledge, a single Jewish member of the Citizens Councils in Virginia.

The question of desegregation as such, in the minds of Jews, tends to be secondary to the possible effects of race violence on their own place in Southern society. The history of anti-Jewish persecutions tells them that an atmosphere of tension and conflict is not "good for the Jews," and they fear that any Jewish involvement on the side of the Negro—whether by a Jewish Senator from New York, a Jewish defense agency, or one of their own leaders or organizations—will bring reprisals. The degree to which this fear is economic has been exaggerated; one is hard put to it to find a half-dozen Jews in the South (let alone in Virginia) who have been hurt by boycotts resulting from the segregation fight. Rather, Virginia Jews are worried about their community status. Many have spent years working in Community Chest and Red Cross drives and other civic activities because of their natural interest in social improvement and in an effort to show their Christian neighbors that they "belong." If Jews now stand apart from the dominant white group, they fear, they may jeopardize the position and prestige they have worked so hard to secure. Besides, many ask, what good can the Jews do the Negroes? They can only bring hostility down on themselves without, they believe, significantly advancing the Negroes' cause.

Virginia Jewry's new fear of anti-Semitism is legitimate. There have been no bombings in Virginia, but the Old Dominion has become a prime dumping ground for anti-Semitic leaflets, magazines, and pamphlets which pour into the state from the North and West. George Lincoln Rockwell, who has had contacts with two of the men indicted in the Atlanta temple bombing, prints handbills and other literature in his native Arlington for his "National Committee to Free America from Jewish Domination." The theme of this literature, whatever its source, is that desegregation is a Zionist-Communist plot to mongrelize the white race so that the Jews can take over.

Last spring, there was a series of anonymous mailings of racist and anti-Semitic pamphlets and letters to seniors at Washington-Lee and

Wakefield High Schools in Arlington.[2] In recent months, Norfolk and Newport News business and professional people have been receiving hand-written envelopes with Los Angeles postmarks which contain literature published by Frank L. Britton, editor of the rabidly racist *American Nationalist*. ("The time has obviously come," says one such piece, "for white Americans to take action if this Jew-inspired program for compulsory mongrelization is to be defeated.")

On the eve of the opening—or, rather, the closing—of half a dozen junior and senior high schools in Norfolk last fall, an estimated 15,000 pieces of hate literature were distributed door to door in many sections of the city, including those heavily populated by Jews. There had been earlier distributions of such material in smaller quantities. The literature included copies of Conde McGinley's bitterly anti-Semitic *Common Sense*, published in Union, N. J.; reprints by the Norfolk Chapter of the Defenders of State Sovereignty and Individual Liberties of an *Atlantic Monthly* article entitled "Mixed Schools and Mixed Blood"; and copies of a monthly magazine called the *Virginian*.[3]

The *Virginian* began in 1955 as a four-page segregationist newsletter published by two young men in Newport News. It is now an ably written, slickly produced magazine with a format similar to *Time*. Its message is racial and religious hate, and it attacks organizations like the American Jewish committee for allegedly leading the "integration conspiracy." Though only 7,000 copies of the *Virginian* are distributed, its very existence at a time of tension is a source of concern.

The organized segregationist movement in Virginia takes three forms. There is the Commonwealth of Virginia Association of Citizens Councils, consisting of units in the Arlington, Brunswick, Lunenburg, Mecklenburg, Fairfax,[4] and Peninsula areas, which has demonstrated

2. See William Korey and Charlotte Lubin, "Arlington—Another Little Rock?" *Commentary* (September 1958).

3. One of the men distributing this material stopped to discuss flowers with a former German Jewish refugee working in her garden. He left some of the literature with her when he moved on. She became ill when she saw it. The material created so much concern among Norfolk Jews that the Jewish Community Council wrote to its members urging calmness and recounting the steps it had taken.

4. The Fairfax Citizens Council has widely distributed a publication called *The Shocking Truth About Northern Virginia's Parent-Teacher Groups*. This publication contains an organization chart showing the "interrelationship" of groups labeled "Fairfax County PTA," "Zionists," "B'nai B'rith," "UNESCO," and the "Southern Regional Council," the latter described as a "Communist Front." *The Shocking Truth* recently

little strength or influence. Another, even smaller organization is the Seaboard White Citizens Council established by John Kasper in Washington, D.C., and active in Northern Virginia. The handful of fanatics in this group are violently anti-Semitic as well as anti-Negro. In the summer of 1955, Kasper set up a unit in Charlottesville, but its members lost interest when they learned that Kasper had danced with Negro women in New York before he became a racist. However, since the closing last fall of the Lane High School and Venable Elementary School in Charlottesville, this group—or at least its leader, George Cason—has begun to stir. (On October 14, Kasper himself said he planned no activity in Virginia: "I believe that, now that the state government and the Governor have taken such an admirable position in defending the people, we truly have no business coming into Virginia.")

The most important of the organized segregationist groups is the Defenders of State Sovereignty and Individual Liberties. Founded in 1954, it claims some 12,000 members. Unlike the Citizens Councils and Kasper's group, the Defenders have attracted to their ranks prominent business and political leaders—among them Congressman William M. Tuck, a former Governor sometimes mentioned as Byrd's successor, and Congressman Watkins M. Abbitt, a Byrd lieutenant. Virginia Jews are uncomfortably aware that many of their co-workers in local civic undertakings are members of the Defenders.

With the growing school crisis, an increasing preoccupation with Jews and Jewish organizations became discernible among the Defenders. The February–March 1958 issue of their official organ, *Defenders' News and Views*, carried a picture of Thurgood Marshall, NAACP special counsel, receiving a plaque from Kivie Kaplan of Boston, described as co-chairman of the NAACP's Life Membership Committee, and Arthur Spingarn, NAACP president. The caption went on to note, "THE NAACP IS NOT A NEGRO ORGANIZATION and never has been." In more recent issues, the publication has urged its readers to obtain copies of "Our Nordic Race," a pamphlet written by a former field representative of the Defenders in Richmond. The pamphlet's theme

---

turned up at the fall convention of the State Congress of PTA's in Richmond and has been distributed at public meetings of the Richmond Chapter of the Defenders. It was also used in interrogating witnesses by the now defunct Thompson Committee of the Virginia legislature.

is Anglo-Saxon "racial purity," and it concludes with a discussion of the "agitation Jews" who, "in close cooperation with a group of Nordic Race Traitors, are almost wholly responsible for the destructive 'one race, one creed, one color' Marxist campaign that has brought strife and disunity to our country and to the rest of Western civilization."

In spite of these indications of religious bigotry, it would be incorrect to characterize the Defenders as an anti-Semitic movement.[5] Actually, it is a loosely structured organization composed of diverse people joined together in the common purpose of seeking to maintain segregation. There is no reason to believe, for example, that Congressman Tuck, who has manifested his friendship for Jews by his support of Israel, has ever read *Our Nordic Race* or even knows of its existence.

Last July 7, an editorial appeared in the Richmond *News Leader* entitled "Anti-Semitism in the South." The South, said the editorial, has honored such outstanding Jews as Bernard Baruch, Admiral Strauss, and, in Civil War days, Judah P. Benjamin. Recent manifestations of anti-Semitism, it went on, must be traced to the activities of the Anti-Defamation League. "By deliberately involving itself in the controversy over school segregation, this branch of B'nai B'rith is identifying all Jewry with the advocacy of compulsory integration." It cited the distribution of "pro-integration materials" by the League's Richmond office to a Charlottesville NAACP workshop as evidence to "embattled whites" of activity that has nothing to do with defamation of Jews. "Such inquiries, once bruited about," the editorial went on, "will be seized upon by the ADL as evidence of anti-Semitic feeling. And having thus stirred up defamation of the Jews, ADL can lustily combat defamation of the Jews. 'Look how much anti-Semitism there is!' " The editorial concluded with an invitation to Jews in the South to get rid of "an organization that foments hostility to Jews."

The *News Leader* is a highly respected newspaper, and its editorial was promptly reprinted elsewhere in the South. Its editor, thirty-eight-year-old James Jack Kilpatrick, is one of the most outspoken and influential segregationist spokesmen. It was he, in a previous series of

---

5. The Norfolk Defenders in November adopted a resolution censuring the door-to-door distribution of "hate literature" by one of its members.

editorials, who revived the old constitutional doctrine of "interposition"—that a state can block the application to its citizens of Federal laws and court decisions—and sold it to seven state legislatures and, apparently, Governor Orval Faubus of Arkansas.

Kilpatrick's editorial on "anti-Semitism" set off worried phone calls, hurried meetings, and other manifestations of alarm among Richmond Jews. Two views emerged from the Jewish discussions of the editorial. Some agreed with it, and said that Jewish organizations should not involve themselves in the integration struggle. Others read the editorial as a veiled threat of blackmail: if Southern Jews did not silence Jewish agencies working in the field of human relations, "embattled" segregationists would strike back at them. (Many Jews also wondered why Kilpatrick, a Roman Catholic, had not held the specter of anti-Catholicism over the heads of his co-religionists, whose parochial schools are integrated throughout the state.)

The theme first stated publicly by the *News Leader* was quickly picked up by the *Arlington* Defenders, the most extreme of the Defender chapters, who chose as their target Rabbi Emmet A. Frank of Alexandria, a suburb of Washington. In a Yom Kippur sermon from the pulpit of one-hundred-year-old Beth El Congregation, Rabbi Frank had charged that Senator Byrd and Governors Faubus and Almond had wrought more disunity in the nation in the last few years than U.S. Communists ever had. The Rabbi, sharply critical of Virginia's "massive resistance" laws, had urged Jews not to remain silent to injustice against anyone. There is only one word, he said, to describe the "madness" of segregationists: "Godlessness, or to coin a new synonym—Byrdliness. . . ." The Arlington Defenders demanded that the Jewish community of Northern Virginia openly condemn Rabbi Frank's "slanderous statements and innuendoes." His remarks, they said, "will cause irreparable damage to the hitherto friendly relations between Jews and Christians unless Jewish congregations . . . move quickly to refute and condemn Rabbi Frank. . . ." A number of newspapers joined their attack on Rabbi Frank. Soon afterward, the Unitarian Church in Arlington had to be emptied as a result of a bomb scare just before Rabbi Frank was to occupy the pulpit.

Northern Virginia Jews remained relatively unmoved; they are mostly Federal government employees of Northern origin and, as such, less susceptible to the pressures that trouble Jews in other parts of the state. Elsewhere, there was considerable anxiety. One Jewish group briefly considered—and rejected—a move to have the organization apologize to Senator Byrd. A number of Jews did write to him, declaring that the Rabbi did not speak for them.

The Kilpatrick and Frank incidents have helped to focus public attention upon the Jewish community. Many white Christians are beginning to look more closely at Jewish neighbors whom they had taken for granted. A Jewish community recently debated whether former Senator Herbert Lehman should be invited to take part in a purely communal affair, since he has been a forthright advocate of civil rights legislation. A Jewish businessman was recently invited to lunch by his dentist, who wanted to know "what the Jews think" about integration, and whether they are the real force "behind" the Negroes. Another Jewish businessman wondered if he should accept a public post if it involved having his picture in the newspaper.

Virginia Jews have joined other Southern Jews in demanding that national Jewish organizations discontinue making public statements on the race issue or the problems growing out of this question. Recently, a national Jewish agency called a meeting of Virginia Jewish leaders to ask whether it should file a friend-of-the-court brief in the case of a Northern Virginia printer, a Quaker named David Scull, who had refused to answer questions put to him by a legislative committee because he believed its purpose was to harass pro-integration organizations. The local leaders succeeded in blocking such action, even though most of them recognized the civil liberties issues involved in the case. They argued that Scull was adequately represented by counsel and that intervention by a Jewish agency was therefore unnecessary and might be harmful to Virginia Jews.

In the face of pressures both outside and within the Jewish community, most of the outspoken Jewish integrationists in the South have, since 1954, retreated into positions of silence. In this respect the Jew is no different from the white Protestant liberal or moderate in Virginia —though he has more cause for inaction. Nevertheless, Jews in Virginia do not live in anything resembling a state of terror. Life, in fact, goes on very much the same for most Virginians. Nor have all Jews surrendered to their fears. A number have been active in Norfolk and Charlottesville pressing for the opening of public schools. Rabbi Malcom Stern of Norfolk publicly urged a city referendum on public school closings last spring, while Rabbi Frank continues to air his opposition to massive resistance. Other rabbis are working through ministerial associations and other groups in efforts to head off violence and mediate the racial struggle.

Nor is there evidence of any appreciable rise in anti-Semitism, as distinct from anti-Semitic activity. Recent temple bombings in other parts of the South have horrified Virginians. Early in November, Governor Almond told Milton Friedman, Washington correspondent of the Jewish Telegraphic Agency, that elements seeking to promote violence and anti-Semitism "are not friends of the South" and were hurting the states rights cause. A Virginia Congressman mailed a check for $50.00 to a prominent Jew in his community to help pay for the restoration of the "Jewish church" in Atlanta.

But Jews in Virginia remain worried nonetheless. And neither their own silence on the race issue, nor the silence of national Jewish organizations, can end that worry. When a society is experiencing crisis, pressures on its Jews usually increase. Virginia Jews can expect peace only when Virginia finds peace—that is to say, when leaders of the Old Dominion recognize the futility of "massive resistance" and begin to adjust their state's practices to the law of the land.

Marvin Braiterman
Mississippi Marranos

MARANO *(plural Maranos, generally written Marranos):*
Crypto-Jews of the Iberian Peninsula.... The name was applied to the
Spanish Jews who, through compulsion or for form's sake, became
converted to Christianity in consequence of the cruel persecutions of
1391 ... who yielded through stress of circumstances, but in their
home life remained Jews and seized the first opportunity of openly
avowing their faith.

(*The Jewish Encyclopedia*, Vol. VIII, p. 318)

I have been in Mississippi as a volunteer civil rights lawyer for exactly
one week. Volunteers from the North are needed because there is
virtually no local legal defense available for the students and staff
workers of COFO, the civil rights movement in Mississippi. Tonight
I am weary of the enemy camp where this campaign is being fought,
and restless from exclusively associating with my colleagues and the
young clients of COFO. A world totally surrounded by the civil
rights movement, and its participants and adversaries, can be grim. I
need relief from crisis and cases and atrocity stories.

This evening, the calendar is a blessing. It is the Sabbath, and there
is a temple in this strange city. Some Jews live here. I can leave everything for a while, and retreat to the familiar sights and sounds of a
house of worship. Perhaps afterwards I will be invited to somebody's
home for the evening. Last week, some of the other Jewish lawyers

had this experience, and it was a pleasant change from Mississippi's Summer Project.

My job in the Project generally keeps me in or near the office every second or third day and most evenings, attending to the details of cases, investigations, legal counselling with clients, and consultations with my colleagues. Our staff usually consists of five or six lawyers—we each have volunteered for two weeks—and three law students. On the other days I am on the road, visiting the small towns and rural outposts of civil rights activities. Freedom schools, community centers, voter registration programs are operating around this state in a battle to the death with the established order.

Our legal staff is somewhat set apart from our clients. We are older and more conventionally dressed. At first, we are somewhat less tense and a bit more lighthearted than they are. For a few days, we retain our sense of humor, along with some of our illusions. The youngsters whom we represent have lost both of these, because they have been here longer. (I constantly think of our clients as "youngsters" and "kids." They are mostly in their teens and early twenties, not much older than my own children, the age of most revolutionaries in history.)

I see them subjected to harassment and abuse in little parishes of misery whose names have become household words. Before this summer, I had never heard of places here named McComb and Canton and Carthage and Camden and Philadelphia. Now I know them all well. These are the Mississippi towns that furnish the datelines on stories of freedom house bombings and church burnings and threats and violence. These towns, and a half-dozen of their counterparts, are our precincts.

After a week, my sense of humor is rapidly vanishing, and I am in tune with the others in the civil rights movement. I understand the youngsters, who are unrelentingly bitter and apprehensive. No longer are the lawyers a jollier group than the clients. Every traffic case and misdemeanor that we handle is a civil rights incident. Repeatedly, the workers are arrested on charges like "distributing illegal literature"— as if the written word calling on the black man to stand up and count and be counted could be a criminal act in the United States. Or "breach of the peace"—where there is no peace. Or "assault" and "resisting arrest"—after they are pistol-whipped by a policeman. One young man is charged with exceeding 130 miles per hour—in a Volkswagen. Another, with failing to obey a Stop sign—where there is no Stop sign. Arrest means jail, even for these petty charges. Jail must be followed by bail and hearings, and hurried calls and telegrams must go forth to a complicated network of sources. Meanwhile, many a defenseless teenage worker, in police custody or in jail, is beaten or otherwise mistreated before we can obtain his release. We investigate and counsel and plead and petition and arrange and appear and make "deals." We do the best we can, usually with meagre results, that frustrate and infuriate. The highways, the courts, and the jails are battlefields. It is like a war.

After a week of frantic days and nights, I walk slowly into the synagogue. Two of the lawyers and a law student are with me. I am very tired and hot, and I look forward to the service. Many times in the past, when I have been excessively comfortable, Sabbath in a synagogue has afflicted me. Tonight I am excessively afflicted. The evening should give me comfort.

I open a prayerbook, and look around at familiar faces. I know Southern Jews. They have regional differences from other Jews, and they usually tend to be apoplectic about the ringing resolutions and activities of Jewish organizations and their "New York professionals" advocating racial justice. They think they understand Southern Negroes, and the Jews outside the South do not. They will not agree with what we are doing in Mississippi, so they will certainly avoid the subject of civil rights. We can spend the evening discussing common problems of synagogues and religious schools. And they will probably ask me about someone in Baltimore who is their relative or acquaintance. Or we may even talk about baseball, or practicing law, or Jewish history. They will be gracious and hospitable, and I am willing to take the night off.

But the evening is not at all what I expect it to be. My surprise begins with the service itself. It has a hollow sound. The rabbi is on vacation, so a lay reader and the congregation rush through the English words by rote. In twenty minutes, the service is done. I am unmoved. The shadows which envelop Mississippi darken even this House of Israel.

The services over, our fellow Jews are effusively hospitable and friendly to us. They quickly learn our names, our home towns, and our missions. Within the synagogue, they are noncommittal when we tell them what we are doing here, but a pleasant couple quickly invite us to their home for the evening.

We arrive at a comfortable home, not unlike those of the East—a ranch house North of the city. (Like most cities, for some odd reason, the "best" neighborhoods are usually on the North side.) Within a few minutes, we are joined by four other couples whom we had met at the temple, and drinks are served. We exchange some of the expected small talk, and I relax. Suddenly, our hosts ask us to describe our work. The talk shifts to civil rights in Mississippi, and will not again leave this subject for over three hours. These people are obsessed with it, even as we have been this week. They insist that we tell them candidly what we have done and seen, and what we think of it all. Somewhat reluctantly, we tell them, and wait for some words of apology or defense of their State. It would only be natural for them to apologize and defend. One man makes a short pretense of assuring us that things were not nearly so bad before we came—that real progress was "in the air," but the "nigras are pushing too fast for everything all at once, and they have themselves to blame for what is happening and going to happen to them."

We are quiet, trying to behave as courteous guests. We do not intend to argue with these people tonight. But we have prejudged them, and assume that they agree with the Mississippi defender. We are wrong.

The others do not agree with him. There are many things they do not understand about what we are doing, but in general they sympathize with the civil rights movement. They think that what is happening is terrible. They deny that the Negroes—they pointedly refuse to mispronounce that word as the first man does—would have a chance of making any gains, economic, political, or social, without substantial intervention from outside. They are full of regret that the so-called "army of agitators" is not protected by more forceful action of the

Federal government. We, the lawyers here to defend them, are to be congratulated for what we are doing. But why have we waited so long to get here? Things happened to these youngsters before and they were legally defenseless. Of course, they couldn't expect any defense from resident lawyers in Mississippi. There are "some" such lawyers whose conscience hurts them, but "of course, they just can't help these people."

Yes, some of these are Jewish lawyers, but "if they go too far, they will have to leave the State." So will our hosts and fellow guests have to leave if they go too far.

"We would lose everything we have. Some of us are fourth and fifth generation Mississippians, and you can't expect us to sacrifice everything, even though we hate what is going on here. We have our businesses, our families, even our lives to think of.

"But we do try to do things. The truth is that we usually fail. Like with the newspaper, the *State-Times*. It wasn't a liberal paper, just objective and not bigoted or inflammatory. We invested money in it, and looked on it as a potential salvation of moderation and common sense in Mississippi. But when the Citizen's Council got after it, the paper was ruined, bankrupt, a million dollars down the drain. Its building and plant are for sale now. The TV and radio stations are terrible, like the newspapers are. There is no medium to express a moderate point of view. We can't even find out who, or how many, we are.

"We are all active in a campaign to preserve the public schools against the private school plan the legislature has just adopted. If we fail in that, God help us. We are not ignorant rednecks. We have tried, but we just can't get anywhere. The Citizen's Council smashes everything we try to do.

"Some of the people in the Citizen's Council are more moderate than others, but the moderates are scared to death of the Klan.

"We are suffering every day over the treatment these kids in the civil rights movement are getting. Their parents must feel awful. Many are Jewish kids, like ours. We are parents. We know right from wrong, and the difference between our God and the segregationist God they talk about down here. But their God runs Mississippi, not ours.

"We have to work quietly, secretly. We have to play ball. Anti-Semitism is always right around the corner. We are a tiny, tiny minority here. In Mississippi, the Jews are about one-half of one percent of the population. Our children are lucky if they ever have one or two other Jewish children in their class. They can't be different. They don't want to be different. They are just children. Yes, we are really frightened for them. What will happen to their morals and values, living in such an environment? We try to send them away to college. We take them on trips. We try to let them have as much contact as possible with children from the outside, especially with Jewish children.

They did not voluntarily take their children to the baptismal font; and if obliged to do so, they on reaching home washed the place which had been sprinkled.

(The Jewish Encyclopedia, Vol. VIII, p. 318)

"It is an awful tough job just to remain a Jew in Mississippi. Our people leave the State, or they intermarry and leave Judaism, or they just stop being Jews. Many of us already have many non-Jewish relatives. We can't commit Mississippi Judaism to open support of the civil rights movement—it would be doomed.

"But we try in little ways. We work in the PTA for more moderate attitudes. We try to teach our children some relationship between our Jewish heritage and what is happening. We try. We try. We try. But we are very disturbed by what is going on.

"We don't want to have our Temple bombed. If we said out loud in Temple what most of us really think and believe, there just wouldn't be a Temple here anymore. They let it alone because it seems to them like just another Mississippi church. And if it ever stops seeming like that, we won't have a Temple. We have to at least pretend to go along with things as they are.

"Don't you see? Can't you understand? This is a dangerous, violent place. Our phones are probably tapped. Most everybody in the State has a gun in his house. People here get lost or killed or sent away. We are constantly watched and we are afraid."

Were these converts convinced of the truth of Christianity? . . . Obviously, the acceptance of baptism was in almost all cases merely a means of escaping violent death. They must have hoped that, the storm over,

they would be able to return to the faith of their fathers. This, however,
was not permitted them.

(Grayzel, *A History of the Jews*)

It occurs to me that the conversation, the situation is incredible, but
it goes on. We ask them:

"How can you be so sure that a public statement would ruin you
here? Come out in the open. Go to a Freedom School. See what they
are doing there. Give them some support and help. You have little
more to lose. Your silence either makes things get worse, or things get
worse in spite of it. You might as well open your mouths and do something about what you think."

"No. No. What you're talking about is suicide. What would you
do if you were me?"

"I don't know what I would do if I were you. But being me, I think
I would take my family and leave. Mississippi in 1964 is like Germany
in 1934. But *you* are still in the United States. You are not nailed to
this damned place."

"But if we leave, what good does that do? We abandon everything
here to *them*, and we are ruined."

"Haven't you just said that you can accomplish nothing here—that
in Mississippi they win and you lose? At least, get away and save your
own souls and make a life for yourselves where your children can
breathe air that has some future and some hope."

"What about our Temple?"

"If your Temple must imitate a racist church, it is not worth
worrying about."

"You don't understand. You just don't understand."

The converts were forced to remain Christians just as they had been
compelled to become Christians . . . some among these New Chris-
tians . . . early gave up the struggle. . . . There were others . . . who
made up their minds to profit from the situation. Still others fled the
country and sought a new home where they could worship God in
accordance with the dictates of their conscience. But many, perhaps
a majority of the New Christians, continued to hope and wait for a

change of fortune, for the time when they could return to Judaism within the borders of their native land. In the meantime, they tried their best to observe in secret the religion which was forbidden them in public. (Grayzel, *A History of the Jews*)

The evening ends at last. I am filled with pity for these terror-stricken people. They are the best of the "white community" I have met here. At least they are decent, and they see the truth of what is happening around them. But only in the secret sanctuary of their homes can they speak this truth.

In the city of Seville an inquisitor said to the regent: "My lord, if you wish to know how the Maranos keep the Sabbath, let us ascend the tower." When they had reached the top, the former said to the latter: "Lift up your eyes and look. That house is the home of a Marano; there is one which belongs to another; and there are many more. You will not see smoke rising from any of them, in spite of the severe cold; for they have no fire because it is the Sabbath.

(*The Jewish Encyclopedia*, Vol. VIII, p. 319)

Even at home they are afraid. The telephone may not be safe. They will call us in a few days, they say, to arrange for us to come again next Friday night. They want us to meet their teenage children, so that we can hear directly from them of the life of the young ones in Mississippi. And they can learn from us something of the spirit of this Movement that has brought us all the way down here. It would be good for their children to have a chance to speak to us.

But they will call us from a coin telephone, not from home. And, of course, we will meet at home, unofficially, not at the Temple.

As the evening ends, we sit in our automobile alongside the house. The elegant suburban street is dark and quiet. Our door is slightly ajar, and the dome light shines as we talk quietly with our hosts about the arrangements for next week.

"Close the car door, please. Our neighbors might see you in the light, and recognize you or wonder who you are. We wouldn't want them to know . . ."

At the festival on which the Jews blew the shofar, the Maranos went into the country and remained in the mountains and in the valleys, so that the sound might not reach the city.
(*The Jewish Encyclopedia*, Vol. VIII, p. 319)

Now we are returning to the homes of the courageous Negroes who house us in the city. But on the way, we stop briefly at our make-shift law office. It is past midnight and the place is still and deserted. We go in to check our messages. There are none, thank God—in Mississippi, no news is good news. We are leaving now for home and bed. From the stairway, we hear the telephone ring.

"There is trouble in Laurel. We need a couple of you fellows there tomorrow at 10 a.m. The rabbi who got hit on the head with an iron pipe is in the hospital in Hattiesburg. Laurel is just about twenty-five miles from Hattiesburg. You can drop in on the rabbi there tomorrow afternoon, when you've finished in Laurel."

The rabbi in the Hattiesburg hospital is also an "outsider"—Arthur Lelyveld, from Cleveland. The next day, my business in Laurel takes longer than expected, and it is five o'clock when I arrive in Hattiesburg. By that time, he is gone. I am told that he left town a couple of hours before, on his way out of Mississippi. In a week, I will be leaving Mississippi, too.

Comparatively few of the secret Jews survived this struggle; but the Inquisition, too, was destroyed; and wherever men have valued freedom they have been ashamed of the Inquisition and its works.
(Grayzel, *A History of the Jews*)

And the Mississippi Marranos? May God be merciful to them.

The Jews of the time judged the Maranos gently and indulgently; in Italy a special prayer was offered for them every Sabbath, asking that God might lead them from oppression to liberty, from darkness to the light.
(*The Jewish Encyclopedia*, p. 319)

Allen Krause
Rabbis and Negro Rights
in the South, 1954–1967

For MANY YEARS the American vocabulary has in-
cluded the phrase *Solid South*, but the phrase is more romantic than
realistic, especially if from *solid* one infers *uniform*. Where Negro
rights are concerned, there are within the southern region—within,
that is, Alabama, Arkansas, the Carolinas, northern Florida, Georgia,
Louisiana, Mississippi, Tennessee, northeastern Texas, and Virginia—
many degrees of what James Silver calls "the closed society." Atlanta
and New Orleans are worlds apart from, say, Cleveland, Mississippi,
or Macon, Georgia. A continual awareness of this diversity in the
makeup of Dixie is important, for, when we discuss, as we propose
to do here, what the Reform rabbis[1] of the South have or have not
done in the realm of civil rights since 1954, it is necessary for us to
pose the question: Which South? Once this is understood, a generalization about the mood of the South as a whole might prove helpful as
a point of departure.

Our generalization is simply this: The reaction of the South toward the so-called civil rights movement has been one of, at the least,

1. This investigation is limited to the Reform rabbi, first because adequate data
on the southern Conservative and Orthodox rabbinate have not been available to the
writer, despite his efforts to get in touch with such rabbis, in sufficient quantity to
merit inclusion; then, because the writer's information about non-Reform rabbis has
come, in the great majority of cases, from their Reform colleagues, and this might,
rightly or wrongly, be open to charges of excessive subjectivity; and, finally, because
there are simply not many non-Reform rabbis in the South. In the entire state of
Mississippi, for example, there is only one Orthodox *minyan* served by a rabbi: see
Charles Mantinband, "Mississippi, the Magnolia State" (Cincinnati: American Jewish
Archives, Nearprint File, 1961).

antipathy, if not indeed sullen defiance. Surely it is no exaggeration to say that not a single city or town in the South welcomed the Supreme Court decision of 1954.[2] And if this applies to cities like Atlanta, New Orleans, and Nashville, how much the more so does it apply to the four "hard-core" southern states—to South Carolina, Georgia, Alabama, and Mississippi? As John B. Martin has put it, "Segregation is not a principle upheld only by louts and bullies. It is viewed as inherently right by virtually every white person in the four-state South of which we speak." [3]

"They Are Not With It"

The South, aside from occasional Catholic enclaves, is essentially "Protestant country," and the Protestant churches of the region have been basically supportive of the typical southern views on segregation. A survey reported in *Time* on October 27, 1958, placed nearly 50 percent of southern ministers in the segregationist camp, while the remaining 50 percent gave few outward signs of non-approval. Especially during the 1950s, then, it was no easy task to find Protestant clergymen aligned with the forces seeking social change in the South. Little difference between pulpit and pew has been evident in this matter.

Defiance, violent opposition, go-slow tactics, at best a grudging acceptance of the inevitable—such has been the mood of the South during the last two decades. There is in the South a local or regional patriotism that dies hard, if it dies at all. As much as any other incident, one related by Robert Penn Warren offers insight into this atmosphere and underscores the problem that a "Liberal" faces in Dixie Land: "I remember sitting with a group of college students and one of them, a law student it develops, short but strong looking, dark-haired and slick headed, dark, bulging eyes in a slick, rather handsome, arrogant—no, bumptious—face, breaks in: 'I just want to ask one question before anything starts. I just want to ask where you are from?' " [4]

There are approximately two hundred thousand Jews in the South, as this study defines the region—that is, less than 1 percent of the total

2. *Brown* v. *Board of Education of Topeka* was the key decision regarding school desegregation.
3. John B. Martin, *The Deep South Says Never* (New York, 1957), 9.
4. Robert Penn Warren, *Segregation: The Inner Conflict of the South* (New York, 1956), 24–25.

population.[5] Socioeconomically, they are to be found mainly in the middle and upper-middle class. Most are businessmen, many are professional men, others are engaged in various other white-collar occupations, a few are planters. Their attitude toward segregation is not easily established. One rabbi of a Louisiana congregation told a northern audience that the "vast majority of southern Jewry" is neither voiceless nor supine, but that in southern cities, both large and small, Jews have taken "the courageous (though frequently unpopular) stand." Sociologist Theodore Lowi, however, in his analysis of pseudonymous Iron City, characterized probably all the Jews there as "publicly conservative," and, of key importance, "easily a majority are privately conservative as well . . . the manifest values of Jews . . . are homogenized under the pressure of Southern consensus on the most important political and social issue of all." [6] The Reverend Fred Shuttlesworth, who was one of Dr. Martin Luther King's right-hand men, prefers an in-between position: "The response of southern Jews to the [civil rights] movement certainly compares favorably with that of numerous other white groups." [7] But Mississippi's NAACP leader Aaron Henry shows little sympathy with Shuttlesworth's words. "You ask about the Jews in the South and rabbis in particular," he responded to the writer, "sorry, they are not with it."

Where, then, does southern Jewry stand on the issue of segregation? Are they fighting friends, frightened friends, or foes of the Negro activists? They are, in the writer's opinion, something of all three—with emphasis on the middle designation. Without a doubt, southern Jews do include vocal and active desegregationists—but their number is small. They would usually be members of the groups that Lowi called "new Jews" (oversimplified that means first-generation Southerners)—people like Harry Golden.[8] In addition, they are to be found almost invariably in other than Deep South communities. There are also vocal, card-carrying Jewish segregationists—who are so not out of fear, but out of conviction. More often than not, they will be (again

5. *American Jewish Year Book*, LXVI (1966), 83 ff.
6. Theodore Lowi, "Southern Jews: The Two Communities," *Jewish Journal of Sociology*, VI (July, 1964), 111.
7. Taped interview with the Reverend Fred Shuttlesworth, July 15, 1966, American Jewish Archives.
8. Lowi, "Southern Jews," 111.

using Lowi's terminology) "old Jews," but they, too, are a definite minority—amounting most likely to a percentage about equal to their liberal coreligionists. The vast majority of southern Jews—some 75 percent of them—are in the middle; somewhat ambivalent about the whole issue, but tending toward thoughts sympathetic to the Negro. Fear of repercussions keeps their sympathies unspoken and makes them very difficult to live with, if one happens to be on either "extreme." They would no sooner join the White Citizens Council than the NAACP—unless abnormal pressure were applied. Absolutely essential, if they are to be understood, is their minority status. As Marvin Schappes points out: "Jews who live in the North and West . . . need to keep in mind . . . [that the] Jews of the South constitute seven-tenths of one percent of the total population of the South! . . . We who think of ourselves as a minority when we are approximately one quarter of the population of New York, need perhaps to shift gears a bit when we think of the minority status of Jews in Southern States." [9]

It is to these people that the rabbi of the South preaches, it is with them that he lives, and it is before them that he is called to account for his words and deeds.

"The Question Has Not Been Discussed"

Many rabbis and Reform congregations in the South have reacted to the trials and heart-rending conflicts of the struggle for human equality in their area with courage and with fortitude. They have spoken bravely their convictions and ours, and they have put into actions their preachments and ours. Their words and deeds are precious to us. . . . In the face of threats and violence they have continued to adhere to the teachings of Judaism in word and deed. May God grant them vigor and continued courage! [10]

You asked about Jews in the South and rabbis in particular. Sorry, they are not with it.

If the reader is somewhat confused, he need not apologize. The first statement above, a resolution passed by the Board of the Union of American Hebrew Congregations in 1958, and the second, Aaron Henry's comment, stand in sharp contrast to each other. Have the southern rabbis been activists, or have they "not been with it?"

9. "Jewish Young Freedom Fighters and the Role of the Jewish Community: An Evaluation," *Jewish Currents*, XIX (July–Aug., 1965), 22.
10. Emmet A. Frank file, American Jewish Archives.

A majority of southern rabbis would fall into the category of men holding pulpits in small, deeply "Southern" cities and towns. Their participation in civil rights activity has differed on the whole from rabbinical efforts in cities whose liberal element is larger and more vocal. Although there have been one or two notable exceptions—especially Rabbi Charles Mantinband, of whom we shall have more to say—these rabbis have a record of being less noticeably involved in local desegregationist activity. But this is a far cry from saying that they have not been involved at all. In order to determine just how active they have been, one must look at their "civil rights" activity within their community.

When it comes to espousing civil rights causes from their own pulpits, most—the vast majority of—southern rabbis have let it be known to their congregants that they favor change in the South's social system. Of course there are exceptions, one of them a rabbi who has served two communities during his nearly twenty years in the South. This man informed the writer: "I don't preach to my congregation what to do with regard to this. I have my own ideas on civil rights which I don't foist upon my congregation. They know—in private groups we discuss these matters. From the pulpit, I very rarely discuss it, because I don't want to harm the Jewish community in any way, shape, or form."

Another rabbi, asked to estimate how many of his congregants held prosegregationist feelings, responded: "I wouldn't know, because the question has not been discussed." Although ultimately this rabbi chose to deliver occasional remarks on civil rights matters from the pulpit, the limitations he placed on such sermons appear to have all but negated their purpose: "The question's always been how you think, whether you deliver an agitating speech or discuss . . . problems. If you discuss problems, you can discuss any problem. But, *if you are going to take sides* and agitate, you accomplish nothing except the hostility of people. So I have always, in my discussions with individuals and within groups, just plainly discussed the problems and how to solve them." (Italics added.)

Other rabbis, too, have been unwilling "to take sides." In March, 1957, one of them, since deceased, addressed a letter to Dr. Jacob R.

Marcus, director of the American Jewish Archives: "In answer to your inquiry on the subject of desegregation, I wish to say I have made no public pronouncements on this subject either from my pulpit or in the columns of our daily press. Since you, yourself, say you appreciate the problems involved, I know you will understand why I have felt it impossible to discuss this very pressing problem."

One other rabbi should be considered here. He is unique among his colleagues in that his utterances have been used by prosegregationists in support of their position. "With a few clergymen in modest rebellion against the status quo," wrote James Silver in *Mississippi, the Closed Society*, "the Citizens Council eagerly grasped to its bosom a strange new reinforcement in the person of Rabbi B——— S———," who soon after his arrival in Mississippi "laid down the principles which could save America": "If Mississippi had prevailed, pro-communists would be off American college faculties . . . "red-baiter" would not be a dirty word. Traditional patriotism would sweep the land to . . . insure victory in the international crisis. As it is, America is losing, mostly because of decay among its own intellectuals." [11]

This rabbi finds little support for his views among his southern colleagues. Although some men do not speak on civil rights or, on occasion, in the privacy of the Jewish community, speak against certain aspects of the civil rights movement, no other man seems ever to have been even peripherally associated with the segregationist position in the eyes of his community, congregants, or colleagues.

"Father Forgive Them"

More common among the rabbis of the Deep South are those who advocate desegregationist goals, when they speak within the walls of their congregation. But here again caution must be exercised in an evaluation of the "fervor" of their involvement, since many a rabbi prefers mild, carefully worded and carefully "non-inflammatory" rhetoric to a more "activist" advocacy. Thus, in November, 1955, when one man in a large Deep South city sermonized against the White Citizens Councils and in favor of school integration, he employed arguments similar to those reflected in this excerpt:

11. James Silver, *Mississippi, the Closed Society* (New York, 1964), 131.

There are other and better courses open. As no good comes from calling names or using measures of force, much good can come from the realization that most of us on both sides are decent people, and that, if we sat down together in good will, we could work out a course of action that might be acceptable to all. . . . I believe that such a procedure would produce this situation: That *the overwhelming majority of colored children, at least 90 or 95 percent, would remain right where they are. From previous experience, it seems that they definitely prefer it this way.* [Emphasis added.]

The sources available to this writer would indicate that such statements—in favor of desegregation, but apologetic, fearful, lacking specific demands and hence easily overlooked—have been very much in evidence in Deep South Jewish congregations. It is this fact that caused many a non-rabbinic informant to judge the rabbinate as strong in thought, but weak in word and deed when it came to involvement in civil rights.

Still, there are some men whose pulpit preachments have gone forcibly and directly to the issue. One rabbi in a Deep South city has for years welcomed Negro servicemen to the synagogue, has been a member of both the regional and state branches of the antisegregationist Southern Regional Council, has played a role in the somewhat successful desegregation of the city's schools, playgrounds, libraries, and theaters, and has, in addition, become a spokesman for desegregation in the general community. Another, in an even more "closed" community, convinced his congregants to give hospitality to Jewish "Freedom Riders" and has used his pulpit to denounce the White Citizens councils and all they stand for. This rabbi was also the first in his state to become intimately involved in aiding Jewish and non-Jewish Freedom Riders incarcerated in his region.

The point has been made that in Deep South "closed" communities, men like these appear very much in the minority. It is true that the majority of the southern rabbinate in such communities have been hesitant to speak out boldly and in specific terms within their own congregations; it follows that an even greater number have failed to do so in the community at large.

One interviewee, when asked if he had ever felt the need to become involved in the civil rights struggle outside the confines of the synagogue, responded: "Yes, but it would have been limited to twenty-four hours. Twenty-four hours later I wouldn't be there in the state anymore. . . . The majority of the people of the city have been vehemently opposed to integration . . . including a great number of the Jewish community. . . . The Jewish community could not exist . . . if they had been in any way involved in the civil rights movement." This rabbi did occasionally speak to civic groups with sporadic references to "general community problems," and he noted that there was no hostile response so long as the rabbi "did not agitate."

Lest the reader be tempted to stand too quickly in judgment let it be remembered that this man lives in the heart of the Deep South. Alfred O. Hero, Jr., discusses another rabbi's response to life in such an "Antebellum Town": "He had tended to voice disagreement with views expressed in face-to-face conversations when he first returned there. However . . . he had given up trying to change people's thinking. When someone next to him at a . . . meeting expressed irresponsible . . . views, by 1961 he either let him 'rave' or changed the subject." [12] This response has not been uncommon among the Deep South rabbinate, yet it has not been the only response evident.

A rabbi, invited to speak to a local church on "any subject except the 'Niggers,' " responded to the invitation: "While I had not intended to speak on 'The Negro,' now the issue is such that I will speak only on 'The Negro'." The invitation was rapidly retracted.

Ira E. Sanders, of Little Rock, appeared in 1957 before an open hearing of the Arkansas Senate to testify in opposition to four prosegregationist bills. He began by recounting his long connection with Arkansas and his love for the state. He then continued:

Above my love for Arkansas comes my devotion to America. . . . I regard the (United States) Supreme Court as the final democratic authority of the land. . . . Once they pass on the constitutionality of the law, it should become operative as the law of the land. Higher than the legal law, however, stands the moral law. . . . When Jesus died on the cross, he repeated these immortal words: "Father, forgive them for they know not what they do!" Legislators! May future generations reading the statute books of laws not be compelled to say these words of you . . . defeat, I pray you, in toto, these four measures.

12. Alfred O. Hero, Jr., *The Southerner and World Affairs* (Baton Rouge, 1965), 499.

Rabbi Sanders' voice was one of the few moderate utterances to be heard in Arkansas during the black year of 1957, and it took no little courage to stand up and be counted in so open a manner.

Two years earlier another man had become involved in a situation that unexpectedly forced him to make a civil rights stand in his community. This rabbi was asked by the Jewish Chautauqua Society to take part in a religious emphasis program at the University of Mississippi. Along with the Jewish clergymen, an Episcopal minister, a Catholic priest, three additional Protestant ministers, and a layman were invited to participate. About two weeks before the program, the Episcopal minister attracted public notice when, on the then popular $64,000 Question television show, he won a large sum of money. When asked what he planned to do with his winnings, the minister responded—on a coast-to-coast hookup—that he was going to donate a percentage of them to the NAACP. The Mississippi legislature, in a fit of pique, ordered the university's chancellor to cancel the invitation that had been extended to the Episcopal minister. The rabbi then began to have misgivings about participating in the University program. He placed calls to the six other participants and asked them to join him in rejecting the university's request that they take part in the religious emphasis program. All except the layman agreed. After much backstage maneuvering, eventually the rabbi sent his friend, the chancellor, an individual telegram canceling his participation. The next day the local newspaper headlines proclaimed: "Rabbi Refuses to Speak at University." In the months that followed, telephone harassment and threats made it necessary for the F.B.I. and the local police to provide constant surveillance for the rabbi and his family. In the whole incident, this clergyman played the central public role in opposing an act demanded by the Southern Way of Life.

There are a few other Reform rabbis who have played some role in opposing segregation and its manifestations in the public school systems of the Deep South. For all this, however, the available sources do not permit the assertion that most or even many rabbis in these very difficult communities played a significant part in abetting or hastening implementation of the 1954 Supreme Court decision.

Three Sermons

We turn now to the rabbis in the "less closed" societies of the South. In general this category includes most cities and towns in Kentucky, Tennessee, Virginia, Florida, Texas, and western and southern Louisiana. To this list must be added Atlanta, Georgia, which stands out as an enclave of "Northern" ideas and influence in the land of Civil War Dixie.

In the congregations of these communities, there has been no dearth of sermons, especially since 1954, dealing with the civil rights movement. Many of these pulpit texts are presently on file in the American Jewish Archives, and they speak quite well on their own behalf. Although some are vague and are content with skirting the important issues of their time and place, several come directly to the point and evidence strong desegregationist feelings. A recurrent theme is the necessity of abiding by the law of the land, and the need for the Jewish community to show the way in such acquiescence. Brief quotes from three will provide the reader with a taste of these pulpit messages. Each was given in a different pulpit, by a different rabbi. The first was delivered on Yom Kippur eve in 1954:

We have reached that time in American history when certain changes are to be made in our culture which will radically modify some of our customs and mores, especially in certain sections of our land. Our society is governed by . . . laws, and . . . it is the responsibility of every good citizen to abide by the laws as they are interpreted. . . . Since certain significant decisions were rendered by the highest tribunal of our judiciary last Spring, certain hate groups have been organized to resist the decisions that have been handed down. . . . Let the name of no Jew be found on the roster of these hate organizations. If there are those among us who cannot be in the vanguard striving for a better humanity, then at the very least, let us not be among those who would stifle the moral progress of mankind.

The second excerpt is from a sermon preached on November 18, 1955:

To the newspaper reporters and visitors to the Congregation this evening I want to bid a warm and most cordial welcome. Then I want to hasten to add that whatever is written or spoken about my remarks this evening must make clear that I am speaking only for myself . . . as a rabbi of the Reform Jewish faith who has been trained in a faith founded upon the prophetic message of the Bible . . . . This sermon I must preach for myself and for the sake of my soul if for no one else. . . . Anyone of intelligence who lives here and understands and loves the South knows full well the race problem is going to take time and intelligence, patience and good will on both sides, before it will be solved. But it will not be solved by unyielding, unmoving, unthinking resort to prejudice and Shintoist slogans that scream about keeping the Southern Way of Life. Greater than the Southern or Eastern or Western way of life is the American Way of Life, and still greater is the Judeo-Christian Way of Life.

The third sermon, delivered from a Virginia pulpit, alluded to the segregationist views of Senator Harry F. Byrd:

I speak as a rabbi on this issue to a Jewish congregation on our holiest evening in that I have chosen one of our holiest days to devote it to root out the evil in our midst in the form of bigots and hate peddlars who, for a headline, a misplaced vote, would attack minority after minority. When those who are not afraid to speak . . . sound like a voice crying in the wilderness—it is our moral obligation as Jews not to desist from being a light unto the nation. . . . I am afraid of silence. . . . The Jew cannot remain silent to injustice. . . . Let the segregationists froth and foam at their mouth. There is only one word to describe their madness—Godlessness, or to coin a new synonym—Byrdliness. Byrdliness has done more harm to the stability of our country than McCarthyism. . . . I am an American, and yes, I am a Virginian; but not of the vintage of Byrd and his invertebrate crew that follow him like subdued puppies, but I am a Virginian of the vintage of Jefferson, who said: "I have sworn upon the altar of God eternal hostility against every form of tyranny over the mind of man."

These are but three excerpts from numerous sermons preached by a large number of non-Deep South rabbis. Although some of their colleagues have never devoted an entire sermon to a civil rights issue, it is no exaggeration to say that nearly all Reform rabbis in these cities and towns have touched on the subject at least occasionally. Of this large majority, a lesser number (but still a majority) have spoken several times a year, often on the High Holydays and in specifics, as sermon texts on file in the American Jewish Archives document. But the sermon has been far from the only tool employed within the congregation by rabbis who serve these communities.

"The Ticklishness of the Situation"

Very important has been the use of integrated worship services—even before the United States Supreme Court decision of 1954. One rabbi, on Washington's birthday in 1951, "despite some serious qualms on the part of my board," organized an interracial service complete with an integrated choir and a sermon by the president of a local Negro divinity school. Another man invited a Negro to occupy his pulpit in 1955, as a dramatic gesture in order to "indicate at a time of tension, the support of Reform Judaism not only for the decision of the Supreme Court, but to take a stand in behalf of the Negro." Not all rabbis have been as firm, when it comes to encouraging integrated worship services within their synagogues. One told of the evening when just prior to services:

A well groomed Negro came to my office. . . . He asked for the privilege of attending Temple that night. In answer to my query what led to this request, he said that he was indeed a Jew who had been converted by a colleague in Arkansas. I immediately telephoned this man . . . and he verified the fact of the man's sincere conversion. I then suggested to the gentleman that, because of the ticklishness of the situation, I ought to discuss his request with those who had already begun to arrive. . . . Their answer was: that if anyone objected to this Jewish Negro worshipping that night, they themselves would leave in protest rather than have him embarrassed. I was proud of them as I was some years later, when, a Negro sergeant from a nearby Army base asked to worship with us—for again their answer was the same.

The question that comes to mind, of course, is what the rabbi would have done if his congregation had refused the man permission. The data at hand lead one to believe that at least some of the rabbis would have made peace with the decision and would have done without Negro worshippers.

Along with sermons and integrated services, rabbis have used bulletin messages, study groups, personal contacts, and creative "social action" projects to influence their members to support local efforts at desegregation. Mention should be made, if only in passing, of a major project implemented in Nashville, Tennessee, by Rabbi Randall M. Falk. His Social Justice Committee, during October and November, 1963, initiated a series of parlor meetings which eventually involved a sizable percentage of the Nashville Temple's membership. These meetings resulted in the adoption by the congregation of a highly liberal and responsible "Decalogue on Race Relations."

Directing our gaze to the outside community, we find many examples of rabbis in non-Deep South communities playing at least some role in local desegregationist activities. In most cases much of this work has been done in conjunction with the liberal ministerial groups that have blossomed during the last two decades. For example, such was the circumstance that brought Rabbi Marvin M. Reznikoff, of Baton Rouge, Louisiana, to national attention in 1961, when his telephone conversations with other ministers were monitored by segregationists aiming at undermining the clergy's liberal intentions.

In the school desegregation crises that shook the South following 1954, at least a few Reform rabbis played significant roles. One, the rabbi of a community with slightly fewer than ten thousand Jewish inhabitants, decried his state's defiance of the Supreme Court decision. Speaking in 1957 to a Methodist congregation, he warned: "If we don't rise above our partisan feelings of segregation versus integration, we'll have disintegration in our public schools." Within a few weeks' time, largely through the efforts of this man, a Committee for Public Schools was formed, which played a major role in influencing the community's business forces to apply sufficient pressure for the schools to be reopened so that children would not lose the entire school year of 1957–1958. Although differing in details, the roles of two of this man's colleagues, one in a border state, the other in a cosmopolitan port city, were basically the same. In these latter two cases, the rabbis involved were clearly recognized by the community as leaders in the push for integration, and many recriminations and acts of harassment followed. On the whole, however, rabbinical involvement of this sort appears to be quite exceptional. More common were rabbis who occasionally lent their moral support to the struggle toward implementation of the 1954 decision, but who took little part in the actual behind-the-scene and public fighting. Prominent among those who do not fit this latter pattern have been two men who merit separate consideration.

The Bombing Created a Reaction

Rabbi Jacob M. Rothschild came to Atlanta, Georgia, in 1946. Even at that early date the city already had the makings of what was to become the atmosphere most "open" to racial liberalism in the South. Rothschild has proved eminently suited to take advantage of the opportunities that such a milieu can provide the religious leader. From the very beginning, he expressed himself as a racial "liberal" and had every intention of guiding his congregants along the same path. In a Yom Kippur sermon delivered on October 3, 1948, during the early years of his Atlanta ministry, he confessed to a sense of shame at "the growing race hatred that threatens the South" and called for his people to "be among those who are willing to do something" to reverse the tide.

Rothschild himself has not neglected the deed. In 1957 he joined with seventy-nine other Atlanta clergymen in order to issue the now famous "Atlanta Manifesto"—one of the earliest and most influential clerical statements proclaimed throughout the South. In his congregation, to supplement his frequent antisegregationist sermons, he began seminars to help prepare his people for desegregation. In 1958, chiding his fellow members of Rotary, he advised them that the Negro had every right to be impatient with a white community unreceptive to racial progress. At the mayor's request, Rothschild gave the key speech to a meeting of hotel and restaurant owners during a time when the public accommodations issue was especially urgent. In 1961 he was one of the founders of and speakers for a group created to prepare the community for school integration; it was called HOPE (Help Our Public Education). In short, Rabbi Rothschild was involved in practically every civil rights issue in Atlanta.

This multilevel involvement with the Negro's struggle for equality has, of course, brought the rabbi into touch with many members of the Negro community. He has often graced their pulpits and they his. One striking example of an activity that Rothschild carried on in contact with the Negro community was the 1965 testimonial dinner for the late Dr. Martin Luther King, Jr. The idea was Rothschild's, and, although some elements of the Negro power structure wished to turn it into a money-raising function, the rabbi persisted in his desire to keep it nothing more than a community's way of expressing its pride in its first Nobel Prize winner. Mainly because of Rothschild's labors, the evening proved an enormous success—sixteen hundred people were in attendance, and many more had to be turned away for lack of room.

At the dinner's close, all these people, Negro and white alike, stood up and sang the civil rights anthem, "We Shall Overcome." It was in Rothschild's words, "the most significant meeting that Atlanta ever had—everybody said so."

But the events of 1965 take us too far ahead of our story. On October 12, 1958, Atlanta had become the fifth southern city within eight months to look upon the crumbled walls of a Jewish community building. Only hours after it rang with children's voices, Rabbi Rothschild's synagogue echoed with the sound of a dynamite blast that caused well over two hundred thousand dollars in damages. Why his synagogue? According to the rabbi:

I suppose that part of it was because I was so obviously identified with the civil rights movement. . . . What happened was . . . a small group of so-called Nazis . . . took advantage of the atmosphere of violence. . . . They used the atmosphere to bomb a synagogue, because they were specifically anti-Semitic. . . . [But] they misread the attitudes of the community. . . . The bombing . . . created a reaction . . . of such outrage that it backfired, and as a *result* of the bombing of the Temple, it now, for perhaps the first time in Atlanta, became possible to speak out. I'm firmly convinced that it was *this* episode that prevented Atlanta from becoming the same kind of closed society that Birmingham became, or Mississippi became.

In his congregation, in his community, in the South as a whole (Rabbi Rothschild has been a member of the Southern Regional Council), Rothschild has been a constantly outspoken opponent of segregation. Protestant civil rights workers, Negro activists, writers on the contemporary South—if they had heard of any "activist" rabbis—offered or recognized the name of Jacob M. Rothschild more often than any other name—except that of Rabbi Charles Mantinband.

"Too Smart for Your Pants"

Since 1946 Charles Mantinband, for all practical purposes a native of Norfolk, Virginia (his family settled there before his fifth year), has served three southern communities. His pulpit from 1946 to 1952 was in Florence, Alabama. In 1952 he left for Hattiesburg, Mississippi, remained there until 1963, and then departed for his present home in Longview, Texas.

Hattiesburg, Mississippi, not unlike Florence, Alabama, is about as closed as the closed society ever becomes. It is a small community, numbering fewer than fifty thousand residents—with a Jewish population of about 175. The mood of Hattiesburg, when Rabbi Mantinband first arrived, and even more so after 1954, was sullen and defiant. It is Klan country and not a place to look for liberals. Nevertheless Charles Mantinband had made certain vows to himself at the beginning of his years in the rabbinate, and he intended to live by them in Hattiesburg. As he told the writer:

From the very beginning, I had to make up my mind to two things as to what I would do. . . . The first thing was that the pigmentation of a person's skin would make no difference to me in my relationship to him. . . . I would judge a man, if I would judge him at all . . . in terms of his merit, his worth. That means that Negroes came to my home, through the front door, sat at my table, all the time, and that was my private affair. That was not too difficult. . . . The second thing was much harder. I vowed that I would never sit in the presence of bigotry and hear it uttered . . . that I would not [fail to] voice a contrary opinion, and make my opposition felt. . . . I wouldn't try to make a speech. I would just register . . . what my religion compels me to think, and feel, and be, and how it makes me behave. And when they would say to me, "God is a segregationist, because the Bible is full of it," I always ripped out a Bible, and I would open it to where the opposite is stated and say, "Do you mean here? Or do you mean there? Or do you mean the other place?" And then they would say, "You're too smart for your pants."

Rabbi Mantinband's open association with Negroes on an at-home social basis, his refusal to keep to himself his ideas about the evil of segregation, his very active participation in the Southern Regional Council, and numerous speeches he made at nearby Negro colleges all precipitated many a crisis between him and his congregation and community. One of his board members claimed that the rabbi's home was Temple property and attempted—unsuccessfully—to pressure the rabbi into closing the door of his home to Negroes. The response was: "Yes, it is your house, but it is my home. If you want your house back I'll give it to you . . . but you can't tell me how to live my private life."

Equally unsuccessful was an act of intimidation by one of Hattiesburg's former mayors, who was at the time, in 1958, the president of the local White Citizens Council. Following the bombing of the Atlanta synagogue, Mantinband happened to meet this man on the street. In the ensuing conversation, the ex-mayor informed the rabbi that, at the last meeting of the White Citizens Council, he had advised the membership that bombing a synagogue was silly, for if they wanted to get to the bottom of the trouble in their own city, it was not a building but a person. "His name," he related, "is Rabbi Mantinband. I know his personal habits, I know where he lives. I can tell you how to get at him if you decide that's what you really want to do." Thinking quickly, Mantinband pulled out a pen and pad, recorded what had been said, and told the ex-mayor that he was going to have it "signed by the first five representative white Christians I meet," and that he would then send it on to the f.b.i. As Rabbi Mantinband told the writer: "That fellow and I lived in that town—he never looked me in the face again because I had called his hand."

How could a man so decidedly at odds with the closed society remain eleven years as rabbi in Hattiesburg, Mississippi, and be given the key to the city when he finally decided to leave? Harry Golden has one answer, which he related to Rabbi Mantinband. Respect for religion is so great in the South, he suggested, that people there will not molest a man of the cloth, even if he is attacking the Southern Way of Life. Of course, this explanation fails to take into account a fact which Golden himself has noted—scores of Protestant ministers have been driven from their pulpits by these very same people.[13] Much closer to the South, in the present writer's opinion, is a statement made in the *New South*, the official publication of the Southern Regional Council: "It is possible in the South for a man to be what he is, speak what he believes and stand up to segregationist hatred, as our Rabbi, Charles Mantinband, has stoutly demonstrated for 15 or 16 years in darkest Alabama and Mississippi. . . . I think Rabbi Mantinband . . . survived his environs so handsomely, despite his freely and frequently expressed views that all men are equal, because he sees no man as his enemy. . . . The first time I saw him . . . I figured that if you're good enough you can say and do what you believe anywhere." [14] Viewed in the light of this perspective, Rabbi Mantinband has indeed been good enough.

13. Harry Golden, *Mr. Kennedy and the Negroes* (Cleveland, 1964), 191 ff.
14. Margaret Long, editorial, *New South*, XVII (October, 1962), 2, 17.

Community Characteristics

By now it should be fairly clear that the southern rabbinate has been far from monolithic in its degree of involvement in the struggle for Negro civil rights. Although some attempt has already been made to point out a few of the causes for this phenomenon, it might be helpful to concentrate a little more fully on the matter.

One of the most important factors in determining rabbinic involvement has been the nature of the general community. There are, as we have noted, many Souths, and thus many milieus in which southern rabbis have functioned. On one end of the spectrum is the tightly closed society of Mississippi, which James Silver calls "the South exaggerated." On the other end is Atlanta, Georgia, which many of my informants considered comparable to a non-southern city. And in between—hundreds of locales, each slightly different, each with its "open" and "closed" qualities.

If one were to attempt a characterization of "the South exaggerated" he would come up with something along the following lines: a city or county which has a rural, non-cosmopolitan orientation, contains a large percentage of Negro inhabitants, and is serviced by mass media unequivocally supportive of the "Southern Way of Life." In addition, the local population would be more than 90 percent fundamentalist in their approach to Christianity (they would be Protestants), their level of educational attainment would be markedly below the national average, and their local leadership would be dedicated to maintaining the racial status quo. This is, of course, a fairly accurate description of most communities in the "Deep South." To a very considerable extent, it follows that the more cosmopolitan the area, the lower the percentage of Negro inhabitants, the less supportive the local mass media and community leadership are of the "Southern Way of Life"; the higher the level of educational attainment, and fewer the number of fundamentalist Protestants, the more permissive that community will be in allowing verbalized dissatisfaction with the racial status quo. Such community characteristics are of no little influence on rabbinic involvement in the struggle for Negro rights. Yet this is not the whole story, for the rabbi works within a Jewish community as well.

The enclaves of Jews in the South generally reflect the broader communities of which they are a part. I qualify this statement because southern Jewry does tend to be more moderate on the race question than are their Christian neighbors. This would follow from the fact that they are usually better educated, are mainly to be found in white collar occupations, and are more frequently exposed to national (including Jewish) mass media. Nevertheless, Jewish communities likewise differ from one another.

Of crucial importance is the proportion of "old Jews" to "new Jews" within the Jewish community. Usually the stronger the influence of the "old Jews," the less liberal the rabbi will find his congregants to be. Thus one would expect a city like Charleston, South Carolina, where more than 50 percent of the Jewish community are native Southerners, and 12 percent have been Southerners for at least three generations, to be more "Southern" than the Jewish communities of Atlanta or Nashville, which have larger proportions of "new Jews."

Another factor influencing the nature of any specific Jewish community is the source of its members' income. Those communities in which the majority are merchants, highly visible on Main Street, and dependent in large part on the favor of the gentile populace, are more "nervous" on the matter of civil rights activity than communities in which most Jews are in services or the professions. Thus, the Jews of a rural town in Alabama will almost certainly have far less patience with a crusading rabbi than those in a bustling metropolitan area.

Worth noting is the fact that there are a number of exceptions to the general rules thus far stated. For example, although most "new Jews" are moderates or liberals, the phenomenon of a recently arrived Northerner "out-Southerning" the Southerners is definitely not uncommon. And, conversely, there are some third- or fourth-generation southern Jews who represent the most liberal thought to be found in the South. But these are atypical situations, and should not be accorded more weight than they numerically deserve.

One additional factor might be mentioned. The Jew is, throughout the South, an infinitesimal minority of the total population. In the South as a whole, including southern Florida, he amounts to slightly more than one-half of one percent of the populace. And in states like

Arkansas, Mississippi, Alabama, and South Carolina, even that ratio is extravagant.[15] There is security to be found in numbers—a security which most southern Jews lack. This is especially the case in the smaller towns and cities. For example, the largest Jewish community in the state of Mississippi numbers only seven hundred souls. Only in the few major metropolitan areas in the South—in Atlanta, New Orleans, Memphis and the Alexandria, Virginia, urban complex, does the individual Jew approach the feeling of being able to hide behind the number of his coreligionists. And even this should not be exaggerated, for Atlanta, with the largest concentration of Jews anywhere in the South (about fifteen thousand), still is 97 percent Gentile. Thus the rule that we can derive regarding population is of limited value, since it is so much the same story throughout the South. Understanding this, one may state hesitantly that, the larger the Jewish population in a city, the more permissive that Jewish enclave will be to civil rights activity of a moderate or liberal nature.

Feeling so small in numbers, and carrying in his inner consciousness a four-thousand-year tradition of being different, the southern Jew is highly susceptible to real or imagined anti-Semitism. Especially in the smaller or more "closed" communities, he avoids like the plague any suggestion that he is "different" on the civil rights issue. In the privacy of his home or synagogue, he might admit to being a moderate or liberal, but in the outside community, almost never. Only in the large, "open" cities, where he can find some security in numbers, will he consider casting his lot with those who criticize the Southern Way of Life. A rabbi, serving a southern Jewish community, must inevitably be affected by the character and size of the group to whom he ministers.

"Shall We Start a Messianic Movement?"

The nature of the general community is important; the character of the Jewish community is a major consideration; likewise, the personality and the philosophy of the rabbi influence the role he will play in the struggle for Negro equality. There are "open," relatively "safe" communities in which some of the rabbis have done little or nothing,

15. *American Jewish Year Book*, LXV, 83–84.

there are also tightly closed communities where the rabbi has been a vocal and consistent opponent of the accepted racial system. Here clearly the man has made the difference.

Not all rabbis agree with the necessity of involving themselves in the civil rights struggle. One, mentioned earlier, appears almost a segregationist at heart. Others are far from being "activists" in personality and personal philosophy. For example, one rabbi wrote:

The Negro has just experienced his second emancipation. Now he and his leaders, including Dr. King, expect a sudden and miraculous transformation. By the magic hocus pocus of President Johnson, Secretary Katzenbach, the Department of HEW and Congress they should all now be white collar men of the upper middle class. . . . The age of miracles is gone. Gold is not found on the streets of American cities. The Irish came to this country and struggled hard to establish a place of social equality and economic security. They lived in rat infested slums too. So did the Italians. So did Polish immigrants . . . they had it much harder than the Negro has it today. I grew up in the _____ ghetto; I understand conditions were even worse in Chicago and New York. The Negroes and Puerto Ricans now occupy what was formerly the Jewish slums. Like the other strata of American society, the Negroes will have to pull themselves up by their own bootstraps. . . . Negroes are not as pretty as Cinderella and do not have a fairy godmother.

Another rabbi explained to the writer why he had not yet sponsored an integrated program in his synagogue: "You have to find first a Negro who is intelligent enough, who is willing, or who has the educational background [so that] you can talk to him in a civilized manner. I have not been able to find [one]." Another rabbi explained his inactivity to his colleagues by telling them he would retire in eight or nine years, and he didn't intend to get fired in the meantime. Finally, three men presented their overall goals in the following words:

I don't know, I've never really thought about the question, to tell you the truth. I would like to see, of course, the Negro have fair treatment . . . but I think . . . he's going to have to earn it to a certain degree himself. We're going to have to help him. . . . this is not going to happen overnight, even with legislation, because you can't legislate sociology . . . and the background of the Negro is such that he is going to have to prove himself— through education, through his own morals—which he will do, but it's going to take time. I think that rushing these things through with Freedom Marches and, all kinds of picketing and strikes—this is not going to do it— it's only going to create ill will.

Shall we start a Messianic movement? . . . The Negroes won't follow us anyway. They identify us with the possessing classes. It often seems as though the task of trying to clarify issues and teach simple truth is beyond us. It's like ladling out the ocean with a spoon.

We must abide by the laws of the land. . . or we shall have anarchy. We don't like all the laws that are passed . . . but we obey them. . . . the same thing goes as far as desegregating . . . this is the law. *But*, whatever goes for the general population, the White population, must go for the Negro population too—they also must obey the law.

This last rabbi, when discussing the struggle for Negro equality commented: "I feel that this problem is not a Jewish problem, it is an American problem. . . . a lot of people feel that the synagogue is bankrupt . . . so that social action is regarded as an opportunity to revitalize . . . the synagogue. My feeling in the matter is that if the synagogue has to look for issues to survive, it's in a bad position."

The role that personality and personal philosophy have played with regard to these men is at least as important as the influence exerted on them by the outside community. The writer would venture to say that most or all of them would be far from active in the arena of civil rights, regardless of which community they served. But, as inner influences determine a man's lack of participation, so also do they determine his involvement in the struggle for Negro equality.

"My early school and social life was in a segregated society. After considerable struggle I learned to exercise control in my attitude and make no distinction between one man and another." Thus Rabbi Charles Mantinband partially explained why he has become the activist he is. Among his colleagues there are many like him, men who have felt an inner drive goading them to action. They have not been silenced by fear or pessimism, nor have they been willing to settle for limited objectives. They expect more of their people than a grudging obedience to the law of the land, they see the value in standing up and being counted in a physical manifestation of their support, they indeed wish to start a messianic movement. Their goals sound much less negative than those of some of their colleagues:

My goal is to bring the community to a position where every man would be judged by what he is, rather than by the color of his skin—which is, of course, the traditional Jewish attitude.

My goal is complete desegregation and that there would be an acceptance, in *good* spirit, on the part of the people of the community. They weren't just giving in, but they believed that it was the right, moral thing to do.
I believe that any spiritual leader who does not speak forth and lead his congregation on moral issues is not worthy of being the Rabbi of this or any other congregation—and I speak clearly and without equivocation that all may understand: Together with the Central Conference of American Rabbis and the Union of American Hebrew Congregations I favor integration.

The division is not a clear-cut one. Even the hesitant almost always are in general sympathy with the goals (if not the methodology) of the civil rights movement. Similarly, even those most committed to the struggle know their moments of pessimism, fear, hesitancy—they have not done all they would like to do. And the gradations from pole to pole are as numerous as the rabbis laboring in southern vineyards.

Who the man is, where he comes from, what he believes, and how great his need is for acceptance and security—in the final analysis these elements must be considered. It is true that a rabbi responds to external pressures and stimuli—this, however, is but half the story. There is a piper who pipes a tune within as well as without.

"A Force in Readiness"

Some of the facts have been presented. Statements have been made by and about the southern rabbinate. It seems appropriate to return to an earlier concern, namely, in the field of Negro rights, just what have the southern rabbis done, and what more could they do?

Obviously, any answer will necessitate a certain degree of generalization—a most insensitive scholarly tool. There have been many different levels of involvement among the southern rabbis, from the few fully engaged in the civil rights struggle, battering at the walls of the old system, to the one who might be considered a keeper of the gates. There are men who speak and act, men who speak, but rarely act, and men who rarely speak. It is hoped this point has been made. Still, though faulty instruments, generalizations have their use, especially if the reader is forewarned to accept them only as the view of the forest which cannot fully do justice to its individual trees.

Our first generalization, then, is that the Orthodox and Conservative rabbinate in the South has been conspicuous by its absence from the fray. According to the writer's informants and also the written sources at his disposal, these representatives of the more traditional branches of Judaism "haven't participated to any great extent." The highest praise accorded to some of their number was that they signed petitions prepared by other clergymen, or that they discussed the subject within their congregations. One informant, a past Regional Director of the Anti-Defamation League and himself a member of a Conservative synagogue, was asked if he detected a difference between the involvement of southern Reform, Conservative, and Orthodox rabbis in the civil rights struggle. His reply was: "I guess I would have to say yes. In the first place there were more Reform rabbis in the Southern region. . . . Also the Reform rabbis . . . by philosophy and background felt that they had a greater involvement publicly in community affairs than either the Conservative or Orthodox did. Matter of fact, the Orthodox rabbinate, where it existed, was not at all involved."

Although the Conservative and Orthodox rabbis in the South have done little or nothing, their Reform colleagues, on the whole, have played a respectable, if not an overly important role. They have been, as Reverend Shuttlesworth describes them, "a force in readiness . . . giving some support . . . some tacit, some active." Much of what they are doing is unpublicized and behind-the-scenes. Many among them speak in their congregations and in the outside community; a few have involved themselves in civil rights groups and activities. There is probably not a single community where the Reform rabbi has played *the* key role in battling segregation (although Hattiesburg, Mississippi, might be an exception), but there are a number of communities in which Reform rabbis have played valuable secondary or supportive roles. Such has been the case especially with regard to the battles for school integration. And the fact that this is so—that the rabbis have not led the parade—is not necessarily a derogatory evaluation. At least Harold Fleming, the former Southern Regional Council director, was hesitant to condemn the southern rabbinate because of this: "I'm not sure that the more defeatist rabbis were not right, in practical terms, that there were very stringent limits on how much direct or unilateral action by rabbis could have changed the situation in those days. . . .

I wasn't one of those who felt that if every rabbi would get 'gung ho' on this issue that it would change it substantially. I think a whole predominantly WASP . . . region had to be moved on this." The rabbis have played a respectable role. The question is, have they played as great a role as they could have played? The answer must be no.

After Watts

In 1964, when this study was begun, it seemed quite natural to focus attention on the southern United States. With regard to Negro rights, there has been a widespread feeling for well over a century that the situation in the South is more oppressive and "un-American" than elsewhere in the United States. Events of recent years—beginning abruptly with the Watts riot at the end of 1965's long, hot summer—have blurred the line considerably. The façade has been lifted to expose a national, not a regional malady. But, in one way at least, a quantitative (if not qualitative) difference remains—the society above the Mason-Dixon Line is still more "open" than the one below it. Put in a slightly different way, even today it requires less courage to take the unpopular stance in a northern city than in a southern one.

That this is so has enabled some who sit in northern cities to condemn the southern rabbi as a disgrace to prophetic Judaism. Many have done so. Many have made weekend trips down South to teach their colleagues some Judaism. This writer, however, feels obliged to question the reasonableness of their words and deeds. If we must condemn those who minister to southern Jewry, it should not be because they have not been outspoken liberals, leading the picket lines in their Deep South communities. It should be because they have not done what it was within their power to do.

For indeed there are things that any man can do, even in the Deep South, if he feels strongly enough about the issue of Negro rights. In another place I have attempted to treat this subject at some length[16]— suffice it to say that a minimal program for such a rabbi would include: (1) sensitizing and educating his congregation; (2) gaining access to the community power structure; (3) joining himself (quietly) to the

---

16. P. Allen Krause, "The Southern Rabbi and Civil Rights" (M.A. thesis, Hebrew Union College, Jewish Institute on Religion, Cincinnati, Ohio, 1967), 248–54. Thesis is on file at American Jewish Archives.

city's liberal elements—especially the liberal clergy; and (4) making it known (undramatically) where he stands. Granted that this is very much a minimal program, but, in many communities, it might very well be the most effective program possible. Melvin Tumin seems convinced of the merits of such an approach:

The principal advocacy of social change . . . comes from those who have the widest perspective on themselves and their communities. The development of this sense of perspective leads one to be deliberate rather than impulsive; to be reflective rather than hasty; to be willing to bargain delayed gratification of several desires against immediate impulsive gratification of only one; to be concerned for the obligations of one's membership in the larger society along with the obligations of membership in one's local province; and finally, to take into account, in deciding upon a course of action, some notion of responsibility to one's community and its organized patterns of life, as well as listening to the clamor of the inner voice.[17]

President John F. Kennedy, during a White House conference of southern clergymen, advised his audience that "they were a most fortunate group—that it was not often that people have had such a role to play in history." So far the clergy of the South have played their role halfheartedly, even badly. Rabbis, though small in number, must be considered among those men of all generations to whom the well-known dictum was addressed: "The only thing necessary for the triumph of evil is for good men to do nothing."

One of the key challenges, if not *the* key challenge of our age is the white-black confrontation. In America power and numbers are on the former side. If the odds are to be lessened and overcome, it will take all the moral force available to the American people. Few would doubt that morality is a central concern of religion—as such, it must also be a central concern of the church and the synagogue. In the past neither clergy has distinguished itself on the southern battlefield. From a Jewish viewpoint, the verdict can be put without froth or frills: the southern rabbi has done a good deal, but he could do so much more.

17. Tumin, *Desegregation: Resistance and Readiness* (Princeton, 1958), 199-200.

Contributors

DAVID BERNSTEIN has been editor and chairman of the board of the *Sun-Bulletin* (Binghamton, N.Y.) since 1960. Both he and his wife, Adele, who at one time was a reporter for the Washington *Post*, have collaborated on numerous magazine pieces. Mr. Bernstein has also written *The Philippine Story* (1947).

MARVIN BRAITERMAN resides in Baltimore, where he practices law and is active in local Temple affairs. He is counsel, Commission on Social Action of Reform Judaism; director of education and research, Religious Action Center, Union of American Hebrew Congregations; and author of *Issues of Conscience: Religion and the Public Schools.*

THOMAS D. CLARK is Distinguished Professor of American History at Indiana University, and Professor Emeritus, University of Kentucky. He also wrote *Pills, Petticoats, and Plows* and *Southern Country Editor.*

LEONARD DINNERSTEIN is Professor of History at the University of Arizona. He is the author of *The Leo Frank Case;* co-editor, with Frederic Cople Jaher, of *The Aliens: A History of Ethnic Minorities in America,* and editor of *Antisemitism in the United States.*

JOSHUA A. FISHMAN is Research Professor of Social Sciences at the Ferkauf Graduate School of Humanities and Social Sciences, Yeshiva University, New York City. He has been a Fellow at the Center for Advanced Study in the Behavioral Sciences and a Senior Specialist at the Institute of Advanced Projects, East-West Center.

MURRAY FRIEDMAN is director of the Pennsylvania, Delaware, and Maryland Office of the American Jewish Committee. He also teaches intergroup relations at the Albert M. Greenfield Center of Human Relations at the University of Pennsylvania and LaSalle College. His articles have appeared in *Commentary*, the *New Leader*, the *New Republic*, and the *Progressive*.

SIDNEY I. GOLDSTEIN is Rabbi of Temple Bnai Israel in McKeesport, Pennsylvania. He has also served a congregation in Meridian Mississippi (1959–62). Rabbi Goldstein also wrote "A Footnote on Mississippi," *Negro Education Review*, XVII (January, 1966).

ABRAM VOSSEN GOODMAN, who holds both the Ph.D. and D.D. degrees, has served as Rabbi in several communities and also as president of the American Jewish Historical Society. Before attaining this present position, he held the posts of curator and vice-president of the Society.

FOSTER B. GRESHAM was awarded a Ford Foundation fellowship in advanced education for 1953–1954. The author of *Teaching English in Virginia High Schools* and co-author of *Better English*, he is now on the English faculty at Longwood College, Farmville, Virginia.

JACOB HENRY (1776?–?). Born Jacob Gratz of Philadelphia, Henry moved South and served two terms in the North Carolina legislature. Aside from his famous speech defending his right to a seat in the legislature in 1809, little is known about him.

ALFRED O. HERO, JR. is the executive secretary of the World Peace Foundation and the author of numerous works on religious groups and American foreign policy, including *The Southerner and World Affairs* (1965).

LEON HÜHNER (1871–1957) served as curator of the American Jewish Historical Society, 1903–1957. He pioneered in the writing of American Jewish history and is author of numerous essays on the subject. He also wrote a biography of Judah Touro.

BENJAMIN KAPLAN (1911–1972) was Godchaux Professor of Sociology at the University of Southwestern Louisiana until his death. He wrote *The Eternal Stranger* and *The Jew and His Family*.

LUCIAN LAMAR KNIGHT (1868–1933). Literary editor of the *Atlanta Constitution* (1892–1902), an ordained Presbyterian minister, and first director of the state of Georgia Archives. He wrote the six-volume *Standard History of Georgia and Georgians*, and edited volumes 22 through 26 of *The Colonial Records of the State of Georgia*.

BERTRAM WALLACE KORN, senior Rabbi at Reform Congregation Kneseth Israel in Elkins Park, Pennsylvania, since 1949, is also a distinguished scholar. He engages in a myriad of activities and in addition to being author and editor of twelve books, including *The Early Jews of New Orleans*, he has been past president of the Association of Jewish Chaplains of the Armed Forces of the United States, of the American Jewish Historical Society, and of the Alumni Association of the Hebrew Union College —Jewish Institute of Religion.

RABBI ALLEN KRAUSE, a Leon Watters Fellow of the Hebrew Union College—Jewish Institute of Religion, is on the faculty of the University of Santa Clara, and is Rabbi of Temple Beth Torah, Fremont, California. His 1967 master's thesis, at the Hebrew Union College, "The Southern Rabbi and Civil Rights," probed the involvement of southern— principally Reform—rabbis in the struggle for Negro rights since May, 1954.

THEODORE LOWI, Professor of Political Science at the University of Chicago, has written numerous scholarly articles, as well as *At the Pleasure of the Mayor, The Pursuit of Justice* (with Robert F. Kennedy), and *The End of Liberalism* (editor).

LEONARD REISSMAN is chairman of the Department of Sociology at Cornell University. Formerly the Favrot Professor of Human Relations in the Department of Sociology at Tulane University, he also was director of the Tulane Urban Studies Center. His writings include numerous articles, as well as *Class in American Society* and *The Urban Process*.

IRA ROSENWAIKE, as statistician with the Maryland Department of Health and Mental Hygiene, has written on health and demographic topics. He has published numerous articles dealing with Jewish experience in eighteenth- and early nineteenth-century America. He is recognized as an authority on American Jewish demography, and is the author of *Population History of New York City*. Currently Mr. Rosenwaike is engaged in historical research on a study of the early Jewish settlement in Baltimore.

ALBERT VORSPAN is director of the Commission on Social Action of the Union of American Hebrew Congregations. He is author of *Giants of Justice*, coauthor of *Justice and Judaism*, and coeditor of *A Tale of Ten Cities*.

Bibliographical Essay

The literature on southern Jews is thin. There is no single history of Jews in the South and there are few monographs. The only general surveys are Alfred O. Hero's essay, reprinted in this volume; and Leonard Dinnerstein, "A Note on Southern Attitudes Toward Jews," *Jewish Social Studies*, XXXII (January, 1970), 43–49, and Dinnerstein, "A Neglected Aspect of Southern Jewish History," *American Jewish Historical Quarterly*, LXI (September, 1971), 52–68. The best articles from the *Publications of the American Jewish Historical Society*, which is now the *American Jewish Historical Quarterly*, have been collected by Abraham J. Karp and published in five volumes under the title, *The Jewish Experience in America* (New York: KTAV Publ. House, Inc., 1969); while some of the notable articles from *American Jewish Archives* have been published in three volumes entitled *Critical Studies in American Jewish History*, edited by Jacob Rader Marcus (New York: KTAV Publ. House, Inc., 1970). Both of these collections contain some good essays on southern Jewry.

For the colonial era, one might look at the relevant chapters of Jacob Rader Marcus, *The Colonial American Jew: Fourteen Ninety-Two–Seventeen Seventy-Six* (3 vols.; Detroit: Wayne State University Press, 1969). Marcus also provides an extensive bibliography.

For the period between the Revolution and the Jacksonian era, there is a good deal of material on the South in Joseph L. Blau and Salo W. Baron (eds.), *The Jews of the United States, 1790–1840: A Documentary History* (3 vols.; New York: Columbia University Press, 1963). Peter Still, *The Kidnapped and the Ransomed: The Narrative of Peter and Vina Still After Forty Years of Slavery* was originally published in 1856, but it has been reissued (Philadelphia: Jewish Publication Society of America, 1970), with an introductory essay on Jews in the antislavery movement by Maxwell Whiteman. Bertram Wallace Korn, "Factors Bearing Upon the Survival of Judaism in the Ante-Bellum Period," *American Jewish Historical Quarterly*, LXIII (1964), 341–51, is a revealing contribution.

The Civil War period has attracted the attention of Jews as well as gentiles. One of the best historical monographs on Jews for any era is Korn, *American Jewry and the Civil War* (Philadelphia: Jewish Publication Society of America, 1951). *American Jewish Archives*, XIII (April, 1964), devoted that entire issue to "Civil War Centennial: Southern Jews."

There are few biographical studies of southern Jews. Robert Meade, *Judah P. Benjamin: Confederate Statesman* (New York: Oxford University Press, 1943) is still the standard work. For the late nineteenth century, the following articles are worth reading: Selig Adler, "Zebulon B. Vance and the 'Scattered Nation,' " *Journal of Southern History*, VII (1941), 357–77; Stanley F. Chyet, "Ludwig Lewisohn in Charleston, 1892–1903," *American Jewish Historical Quarterly*, LIV (1964–65), 296–322; and Joseph Proskauer's reminiscences of his Mobile years, "Southern Boyhood," in Harold U. Ribalow (ed.), *Autobiographies of American Jews* (Philadelphia: Jewish Publication Society of America, 1965).

A number of community histories have been written. Some cover short periods of time, others are more expansive. Most lack depth but they do provide factual background. For Maryland see E. Milton Altfeld, *The Jew's Struggle for Religious and Civil Liberty in Baltimore* (Baltimore: Martin Curlander, 1924); Isaac M. Fein, *The Making of an American Jewish Community: The History of Baltimore Jewry from 1773 to 1920* (Philadelphia: Jewish Publication Society of America, 1971); and Isidor Blum, *The Jews of Baltimore* (Baltimore, Historical Review Publishing Co., 1910). On Richmond, Virginia, there is Herbert T. Ezekiel and Gaston Lichtenstein, *The History of the Jews of Richmond from 1769 to 1917* (Richmond, Va.: privately published, 1917). Barnett A. Elzas, *The Jew of South Carolina* (Philadelphia; J. B. Lippincott Co., 1905) has been improved upon by Charles Reznikoff and Uriah Z. Engelman, *The Jews of Charleston* (Philadelphia: Jewish Publication Society of America, 1950). Engelman added more detailed information in "Jewish Education in Charleston in the 17th and 18th Centuries," *Publications of the American Jewish Historical Society*, XLII (1952–53), 43–67. Especially revealing, and much broader than the title implies, is Allan Tarshish, "The Charleston Organ Case," *American Jewish Historical Quarterly*, LIV (June, 1965), 411–

BIBLIOGRAPHICAL ESSAY / 391

49. Leo Shpall detailed what many Jews like to forget in "Some Anti-Semitic Incidents in South Carolina," *Jewish Forum*, XXX (1946), January, 19–20; February, 43–44; March, 66 and 88; April, 104.

A penetrating analysis is Solomon Sutker, "The Jews of Atlanta: Their Social Structure and Leadership Patterns" (Ph.D. dissertation, University of North Carolina, 1950). Rabbi David Marx wrote a brief "History of the Jews of Atlanta," *Reform Advocate*, November 4, 1911; while Janice O. Rothschild, *As But a Day* (Atlanta: University of Georgia Press, 1967) is a history of the city's Hebrew Benevolent Congregation. Atlanta's largest department store, founded by a Jewish peddler in 1867, is approached from a businessman's point of view in Henry Givens Baker, *Rich's of Atlanta* (Atlanta: University of Georgia Press, 1953).

The Louisiana Jewish community has attracted a number of scholars. Bertram Wallace Korn, *The Early Jews of New Orleans* (Waltham, Mass.; American Jewish Historical Society of America, 1969) utilizes a biographical approach; Samuel Proctor, "Jewish Life in New Orleans, 1718–1860," *Louisiana Historical Quarterly*, XL (April, 1957), 110–32; and Julian B. Feibelman, *A Social and Economic Study of the New Orleans Jewish Community* (Philadelphia: Jewish Publication Society of America, 1941) are more conventional narratives. Leo Shpall, *The Jews of Louisiana* (New Orleans: The Steeg Printing and Publishing Co., 1936) covers the state, while Benjamin Kaplan, *The Eternal Stranger* (New York: Bookman Associates, 1957) is an extraordinarily sophisticated analysis of three of its small Jewish communities.

Leonard Dinnerstein, *The Leo Frank Case* (New York: Columbia University Press, 1968), also surveys the background of southern Jews. Uriah Zevi Engelman, "Jewish Social, Educational, and Religious Developments in Charleston, S.C., 1900–1950," *Reconstructionist*, XVIII (March 21, 1952), 26–30, brings the story up to modern times.

For the more recent period, there are a number of insightful essays. Among the best are: Harry L. Golden, "Jew and Gentile in the New South: Segregation at Sundown," *Commentary*, XX (1955), 403–12; Calvin Trillin, "U.S. Journal: New Orleans," *New Yorker* (March 9, 1968), 138–43; Harold Mehling, "Is Miami Beach Jewish?" *The Most of Everything* (New York: Harcourt, Brace & World, Inc., 1960), 129–44; Irving Goldberg, "The Changing Jewish Community of Dallas," *American Jewish Archives*, XI (April, 1959), 82–97; and James Lebeau, "Profile of a Southern Jewish Community: Waycross, Georgia," *American Jewish Historical Quarterly*, LVIII (June, 1969), 429–42. Three attitudinal surveys sponsored by the

American Jewish Committee and prepared by Manheim S. Shapiro are: "The Baltimore, Md., Survey of Jewish Attitudes" (1963); "The Bayville (Dade County, Fla.) Survey of Jewish Attitudes" (1961); and "The Southville (Memphis, Tenn.) Survey of Jewish Attitudes" (1959).

The desegregation crisis after 1954 gave rise to a number of analyses of southern Jews. Leonard Dinnerstein synthesizes their feelings in "Jews and the Desegregation Crisis in the South, 1954–1970," *American Jewish Historical Quarterly*, LXXII (March, 1973). The following three cover specific temple bombings, but their analyses are much broader: Nathan Perlmutter, "Bombing in Miami: Anti-Semitism and the Segregationists," *Commentary*, XXV (June, 1958), 498–503; Jackson Toby, "Bombing in Nashville: A Jewish Center and the Desegregation Struggle," *Commentary*, XXV (May, 1958), 385–89; and Arnold Shankman, "A Temple Is Bombed—Atlanta, 1958," *American Jewish Archives*, XXIII (May, 1971), 125–53. Harry L. Golden and Albert Vorspan, "Unease in Dixie," *Midstream*, II (Autumn, 1956), 38–51, is a perceptive article.

The *Southern Israelite, One Hundred Years' Accomplishments of Southern Jewry* (Atlanta: Southern Newspaper Enterprises, Inc., 1934) is filiopietistic but informative nevertheless.

Alfred O. Hero, Jr., *The Southerner and World Affairs* (Baton Rouge: Louisiana State University Press, 1965), has the best published bibliographical essay on southern Jews.